# Printing terror

Manchester University Press

# Printing terror

## American horror comics as Cold War commentary and critique

Michael Goodrum and Philip Smith

Manchester University Press

Copyright © Michael Goodrum and Philip Smith 2021

The right of Michael Goodrum and Philip Smith to be identified as the authors of this work has been asserted by them in accordance with the Copyright, Designs and Patents Act 1988.

Published by Manchester University Press
Oxford Road, Manchester M13 9PL
www.manchesteruniversitypress.co.uk

British Library Cataloguing-in-Publication Data
A catalogue record for this book is available from the British Library

ISBN   978 1 5261 3592 6   hardback
ISBN   978 1 5261 7900 5   paperback

First published 2021

The publisher has no responsibility for the persistence or accuracy of URLs for any external or third-party internet websites referred to in this book, and does not guarantee that any content on such websites is, or will remain, accurate or appropriate.

Typeset by
Servis Filmsetting Ltd, Stockport, Cheshire

# Contents

# List of figures

Where we have been able to identify the creators behind a comic we have used the following notations: 'a' artist, 'c' colourist, 'e' editor, 'i' inker, 'l' letterer, and 'w' writer.

# Acknowledgements

I would like first and to foremost express my gratitude to Phil, without whom this book would never have happened. I am also grateful to my wife, Emma, for putting up with all the research materials I have had lying around, Frankenstein-like, during its creation. Thanks to Anna for the picture of the Creature from the Black Lagoon she drew for me. Thanks to Elise for all the letter 'e's you typed in the conclusion. This book was written while I was teaching at Canterbury Christ Church University; I am grateful for the research leave that allowed me to make so much progress on this, and other projects. Stephen Hipkin went above and beyond by offering me space in his beautiful home, and even sometimes lending me his bike, while I was in Canterbury. Thank you for putting me up, and for putting up with me. Some of my students at CCCU also warrant thanks, especially those who took up research placements through the Applied Humanities module: Josh Owens, Alexandra Owen, and particularly Holly Bringes. Alex Clifford constructed a helpful index of *Famous Monsters of Filmland* and I am also grateful to my students on the Spectres Haunting the West module. Long and frequent discussions with Jordan Newton were also extremely productive and brimming with his usual line of insight. For unrivalled guidance and friendship, I shall forever be indebted to Kevin Ruane. In Oxford, I am grateful to Mara Keire for her thoughts on zombies and mouvance. I am also particularly grateful to two people who had a transformative impact on me, but who will not get the chance to read this: my uncle, Mervyn Goodrum, and my friend and mentor, Hugh Brogan, both of whom passed away while we were writing this book. *Michael Goodrum*

I am grateful to Mitch. We first met when we were both PhD students living in Oxford. We have maintained our friendship over more than a decade despite (on my part) numerous moves across continents into awkward time-zone conflicts. You are a wonderful, beautiful, human

being, Michael Goodrum. After so many read-throughs and redrafts, the question of whose passage is whose in this book has no meaningful answer, but I can state with confidence that the idea for this book was Mitch's, as was the sourcing of much of the primary material, and full credit goes to him to the deep dives into history. (The contributions I can definitely identify as mine are far more pedestrian; where a sentence is in the active voice, a modifier is attached unambiguously to a noun phrase, a structure is parallel, or Shakespeare has been crowbarred in, you may feel the phantasmal presence of my hand.) I did the majority of my work on this book while I was a faculty member at the University of The Bahamas and completed the rewrites as associate chair at Savannah College of Art and Design, Hong Kong. These two institutions have made me a part of an academic community; something sacred, pleasant, and steeped with purpose. Many of my ideas for this book arose and were refined in my Popular Fiction, Introduction to Film, and Graphic Narrative classes. Particular thanks go to Raven Scott who directed me to the 'Crawling Evil' comic, which appears in Chapter 2. I am grateful to colleagues at the Comics Studies Society, the Canadian Society for the Study of Comics, and the TORCH research network at Oxford, all of whom gave me feedback and ideas when I presented parts of this project. I am especially grateful to Aaron AuBuchon, Mike Phoenix, and Dan Yezbick. My father, Paul Smith, keeps track of my research interests and forwards me pertinent articles he stumbles across in *The Guardian*, which is both useful and a kind reminder that he cares. My mother, Grace Pearn, among her innumerable acts of kindness, has housed most of my library of academic books in her attic for what will soon be a decade. My wife, Stephanie, has travelled across the globe with me and has done me the wholly unearned honour of taking what I do seriously.
*Philip Smith*

We would like to thank our editor, Matthew Frost, and our copy editor, Gemma Marren. We are indebted to the reviewers who offered their enthusiasm, expertise, and advice in shaping both the proposal and the draft manuscript of this book. We offer our gratitude to everyone who has trodden this ground before us, especially to those with whom we disagree.

# Introduction

> In none of these later war memoirs is there anything to recall that queer quality of the 1914–18 stories, of men who felt they were going out from absolutely sure and stable homes and cities, to which with reasonable good fortune they would return and live happily ever after … The men of this later cycle of wars felt that there would be no such homecoming. They knew that they went out to misery and left misery in active possession at home. Their war was not an expedition; it was a change for ever. (H. G. Wells, *The Shape of Things to Come*, 1933)[1]

The war described above by Wells did not happen; it is a traumatic future history transmitted through dream and recorded by Dr Philip Raven, a prominent international diplomat. Published in 1933, *The Shape of Things to Come* probes the near future and recent past and finds only horror. In the wake of the real war, which contained nightmares unimagined by Wells, horror comics served a similar function, investigating the war, its aftermath, and the anxieties to which it gave rise. They both anticipated and documented some of the traumatic effects of the war – the dislocation of dream and reality, of the past, present, and future, and of values from their social mooring. Although horror comics preceded the Second World War, it was in its aftermath that they attained their greatest popularity, and notoriety, both in the US and abroad. The world was certainly a more horrifying place after the mass destruction of the war, after the massacre of civilians through bombing campaigns (predicted by Wells), and the Holocaust. It was horrifying in different ways for different demographics; many of those who had historically enjoyed a position of social privilege felt threatened by social upheavals along the lines of gender and race brought to prominence by the war. In this sense, the horror comics under consideration here contributed to a relatively one-sided dialogue on the boundaries of acceptability and of monstrosity, where the agents of fear 'have to be everything the human is not and, in producing the negative of human … make way for the invention of human as white, male, middle-class, and heterosexual'.[2] In dramatizing this process of dialogic construction, comics, particularly the crime and horror genres, attained the status of a moral panic. This panic was both domestic and international, and in both cases was explicitly tied into Cold War concerns around communism, race, and perceived 'deviance' in sexuality and gender roles. Comics were therefore swept up in the internalization of the doctrine of containment (then being applied by the US to international relations). In 1954, following a Senate subcommittee hearing on juvenile delinquency that took comics as its focus, the comics industry implemented a self-regulatory code that removed everything essential to horror. However, horror comics were subsequently reanimated after changes to that code in 1971, and thereafter served as a similar nexus of anxiety during and after another war: Vietnam. As in the 1950s, there were similar domestic patterns of containment in the 1970s, such as the War on Drugs and the monitoring of Civil Rights groups; horror comics drew on past practice as well as contemporary resonance to create shocking moments for their readers.

Contemporary resonance is at the core of this book. Horror comics exist in dialogue with the social, cultural, and political movements of their time – both the comics themselves and the narratives they contained became, following Jack Halberstam, monstrous machines of meaning.[3] In the Cold War climate under consideration here, these comics engage with the national trauma of war, feminist projects, and public conversations on civil rights, but they do so in a manner centred primarily on the experience of white middle-class heterosexual men. We take up an argument presented by Aviva Briefel and Sianne Ngai, that in horror comics the 'experience of fear' can be read as emotional property, access to which is restricted to specific privileged individuals – while these comics often seem to condemn overt racism and misogynistic violence, they consistently present women and people of colour as a threat to both individual white males and the social fabric.[4] This is partly related to spatial politics. Economic shifts, the rise of political movements, and patterns of urban and suburban development placed the 'wrong' bodies in the 'wrong' places, rendering both the body and the space it inhabits uncanny; as something that does not belong within the lived experience of white men living in and moving around the US.[5] In this introductory chapter we seek to outline the perception and conception of the reality in which horror comics circulated, both in terms of the development of the genre and in the socio-cultural milieu in which horror comics were produced. This contextual study paves the way for the close readings in subsequent chapters. We also offer a framework for the study and an overview of the chapters to follow.

## American horror

Critics generally recognize Horace Walpole's *The Castle of Otranto* (1764) as the first horror novel in the sense that it codified many of the markers we now associate with the genre.[6] The novel includes a pervasive sense of threat, trap doors, secret passages, mysterious sounds, and doors opening seemingly of their own volition. Monstrous manifestations emerge, as in *Hamlet*, from something being rotten in the state, indicating an early example of anxieties around leadership in a time of war being mediated through the horror genre.[7] Poet Thomas Grey told Walpole that the novel made 'some of us cry a little, and all in general afraid to go to bed o'nights'.[8]

While Walpole's work was an important intervention in the genre, critics also acknowledge that fear is so essential an experience that it would be fruitless to attempt to establish the first occasion in which one human sought to horrify another through storytelling.[9] We find elements of the Gothic, S. T. Joshi argues, in *The Epic of Gilgamesh* from around 2100 BC and Noël Carroll identifies horror elements in Petronius' *Satyricon* (late first century AD) and Ovid's *Metamorphosis* (8 AD).[10] Renaissance theatre, too, included elements of supernatural horror in Marlowe's *Doctor Faustus* (1592) as well as Shakespeare's *Macbeth* (1606) and *The Tempest* (1611). Indeed, in *The Castle of Otranto*, Walpole quotes both Shakespeare and various poetic 'odes to horror' such as Collins' *Ode to Fear* (1747).[11] We can detect horror elements, too, in the earliest attempts to record folk tales in seventeenth-century France. The story 'Blue Beard', for example, which appears in Charles Perrault's *Stories or Tales from Times Past, with Morals* (1797).

Despite his stated desire to create 'a new species of romance', Walpole did not invent horror.[12] Walpole drew on imagery from the eighteenth-century 'Graveyard School' of poetry as well as earlier forms of horror and codified these elements into a recognizable and reproducible structure. Such was Walpole's influence that the *Encyclopaedia Londinensis* of 1827 specified a sub-genre of romance called the 'horrible romance' in which the anonymous author included John Polidori's *The Vampire* (1819) and Mary Shelley's *Frankenstein* (1818).[13] The horror romance, the author argued, typically contained 'a dark and wicked man [...] a lady whose purity and transcendent virtue are continually displayed by her aversion to ravishment [...] dungeons deep, fortified castles, assassins, bandits, and sometimes a treacherous priest'.[14] After Walpole, and certainly after the huge success of Ann Radcliffe, writers were mindful that when they wrote to evoke a sense of threat, they were contributing to an established genre of fiction with its own semiotics and codes.

Many of these formal elements have come to be recognized as a distinct sub-genre of horror, the Gothic, from which later versions of horror have evolved.

In Victorian England, Royce Mahawatte argues, horror was 'encompassing and intricate'.[15] The language and imagery of horror found its way into genres and forms beyond its original scope. Horror also continued in novels such as Wilkie Collins's *The Woman in White* (1860), the emergent 'penny dreadful' novel such as *The Mysteries of London* (1884–1888), in the explosion of print culture during the 1880s and, most famously of all, in Bram Stoker's *Dracula* (1897).

In the US, the language and imagery of horror were invoked in anti-slavery tracts of the late eighteenth and early nineteenth centuries.[16] American writers such as Charles Brockden Brown and Washington Irving adapted the form to the emergent American literary palate. Horror in the US, Agnieszka Soltysik Monnet argues, had both literary precedents in the form of 'captive narratives' – women's accounts of being captured by Native Americans – and historical events, most famously the Salem Witch Trials of the 1690s.[17] The American Gothic form was later developed by Edgar Allan Poe, Nathaniel Hawthorne, and Charlotte Perkins Gilman, taking distinct American forms in such developments as Southern Gothic, with decaying plantations and racial politics supplanting the decaying castles of medieval Europe.

David J. Skal identifies another American innovation in horror: the carnival. P. T. Barnum's American Museum, founded in New York in 1841, made '[d]warves, pinheads, Siamese twins, albinos, giants of height and girth […] staples of American diversion'.[18] The carnival grotesques found their way into the works of Mark Twain, James Otis, and, later, Ray Bradbury.[19] Indeed, Leslie Fiedler argues that American literature often seems like 'a chamber of horrors disguised as an amusement park "fun house," where we pay to play at terror and are confronted in the innermost chamber with a series of inter-reflecting mirrors which present us with a thousand versions of our own face'.[20] During the early twentieth century the horror genre was popular on the stage as well as in print. Horace Liveright's 1927 American stage adaptation of *Dracula* was a huge success, generating $2 million in profits.[21] American horror fiction also gained some momentum. Gertrude Atherton's *Black Oxen* was the second-best selling book in 1923. Howard Phillips Lovecraft's 'weird fiction', which would not gain a significant readership until later in the twentieth century, described monsters lurking in Manhattan's lower East Side, while also developing the genre of 'cosmic horror' – the notion that humanity was an insignificant presence in a hostile, or worse, indifferent universe.

While the carnival grotesque, theatrical adaptation, and particular types of horror fiction were key American developments, the US and its audiences were slower to warm to the possibilities of film. Although audiences had been thrilled by the Edison Company's production of *Frankenstein* as early as 1910, the first cycle of horror films to truly fire international imaginations were made not in the US, but in Weimar Germany. *The Cabinet of Dr. Caligari* (1920, released in America 1921), Skal argues, 'built up a pretentious head of steam, capitalizing on postwar xenophobia and traditional American self-doubts in matters artistic. *Caligari* was a kind of cultural sputnik, launched out of nowhere by Europe, a gauntlet not thrown down but projected up on the shivering screen of America's insecurities'.[22] It was followed by similar German masterpieces of horror film such as *Nosferatu* (1921) and *Orlacs Hände* (1924). This cinema resonated with the American preoccupation with the grotesque in a different format; in *Anxious Visions*, Sidra Stitch argues that the Surrealists' preoccupation with altered bodies is a direct response to the crippled and mutilated veterans who returned from the First World War.[23] These images of disfigured bodies also found a home in cinema in the form of the rat-like vampire in *Nosferatu* and the autonomous hand in *Orlacs Hände*. European horror cinema, then, offered a window into the cultural unconscious after the First World War. American filmmakers found themselves scrambling to catch up.

The earliest film interventions in horror came from Universal Studios, which began production of what is now known as the Universal Monsters series of films in 1923. Universal produced six films during the 1920s, the most successful of which featured the startling performances and make-up of the actor, Lon Chaney. After the American release of *Nosferatu* in 1929 proved a significant box office success, production increased. As an unlicensed adaptation of *Dracula*, however, the estate of Bram Stoker sued the producers of *Nosferatu*. As a result of the lawsuit, which found in favour of Stoker's estate, all prints were supposedly destroyed (though fortunately for later audiences, some survived). An American adaptation of *Dracula*, based on the successful Broadway play and also starring its lead, Bela Lugosi, filled the void in 1931. The film proved sufficiently popular to spark major American production of horror films throughout the 1930s and 1940s.

The initial success of American horror cinema can in part be attributed to director Tod Browning and leading actor Lon Chaney, the latter of whom took many roles that involved prosthetic disfigurement. Browning's directorial work appeared as early as 1915, but it was not until the 1920s and 1930s that he learned the lessons of German horror cinema and directed films such as *London After Midnight, The*

*Unknown* (both 1927), and, most famously, *Dracula* (1931) and *Freaks* (1932). Kendall R. Phillips argues that *Dracula* was 'the film that began America's love affair with horror'.[24] Films that immediately followed represented a wide range of horror genres from monster films to psychological thrillers. They included, to name a few, *Frankenstein, Dr. Jekyll and Mr. Hyde* (both 1931), *The Mummy* (1932), *Mystery of the Wax Museum* (1933), *King Kong* (1933), and *The Black Cat* (1934). The production of horror films remained high after 1934, with *The Bride of Frankenstein* (1935), *The Devil Doll* and *Dracula's Daughter* (both 1936), *Face at the Window* (1939), and *The Wolf Man* (1941). However, the post-1934 era, most critics agree, saw a decline in quality due to the enforcement of the Hays Code, which controlled the content of film and rendered horror more difficult to realize, and the end of Carl Laemmle Jr's period as head of production at Universal, a major advocate of horror cinema, in 1936.

In many cases, the early films of the 1930s established the model to which subsequent versions of a given character, including those found in comics, would refer – Bela Lugosi's Dracula and Boris Karloff's Frankenstein, for example, were quickly adopted as cultural icons. The genre was sufficiently established by 1933 to spawn parody such as the Disney film *The Mad Doctor* (1933), in which Mickey Mouse seeks to rescue Pluto from a deranged scientist. It also spawned imitators in radio, perhaps most famously Arch Oboler's series 'Lights Out' (1938–1939 and 1942–1943) which, thanks to the absence of visuals and more relaxed censorship laws, told stories even more gruesome than those found on screen. Oboler's drama 'Burial Service', for example, comprises a monologue of a woman who is being buried alive.

American horror cinema of the 1930s inherited some of the interest in bodily disfigurement from European film while addressing more contemporary concerns. Cinema was one outlet for those who fell victim to the Great Depression. As Gilbert Seldes asserts, the American public craved escapism, and while '[t]he rich could still go to the South Seas Islands [and] the intellectuals went to Mexico[,] the poor went to the movies'.[25] In films such as *King Kong*, the poor could even see themselves on screen: film producer Carl Denham plucks Ann Darrow from the Depression-era streets of New York to star in his new film after he sees her stealing food from a stall. Popular cinema under Prohibition had turned to the gangster genre, revelling in images of unsanctioned opulence, and failing social and legal structures; in the wake of Prohibition's repeal, the monster film seemed to speak more directly to the cultural moment.[26] As Skal asserts, 'America's worst year of the century would be its best year ever for monsters', suggesting an affinity between the horror of existence under the Depression and the desire to see that, in some way, played out culturally.[27]

Kendall R. Phillips argues that horror cinema enjoyed significant success because it 'connected to existing cultural drifts and directions in such peculiarly poignant ways as to be recognized as somehow "true"… that somehow what they saw up on the screen was an accurate, if allegorical, depiction of their own collective fears and concerns'.[28] Such an approach can be seen to take us so far – clearly, people in the 1950s were concerned about atomic warfare and species-level threats – but horror must also, by definition, horrify. Part of this is through spectacle, and horror is quick to harness new production techniques. For instance, Kevin Heffernan discusses how the same story of a crazed wax sculptor was used to herald Warner's 'brief excursion into two-strip Technicolor' in 1933 (as *Mystery of the Wax Museum*), and, as *House of Wax*, was the first film by a major studio made in 3-D.[29] Horror, like Modern Art in the terms of Robert Hughes, can derive much of its power from 'the shock of the new'.[30] Technological developments, like colour or 3-D, can provide such a shock. This is not to say that pleasure cannot be gained through meeting expectations – this is one of the major appeals of genre fiction, after all – but that it is the texts that deviate from them in particularly interesting or culturally resonant ways that attain the greatest success and notoriety.

## Film to comics

The increasing scrutiny of Hollywood, the postwar channelling of Cold War anxieties, and economic shifts all had a dramatic effect on horror cinema and the horror comics that would follow. During the late 1940s, Hollywood saw dramatic changes that profoundly affected horror film production and distribution. Cinema as a whole faced a decline in ticket sales resulting from competition from television. These problems were compounded in 1948 when the US Supreme Court issued the Paramount Decree that, among other anti-trust rulings, made it illegal for studios to 'block-book' films by selling A and B list films as a package to theatres. The end of block-booking meant that B-movies became dramatically less profitable, causing a decline in their output. Studios began to produce a small number of high-budget films rather than a combination of A and B titles. Horror, which made up a significant portion of B films, declined as a result. Horror film was also under threat from shifting perceptions of respectability; even before the Paramount Decree, Universal had chosen to stop making horror films and serials in order to reinvent itself as a higher-brow film company. As a result of these industrial and broader technological shifts, the film industry suffered what Kevin Heffernan calls 'the most precipitous and sustained decline in box-office attendance in the postwar period', moving from a central component of the lives of the vast majority of Americans to a more marginal presence that attracted more marginal audiences.[31]

The 1940s saw a general decline in the quality and quantity of horror cinema, with the most notable works being a series of thoughtful, low-budget, films such as *Cat People* (1942), *I Walked With a Zombie* (1943) and *The Leopard Man* (1943), directed by Jacques Tourneur and produced by Val Lewton at RKO. By the late 1940s, older forms of horror were ripe for parody: the comedians Abbott & Costello appeared in several horror comedies, beginning with *Abbott & Costello Meet Frankenstein* (1948). Horror film did not vanish entirely, however; Maila Nurmi began a popular turn as Vampira in 1954, a host for a late-night schedule of horror films on KABC-TV, a Los Angeles station.[32] This became an increasingly popular concept for promoting late-night screenings particularly as, in 1958, Universal signed a deal for television syndication of their 1930s horror productions. The horrors of the 1930s stalked the screen once more, though the audiences watching them were now haunted by new fears. Invasion, not immigration, and communism, not the crypt, were the new spectres haunting the US. This is not to say they were discrete issues: aspects of former horrors were overlaid with new meanings in this new context. While the Gothic prowled the imagination of filmmakers and audiences in the 1920s and 1930s, leading to and resulting from a sustained period of horror film production between 1931 and 1934, the postwar period faced more concerns about their future than the secret pasts of Gothic fiction.[33] These issues were, certainly, still historical. The changed circumstances of the world, and of the US within it, gave rise to new fears born of atomic warfare, space travel, and escalating conflicts between superpowers. Threats from the 'Old World', such as European vampires, were largely replaced by enemies from new worlds, aliens bent on conflict or conquest, or the results of science probing areas it did not, and should not seek to, understand. Phillips argues that 'if the interwar years were haunted by legacies of the past, the post-war years were filled with uncertainties about the future [...] By 1950, Americans had developed a cultural replacement for the Gothic ghouls from the crypt – little green men from flying saucers'.[34] These alien bodies, however, were usually still marked as Other, whether through conforming to the stereotype of 'little green men', or through more subtle differences, the subtlety of which, as in *It Came from Outer Space* (1953), might be stripped away at any moment to reveal the true threat posed by the alien – not just through its destructive capabilities, but through its ability to cross boundaries, to move from the category of apparently safe and homely to deviant Other. More threatening was the suggestion that the space itself, the home(land) could be rendered alien, often through the restaging of models of violent imperial intervention that the US was exporting alongside its cultural imperialism: its popular culture.

Like many of the creatures they depicted, horror comics crept up on the 1950s. It is beyond the scope of this project to detail the lives of various horror properties across different media or to document the entirety of the discourse between comics and film throughout the twentieth century. It is of note, however, as critics such as Dru Jeffries and Blair Davis have shown, that there has always been considerable traffic of ideas, properties, and stylistics between comics and film.[35] The inaugural issue of *Movie Comics* (1939), for example, adapted horror film to the comics page by combining promotional movie stills from *Frankenstein* (1931) with hand-drawn backgrounds and colour – a technique referred to as the 'fumetti' method.

As Mark Jancovich notes, 'most people's understanding of a genre is developed through their awareness of a number of different cultural forms', indicating that even if there is little obvious influence of one form on another at the level of creation, readers of horror comics were likely to position a given text within their consumption of a broader milieu drawing on film, literature, radio, and other forms.[36] There are, however, clear points of crossover between horror film and comics. To name a few, the Batman villain Two-Face, who first appeared in 1942, was inspired by the film adaptation *Dr. Jekyll and Mr. Hyde* (1941) and, more famously, Joker has a clear debt to Conrad Veidt in *The Man Who Laughs* (1928); the title and intermission screens of the now cult classic, *Robot Monster* (1953), are set to a backdrop of horror comics; in 1940, *Wonderwall Comics* advertised a 'Comic-Scope' projector that promised to turn comics pages into film; and comics artist Bob Powell, who drew for various publishers during the early and mid-twentieth century was, Howard Nostrand asserts, greatly influenced by Hitchcock.[37]

American cinema has sought to capitalize on the 'presold' audience for comics ever since the short film *Happy Hooligan in Jail* (1903). The reinvention of comic characters in film began with a series of 'funny page' characters in cinema of the 1930s, as well as superhero serials and film franchises from the 1940s onward. Unlike other genres, horror has tended to be derivative of, rather than in dialogue with, film. This might be explained by the fact that horror lacks a recurring transmedia presence with its origin in comics – the majority of transmedia horror characters have origins in either literature (such as Dracula and Frankenstein's monster) or film (Freddy Krueger or Aliens). Vampirella came close to being such a figure in the 1960s and 1970s, but during the 1940s and 1950s horror comics, for all of their popularity, lacked the brand recognition of a Superman, Dick Tracey, or Li'l Abner to draw in a presold audience. As a result, the flow of content between horror cinema and horror comics seemed to go in one direction. It was not until *Tales from the Crypt* (1972) and *Creepshow* (1982) that horror comics would repay some of their debt to horror cinema.

## The comics industry

The question of an origin, such as one can be said to exist, for the comics form is as problematic as identifying an origin to the horror genre. This is for many of the same reasons, the most central one being that for us to establish a beginning to comics, we must first agree what comics *are*. Scott McCloud understands comics as a means to tell stories through images and so cites the Bayeux Tapestry and other artefacts as early examples of comics.[38] David Kunzle, similarly, starts the history of the comic book in the 1400s with church frescos and, later, early broadsheets and chapbooks.[39] If one wishes to trace a more direct lineage from modern comics, however, then one must read comics not only as storytelling through images, but in terms of their production and distribution as well as semiotic codes that they employ such as motion lines and speech bubbles, or what cartoonist André Franquin calls 'krolle-bitches'.[40] In this sense, the origins of American comics might be traced to newspaper cartoons from nineteenth-century Europe, the most frequently cited of which is *Puck*. These newspaper cartoons, in turn, were inspired by the woodblock prints of Rodolphe Töpher, Gustave Doré, and the Forrester brothers.

Early American comics appeared in newspapers and were collected in hardback books – Mike Benton asserts that seventy or more such collections were published between 1900 and 1909.[41] In 1929, the publication *The Funnies* was the first to print a collection of comics not previously published in newspapers. In 1933, Eastern Color Printing Company began publishing *Funnies on Parade* in seven-by-nine inch dimensions. The project was the brainchild of salesman Max C. Gaines, who also decided on the iconic ten-cent price tag. In November 1936, Comic Magazine Company, publishers of *The Comics Magazine*, released *Detective Picture Stories* – the first anthology devoted to a genre other than comedy. Other genres quickly followed, most prominent among them being the superhero, arguably the dominant genre from the first appearance of Superman in 1938. The Second World War proved to be particularly fertile ground for superheroes – they were, after all, well-suited to nationalistic and unnuanced stories of good versus evil. Comics were inexpensive and, during the 1940s, faced little competition from television or radio. By 1944, 91 per cent of children read comics.[42] By 1950, adults made up 54 per cent of comic book readers, and the American comic book industry produced 50 million comic books each month.[43]

**The horror comic**

Bradford Wright and Mike Benton identify the beginning of the horror comic genre as 1950, when EC launched the hugely successful series *Tales from the Crypt, Vault of Horror*, and *The Haunt of Fears*.[44] Robert Michael 'Bobb' Cotter, similarly, asserts '[i]t all starts with E[ntertaining] C[omics]'.[45] EC (then Educational Comics) was founded by Max C. Gaines, who began as a publisher of educational and religious comics. His son, William Gaines, took over the company in 1947 at the age of twenty-five, changed the name, and introduced crime and war comics to the company's offerings. In 1950, Gaines, along with his editor Al Feldstein, decided to launch a 'New Trend' of comics. They ceased publication of their existing six titles and instead began publishing high-quality provocative works in the horror, science fiction, and war genres. In the most commonly told version of this story, in 1949 Gaines and Feldstein decided that they wanted to bring the style of horror radio drama to comics and thus gave birth to the genre.

The narrative is not quite so straight-forward – Shelly Moldoff claims to have pitched the idea of a horror series to Gaines in 1948. More importantly, EC's intervention in horror comics also had many antecedents; exactly which comic might be described as the 'first' horror title is the subject of some debate and depends upon the problematic question of how we define horror. Harry A. Chesler's team of artists, for example, produced some stories that contained horror elements in late 1936.[46] The previously mentioned *Movie Comics* featured a comic adaptation of the film *Frankenstein* in 1939, making it another contender for a first horror comic. While occupying a different evolutionary branch of the comics industry, Charles Addams' *New Yorker* cartoons beginning in the 1930s contained a strong allegiance to the Gothic.[47] Greg Sadowski also identifies horror elements in stories that ran in *Amazing Mystery Funnies* as early as 1939, such as the story

'Madhouse Murder Mystery', which features the now-familiar trope of a beautiful woman being abducted by a monster (Figure 1). In 1939, *Detective Comics* #31 and #32 pitted Batman against, in the words of Glen Weldon, 'a mysterious supervillain called the Monk, hypnotism, a giant ape, werewolves, and vampires'.[48] Superhero stories continued to feature horror elements such as the Frankensteinesque Solomon Grundy, who first fought the Green Lantern in 1944, or Two-Face, the recurring Batman villain who debuted in *Detective Comics* #66 in 1942. Prize Comics' *Frankenstein* series (1940–1954) evoked an icon of horror fiction and cinema, although its overall tone seemed to vacillate between humor and action rather than a sustained attempt to evoke fear. Other adaptations of literature contained far more horror elements, however; *Classics Illustrated* #12 featured the stories of Rip Van Winkle and the Headless Horseman. Evelyn Goodman and Allen Simon's adaptation of *The Hunchback of Notre Dame*, which appeared in *Classics Illustrated* #18 (1944), was so violent that eight pages were removed from the 1949 reprint.[49] *Suspense Comics*, which began publication in 1943, featured horror themes on the cover, although the comics within seemed to more closely resemble the already well-established crime genre. *Yellowjacket Comics* also featured horror stories in the mid-1940s.[50] *Eerie Comics*, which first launched with a single issue in 1947, featured ghosts and bloody murders as well as the iconic formula of a monster menacing a pin-up girl in a red dress on the cover, and is likely the comic series that served as the template for the genre.[51] William Schoell identifies American Comic Group's *Adventures into the Unknown* (1948–1967) as the earliest, and longest-running, example of the horror genre in the sense that it introduced elements from supernatural horror cinema, pulp fiction, and radio into a comic book format.[52] By early 1950, before EC launched their three horror titles, the horror genre had already reached a level of ubiquity that it was ready for parody; Jerry DeMatt's 'Scoopy' strip, which appeared in *Sparkler Comics* #91 of January 1950, showed the eponymous hero and his friend visiting the house of cartoonist Ernie Bushmiller, where they are confronted by (what transpired to be) horrifying Halloween props.[53] This volume does not seek to offer an answer to the question of a 'first' horror comic because the concept is somewhat misleading – rather than the horror genre being the invention of a single publisher or single creator, we can identify from the above examples a coalescence of different themes and styles across several publications. These disparate elements collectively gave rise to a codified genre in early 1950.

Even if EC were not the first to produce a horror comic, they inarguably left the largest footprint. Artists such as Dick Beck and Bill

**I** 'The Madhouse Murder Mystery', *Amazing Mystery Funnies*

Savage, for example, who wrote for *Mysterious Adventure*, and Howard
Nostrand at *Chamber of Chills*, unashamedly mimicked the EC style.[54]
The editor of *Black Cat Mystery*, Sid Jacobson, states that 'I think that
[before my arrival], everyone knew we were doing hack things, and
then I came in, new to the whole business and I looked at EC and I said
'Oh my God!' I mean, no one else knew anything except them. And I
said, 'Why don't we strive to do this? ... That's what we were trying to
emulate'.[55]

Although EC loomed large, they were certainly not the only horror
publisher. EC's place at the centre of horror comics publishing is at least
in part due to the contemporary marketing efforts of Bill Gaines and his
status as a key witness in the Senate subcommittee hearings on juvenile
delinquency of 1954. This contemporary visibility sits alongside later
attempts to curate the content and reputation of the company by both
Gaines and fans of horror and comics and goes some way to explaining
the endurance of the EC myth. Recent comics historians have been more
cautious in describing EC's position as the first mover of the horror
genre – Terrence R. Wandtke speculates that his work 'may knock EC
Horror a bit from its pedestal' while John Benson, for example, asserts
that EC were responsible for just 7 per cent of horror publishing output.
He further notes that Atlas (later Marvel) were by far the most prolific
publisher, producing 25 of the (by his count) 130 horror titles released
between 1950 and 1954.[56] This project, while aware of the significance
of EC, takes a wider focus, reintegrating the scores of other horror titles
that constituted the bulk of the boom and led to the censorious interest
of the Senate subcommittee hearing on juvenile delinquency of 1954.[57]

The fact that horror comics were derivative of horror film did not
mean that they simply recycled the same themes and images.[58] As Linda
Hutcheon argues, transmedia adaptation involves different modes. Print,
audio/visual, and interactive texts are all immersive media, but they are
immersive in different ways.[59] As a medium, comics function differently
from film, allowing the reader to access the simultaneity of a page and
creating chemistry between panels.[60] Unlike film (in the era before home
video, at least), readers can choose the speed at which they apprehend
images in a comic, facilitating different forms of horror and removing
the possibility of others. Where a horror film, for example, might suddenly cut to a horrifying image accompanied by an orchestral stab of
high-pitched strings, the closest equivalent in a comic would be to reveal
a horrifying image through the turn of a page.[61] The time that the reader
spends looking at the image once confronted with it, however, is beyond
the creator's control. Unlike film, a comic can build dramatic irony by
showing a character in a safe position in one panel and imperiled in

another within the same page. Entire sequences can be dominated by the presence of a single image around which other panels are oriented. The effect of one panel, in other words, can bleed through to others.

Comics were also subject to different censorship laws (the Hays Code, which controlled film content, preceded the Comics Code Authority (CCA) by more than two decades), different budget constraints, and a different range of visual possibilities than film. As Douglas Wolk asserts, comics have an 'unlimited special effects budget'; comics are drawn rather than filmed, which means that the content is limited only by the imagination and skill of the writer and artist – while horror cinema had to make do with prosthetics and wires, monsters in horror comics could be made subject to what Scott Bukatman calls 'cartoon physics'.[62] The obvious artificiality of drawn images also mitigated their capacity to shock, meaning that horror comics could be (and frequently were) far more grotesque than the horror films that in many cases inspired them. Comics also faced fewer risks than film because the financial stakes were far lower; a film in the 1950s cost hundreds of thousands of dollars to produce (the low-budget films of Val Lewton in the 1940s, mentioned above, had to be produced for less than $150,000), meaning that the box office performance of one production could alter the trajectory of an entire studio, or even the entire industry. A single story in a comic was comparatively inexpensive to write and print and, even if it sold poorly, would be replaced on the comics rack within a few weeks. Comics adapted film, then, but the change of media and audience meant that the appropriation of horror properties from film served as, in Hutcheon's terms, 'repetition without replication'.[63]

Those working in comics were afforded a degree of freedom, and a far greater capacity for profanity, in terms of both art and content, than their peers in film. It is prescient that in a story from one of the early horror comics, *Eerie*, in 1947, the protagonist's inspiration for murdering his wife comes from watching a film – 'That's no way to pull a murder!', he muses, 'You've got to be clever ... Much cleverer'.[64] Film and comics, then, fed on each other, and both drew inspiration from horror literature and films of the past – comics writers and artists saw the work being done in horror film and, like the protagonist of the story, sought not only to be cleverer, but more shocking, more bloodthirsty, and more grotesque. Fredric Wertham may have been correct when he asserted that 'comic books make other media worse'.[65]

The heyday of American horror comics occurred during the period between 1950 and 1954, which was also a boom period for horror and science fiction film. Depending on one's criteria for inclusion, the industry amounted to roughly 110 titles published by 30 companies.

Very few publishers exclusively produced horror titles; Ace Comics, for example, which published *Baffling Mysteries*, *Hand of Fate*, and *Web of Mystery*, also published funny animal, romance, superhero, western, and crime comics. Even during the heyday of the horror boom, EC, the company perhaps most strongly associated with horror, also published crime, science fiction, and war comics. Runs of horror series vary from a single issue such as *House of Terror*, published by St John in 1953, to the 174 issues of *Adventures into the Unknown*, which began publication in 1948 and continued, with CCA approval, until 1959. The industry comprised both large publishers like EC, and smaller houses such as Superior Comics. During the 1940s and 1950s it was relatively easy for a publisher to enter the comics market. Aspiring publishers simply needed to purchase artwork from one of several studios or newspaper syndicates, arrange printing, and then send the comics to newsstand distributors where they would be sold on a sale-or-return basis. Printers were often happy to work for credit and so there were few financial barriers to entry.

Most horror comics were published without attribution to any member of the creative teams who worked on the stories. While some publishers had in-house teams, others, such as Centaur, purchased their content entirely from studio shops. The most common comic book publishing operation comprised a single-room office in New York, housing just a receptionist and an editor. Artists and writers, who typically created their works at home, would work for various publishers and studios at a time; this meant that, while some publishers sought a particular house style, the individuals producing the work were interchangeable from the publisher and reader's perspective. Artist turnover was high and their works were often published with little expectation that a given story would be remembered after it left the shelves. It is often only the editorial staff, most famously William Gaines, whose names are associated with the genre. Things at EC were strikingly different, however, as not only were writers and artists credited, they were also given profiles in the comic so that readers knew a little more about them. On occasion, the creative team even appeared in the stories as themselves, usually in a satirical vein in keeping with the editorial approach at EC. Comics from other publishers occasionally offer insights into the writing and editorial process by way of the 'monster come to life' trope. 'Gateway to Death', which appeared in *Witches Tales* #16 (1952), is one such example. In it, a writer for *Chilling Tales* (a genuine publication) has a story rejected. His editor hints that alcohol may be to blame and asks him to write him something 'chilling – really chilling'. The writer does just that, only for the monsters that he has imagined to spring from the page. On the final page he runs to his editor's large country house seeking sanctuary, only to be told to come back when he is sober. The editor slams the window shut, leaving the writer to his fate.

The editor in 'Gateway to Death' is at least moderately kind-hearted. In a similar story, 'Mask of the Monster', a female editor, described as 'beautiful – and hard as coffin nails', fires a writer (who is also her former boss) over his failure to write good horror scripts. She tells him: 'You're too much of a milksop to write horror comics! Your monsters are pathetic things and your stories don't have any zing to them! Hundreds of our readers are complaining! Your stories just don't scare people'. He crafts a story in revenge in which a monster attacks his former editor. He dresses as the monster in order to scare her, driving her to leap from her office window. He removes the mask only to be confronted by the monster itself, and similarly falls to his death.

The world presented by these stories is cut-throat. Writers are under constant pressure to create stimulating plotlines, loyalty is minimal, and memories are short: 'I tried', complains the hapless writer of 'Mask of the Monster', 'I worked hard, but they kept cutting my salary and threatening to fire me!' Such depictions may not be too far from reality – publisher Harry A. Chesler described the Manhattan studio of Detective Comics as a 'sweat shop'.[66] It is perhaps little wonder, then, that horror writers returned to familiar tropes and borrowed liberally from existing horror properties in order to create their own comics.

The question of who horror comics were written for is somewhat contested. Fredric Wertham and fellow opponents of the medium maintained that children made up the majority of comics readership and, further, that young readers were damaged by exposure to comics of all genres, including horror. Al Feldstein, conversely, asserts that children were not the intended audience; he and his colleagues at EC, he asserts, 'were writing for teenagers and young adults; we were writing it for the guys in the army'.[67] His assertion may well have been a retrospective one and difficult to disentangle from the accusations levelled against comics during the Senate subcommittee hearings of 1954. A consideration of the advertising offered in horror comics suggests that Feldstein's claim was at least partly true – *Witches Tales* #9 (1952), for example, carried an advertisement for lingerie, and *Tomb of Terror* #7 (1953) carries an advertisement for a car manual, both of which suggest (at least the expectation of) an adult readership. The likely answer is that both Wertham and Feldstein were correct – that comics were written for young adult men but were read by all. Ruth Morris Bakwin reports that, for example, in 1944, 41 per cent of men and 28 per cent of women read comics, while Shirley Biagi and Marilyn Kern-Foxworth report that in the same year, 91 per cent of American children also read comics.[68] In 1950, the comics industry generated an annual profit of almost $41 million dollars and published 50 million comics a month: everyone read comics.[69]

In 1954, the resistance to comics came to a head. For several years, church and parenting organizations, buoyed by the works of academics and psychologists, had protested against comics content. One work often credited as the tipping point in this campaign is Fredric Wertham's *Seduction of the Innocent* (1954), which argued that comics were part of socio-cultural conditions that caused juvenile delinquency. Not all criticism came from outside the industry. Artist Alex Toth, for example, reports that he felt uncomfortable with the gory images he was asked to draw by his editors at Better Publications.[70] 1954 also brought the Senate subcommittee hearings, during which William Gaines made a poor attempt to argue that the content of the comics published by his company was in good taste. The hearings were quickly followed by the adoption of the Comics Code Authority, a self-regulatory body that forbade certain types of content in comics. A key component of the panic around horror comics was the notion among their critics that children read these texts seriously. As evident from the pun-laden introductions of horror hosts and reader correspondence (particularly in EC titles), however, it is clear that at least some members of the audience adopted a degree of ironic distance from the text.[71]

The CCA did not destroy the horror genre, but it dealt it a huge blow. The immediate aftermath of its introduction saw publishers desperately inking over anything that the code forbade in order to publish stories that had already been created. In the months that followed, many publishers, such as EC, ended their horror titles and switched to other genres. Around 800 comics professionals found themselves without work.[72] EC eventually left comics entirely and became a magazine publisher, pinning what was left of their business on their surviving publication, *Mad*. Others, such as Fiction House Comics, Comic Media, Timor Publishing, Stanhall Publications, Star Publications, Sterling Comics, Toby Press, and United Feature, went out of business. The CCA affected all of the comics industry, but horror and crime comics were the hardest hit. Some publications continued while dramatically toning down the gore and sexualization in order to meet the requirements of the Code. DC and Charlton Comics launched their suspense-driven *My Greatest Adventure* (1955) and *Unusual Tales* (1955) in order to capitalize on the gap in the market left by more violent titles. In 1960, ACG launched *Unknown Worlds*, which included some restrained and largely bloodless ghost stories. The horror genre limped along, then, but the boom was at an end. By 1959, even *Adventures into the Unknown* ceased publication.

The horror comic did not stay dead for long. During the 1960s, EC veterans Russ Jones, Larry Ivie, and Al Williams partnered with publisher James Warren, editor Forrest James Ackerman, and new writer Archie Goodwin to launch a series of black and white horror magazines that broadly followed the style of the 1950s horror genre. The distinction between 'comic' and 'magazine' in this sense had more to do with avoiding the scope of the CCA than content, as Warren's magazines largely contained comics. Warren Publications launched *Creepy* in 1964, *Eerie* in 1965, and *Vampirella* in 1969. The success of Warren Publications' horror line led to the rise to similar magazines, which featured reprints of 1950s horror comics and original material from companies such as Eerie Publications and Skywald Magazines. While these magazines were similar in content to the comics of the 1950s, they catered to a different audience; the 1960s saw the rise of the 'monster kid' subculture, for which Warren's lead publication, *Famous Monsters of Filmland*, served as a rallying point.

By the end of the 1960s the comics industry, burdened by the yoke of the CCA and unable to compete with television, was floundering. Benton asserts, '[d]eclining sales, increasing prices, a lack of direction, and almost no new titles or characters made 1969 the most disappointing year of the decade for comic books'.[73] Rather than attempting to attract new readers, the industry catered increasingly to a subculture of collectors and fans increasingly immersed in networks of continuity, providing intricate plotlines that spanned multiple titles. In 1971, however, both DC and Marvel published comics that made explicit reference to drug abuse. Marvel breached the Code after a request from the Nixon administration to intervene in the fledgling War on Drugs, which was being pushed as a re-election pledge. Stan Lee saw an opportunity and wrote an anti-drugs story featuring reference to drug addiction at both the core and periphery of society, from fashionable white college students to a marginalized young man of colour. This content meant that Marvel's *Spider-Man* #95–97 were published without approval from the CCA. As a result of the significant success of these issues, the CCA reviewed their standards, not only removing prohibitions against the depiction of drug abuse, but those which had made horror comics practically impossible for the previous fifteen years. The first titles to launch were *Marvel Spotlight* (1972), which featured the first appearance of Ghost Rider in #5. In the same year, they also launched *Tomb of Dracula*, *Chamber of Chills* and *Supernatural Thrillers*. Marvel also discussed *The Mark of Satan*, a comic that would star the devil, but abandoned the idea.[74] In the same year, DC launched *Swamp Thing* and the

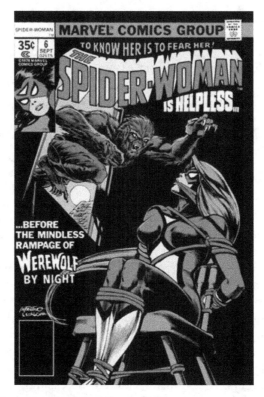

**2** Carmine Infantino's cover for *Spider-Woman* #6

anthology, *Forbidden Tales of Dark Mansion*. By 1974, horror rivalled the superhero genre in terms of output – Benton counts forty-five superhero titles and forty horror titles published that year.[75] Charlton Comics produced several horror titles in 1975 such as *Beyond the Grave* and *Monster Hunters*. By 1978, the superhero genre, once again, fed from the success of horror. In *Spider-Woman* #6 (1978), for example, the titular heroine appears tied to a chair as a werewolf bears down on her in a superhero variation of the classic 1950s imperiled-woman-in-red-dress trope (Figure 2).

1970s horror borrowed some of the tropes of the 1950s, featuring Gothic characters such as Frankenstein's monster and Dracula – characters who had largely been abandoned by 1970s cinema in favour of more psychological or bloody horror. In comics, these characters were somewhat different in kind, though, as they existed as recurring characters within the Marvel superhero universe. Where 1950s horror had generally been made up of stand-alone stories, the horror of the 1970s featured the titular monster as the protagonist in a series of adventures.[76] Unlike most of 1950s horror, the comics of the 1970s also gave credit to the creative team.

We thus have a broad history of the comics covered in this volume. This history is not, itself, the focus of this book. While it is impossible to separate horror comics from the circumstances of their production, our interest lies in using the text as cultural artefact – in looking not at the travails of the comics industry, but at the way in which horror comics commented on the world in which their creation and reception were enmeshed. In order to do so, we must first understand how the horror genre functions as a cultural force.

## Defining horror

In the section above we have offered a history of the horror genre. To offer a convincing interrogation of the social function of the horror genre, however, we must first offer a more precise definition of its properties.

An immediate challenge that faces anyone who wishes to engage with the horror genre in any of its manifestations is the question of defining what, exactly, we mean by 'horror'. The question is certainly relevant to this study; Jim Trombetta's collection of horror comics, *The Horror! The Horror!* for example, includes several texts that first appeared in publications marketed as belonging to the crime or science fiction genres.[77] Trombetta is not alone in his struggle to define the boundaries of the genre; when deciding which texts were eligible for inclusion in his volume, Greg Sadowski, editor of the collection *Four Color Fear*, deems *Frankenstein* (1940–1954) to be horror, for example, but only from issue #18 (in 1952) onward. Even Fredric Wertham, a man who had significant professional interest in the genre, considered *Wonder Woman* – otherwise universally read as a superhero comic – to be horror, although his grounds for classification are never eluci-dated.[78] One might argue that Trombetta, Sadowski, and Wertham's works mediate the same genre-mutability found in the comics industry at the time, where the question of genre was often determined by the publication in which a given story appeared, rather than any adherence of that story to any standard of form and content. To offer an illustra-tive example, while superheroes were firmly on the decline after their peak of popularity during the Second World War, an attempt was made to bolster the popularity of one declining genre through grafting it on to another. One such creation was *Captain America's Weird Tales*, which ran for two issues (#74 and #75) in 1949 and 1950. Issue #74 pitched

the super-patriot into battles with monsters, while #75 retained the title
but dropped Captain America. The series followed its titular protagonist
into the void soon after.[79] The interchangeability of horror and other
genres was likely less a question of mutual compatibility and more a
case of publishers being ready to respond to changing tastes. The most
successful comic manufacturers were those that were able to rapidly
respond to changes in demand, and savvy publishers were unlikely to
let a lack of content stop them from capitalizing on trends. If readers
wanted crime stories one day and horror the next, then publishers would
take the crime stories they had available, package them inside a cover
that featured a monster and a woman in a red dress, and sell them as
horror. Despite the somewhat mercenary approach to genre, however,
there were characteristics and themes that most horror comics shared.
Defining those themes, however, requires us to look to attempts to
define the horror genre.

Adriana Cavarero argues that horror is that which seeks to evoke
disgust.[80] Xavier Aldana Reyes builds on this definition:

> [H]orror fiction may be best understood as the literature that actively, and
> predominantly, seeks to create a pervasive feeling of unease and which,
> consistently, although not always successfully, attempts to arouse the emo-
> tions and sensations we would normally ascribe to feeling under threat.[81]

As Reyes demonstrates, horror is an emotion that contains, but is distinct from, fear, terror, or disgust. As Stanley Cavell asserts, 'terror is of
violence, of the violence I might do or that might be done to me. I can
be *terrified* of thunder, but not *horrified* by it'.[82] The distinction between
terror and horror can be traced back to Edmund Burke's discussion in
*On the Sublime and Beautiful* (1757) in which he asserts that terror is
'the ruling principle of the sublime'.[83] Ann Radcliffe agrees, remarking
that terror 'expands the soul' while horror 'contracts, freezes, and nearly
annihilates' it.[84]

This definition is complicated, however, by the fact that it is built on
the somewhat unstable ground of audience response. This is problematic
first, because what terrified one generation may amuse another, and,
second, because horror is ripe for parody. We can recognize the codes
and generic architecture of the horror genre in the *Scary Movie* (2000–
2013) films, for example, without feeling a sustained sense of threat
– viewers are able to enjoy feeling the threat but it is swiftly dispelled
through laughter (a phenomenon sometimes termed as [s]laughter).[85]
A working definition of horror, then, requires us to recognize the ways
in which certain images, sounds, words, and narrative structures have
come to signify horror beyond its originary intent.

The horror genre can be broadly defined through various characteristics and conventions encompassing both style ('jump cuts', a restricted view point, or loud discordant strings in horror cinema, for example, or hyperbolic language and mechanisms to build suspense in horror fiction), and substance (vampires, blood, serial killers, etc.). None of these are either necessary or sufficient for a particular text to be considered horror, however; both formal and material elements of Gothic fiction appear in, for example, Jane Austen's *Northanger Abbey* without it being considered horror. Indeed, many critics argue that seeking out a formal taxonomy of genre is a fruitless exercise; James Naremore argues that genre is largely determined by paratexts and extra-textual discourse rather than content – he describes genre as a 'loose evolving system or arguments and readings', while Andrew Tudor contends that genre is no more than 'what we collectively believe it to be'.[86] Mark Jancovich pinpoints crucial difficulties in any project of definition, arguing that it leads to a 'tendency to conflate very different forms in a manner which can ignore or minimise both historical change across periods and differences or struggles within any particular period', and a secondary problem where critics 'define specific genres in ways that will mark them off as distinct and different from one another', which overlooks questions of definition by audiences and also hybridity, where a text draws on elements of more than one genre.[87]

Such arguments recognize the instability and mutability of genre but restrict our ability to place a given work in relation to its textual antecedents. Horror comics cannibalized a range of other material both within the genre (adapting stories by Edgar Allan Poe, for example) and within the medium (borrowing tropes from crime, science fiction, and romance comics), so an awareness of intent and content helps to build an understanding of degrees of continuity and discontinuity in how they functioned. Even if genre is no more than a question of, as Kendall R. Phillips argues, 'collective understanding and expectation', then we need, for the purpose of this study, to attempt to define the understandings and expectations of the genre in the time when the comics in question were published.[88] If attempts to define horror prove illusive, it is perhaps because we need to understand the genre as a practice rather than through genre signifiers and audience response. Attempts to define horror cannot occur in a vacuum. In order to define what horror *is*, we must examine how, and when, it *does*.

Horror serves a social purpose; as Stephen Schneider argues, '[l]ike tragedy, horror promotes emotional catharsis in audiences; like fantasy, it offers viewers an escape from the tedium of everyday life; like comedy, it provides a relatively safe (because relatively disguised/distorted) forum

for the expression of socio-cultural fears'.[89] Our attempts to define
horror, then, must also constitute a history of how it has been seen and
some of its contemporary concerns.

Stephen Schneider argues, using a psychoanalytic framework, that
all monsters embody surmounted beliefs – those which we know to
be untrue. Successful monsters (those that evoke horror), he argues,
are those that reconfirm previously surmounted beliefs.[90] Darryl Jones
describes horror as a 'phobic cultural form', by which he means that it
documents and responds to dominant cultural and historical shifts first
by presenting something that exists outside of existing social practices,
and then resolving that threat, producing a sense of catharsis.[91] Reyes
similarly argues that:

> [T]he best horror, or, at least, the horror that has been retrospectively
> recuperated as the richest, is the one that manages to contain social and
> historical preoccupations within a narrative that may be experienced very
> differently by its initial, or non-scholarly trained, readers.[92]

In this sense, horror has often been read as the place in which the
otherwise unspoken anxieties and preoccupations of an era are given
form and brought to some kind of resolution. Successful horror,
Phillips argues, presents the audience with 'an accurate, if allegorical,
depiction of their own fears and concerns'.[93] Noël Carroll, similarly,
argues that horror challenges and complicates boundaries between,
for example, life and death, human and animal. The resolution of a
horror story represents a reassertion of those boundaries, representing a cathartic return to normal and the resolution of threat.[94] Many
horror stories are, at their heart, morality tales – the monster of the
typical horror story is punished (most often killed) for his or her par-
ticipation (willing or otherwise) in the events that have unfolded; if
it is not killed, then the monster may well be the agent policing the
morality of the protagonists. The catharsis arising from the end of the
narrative is a means by which order is restored, threats are symboli-
cally resolved, and the values of a given society are reaffirmed. This
puritanical streak is as visible in Matthew Gregory Lewis' 1796 novel
*The Monk* as it is in the classic modern slasher trope of sex leading
directly to death. This puritanical impulse has survived numerous
iterations of the genre, as, Roger Luckhurst argues, the ascendency
of science during the Victorian era led to H. P. Lovecraft's indifferent cosmos eliminating the possibility of a 'just' universe. Luckhurst
proposes that 'modern horror is what is left when Christian dread has
drained from the body Gothic', when the ordering principle of the
universe no longer stands.[95]

As Curtis Harrington, among others, argued, 'the ghost and horror story in literature rises during times of outward stress in society, and certainly the vogue for this genre of film follows the same pattern'.[96] This assertion certainly holds true when we consider, for example, that the explosion of horror cinema in the 1930s coincided with the Great Depression, and that *Rosemary's Baby* (1968) followed shortly after the Thalidomide tragedy of the 1960s and at a time more broadly concerned with women's reproductive rights. We should perhaps not place too much stock in such totalizing theories, however. Harrington commits a fairly obvious false cause error – when has any society been free from some form of 'outward stress'? Certainly, every work of art is, in some way, a mediation of its age, but a simple model of horror as an indicator of societal unease requires more nuance to be useful.

Readings of horror as affirmation of social values are also problematized by the fact that, as Robin Wood observes, monsters rarely stay dead.[97] As Noël Carroll argues, '[m]onsters are not only physically threatening; they are cognitively threatening. They are threats to common knowledge. [M]onsters are in a certain sense challenges to the foundations of a culture's way of thinking'.[98] Luckhurst describes the Gothic (a central sub-genre, distinct from other manifestations of the horror genre) as 'the underside of modernity, its persecutory double or secret sharer. Wherever Victor Frankenstein is, there his monster shall also be'.[99] The Gothic, particularly, haunts modernity with the threat of what Chris Baldick calls 'historical reversion; that is, of the nagging possibility that the despotisms buried in the modern age may yet prove to be undead'.[100] This function of the Gothic has made it fertile ground for exploring that which might otherwise be marginalized. Reyes argues that '[p]art of the attraction of horror derives from its transgressive nature – from the fact that it can deal in matters often left out of other genres or considered too extreme, maybe even harmful'.[101] Horror is able to maintain a form of permissiveness (and particularly sexual permissiveness) not found in other genres. George Haggerty argues that the Gothic articulates a 'queer' sensibility in the sense that it facilitates the exploration of desires that 'violate the terms of conventional social intercourse and defy the confines of novelistic expression'.[102] We might consider, for example, not only Dracula's 'red lips' in Stoker's novel, but the extratextual adoption of the Babadook (of the 2014 film by the same name) as a queer icon – and similar processes of adoption have occurred for other horror icons.

Adam Lowenstein positions horror films as a way of recognizing 'our connection to historical trauma across the axes of text, context, and spectatorship [...] through the agency of an allegorical moment situated at the unpredictable and often painful juncture where past and present collide'.[103] Horror comics can serve a similar function, though in a more complex way. While horror remains a marginalized scholarly genre in the sense of its being regarded as 'popular', many individual horror films have risen to prominence as artistic texts, albeit in a way that often distances them from the generic conventions and functions in which and through which they operate. These elevated texts then become part of a 'national cinema' 'that mirrors dominant narratives of national history', narratives through which the nation itself evolves and is continually constructed as a nation.[104] Horror comics have not been subject to a similar process – those comics or graphic novels taken up as emblematic of the medium's claims to higher cultural status tend to be from more 'acceptable' genres.

What these different theories of horror perhaps miss is that the genre does not have a single effect. Clearly, a defeated monster means something different from a monster at large. Can we still call a text conservative if, rather than being an aberration, the monster represents a part of social norms? Joan Hawkins, for example, argues that in Jésus Franco's films 'the monster-criminal seems to emerge from and, in some ways to represent, the dark side of the legal/penal system'.[105] What if our response is conflicted as in, for example, *I Spit on Your Grave* (1978), where the audience may sympathize with the threat (in this case a rape victim turned serial killer who is taking revenge on her assailants)? As Tudor argues, 'precisely the same representations of a monster can be found frightening, repulsive, hideous, pitiful, or laughable by audiences in different social circumstances and at different times'.[106] Clearly, then, totalizing theories of horror must be tested against specific manifestations.

Lowenstein seeks to disrupt this process, trying to construct 'national cinema' as 'a contested process of debate and dialogue', a space in which meaning is created through multiple voices, with all the attendant tensions that implies.[107] Horror operates in a number of different ways for a number of different ends, with no guarantee that the intended aims will be the messages taken from texts by their audiences. This is especially true given the heterogenous nature of horror audiences, divided as they are by age, race, class, gender, sexuality, wartime experience, and so on. Film has gradually become accepted, at least in part, as a medium capable of 'high art'; comics can still carry associations of simplistic narratives and childhood.[108] In the 1950s, for instance, horror comics were the most marginalized of all genres within the medium, and as such the images in the 'mirror' that they offered to contemporary American society were violently rejected – even as international campaigns against horror comics initially defined them as 'American Style' comics.[109]

While acknowledging the problems outlined above, this study is founded on the assumption that to understand the purpose of horror we must understand its historical context(s). A historical approach raises important issues about how we, from our present vantage point embedded in its own tangled web of reference points, come to understand the past. We are sensitive to the danger of reducing texts, to use Stuart Clark's words, to 'epiphenomena', – a means of tracing the 'periodic social need to relocate moral and cultural boundaries by means of accusation of deviance'.[110] At the same time, we hope to convince our readers that horror comics offer a lens through which we can locate and understand social anxieties present in American life during the Cold War era. By 'thinking with demons', as Stuart Clark urges us, we can begin to reconstruct the contours of a society and its subcultures through what, when, and how it feared.

## The historical context of horror

This project draws upon a large body of work from both Horror Studies and Comics Studies. Comics scholars often point to horror as a key part of the demonization of comics from the 1950s onward, but the thrust of their argument is usually elsewhere. Amy Kiste Nyberg, for example, writes about the history of the Comics Code Authority, the result of the hearings of 1954, rather than explicitly about the material itself.[111] Bradford Wright discusses the implementation of the Comics Code Authority in his impressive narrative of American comics, but the nature of his project and approach means that the horror boom can only be one moment in a series of moments.[112] Martin Barker's excellent study of the horror comics of the 1950s looks at the reception of these products in Britain, rather than America, and analyses the ways in which political alliances were forged to fight against them.[113] Other studies of horror take a more periodic approach, such as Mark Jancovich's account of 1950s horror, and such studies also tend to focus on films rather than comics.[114] There have been several academic and popular histories of the horror comics genre by, to name a few, Terrence R. Wandtke, Jim Trombetta, Michael Walton, and Greg Sadowski.[115] This study departs from existing works in two ways; first, we position horror comics in their historical and industrial context, considering the way in which they engage in dialogue with each other as well as with other influences, such as film and literature, whether contemporary or from an earlier period. Perhaps more crucially, unlike our colleagues, we read horror comics not as a disruptive social force that challenged

McCarthy-era sensibilities, but as primarily preoccupied with threats to, and the preservation of, white heterosexual male subjectivity.

For the purpose of this study we read horror comics as, broadly, speaking with one voice. There are, as noted above, problems with this approach; individual creators had their own style and particular companies preferred certain types of story and art – *Ghost Comics*, for example, preferred stories that featured ghosts, and EC were typically seen to produce higher quality work than their competitors. During the 1970s, there also emerged two distinct styles of horror comic; those by Warren Publications, which retained the single-story format from the 1940s and 1950s, and those by Marvel (and later DC), which had character-centred ongoing storylines and made horror properties a part of the broader Marvel universe developed during the 1960s.[116] As a whole, however, the various manifestations of the horror genre of the mid-twentieth century were more similar than they were different; various companies sought to imitate the EC style, the woman-in-red-dress was a ubiquitous figure, story-length and theme were consistent, and many of the same writers and artists moved between titles with, for example, Warren building its initial staff of contributors from veterans of EC from the 1950s, and Archie Goodwin moving from Warren to Marvel during the 1970s. While acknowledging differences are important, we choose to view the various manifestations of the horror genre as coalescing around particular themes and ideas. This book does not attempt to cover the entirety of mid-twentieth-century horror comics but a representative sample, with particular interest in comics that have previously not been covered, or covered to a lesser degree, in horror scholarship.

Much of the work in this book builds on gendered readings of horror. Barbara Creed's work on the 'monstrous feminine' is key to this, though it requires some reframing to take it from film screen to comics page. Creed states that 'the horror film's obsession with blood, particularly the bleeding body of woman, where her body is transformed into the "gaping wound", suggests that castration anxiety is a central concern of the horror film', and this maps splendidly on to the examples she deploys, particularly *Carrie* (1976).[117] Comics, however, were not generally characterized by blood, even before the introduction of the Code in 1954, which prohibited its display as overly gratuitous. Instead, comics were far more focused on the visibility of that which should be invisible – internal organs, bones, rotting human flesh. Violence is committed, frequently against women, but it is often bloodless; it may well have been the intention of creative teams not to mar the beautiful bodies offered up for the male gaze, while simultaneously punishing them for the perceived lack they project back on to the assumed male reader.

There is still castration anxiety, it is just doubly acted upon: lack is punished, but the act of punishment, and the body being punished, are also positioned as acts of rephallusization. Women are put 'in their place', which consequently reinforces the 'place' of the male reader, through sexualized violence. Creed continues along similar lines, arguing that 'as a form of modern defilement rite, the horror film works to separate out the symbolic order from all that threatens its stability', although this is another position that requires some adaptation in order to fit the horror comics under examination here.[118]

There are certainly acts of projection in these comics that involve the expulsion of the abject from the symbolic order underpinning American society. However, there are equally large numbers of stories and images where the abject is firmly located within the socio-political and economic structures that constitute and construct white patriarchal America. If, however, we follow Creed's line that horror films are essentially laying bare the abjection of women as necessary for the construction of that patriarchal society, our paths begin to converge. Horrifying things might be both inside and outside white American men and the power structures they inhabit, but it is only their fear that is taken seriously by the narratives under analysis here. There are crises within and without American society that threaten its stability, these comics seem to say, but the narratives and images they contain serve a double, or even triple, function: first, to identify the crises and the groups from which they emanate (women, departures from heteronormativity, people of colour); second, to work towards the containment of crises through violent spectacle that restages one of the crises in American masculinity – the practices and consequences of war – and simultaneously demonstrates the functional role of violence, both physical and cultural, in structuring contemporary society; and third, to contribute to a process of empowering the already empowered, white men, who perceive potential advances for women and in civil rights as a threat to their socio-economic and political position. Crises and groups that threatened the ascendancy of the white American male were experienced as challenges to the 'wages of whiteness' and the purchase of a privileged position within American society.

Our central thesis builds on the theory proposed by Aviva Briefel and Sianne Ngai, who argue that in horror film, fear is often tied to privilege: property owners, they argue, 'occupy the subject position of the haunted. It is with this secondary, derivative fear that the horror film begins, while the fear of the haunter is relegated to a historical past that is never represented'.[119] Fear, they argue, is a form of emotional property to which only those with privilege have access. They trace this trend to the Gothic theme of the haunted mansion, where access to fear is tied directly to property (in order to have a haunted mansion, one must own a mansion). The subaltern, who does not have access to property, is also denied access to fear. He or she, by default, occupies the position of the monster. Briefel and Ngai argue that the victim of a horror narrative is typically presented as generically white and middle-class (in films of the 1990s, 'the jock, the prankster, and the preppy prude' and in comics of the 1950s, typically a good-looking middle-class white couple in their thirties):

> Whereas the horror genre standardizes the constituency of the victim group, the subject position of the haunter fluctuates. In this manner, the white middle-class' ability to maintain itself as cohesive, autonomous group from film to film ultimately suggests a fantasy of its resilience to the changes embodied in the many vicissitudes of the haunter, who functions as an emblematic representation of change itself. The horror film is thus primarily a survival narrative of a homogenous class of property owners.[120]

If this was true of 1990s horror film, it was doubly true of horror comics from the mid-twentieth century. The socio-political, and literal, injuries of the Second World War and Vietnam constituted a historical trauma, a moment that disrupted the functioning of the practices that continually constructed the heteronormative patriarchal ideologies that underpinned and defined American society. A white masculine hegemony, such as one ever existed, faced challenges to definitions of manhood from the reverberation of war, the entry of women into the workplace, increasing public awareness of non-normative sexual practices, changing global politics, and the rising visibility of people of colour through the Civil Rights movement. In visualizing traumatic wounds, horror comics attested to anxieties around white middle-class masculine identity.

Our thesis, then, is that for all of their capacity to shock, American horror comics of the mid-twentieth century are primarily concerned with cathartically playing out and resolving threats to white male subjectivity. In this sense, we depart dramatically from other criticism of horror comics and a more general tendency in cultural studies to read popular media (and, in particular, popular media that incites the ire of a conservative establishment) as essentially aligned with the values of cultural liberalism. Terrence R. Wandtke, for example, describes horror comics as a 'seat of cultural criticism' that 'railed against traditional American values'.[121] One can understand why sociological, literary, and historical studies of horror comics have tended to understand these works as subversive; this was, after all, how they were understood by the anti-comics movement and the Senate subcommittee hearings. Even as critics such as Wandtke and Carol L. Tilley challenge the methodology and conclusions of anti-comics intellectual Fredric Wertham, criticism of horror comics has tended to broadly agree with Wertham's thesis that comics of all genres troubled 'traditional' (however problematic such a term might be) American values in that they encouraged anti-authoritarianism and normalized homosexual relationships.[122] While we agree that horror comics resisted dominant narratives of social and economic progress, we argue that they often did so from a position of conservativism and white male supremacy, building monsters from the perceived threats of (proto-)feminism, lesbianism, and civil rights. Horror comics were, we argue, far more resistant to the liberal reshaping of American society than their critics and supporters have historically believed. Ideologically, they have far more in common with the extreme right than contemporary advocates of social change.

This, however, might not always have been conscious. Often, the case we make is that in attempting to craft liberally progressive narratives and images, creative teams demonstrate both their desire for change and their resistance to it; essentially, for change that in no way affects the ability of white men to continue enjoying the full range of privileges to which they have historically had access. The changes for which they agitate increase access on an individual rather than systemic basis, suggesting that uplift is possible and that the system as a whole does not need to be reconfigured in order to achieve greater equality of both opportunity and outcome. In this sense our argument runs counter to that of Robin Wood, who argues that horror at the height of the Cold War refused the chief ideological project of the genre, which is 'the struggle for recognition of all that our civilization represses or oppresses', the creation of a cultural space where contested discussions about what is and is not socially acceptable can occur.[123] This approach is, we demonstrate, too reductive. In the horror comics analysed here, we see the acknowledgement of the marginalized, but all too often the narratives and images either work to justify repression or make too little of it. Cold War horror comics therefore stage the tensions identified by Wood as titillation as much as critique, as a walk on the wild side for possessors of privilege whose greatest fear is the removal of access, or even the widening of access, to that privilege. An approach of this kind, however, continues to construct white men as the bulk of the audience; comic readership was a broader demographic than this, and as such the potential for alternative readings exists. Such alternative readings are best suited to the long-form narratives of the 1970s, when complex monsters were protagonists of series, rather than antagonists of stand-alone scripts covering a matter of a few pages. The shift from margins to centre, in narrative terms, provided more opportunity for characters to develop, and for readers to invest in them, while also offering space for both implicit and explicit commentary on the ongoing nature of problems with race and gender, and the legacy of trauma.

This work divides the horror comics of the mid-twentieth century into two periods, separated by the introduction of the Comics Code Authority and its subsequent revision. These periods follow the popular distinction between the 'gold' and 'silver' ages of comics – a classification created by comics fans but widely adopted by comics scholars. For the purposes of this study we begin the first of these periods in 1947 with the first issue of *Eerie Comics* and end it at 1954 when the majority of comics publishers ceased their lines of horror titles. The second period begins in the 1960s with the growth of the megamonster genre and the first issue of *Creepy*. While many of the titles and characters that appeared during this era have continued into the twenty-first century we consider, for the purposes of this project, the silver age to coincide with the period 1964 to 1975, from the launch of *Creepy* to the end of the Vietnam War.[124]

We consider the periods 1945–1954 and 1964–1979 through the same imbricated lenses, namely trauma, gender, and race. The first chapter examines the cultural trauma of the second World War and the experience of those who served in it or otherwise were affected by it. We argue that horror comics present a counter-narrative to dominant forward-looking narratives of economic and scientific progress. They present, instead, a world in which white male hegemony is under threat from both social change and the horrors of war. The subsequent chapter examines the representation of women during the same period. Female characters, we argue, are presented as a source of horror, wielding, as they do, various forms of supernatural or criminal power. The genre then robs women of this power by representing them as objects to be acted on, or by subjecting them to violence. The third chapter concerns the representation of race. We argue that while horror comics reject overt racism, they reinforce racist assumptions, particularly by presenting people of colour reverting to savagery under stress, and the social movement of them as a group as a threat to 'white' spaces.

Our fourth chapter seeks to bridge these two periods, documenting the changing economics and demographics of the comic book industry after the Code. The subsequent chapter returns to the theme of war, arguing that the rise of the 'monster kid' and the televised violence of the Vietnam War created a shift in the genre – while 1950s horror generally revolves around a white male victim and Othered monster, in the 1970s horror increasingly occurs at the hands of white male perpetrators. At the same time, however, the genre shifted to ongoing storylines featuring evolving and somewhat emotionally complex characters, inviting sympathy for the monster.

While white men had become available as a source of horror during the 1970s, there was no corresponding access to victimhood for women or people of colour. As Chapter 6 demonstrates, despite absorbing some of the rhetoric of the feminist movement, the majority of horror comics continued to present women as sources of horror and/or titillation. The comic *Vampirella*, with a scantily clad horror hostess who flirts with readers, featured a series of misogynistic storylines and exemplifies the genre at the time. Chapter 7, similarly, shows that while people of colour were given limited access to heroic roles, they were only given access to fear in incredibly rare cases. Victimhood remained the province of white men and monstrosity continued to be linked to race. Empowered black characters such as Blade and Brother Voodoo were presented as, at best, allies and protectors of white characters, or as deriving their power from 'white society' in some way, and, at worst, as immune to pain and likely to revert to savagery.

Our conclusion seeks to draw together these themes, demonstrating that neither horror nor comics are intrinsically suited to the exploration of white male anxieties. The stylistics and genre-markers of the comics we have discussed can be appropriated by those they Other. Comics audiences have often been (erroneously) constructed as a space dominated by white men. This book shows that even this form of ownership is tenuous, and subject to assault from multiple different angles. The property through which fears of access are dramatized becomes in itself a space of conflict over access and reading strategies.

## Notes

1  H. G. Wells, *The Shape of Things to Come* (London: Gollancz, 2017), 208.
2  Judith Halberstam, *Skin Shows: Gothic Horror and the Technology of Monsters* (Durham, NC and London: Duke University Press, 1995), 22.
3  See Halberstam, *Skin Shows*.
4  Aviva Briefel and Sianne Ngai, '"How much did you pay for this place?" Fear, Entitlement and Urban Space in Bernard Rose's *Candyman*', in Alain Silver and James Ursini (eds), *Horror Film Reader* (New York: Limelight Editions, 2000), 281–303 (281 and passim).
5  Darryl Jones, *Sleeping With the Lights On: The Unsettling Story of Horror* (Oxford: Oxford University Press, 2018), 20.
6  Horace Walpole, *The Castle of Otranto*, in Peter Fairclough (ed.), *Three Gothic Novels* (London: Penguin, 1986).

7  The Seven Years' War ran from 1756–1763. Despite being a triumph for Britain in the immediate sense of the fact that they won the war, evicting the French from North America in the process, the victory set the scene for Britain's own ejection from the most lucrative of its American colonies in 1783. For more on the relationship between the Gothic and this period, see Angela Wright, *Britain, France, and the Gothic, 1764–1820: The Import of Terror* (Cambridge: Cambridge University Press, 2013).

8  The British Library, 'Gothic Novel *The Castle of Otranto*, by Horace Walpole', retrieved from www.bl.uk/collection-items/gothic-novel-the-castle-of-otranto-by-horace-walpole#sthash.83xwktBX.dpuf (accessed 23 May 2017).

9  According to W. Scott Poole, for example, 'Humanity emerged from the Stone Age dreaming of monsters', see *Monsters in America: Our Historical Obsession with the Hideous and the Haunting* (Waco, TZ: Baylor University Press, 2011), 5.

10  S. T. Joshi, *Unutterable Horror: A History of Supernatural Fiction*, 2 vols (New York: Hippocampus Press, 2012); Noël Carroll, *The Philosophy of Horror: Or, Paradoxes of the Heart* (London and New York: Routledge, 1990).

11  Dale Townshend, 'Gothic and the Cultural Sources of Horror 1740–1820', in Xavier Aldana Reyes (ed.), *Horror: A Literary History* (London: British Library, 2016), 19–51.

12  Horace Walpole, *The Castle of Otranto* (Oxford: Oxford University Press, 2014).

13  The term 'romance' should be understood here to mean 'novel' rather than a story containing a love plot.

14  Anon., quoted in Townshend, 'Gothic and the Cultural Sources of Horror', in Reyes (ed.), *Horror: A Literary History*, 19.

15  Royce Mahawatte, 'Horror in the Nineteenth Century: Dreadful Sensations, 1820–80', in Reyes (ed.), *Horror: A Literary History*, 77–103 (79).

16  Townshend, 'Gothic and the Cultural Sources of Horror', in Reyes (ed.), *Horror: A Literary History*.

17  Agnieszka Soltysik Monnet, 'American Horror: Origins and Early Trends', in Reyes (ed.), *Horror: A Literary History*, 53–76.

18  David J. Skal, *The Monster Show: A Cultural History of Horror* (New York: Faber and Faber, 2001), 30.

19  For more on the notion of the 'freak', see Rachel Adams, *Sideshow USA: Freaks and the American Cultural Imagination* (Chicago, IL: University of Chicago Press, 2001).

20  Leslie A. Fiedler, *Love and Death in the American Novel* (New York: Stein and Day, 1966), 27.

21  Skal, *The Monster Show*, 84.

22  Skal, *The Monster Show*, 43.

23  Sidra Stitch, *Anxious Visions: Surrealist Art* (New York: Abbeville Press, 1990).

24  Kendall R. Phillips, *Projected Fears* (Westport, CN: Praeger, 2008), 14. His assertion, while broadly borne out in audience numbers and popular discourse,

is somewhat belied by the fact that Browning's next horror film, *Freaks* (1932), was a commercial failure.

25  Quoted in Skal, *The Monster Show*, 115.
26  For a detailed account of Prohibition-era America's cultural love affair with the gangster, see David E. Ruth, *Inventing the Public Enemy: The Gangster in American Society, 1918–1934* (Chicago, IL: University of Chicago Press, 1996).
27  Skal, *The Monster Show*, 115.
28  Phillips, *Projected Fears*, 5.
29  Kevin Heffernan, *Ghouls, Gimmicks, and Gold: Horror Films and the American Movie Business, 1953–1968* (Durham, NC and London: Duke University Press, 2004), 24.
30  Robert Hughes, *The Shock of the New: Art and the Century of Change* (London: Thames & Hudson, 1991).
31  Heffernan, *Ghouls, Gimmicks, and Gold*, 5.
32  Skal, *The Monster Show*, 237–247
33  For more on the horror trend of the 1930s, see Alison Peirse, *After Dracula: The 1930s Horror Film* (London: I. B. Tauris, 2013), Chapter 1 of Phillips, *Projected Fears*, and the introduction to Heffernan, *Ghouls, Gimmicks and Gold*.
34  Phillips, *Projected Fears*, 35.
35  Dru Jeffries, *Comic Book Film Style* (Austin, TX: University of Texas Press, 2017); Blair Davis, *Movie Comics* (New Brunswick NJ: Rutgers University Press, 2017).
36  Mark Jancovich, *Rational Fears: American Horror in the 1950s* (Manchester: Manchester University Press, 1996), 13.
37  Davis, *Movie Comics*, 100, 124–125; Howard Nostrand in Greg Sadowski (ed.), *Four Color Fear: Forgotten Horror Comics of the 1950s* (Seattle, WA: Fantagraphics Books, 2017), 314.
38  Scott McCloud, *Understanding Comics* (Northampton, MA: Tundra Publishing, 1993).
39  David Kunzle. *The Early Comic Strip: Narrative Strips and Picture Stories in the European Broadsheet from c.1450 to 1825 (History of the Comic Strip, Volume 1)* (Berkley, CA: University of California Press, 1973).
40  See Jean-Christophe Menu, *Krollebitches, de Franquin à Gébé Broché* (Brussels: Les Impressions Nouvelles, 2016).
41  Mike Benton, *The Comic Book in America: An Illustrated History* (Dallas, TX: Taylor Publishing, 1989).
42  Shirley Biagi and Marilyn Kern-Foxworth, *Facing Difference: Race, Gender, and Mass Media* (Thousand Oaks, CA: Pine Forge Press, 1997).
43  Skal, *The Monster Show*, 230.
44  Benton, *The Comic Book in America*.
45  Cotter refers here specifically to the origins of horror magazines of the 1960s. Robert Michael 'Bobb' Cotter, *The Great Monster Magazines: A Critical Study of the Black and White Publications of the 1950s, 1960s, and 1970s* (Jefferson, NC: McFarland, 2008), 7.

46 Sadowski (ed.), *Four Color Fear*.

47 A 1946 cartoon, for example, shows a group of monsters in the act of pouring oil on carol singers. The image, Iain Topliss argues, pits our 'dark alter egos' against 'our own docile, socialised selves' (Topliss, *The Comic Worlds*, 139). Addams' cartoons also brought horror, including spousal murder, into the home; in one cartoon a middle-aged housewife tells the police, '"and then I disconnected the booster from the Electro-Snuggie Blanket and put him in the deep freeze. In the morning I defrosted him and ran him through the Handi Home Slicer and then the Jiffy Burger Grind, and after that I fed him down the Dispose-All. Then I washed my clothes in the Bendix, tidied up the kitchen, and went to a movie"' (quoted in Topliss, *The Comic Worlds*, 159). What makes Addams' work different from the works studied in this book, aside from audience and medium of delivery, is his conscious and sustained employment of humour. As Topliss argues, 'Addams' cartoon is a stabilizing gesture, reducing fearfulness in laughter rather than increasing it through horror' (Topliss, *The Comic Worlds*, 164). Addams would eventually go on to create the Addams Family. For more see Iain Topliss, *The Comic Worlds of Peter Arno, William Steig, Charles Addams, and Saun Steinberg* (Baltimore, MD: Johns Hopkins University Press, 2005).

48 Glen Weldon, *The Caped Crusade: Batman and the Rise of Nerd Culture* (New York: Simon & Schuster, 2016), 24. *The Monk*, when placed alongside other Gothic types, suggests Matthew Lewis' novel of the same name of 1796.

49 Daniel F. Yezbick, 'Horror', in M. Keith Booker (ed.), *Comics Through Time* (Santa Barbara, CA: Greenwood, 2014), 193.

50 Sadowski (ed.), *Four Color Fear*, and Stephen Sennitt, *Ghastly Terror! The Horrible Story of Horror Comics* (Manchester: Critical Vision, 1999).

51 The use of covers featuring imperilled women in states of undress, which became standard for the genre, began with *Suspense Comics* and owes its artistic genealogy to Margaret Brundage's 1930s covers for the horror short story magazine *Weird Tales* (1923–present).

52 William Schoell, *The Horror Comics: Fiends, Freaks, and Fantastic Creatures, 1940s-1980s* (Jefferson, NC: McFarland, 2014).

53 See Paul Karasik and Mark Newgarden, *How to Read Nancy* (Seattle, WA: Fantagraphic Books, 2017), 207.

54 The title *Chamber of Chills* has been used for two different publications – one by Harvey from 1950 to 1954, and one by Marvel from 1972 to 1976.

55 Quoted in Sadowski (ed.), *Four Color Fear*, 308.

56 Terrence R. Wandtke, *The Comics Scare Returns: The Contemporary Resurgence of Horror Comics* (New York: RIT Press, 2018), xxxiv; John Benson, 'Introduction', in Sadowski (ed.), *Four Color Fear*, i–ii. It is clear, though, that 'largest number of comics' does not always equate to 'largest amount of cultural impact'.

57 For an analysis of EC's 'preachies', its comics dedicated to social and political issues, see Qiana Whitted, *EC Comics: Race, Shock, & Social Protest* (New Brunswick, NJ: Rutgers University Press, 2019).

58 Horror comics were often highly derivative of other media in terms of storyline
if not delivery, taking inspiration not only from cinema but from various tales
in the Gothic tradition. Ray Bradbury, for example, was so struck by the simi-
larities between the story 'What the Dog Dragged In' (*Vault of Horror* #22,
January 1952) and his story *The Emissary* that he wrote a letter to the editors
at EC. Not only did horror comics writers take stories from other media, they
also borrowed storylines from other horror comics – the publishing house
Story, in particular, reworked many EC plots in *Dark Mysteries* and *Mysterious
Adventures* (See Sennitt, *Ghastly Terror!*, 47).

59 Linda Hutcheon, with Siobhan O'Flynn, *A Theory of Adaptation*, 2nd edn
(New York: Routledge, 2013).

60 Thierry Groensteen, *The System of Comics*, trans. Bart Beaty and Nick Nguyen
(Jackson, MS: University Press of Mississippi, 2007).

61 For a good example of this, see Anon., 'The Thing that Walked at Night',
*Ghost Comics* #9 (New York: Fiction House, 1953). Turning the page to see
the opening of this comic genuinely caused me (Phil) to start. Online comics,
which can include moving images within panels, have more means at their disposal to borrow shock effects from film. For an example of this we recommend
the 2011 online comic 'Bongcheon Dong Ghost' (we also recommend putting
down any hot drink you may be holding before you scroll), retrieved from
https://comic.naver.com/webtoon/detail.nhn?titleId=350217&no=31 (accessed
3 June 2020).

62 Douglas Wolk, *Reading Comics: How Graphic Novels Work and What They
Mean* (Cambridge, MA: Da Capo Press, 2008), 68; Scott Bukatman, 'Some
Observations Pertaining to Cartoon Physics; or, The Cartoon Cat in the
Machine', in Karen Beckman (ed.), *Animating Film Theory* (Durham, NC:
Duke University Press, 2014), 301–316.

63 Hutcheon, *A Theory of Adaptation*, 149.

64 Fred Kida, 'The Strange Case of Hen-Pecked Harry', *Eerie Comics* #1 (New
York: Avon, 1947).

65 Fredric Wertham, *Seduction of the Innocent* (London: Museum Press, 1955),
359. The same, of course, can be said of the horror films of the 1950s, which
sought to become increasingly shocking as the decade progressed and culmi-
nated in the rise of the Hammer Horror cycle of films so closely associated with
Christopher Lee, Peter Cushing, and décolletage in distress.

66 Benton, *The Comic Book in America*, 37.

67 Benton, *The Comic Book in America*, 48.

68 Ruth Morris Bakwin, 'Psychological Journal of Pediatrics: The Comics',
*Journal of Pediatrics* 42.5 (1953), 633–635; Biagi and Kern-Foxworth, *Facing
Difference*.

69 Benton, *The Comic Book in America*, 48

70 Benton, *The Comic Book in America*, 97

71 A reading strategy of this kind is represented, and offered to audiences potentially unfamiliar with the practice, in *The Blob* (1958), where the teenage
audience for the midnight screening of the film-within-a-film, *Dementia* (also

known as *Daughter of Horror*, 1955), laugh at on-screen events in a film that was deemed too controversial to be released in the UK until 1970. The upbeat Bacharach and David theme tune urging listeners to 'beware of the blob!' reinforces this reading strategy.

72 Dennis O'Neil quoted in Mike Phoenix, *Comics' Second City: The Gateway History of the American Comic Book* (self-published, 2012), 13.
73 Benton, *The Comic Book in America*, 74.
74 Sean Howe, *Marvel Comics: The Untold Story* (New York: Harper Collins 2012), 112.
75 Benton, *The Comic Book in America*, 77.
76 One letter writer, Bob Margolis, was published in the 4 May 1972 issue of *Werewolf by Night*. He suggests that the title should feature superhero cameos.
77 Jim Trombetta, *The Horror! The Horror!* (New York: Abrams ComicArt, 2010).
78 Wertham, *Seduction of the Innocent*, 34.
79 This was not the hero's last dalliance with the horror genre. He briefly turned into a werewolf in an arc that ran from *Captain America* #402 to #408 (all 1992).
80 Adriana Cavarero, *Horrorism: Naming Contemporary Violence* (New York: Columbia University Press, 2009).
81 Xavier Aldana Reyes, 'What, Why and When Is Horror Fiction', in Reyes (ed.), *Horror: A Literary History*, 10.
82 Stanley Cavell, *The Claim of Reason* (New York: Oxford University Press, 1979), 418.
83 Edmund Burke, *On the Sublime and Beautiful* (New York: Bartleby.com, 2001), retrieved from www.bartleby.com/24/2/202.html (accessed 26 February 2018).
84 Ann Radcliffe, 'On the Supernatural in Poetry', *New Monthly Magazine* 16.1 (1826).
85 See also William Paul, *Laughing Screaming: Modern Hollywood Horror and Comedy* (New York: Columbia University Press, 1994). This strategy can be seen in the Harry Potter series where boggarts, which thrive on causing fear, are dispelled by the riddikulus charm that renders them laughable. Similarly, Mina Seward tries to encourage Lucy Weston to laugh at Count Dracula after their first meeting in *Dracula* (1931). We have already mentioned the early efforts at horror comedy by Abbott & Costello. *Invasion of the Saucer Men* (1957) also combined elements of horror and humour, featuring as it does a disembodied hand, teenage banter, and a bull fond of beers. Jokes can often be found at the beginning of M. R. James' ghost stories, but this most likely indicates their usual purpose, which was after dinner entertainment. Although frequent at the beginning, jokes are rarely found at the climactic moment of fear.
86 James Naremore, 'American Film Noir: The History of an Idea', *Film Quarterly* 49 (1995–1996), 12–28 (14); Andrew Tudor, 'Genre', in Barry Grant (ed.), *The Film Reader* (Austin, TX: University of Texas Press, 1986), 3–10 (7).
87 Jancovich, *Rational Fears*, 10.

88 Phillips, *Projected Fears*, 5.
89 Stephen Schneider, 'Monsters as (Uncanny) Metaphors: Freud, Lakoff, and the Representation of Monstrosity in Cinematic Horror', in Silver and Ursini (eds), *Horror Film Reader*, 167–191 (168).
90 Schneider, 'Monsters as (Uncanny) Metaphors', in Silver and Ursini (eds), *Horror Film Reader*.
91 Darryl Jones, *Horror Stories: Classic Tales from Hoffman to Hodgson* (Oxford: Oxford University Press, 2014), xi.
92 Reyes 'What, Why and When', in Reyes (ed.), *Horror: A Literary History*, 11.
93 Phillips, *Projected Fears*, 5.
94 Carroll, *The Philosophy of Horror*.
95 Roger Luckhurst, 'Transitions: From Victorian Gothic to Modern Horror', in Reyes (ed.), *Horror: A Literary History*, 103–29 (117).
96 Curtis Harrington, 'Ghoulies and Ghosties', in Silver and Ursini (eds), *Horror Film Reader*, 9–20 (11).
97 Robin Wood, 'Return of the Repressed', *Film Comment* (July–August 1978), 25–32.
98 Carroll, *The Philosophy of Horror*, 34.
99 Roger Luckhurst, 'The Public Sphere, Popular Culture, and the True Meaning of the Zombie Apocalypse', in David Glover and Scott McCracken (eds), *The Cambridge Companion to Popular Fiction* (Cambridge: Cambridge University Press, 2012), 68–85 (75)
100 Chris Baldick, 'Introduction', *Gothic Tales* (Oxford: Oxford University Press, 1992), xi–xxiii (xxi).
101 Reyes, 'What, Why and When', in Reyes (ed.), *Horror: A Literary History*, 12.
102 George E. Haggerty, 'Literature and Homosexuality in the Late Eighteenth Century: Walpole, Beckford and Lewis' *Studies in the Novel* 18 (1986), 341–352 (350).
103 Adam Lowenstein, *Shocking Representation: Historical Trauma, National Cinema, and the Modern Horror Film* (New York: Columbia University Press, 2005), 9.
104 Lowenstein, *Shocking Representation*, 11.
105 Joan Hawkins, 'The Anxiety of Influence: Georges Franju and the Medical Horror Shows of Jess Franco's', in Silver and Ursini (eds), *Horror Film Reader*, 193–221 (206).
106 Andrew Tudor, 'Why Horror? The Peculiar Pleasures of a Popular Genre', *Cultural Studies* 11.3 (1997), 443–463 (456).
107 Lowenstein, *Shocking Representation*, 11.
108 Marc Singer argues that this sense of comics as a marginal or villainized medium was once valid but, in 2019, is now largely imaginary and is generally employed as a means to artificially ennoble the work of artists, writers, and comics scholars. Marc Singer, *Breaking the Frames* (Austin, TX: University of Texas Press, 2019).
109 See Martin Barker, *Haunt of Fears: The Strange History of the British Horror Comics Campaign* (London: Pluto Press, 1984).

110  Stuart Clark, 'Inversion, Misrule and the Meaning of Witchcraft', *Past & Present* 87.1 (1980), 98–127 (98).

111  Amy Kiste Nyberg, *Seal of Approval: The Origins and History of the Comics Code, Volume 1* (Jackson, MS: University Press of Mississippi, 1998).

112  Bradford W. Wright, *Comic Book Nation: The Transformation of Youth Culture in America* (Baltimore, MA: Johns Hopkins University Press, 2001).

113  Barker, *Haunt of Fears*.

114  Jancovich, *Rational Fears*; Heffernan, *Ghouls, Gimmicks, and Gold*.

115  Michael Walton, *The Horror Comic Never Dies* (Jefferson, NC: McFarland, 2019). Other texts cited above.

116  Some of the comics we consider here were contemporary to underground comics, which were self-published, iconoclastic, and experimental comics created by and for members of various branches of the counter-culture movement. Many underground horror comics, such as *Skull* and *Death Rattle,* were heavily influenced by EC and, in some cases, featured the work of classic horror comics artists and writers. Mapping the content and reach of underground horror, however, falls outside of this study. Underground comics had such a small and specific audience that their content cannot be effectively mapped onto the trends described here without considerably expanding the scope of our work.

117  Barbara Creed, 'Horror and the Monstrous-Feminine: An Imaginary Abjection', *Screen* 27.1 (1986), 44–71 (51).

118  Creed, 'Horror and the Monstrous-Feminine', 52.

119  Briefel and Ngai. '"How much did you pay for this place?"', in Silver and Ursini (eds), *Horror Film Reader*, 281.

120  Briefel and Ngai, '"How much did you pay for this place?"', in Silver and Ursini (eds), *Horror Film Reader*, 283.

121  Wandtke, *The Comics Scare Returns*, xxxiii, 84; David Hajdu, *The Ten Cent Plague: The Great Comic Book Scare and How It Changed America* (New York: Farrar, Straus, and Giroux, 2008), 179.

122  Carol L. Tilley, 'Seducing the Innocent: Fredric Wertham and the Falsifications That Helped Condemn Comics', *Information and Culture: A Journal of History* 47 (2012), 383–413.

123  Robin Wood, *Hollywood from Vietnam to Reagan* (New York: Columbia University Press, 1986), 75.

124  Comics fans and scholars tend to offer a longer timeline, beginning of the Golden Age in 1938 with the first appearance of Superman, and ending the Silver Age in the mid-1980s when *Watchmen, Maus,* and *The Dark Knight Returns* ushered forth the Bronze Age of comics. Our study uses a smaller date-range because we are only interested in one genre. In 2018 scholar Adrienne Resha suggested that we have now entered into the Blue Age of comics, which offers more diverse characters and appeals to a range of readers, beginning with the launch of ComiXology in 2009.

# 1

## 'The dead – the slain – the unavenged' –
## trauma in the 1940s and 1950s

> When Man entered the atomic age, he opened a door into a new world. What we'll eventually find in that new world, nobody can predict. (Dr Harold Medford, *Them!*, 1954)

In the story 'Hollow Horror', which appeared in *Fantastic Fears* #6 in March 1954, Swilbur, a factory worker, is bullied by his co-workers, who joke that he has 'holes in his head'. His frustration grows until, in a wild rage, he decapitates one of his tormentors, an office secretary. In the final panel he reveals that those who mocked him were unwittingly correct; his head is indeed full of holes that have been patched with plates. 'It was all the doctors could do for me after the war!' he tells the reader.[1] Swilbur, then, is likely a veteran of either the Second World War or the Korean War. He bears emotional and physical wounds from combat and suffers humiliation and emasculation in his postwar life as a result. He has returned to a society that cannot accommodate his injuries and offers him neither understanding nor respect. He is spurned by women who appear to be far healthier, better adjusted, and better equipped for the work environment. Swilbur is the aggressor in the story but he is also a victim – a victim of war and of a society that no longer conforms to his previous sense of order. The promises made to him in exchange for his service, and the ideologies of individual, home, and nation that they promoted, are no longer recognizable to Swilbur. The only means he can conceive of to assert his sense of masculinity is that which was supposed to be the ticket to a new life, not its destination: violence. Whereas war is often established as a means of demonstrating masculine potency, Swilbur's story shows how it could also unflinchingly offer up masculine lack, both individually and systemically. Wilbur fails to reintegrate not only because war has changed him, but because war has changed the world he once thought he knew.

Roughly 60 million people died during the Second World War. Far more suffered physical and psychological injuries that profoundly affected the remainder of their lives. People died on the battlefield; they were blown up, shot, burned alive, and stabbed to death. They also died, in far greater numbers, off the battlefield, as victims of mines, bombs, starvation, and disease. Civilians died in organized and semi-organized massacres when, for example, Japanese soldiers ransacked the Chinese city of Nanjing, collecting trophies and raping women. American and British planes firebombed the German city of Dresden. American planes firebombed Tokyo and dropped atomic bombs on Nagasaki and Hiroshima in August 1945, causing deaths in both the initial explosion and from nuclear fallout in the days, weeks, and months to follow. The Nazi death camps – an entire industry that sought to murder people as efficiently and on as wide a scale as possible – accounted for as many as 11 million deaths. As Gábor Klaniczay states, 'while in earlier centuries it was imaginary magical conflicts that served to resolve or release real social and cultural tensions, now it was social and cultural conflicts that began to assume a somewhat magical dimension', with issues from the war and resettlement being worked out in and through a range of texts.[2]

The war reached the shores of the US in many different forms. Primarily, reports of war arrived in the form of images and letters. As Trombetta argues, by the 1950s 'many Americans had already seen plenty of corpses in dishonoured and distressed condition – if not in person then in newsreels and documentary footage. We too have seen them – populations of emaciated corpses waving sticklike in the jaws of bulldozers, or walking skeletons staring through barbed wire'.[3] Bodies themselves, not just their visual representation, also brought the war home. In 1944, for example, *Life* ran a story about Natalie Nickerson, whose beau had sent her a Japanese skull from the Pacific.[4] In far greater numbers, the war came home in the form of corpses for burial, and in the memories and bodies of those who came home alive. It seemed, for many, as though life had come to resemble and even exceed the most horrific imaginings of cinema and radio – the crimes of doctors Joseph Mengele and Marcel Petiot went far beyond the most depraved mad scientists of 1930s popular culture.

Many of those who came to America after the Second World War, either as returning veterans or refugees, carried the war with them in the form of physical injuries, disease, and psychological trauma. While the killing had, ostensibly, stopped, for them the war remained a recurring and insistent presence in their lives. Many suffered from (often undiagnosed) post-traumatic stress disorder (PTSD), characterized by anxiety, depression, insomnia, a sense of confusion, and a heightened sensitivity to possible danger.[5] In Goleman's words, 'vivid, terrifying moments [had become] memories emblazoned in the emotional circuitry [...] the traumatic memories [became] mental hairtriggers, ready to sound an alarm at the least hint that the dread moment is about to happen once again'.[6] For many, the mental distress resulting from trauma was compounded by a sense of isolation. America's war victims found themselves in a society that was affluent and forward-looking, for which the past, and particularly talk of bloodshed, seemed unseemly and impolitic.[7]

American culture sought to move past this social trauma; while many artists and writers in Europe continued to live with, and build art and philosophy around, the realities of war, America pushed ever-onward with world fairs, widespread industrialization, and rising birth rates. The dominant tone of American culture during this era was famously captured by Philip Roth as follows:

> Our class started high school six months after the unconditional surrender of the Japanese, during the greatest moment of collective inebriation in American history. And the upsurge of energy was contagious. Around us nothing was lifeless. Sacrifice and constraint were over. The Depression had disappeared. Everything was in motion. The lid was off. Americans were to start over again, *en masse*, everyone in it together.[8]

J. K. Galbraith argues that in the 'Affluent Society' of postwar America, production came to be the test of performance. Production, he argues, 'only fills a void that it has itself created', merely burying the wounds of the war under so many consumer items.[9] Horror, however, makes it clear that what is buried will not necessarily stay that way forever; that, as Roger North put it in 1744, 'men that are buried have a sort of life in their graves', a continuing, uncanny, presence that can return to strike against the living.[10]

As established in the Introduction, previous studies of horror comics have tended to emphasise the ways in which the genre resisted dominant cultural trends. In one sense, this chapter affirms that argument; in postwar America, horror comics returned to the genre's traditional role of, to quote Skal, a 'cultural dumping ground for the processed images of men blown to pieces, and the shell-shocked fantasy obsession of fitting them back together'.[11] While American political rhetoric, economics, and mainstream culture spoke of a bright new world, horror comics articulated an aesthetic and ethical commitment to the grotesque, to the inescapability of the past, and to the impossibility of heroism in the face of widespread impersonal violence. They represented a pocket of culture, in other words, which corroborated the experience of warfare in a society that seemed eager not to acknowledge the violence of the immediate past. In their attempts to articulate the terror of the Second World War, horror comics touched upon the veteran's experience, the

Holocaust, and the use of atomic weapons on civilians. In each case, they sought to demolish the geographical and temporal boundaries between the violence of the Second World War and the apparently peaceful and prosperous world of 1950s America. As a grand thesis, spanning the genre, horror comics assert that the violence of the Second World War was both ongoing and deeply imbricated within postwar American life.

Horror comics, then, were profoundly counter-cultural in the sense that they resisted narratives of progress and renewal. However, they were also deeply conservative in that they centre the trauma of warfare on the lives of white American men and omit or decentre the effects of war on people of colour and women. When thumbing through the pages of horror comics from the period, one has a profound sense of a country in crisis, but these representations of crisis limit access to victimhood. These texts present a narrow vision of the effects of war that legitimizes, as we shall see in the following chapters, the positioning of women and people of colour as a source of fear.

### The veteran experience

In 1944, in his book *The Veteran Comes Back*, Columbia University social worker Willard Waller argued that the reintegration of veterans was America's most significant social problem.[12] He claimed that veterans were often resentful of the sacrifices their country had asked of them and that it was of paramount importance that America find an effective means to rehabilitate those who had been affected by war. Waller was less concerned with the welfare of veterans than the threat they, like Swilbur in the story described above, posed to others. He feared that former soldiers, out of anger and a failure to readjust to civilian life, may lash out at their neighbours. Veterans had also been cast as a major source of anxiety in 1932 when President Hoover ordered General MacArthur to use force to clear the 'Bonus Marchers', First World War veterans requesting the early payment of their veterans' bonus to enable them to survive the Great Depression. The veterans' organizations that arose in the wake of the war therefore also sought to shape what it meant to be a veteran, with some positions being more acceptable to governing institutions than others. The American Veterans' Committee (AVC), founded in 1943 by a group of liberal veterans at UCLA, took as its motto, 'Citizens first, veterans second', a position that acknowledged service, but focused on the future and reintegration.[13]

Waller's warnings were not entirely unheeded, but efforts to address the veteran problem were often misplaced. The government provided veterans with opportunities in education, loans, and unemployment insurance – a move away from the bonus system pursued after the First World War and towards the suggestions advocated by groups such as the AVC. However, such provisions attempted to address veterans' economic circumstances rather than their psychological needs. The tacit message conveyed by such legislation was that veterans were expected to move on – that they should put their past behind them and (provided they were white) join America's newly affluent middle classes. Accordingly, recognition of, and treatment for, post-traumatic stress disorder (then called 'combat fatigue') was highly limited. Alcoholism, a form of self-medication common among those suffering from PTSD, was broadly regarded as evidence of a weak character rather than a symptom of psychological distress. High rates of alcoholism among Native American veterans, who were deprived of many of the same opportunities as their white counterparts, reinforced racist stereotypes and perpetuated systems that marginalized them. If a combat survivor continued to be afflicted by war experiences and failed to find a place in postwar America, then they were generally considered to be at fault. Issues related to veterans of colour and their inability to access the same level of services demonstrate that trauma was itself racialized – that the trauma of wartime experience might disrupt the individual but not the systems that contained them.[14]

For many veterans, moving on was impossible. The forward-looking, prosperous, and comfortable lives of the postwar generation belied the realities with which many had been confronted. Veteran Donald Mercier claims that 'when a local airplane would fly over I'd tend to dive into a ditch because when we were on Morotai we were strafed and bombed every day, three or four times'.[15] Mercier, and thousands like him, lived with a sense of still being in a wartime situation – their emotional circuitry was primed for disaster at any moment. Such individuals had a very real sense that, while their country was moving on, they were frozen in the experience of combat. The experience of going from the destroyed cities of Europe, the battlefields of the Pacific, or the barbed wire fence of the death camp to the white picket fence of suburban life in Middle America was, for many, too jarring an experience. The narrative of the Second World War in the American cultural imagination was by and large not one of grotesque tragedy and needless slaughter but of heroism supposed to bring forth a period of abiding peace and prosperity. For many of those who had lived through such experiences, such rhetoric seemed vacuous and empty. Some of this was reflected in popular culture; in *The Best Years of Our Lives* (1946), a film explicitly about reintegration, which starred veterans, Al Stevenson remains Al

Stevenson, but the world changes around him. His experiences have rendered the peacetime world uncanny, as a familiar space characterized not by its familiarity, but by the collapsed boundaries between the safe and the unsafe, the known and the unknown. This attests to the experience of many returning veterans, whose acquired wartime skills relegated them 'even more fully to a marginal social position, since ... they are the traces of a force totally incompatible with postwar America', traces that cannot help but define the way millions experienced postwar life.[16] This must be seen as a failure of the dominant ideology to solicit and maintain belief in itself and the social structures and institutions it underpins. Horror comics explored this liminal terrain, prodding the wounds of war and the scars they had left, refusing to keep them from view and to quietly 'move on'.

The effects of war on the horror genre were profound. The years after the Second World War were characterized by, Jonathan Rigby asserts, a 'sudden, and apparently complete, loss of interest in horror subjects among filmmakers and audiences alike'.[17] This is apparently borne out through a sharp decline in American horror film production, with numbers dropping from the high point of wartime production of fifteen in 1944 to twelve in 1946, then a complete collapse to one in 1947, two in 1948 (one of which was the first Abbott & Costello comedy horror, *Abbott and Costello Meet Frankenstein*), then none at all in 1949. Dziemianowicz argues that the loss of interest, at least in terms of film production, was a direct result of the experience of war: 'a world forced to contend with war's very real legions of the dead and the unalleviated apprehensions of the dawning nuclear age demanded horrors that were more believable than more fantastic'.[18] It is notable that the last of the Universal horror films of the 1940s, *House of Dracula* (1945), coincided with the end of the war and that when the characters returned, in the Abbott & Costello film of 1948, it was as comedic figures. As discussed in the Introduction, there is also the fact that many horror films were B movies, and after the Paramount Decision of 1948, B movies went into major decline, with studios focusing on fewer A grade pictures instead. At the same time, however, horror fiction and, particularly, the short story, began the journey towards immense popularity in the 1950s.[19] One notable example is Shirley Jackson, who first found national prominence with her short story, 'The Lottery', published in *The New Yorker* on 26 June 1948, which describes the process of choosing a human sacrifice in an otherwise convivial town. Perhaps one of the reasons why horror fiction, and horror comics, became popular as horror film declined was that fiction, unlike film, is private and mono-sensory – it offered a means to access the horrors of war in a more controlled format.

There is some evidence to suggest that veterans, in the absence of other relief, may have turned to comics. Many of those who created comics, such as Harvey Kurtzman and Will Eisner, were themselves veterans and their stories, if obliquely, often drew on their experience. Veterans also made up a large part of comics readership; as mentioned in the Introduction, by 1950, adults made up more than half of comics readers, with slightly more men reading than women. Comics had been used as a propaganda tool over the course of the Second World War; some publishers had gone so far as to size their publications to the dimensions of an American serviceman's tunic pocket, and comic books made up a quarter of the books shipped to soldiers serving overseas.[20] Veterans continued to read comics long into adulthood; horror comics frequently carried advertisements for products that could not possibly have been for children, including car manuals (in *Tomb of Terror*) and savings bonds and pensions (in *Beyond*).[21]

Given both the pervasive presence of trauma in the lives of Second World War veterans and the ubiquity of horror comics, it is perhaps unsurprising that the genre mediated veteran experiences. In part, they did so through the invocation of the Gothic, a sub-genre of horror with a primary interest in unearthed trauma. The pervasive persistence of the Gothic can be found in the naming practices of horror comics, which frequently attest to its defining role in shaping Western horror: *Tales from the Crypt*, *The Vault of Horror*, *Tomb of Terror*, *Ghost Comics*, and so on. This is not to say that the preponderance of Gothic naming strategies was similarly constructive of content. In film and fiction, crumbling castles and family curses were replaced by more modern fears of technological warfare and industrialization. The Gothic continued to haunt horror comics, however, in stories that placed an American protagonist (or, more frequently, a pair of American newlyweds) in Europe. In 'The Flapping Head', for example, a couple visit a recently restored castle in 'central Europe', where they uncover the bones of a vampire and unintentionally restore it to life.[22] The story is resolved when the castle collapses on the monster, returning it to its role as a ruined tomb, all of which suggests some familiarity with the Universal monster films of the 1940s, particularly the series of team-ups beginning with *Frankenstein Meets the Wolf Man* (1942) and progressing through *House of Frankenstein* (1944) and *House of Dracula* (1945), all of which end with the destruction of the house that was the locus of the film. The threat that the medieval offers to modernity, often reimagined as a geographical journey westward from Central Europe, is a classic horror trope, articulated perhaps most clearly in Stoker's *Dracula*.[23] After the Second World War, however, the depiction of Europe as a site of ruin where buried traumas erupt into American consciousness took on new resonances. Like the vampire bones that lie beneath a ruined castle, many former servicemen had lost a part of themselves, buried but still dangerous, in Europe.

Other stories located the trauma of the Second World War closer to home. In the story 'Nightmare Merchant', for example, which appeared in *Strange Fantasy* #7 (1953), a veteran and his wife buy a house.[24] It transpires that they have been sold the house by a vampire, who murders them and trades their bodies for blood. The return to America, the acquisition of property, and the tranquillity of suburbia do not mean an escape from the violence of war. Indeed, the seemingly pleasant façade of suburban life does not erase violence but relies upon it – a point made more explicitly in 'Dirt of Death' from *Ghost Comics* #4 in which dead bodies serve as lawn fertilizer.[25] This narrative, with the remarkable absence of subtlety found across horror comics of the 1950s, renders literal the fact that the apparent suburban tranquillity of the 1950s grows from the deaths of millions. Horror comics, it seems, continually resist the possibility of a 'return to normal' by demonstrating continuity between bloodshed overseas and apparent civility and opulence at home – showing normalcy, in other words, to be anything but. Such narratives mediated trends found in short fiction of the era. Murphy argues that 'it was the horror that arose from the conditions of everyday life that would take the lead in the 1950s and after', suggesting that rather than the horror genre, it was the pretence that everything was fine that was truly horrifying.[26]

The persistence of violence in the lives of veterans manifests elsewhere in a recurring trope in horror comics of being awoken by ghosts. Such scenes speak directly to both the invasive presence of the past and the common experience of insomnia among those suffering from PTSD. The comic 'The Demon of Devonshire', from *Ghost Comics* #7, offers an illustrative example. The opening panel shows a man lurching violently awake as ghosts, one of whom is caught perpetually at the moment of being hanged, surround his bed (Figure 3). In his shock, the man relates the fact that this is not a singular occurrence – that he has, in fact, been awakened by these ghosts over a series of nights. In the second panel the ghosts identify themselves as 'the dead – the slain – the unavenged'.[27] This is in keeping with what Owen Davies describes as the 'traditional ghostly fashion to reveal the murder so that justice would be done', an appearance of the past in the present in an attempt to bring about closure on past wrongs.[28] Drew Murdoch's 'The Ghost Gallery', from *Ghost Comics* #2, similarly, opens with a woman waking up at night. The text reads: 'I could feel the evil in the house … It was all around me

**3** Anon., 'The Demon of Devonshire', *Ghost Comics* #7

... Stronger even than the biting cold. I was alone in a strange unfriendly room and the flickering candle was waking hideous shadows on the wall ... As though a man was being murdered'.[29] The past, then, erupts into these characters' apparently comfortable suburban present, insisting on its continued relevance even after the occurrence of violence has long passed. The fact that the ghosts in 'The Demon of Devonshire' consider the circumstances of their deaths to remain unresolved runs counter to the forward-looking narratives of the time. Although out of keeping with the forward thrust of contemporary American rhetoric, the preoccupation with the wrongs of the past fits with the nature of the ghost story, described by Darryl Jones as a:

> Highly conventional, formalized, conservative form, governed by strict generic codes, which often themselves ... reflect and articulate an ingrained social conservatism, an attempt to repulse the contemporary world, or to show the dire consequences of a lack of understanding of, and due reverence for, the past, its knowledge and traditions.[30]

While American culture looked confidently to the future (embodied by modern marvels, science fiction, world fairs, and a rising birth rate), the innumerable trauma victims found themselves drawn, unwillingly but irresistibly, into the horrors of the past.

The insistence of the past in horror comics entails not only psychological but bodily trauma. In many cases, the survivors of a horror comic have only their scars as a record of the violence to which they were subjected. These scars both arrest the individual within the violence of his past (victimhood, as a recurring trope, is reserved for men), and attest to the impossibility of fully expunging or communicating trauma. In 'Found: The Lair of the Snow Monster', the sole survivor of an expedition tells the story of uncovering an otherworldly beast. He finishes his testimony by stating that the experience cost him his 'peace of mind for the rest of my life'. When his interlocutor objects that his story must be 'sheer imagination', the storyteller removes his coat jacket to reveal that he has lost a limb (Figure 4).

The story engages with the veteran experience not only because the storyteller's body serves as a record of past violence, but because his testimony is initially disregarded. Many survivors of the Second World War (and in particular, survivors of the Holocaust) were reluctant to speak of their experiences, first, because they did not wish to relive what they had gone through, and second, because they were worried that if they did speak no one would understand or believe them.[31] The scars the protagonist bears serve as visual evidence to corroborate his

**4** Anon., 'Found: The Lair of the Snow Monster', *Tomb of Terror* #6

story, testifying to the inability to completely eradicate the trauma of the past.

Horror comics do not only grapple with the reality of trauma and survivor guilt; more so than any other genre, they embody a scepticism towards narratives of heroism. While the science fiction, western and, particularly, war comics of the era tended towards narratives in which protagonists overcame an external threat, it was a requirement of the horror genre that its heroes had to fail. To use Trombetta's words:

> In an era that held its values dearly, no dearly-held value survived expo-
> sure to the horror comic universe: not the 'happy ending', not family,
> not science, and not the law. This world seems not merely meaningless
> in an existential sense – godlessness would be a relief – but also actively
> malicious [...] A positive zest is taken in stripping males of their rescuer
> potential, their status, and their prerogatives; not just their maleness goes
> but also their humanity.[32]

Examples of failed heroes abound throughout horror comics. In 'The Survivors', for example, from *Tomb of Terror* #6, a crew of scientists do battle with alien creatures. In a contemporary science fiction story, one might expect the humans to ultimately overcome savage aliens; instead, the only surviving scientist inadvertently transforms himself into one of the beasts he seeks to escape, suggesting that, as was the experience of many soldiers in the Second World War, he found himself not only as a victim of violence, but as a perpetrator; in fighting monsters, he himself became one. Within the horror genre, concepts such as bravery, loyalty, and heroism – concepts that were so fundamental to 1950s narratives of recovery – are found to be misplaced, misguided, and worthless when faced with the impersonal will of violence. Horror comics attested, in other words, to the impossibility of moving on – as did, obliquely, the outbreak of the Korean War (1950–1953), which plunged the US, as part of an international coalition, into another war. As Korea came so soon after the end of the Second World War, and was such an ill-defined and messy conflict without a clear conclusion, its contribution to the national narrative was the introduction of additional confusion and disarray – the perpetuation of trauma rather than its closing off and working through.[33]

## The Holocaust

The veteran experience was not the only way in which horror comics sought (to borrow a phrase from Vietnam War protestors) to bring the war home to America. Just as horror comics allegorically brought combat experience to American soil, the Holocaust, with its terrible implications, was also woven into the fabric of American life.

The Holocaust survivor experience shared characteristics with that of the veteran (indeed, many Holocaust survivors were also veterans). Many survivors continued to live with the violence they had witnessed and been subject to for the rest of their lives.[34] Even decades after the death camps had ceased to operate, Art Spiegelman's father Vladek, an Auschwitz survivor and former soldier, urged his son not to visit Poland because '[t]hey kill Jews there'.[35] For Vladek Spiegelman and those like him, the Holocaust was not consigned to the past but was ongoing and was intimately tied to their daily lives. Indeed, many Holocaust survivors described a sense of the violence of their past drawing closer, rather than diminishing, as time passed.[36]

Art Spiegelman reads horror comics as 'an unconscious post-war attempt to assimilate the atrocities of Auschwitz and Hiroshima', to which Hillary Chute adds, 'we might consider the EC horror comics that blossomed in the 1950s as a secular American Jewish response to Auschwitz – as in the gory 1953 *Vault of Horror* issue whose cover depicts passengers on a subway staring at a disembodied arm and hand gripping a hanging strap'.[37] Indeed, the Holocaust looms large in horror comics. In 'Corpse of the Jury', published in *Voodoo #5* (1953), a concentration camp commander orders that the skin from a Jewish woman's hands be made into a pair of gloves.[38] The woman in question, the commandant asserts, is 'too pretty to die'. He attempts to offer her protection in exchange for, we can assume, sexual favours. She refuses and strikes him, proclaiming that the Germans killed her father. As revenge, the commandant orders a soldier to flay her hands to make a pair of gloves before throwing her, still alive, into a pit filled with corpses. Years later, after the end of the war, the commandant is in hiding in New York. The ghost of the woman visits him and, with the help of the ghosts of others who died in the camp, skins him alive.

The comic engages in part with some of the history of the Holocaust. The men who throw the woman into the pit, for example, remark that they are only doing so because they would otherwise be killed, suggesting that they are Sonderkommandos – prisoners whose work duty involved moving corpses. It is problematic, however, that the text seems to elide the question of the victims' identities. The words 'Jewish' or 'Jew' do not appear in the story and, while there are, of course, blonde Jews, the lead victim is not coded as Jewish. She is, instead, the stock horror comic victim of the attractive blonde woman. If we were to read the text charitably, then we may choose to read this as a deliberate decision; one might infer, for example, that she could be a political prisoner, that she might be Polish, or a member of the many other groups who were murdered in the camps.[39]

While the presence of the blonde female horror archetype in a death camp is perhaps plausible, it remains problematic. The decentralizing of Jewish victims in the comic can be read in terms of what we might call 'Christianizing' the Shoah. Pope John Paul II once stated in an 'Address to the Jewish Community', '[t]hat which threatened you also threatened us'.[40] Certainly, individuals who identified as Christian died in the death camps and their deaths are as much a tragedy as those of Jewish victims, but they did not face genocide and the almost complete annihilation of their culture. De-centring the Jewish experience in narratives of the Holocaust threatens to hijack the Shoah – to mobilize its emotional capital for the political goals of any group.

The one way in which the comic does allude to images of Judaism is in its oblique invocation of the anti-Semitic myth of the blood libel – the belief, dating to the twelfth century, that Jewish rituals involve human sacrifice. There are two sources of horror in the story – the death camp and the ghosts – but that which provides narrative closure is not the violence of the death camps but the ghosts of their victims, who flay their murderer alive. The comic thus evokes not a modern fear of Nazis but a medieval fear of Jews. The image of these Jewish ghosts skinning their victim echoes a later, perhaps more recognizable version of the myth; Shylock taking his pound of flesh. The comic may offer no sympathy for the former commandant but, unlike his victims, it permits him access to fear.

Bernard Krigstein's 'Master Race', which was published in *Impact* in 1955, presents a victim more clearly coded as Jewish and avoids the invocation of anti-Semitic tropes but, like 'Corpse of the Jury', nonetheless decentres the Jewish experience.[41] In the comic, a former prisoner interned in Belsen confronts a former Nazi on the New York subway. Over a series of pages, Krigstein attempts to encapsulate the violence of the death camps, including images of mass beatings, burning chimneys, and a recreation of the iconic image, taken at the Buchenwald concentration camp in 1945, of prisoners behind barbed wire. Krigstein was Jewish, and the comic contains some more deliberate identification of the victims as Jewish with, for example, an image of an individual wearing a yellow star. It is noteworthy, however, that it is immediately followed with a panel in which a home is being ransacked with a crucifix on the wall (Figure 5). Both stories, then, render the attempted genocide of European Jews into a narrative in which the victims (of both the death camps and of the supernatural) are white Europeans.

...OR THE SHOP WINDOWS FROM BEING SMASHED AND THEIR CONTENTS RANSACKED...

...OR THE SANCTITY OF HOMES FROM BEING VIOLATED...

**5** Bernard Krigstein, 'Master Race', *Impact* #1

'Master Race' and 'Corpse of the Jury' are perhaps best understood in the context of their time. Until the trial in 1961 of Adolf Eichmann, one of the architects of the Holocaust, very little written or visual testimony from Holocaust survivors was in circulation. Public discourse concerning the death camps was almost non-existent and survivors overwhelmingly preferred not to discuss their experiences – Anne Frank's *Diary* first appeared in English in 1952, Primo Levi's *If This Is a Man* did not appear in print in English until 1959, and Elie Wiesel's *Night* was first published in English in 1960. Horror comics, in other words, began directly addressing the Holocaust before two of the three major works of survivor testimony were widely available. 'Master Race' was, indirectly, fundamental in paving the way for further conversations. Spiegelman, who went on to write the Pulitzer-winning inter-generational Holocaust survivor testimony *Maus*, asserts, '[w]hen I first saw "Master Race" as a teenager in the mid-sixties, it was like being struck by lightning [...] Here was a singular demonstration that the Nazi death camps could seriously be contemplated in comic books'.[42] It remains problematic, however, that, as discussed above, these comics use the Holocaust in a manner that decentralizes Jewish victimhood and, in both cases, present a white man as the victim of horror.

**6** Anon., 'Midnight Limited', *Witches Tales* #16

'Master Race' and 'Corpse of the Jury' were the first horror comics to engage with the Holocaust in an explicit and sustained manner, but they were not the first to allude to the Nazi killing project. We find throughout the horror genre a recurring image of industry, and in particular, trains, connected with death. In the comic 'Midnight Limited', which appeared in *Witches Tales* #16 in 1952, a man accidentally boards the wrong train, only to find it populated with corpses (Figure 6).

A more chilling, and more surreal, Holocaust allusion, appears in 'Corpses ... Coast to Coast!' published in *Voodoo* #14 (1954).[43] In this narrative, an undertaker dreams of an industry where he gathers and animates corpses 'ready to work for us'.

The fact that the corpses are put to work refers to the labour to which many concentration camp inmates were subjected, as well as the words over the gate of Auschwitz, '*Arbeit macht frei*'. What is perhaps most chilling about the comic is its focus upon process and industry. Under a spectre of death, the character talks dispassionately of the volume of bodies processed and schedules of delivery as production lines of corpses roll before him (Figure 7). Any mention of the humanity of subjects, or recognition of an individual as an end in his or her self, is conspicuously absent. The same imagery appears elsewhere in the horror comics genre, including the story 'Mannequin of Murder', the final panel of which, once again, specifically ties genocide to industry, declaring that the protagonist is 'shipping murder' across America. The accompanying

**7** Iger Studio – Ruth Roche (w), Robert Webb, and David Heames (i), 'Corpses … Coast to Coast!', *Voodoo* #14

**8** Anon., 'Mannequin of Murder', *Witches Tales* #17

image shows a line of people marching, in an orderly fashion, towards a factory (Figure 8).

These comics articulate what Hannah Arendt would, a decade later, call the 'banality of evil'. Arendt wrote of Adolf Eichmann: 'He did his *duty* …; he not only obeyed *orders*, he also obeyed the *law*'.[44] The Nazi death camps, Arendt asserts, were not driven primarily by hatred but by routine, duty, and logistics – all of the signs of industry that, as Adorno and Horkheimer observe, were once celebrated as the path to humanity's enlightenment.[45] Similarly, 'Corpses ... Coast to Coast!' recognizes continuity between the processes of the Holocaust and the factory model that had revolutionized American industry. It is certainly germane to these comics that at the time America was undergoing its own process of widespread industrialization: the mechanical spindle cotton picker, chemical fertilizers, the widespread adoption of tractors, growth in the meatpacking process, as well as, perhaps most iconically, the growth of the American auto-industry. The growth of American industry during the 1950s led to a large increase in the purchasing power of American families, the growth of consumerism, both of which were underwritten by the easy availability of credit, and the ascendancy of America to the status of world superpower, all of which belies the fact that the growth of American industry relied upon the same process of mechanization, scheduling, and infrastructure that facilitated the Holocaust. The protagonist of 'Corpses ... Coast to Coast!' uses the language ('raw material' 'processing plant') and methods (the production line and transportation infrastructure) of a 1950s capitalist to develop an industry that, ultimately, resembles the massacre of those who the Nazi party considered to be enemies of the German people. Once again, horror comics proposed a continuation, or bleeding-through, of the violence of the Second World War into 1950s America.[46]

These comics suggest thematic engagement with the role that modernization played in the Holocaust and, unlike the majority of later examples of Holocaust narratives in popular culture, relocate state-sanctioned genocide to US soil. The threat of genocide, however, is centred, problematically, on white male experience. The growth of white-collar work and the bureaucratic organization that accompanied it was seen by some as depriving men of agency and the individualistic labour that had previously constituted ideas of manliness. Culture dwelt on these ideas in *The Man in the Gray Flannel Suit* (novel 1955, film 1956) and academics analysed them in books such as William H. Whyte's *The Organization Man* (1956), David Riesman et al.'s *The Lonely Crowd* (1950), C. Wright Mill's *White Collar* (1951) and J. K. Galbraith's *The Affluent Society* (1958). It has since proved a rich topic for historical and cultural study.[47] 'Corpses ... Coast to Coast!' draws part of its horror from the dehumanization of victims in the Holocaust, but also through the apparent removal of individual agency in service to overarching bureaucracies intent on world domination. This dehumanization is also evident in the image above from 'Mannequin of Murder' (Figure 8), as the people walking towards Crane's are gradually rendered less human the closer they get to the factory. The factory system drove American growth but, while productive in terms of goods, it was reductive in terms of workers. While a problematic conflation, the narrative and imagery draws on what Roger Luckhurst has termed the 'massification' of the zombie in the postwar period.[48] This scaling up of the zombie is explicitly referenced in 'Corpses ...' when Big Z refers to their ability to create far more zombies than 'those old fools with their voodoo and charms', a statement that suggests the superiority of modern methods of manufacturing, and killing, over those that predate the atomic era.[49] Mass production, the dehumanization of workers, is equated with mass death, suggesting a crisis in American masculinity as a result of its inser- tion into modern bureaucratic frameworks; in recalling the Holocaust, and drawing on imagery of Soviet communism, the story points to a future where the American man might not only be alienated from his labour, but also his life. There is, inevitably, a racial component here as the inefficiencies of folk production, which allude to Haiti through the practice of voodoo, are supplanted by economies of scale in the modern, white, American city.

## The bomb

The violence witnessed and experienced by American soldiers and Holocaust survivors was, for the majority of Americans, tragic but somewhat remote. Certainly, images of warfare and the death camps had found their way into the lives of civilians, and the lives of second-generation Holocaust survivors, as has been well-documented, are deeply imbricated with their parents' trauma.[50] Where in Europe the signs of violence against people and the landscape were very much apparent, America was positioned, both in terms of infrastructure and economics, to forget the war. In part, strategies of forgetting can be seen as a means of obscuring potentially questionable acts; they could also be seen as a means of breaking the momentum of reform movements, such as the Double V campaign, which harnessed wartime experience to drive attempts from the social and political margins to restructure the centre. Moving on from the war was not just about enjoying benefits, it was also about denying them.

Forgetting is a difficult thing, though, and one instance of violence was so spectacular that it permeated everything: the atomic bomb. The casualties in Hiroshima and Nagasaki represented not only the most visible example of violence inflicted upon a civilian population, but a real possibility for America's future. The growth of the USSR, increasing build-up of nuclear weapons (the USSR acquired the atomic bomb in 1949 and the hydrogen bomb in 1953, a year after the US), and the spread of communism across the globe meant that the possibility of nuclear war was very much apparent. Specific flashpoints directed national and international attention to the constant proximity of conventional or, far worse, nuclear attack – after the Soviets developed their own nuclear weapons, the world existed in continual fear of atomic war. The success of conventional communist forces in China led to the establishment of the People's Republic of China in 1949, setting the scene for frequent tension over Taiwan, to which the Nationalist government of China fled, and which the US continued to acknowledge as the legitimate representatives of China until 1978. Geopolitical tension built in Asia with the beginning of the Korean War in 1950, an event that demonstrated that the deaths of the Second World War had only bought a few short years of peace. The war comics of the Korean War era were, in comparison to their upbeat counterparts from a few years previously, on the whole bleak, cynical, and more critical.[51] The film *Duck and Cover*, produced by the Federal Civil Defense Agency, was shown in schools beginning in 1951. Children practised curling up into a ball face-down under their desks in case of nuclear attack.

Many horror comics addressed the issue of nuclear fallout and the possible monsters that would result from this. The image of nuclear blast, reimagined in various guises, recurred throughout the genre. 'Star of Doom', which appeared in *Witches Tales* #17 (1953), for example, opens with the image of a star, from which a witch calls forth monsters to ransack a city. The star appears as an explosion and the red sun that rises beneath it is evocative of the Japanese flag, suggesting a continuum between Second World War violence and the events depicted (Figure 9).

Other comics explicitly reference the bombing of Nagasaki and Hiroshima. In 'The Thing that Walked at Night', which appeared in *Ghost Comics* #9, a war orphan transforms into a murderous monster at night. The girl's adopted mother, it transpires, is her actual mother, who had given birth to her as the bomb fell on Hiroshima. In the final panel, the monster is caught in the moment of killing her mother, even as she assures her (now dead) husband that her daughter poses no threat (Figure 10). The comic suggests that America is unable to control the thing it has birthed, a monster that, even now, threatens to wreak violence upon the homeland.

These panels draw on a range of contemporary anxieties. Atomic fears are clearly evident in the impact of nuclear radiation on Joan; however, there is far more at stake here. The stark black and white background colours foreground the action, which represents two deadly assaults by

**9** Anon., 'Star of Doom', *Witches Tales* #17

**10** Anon., 'The Thing that Walked at Night', *Ghost Comics* #9

women and, as a result, the destruction of the family unit – the basis of postwar settlement in dominant American discourse. Violence is not explicitly depicted – we see the shots fired and the stick raised, but not their results. The transformation of Joan from idealized blonde-haired young girl to a monstrous being with black hair, sallow skin, and hairy arms recalls discussions of the beast within and other racialized discourse. The central panel, blocked out in black, suggests Joan has slanted eyes to go with her black hair, drawing on decades of stereo-

11   Anon., 'Wax Museum', *Tomb of Terror* #3

typical practices for depicting Asians and referring back to her birth in
Japan, an accident of birth marking her as distinctly Other and attesting to fears around immigration. While the black background suggests
mourning for the dead husband, it also draws attention to colour, to
associations based on both a fear of the dark and also a fear of darker
skin colour. These panels can also be read as an allegory of not just the
war returning, but also of war-begotten children returning and their
impact on the family unit.[52]

The effects of nuclear war are also played out, both directly and
obliquely, in the recurring images of melting bodies found on the pages
of many horror comics. In 'Wax Museum' from *Tomb of Terror* #3, for
example, two individuals are transformed into wax and wreak vengeance on the man who imprisoned them, even as their bodies melt away
(Figure 11). The images of melting bodies mediate those of Japanese
casualties from Hiroshima and Nagasaki and anticipate the style of the
Hiroshima survivor manga *Barefoot Gen* (1973–1974) (Figure 12). The
same imagery appears more overtly in '8.30', which ends with a character consumed by x-rays (Figure 13).

Other comics were also concerned with the aftermath of nuclear
war. A recurring scenario is that of an individual emerging from underground to find his city destroyed. In 'Fog Was My Shroud', which
appeared in *Voodoo* #16, a man finds himself the sole human survivor
of an atomic blast (Figure 14). He finds his wife, now horribly disfigured, among the mutants who populate the ruined city. While he
attempts to rehabilitate her, another bomb falls, this time engulfing him
in flame (Figure 15).

Horror comics played out the possibilities of nuclear war and its

**12** Keiji Nakazawa, *Barefoot Gen*

**13** Anon., '8.30', *Witches Tales* #25

consequences, but also sought to address the politics that surround access to nuclear weapons. In 'Shower of Death', which appeared in *Witches Tales* #12, scientists create a destructive rain cloud that responds to the owner's will. The scientists are unsure what to do with their monstrous

14 Anon., 'Fog Was My Shroud', *Voodoo* #16

15 Anon., 'Fog Was My Shroud', *Voodoo* #16

creation and a group of journalists seize control of the cloud, only for it to turn upon them (Figure 16).

The comic indirectly references the tension between the politicians who controlled American nuclear weapons and the scientists who created them. In July 1945, seventy scientists involved with the Manhattan Project signed the Szilárd Petition, wherein they asked President Harry Truman to inform Japan of America's new weapon, perhaps through an observed demonstration in a non-populated area, and to offer the Japanese the opportunity to surrender.[53] Robert Oppenheimer, famously, devoted much of his later career to campaigning against nuclear stockpiling.

**16** Anon., 'Shower of Death', *Witches Tales* #12

In the scenario played out in 'Shower of Death', the promise of power by way of nuclear weapons is too great, and, ultimately, leads to the murder of both the scientists who create the weapons and the people who control them.

'Shower of Death' is one of a series of horror comics that express distrust of scientific discovery. The scientist as horror subject has a long literary precedent; Luckhurst argues that Victorian science fiction contained a large number of 'men of science – physicists, medical doctors, experts in the uncanny and weird phenomena – whose experiments blur the boundaries of the natural and the supernatural'.[54] One such prominent example would be R. L. Stevenson's *Dr. Jekyll and Mr. Hyde* (1886). The aspect of the scientist-as-horror-subject that horror comics developed in the wake of the bomb was the theme of science as dangerous. A recurring scenario, played out in various

**17** Sid Check (i), 'Death Sentence', *Tomb of Terror* #14

guises, is that of a scientific discovery turning on its creator. In 'Evolution', a comic that opens with yet another image evocative of nuclear attack, a scientific discovery leads to the death of a scientist and the destruction of a lab.

As evident in Figure 17, mass panic was not restricted to nuclear anxiety. Experiments with bodies, germs, and chemistry more generally were all mined by horror comics to produce images such as the above. Such images testify to anxieties around biological warfare and its effects on the body individually and, more abstractly, the body politic. There is also the classic horror trope of the unidentifiable agentic ooze, the mass that suggests life and thought but shows no traces of humanity, just a physical and psychological threat to mankind. In horror comics, goo is often the product of science straying into new areas and probing that which should not be probed. The Otherness and physical threat of such gelatinous masses, their ability to absorb what they touch into a uniform mass, also dramatizes fears around American understandings of communism as a homogenous entity, shorn of individuality and agentic identity.[55] The science-gone-wrong story therefore operates as an over-determined space, suggestive of fears as to what American science might unleash in its quest to defeat the Soviets, while similarly suspicious of the Soviets both as a faceless entity, both distant and potentially near, and as the source of a scientific threat.

Discovery, then, does not lead to humanity's betterment, but to its destruction. Progress is not, any longer, a space that can be broadly

18 Anon., 'The Torture Jar',
Witches Tales #13

viewed as carrying a rational population into a blissful Kingdom of Ends.
Rationality and what it makes possible,
even the potential of rationality as previously understood, is therefore itself under
assault. This sentiment is explicitly stated
in 'The Torture Jar' from *Witches Tales*
#13, in which a scientist discovers a race
of creatures who consider humans to be
'inferior' and thus insufficiently threatening to act against – Lovecraftian cosmic
horror writ, and drawn, large. The scientist concludes that the only way to avoid
the destruction of humanity is to cease to
make new discoveries – a future-oriented
'warning to the curious' (Figure 18).

Horror as a genre therefore often presents itself with luddite sentiments. This
is not always the case – in horror and
science fiction film of the period, science
is often both the cause of, and at least
part of the solution to, the source of
horror.[56] When science is the cause alone,
the military are typically able to step in
and restore order.[57] Horror comics offer
a rather bleaker vision, establishing connections with the themes
outlined above with regard to both the lives of veterans and the
Holocaust. The genre positions the violence of the Second World War
as a force that remains prescient for the white men of contemporary
America, suggesting that industrial, scientific, and economic progress
do not represent a departure from past violence, but an acceleration
of America's march towards further destruction. Charges of Ludditism
resonate in peacetime, too, with the increased mechanization of labour
that 'streamlined' jobs, meaning that technology, while heralded as
the future, harmed prospects at home just as it had harmed enemies
abroad. Those prospects were classed and racialized, though, continuing to construct an affluent white middle class as the representative
and only 'true' version of what it meant to be American. The shifting
sands under that position, though – the ferment around race, gender,
sexuality, and access to opportunity – meant that its foundations were
inherently unstable. Horror comics were one place where the cracks in
the structure started to show.

## Conclusion

Horror comics resisted uncomplicated narratives of the war as the foundation of a better future. They presented, instead, a world destroyed by war and under immanent threat of nuclear destruction and/or genocide. Science, rather than being humanity's saviour, promised to usher in an era of destruction and further violence. A theme that unites these narratives is that they centre, universally, on the experience of white men. The world they present is one in which white masculinity is in crisis due to external threats; the ghosts of the Second World War, the Holocaust, industrialization, communism, and the threat of nuclear war are shown to enact violence on, and elicit violence from, white American men. The victims in these stories are, with the possible exception of former Nazis, largely interchangeable, suggesting, as Briefel and Ngai assert, a fantasy of resilience among the white middle class, but also of the white male as the real, and sole, victim of the war and resettlement.[58]

Even though American society continued to be orientated around the interests of white men, women and people of colour had made significant social gains. As Kaja Silverman argues, the Second World War was followed by a 'second historical trauma threatening American masculinity – that posed by a social formation which had proven itself capable of managing without the absent soldier'.[59] The trauma described above, then, was specifically gendered; men were not the only victims of war but, Silverman argues, the war profoundly disrupted the social order, causing crises in masculinity not only on the individual level, when men who had imagined themselves brave and invincible were forced to reconcile themselves to terror and injury, but in the social fabric itself, as women entered the workforce and successfully took up what were once thought of as exclusively 'masculine' roles. Men returning damaged from the war found that the women they had fought to protect were more capable than they had imagined, or been able to imagine within the terms offered up by the dominant fiction of contemporary American society, and found themselves having to question whether they, in their damaged state, were as capable as, and whether their military victory depended on, female labour.

Understood in this way, themes of war, trauma, and immanent destruction in horror comics should not be read as a radical counter-narrative, but as a conservative one. While acknowledging the damage of bodily and spiritual trauma, horror comics centre the experience of fear on the white male victim, seeking to recast the horror of war within the language of property and an erstwhile social order. These narratives suggest that the horrors of war, while pervasive, are something that

happens to middle-class white men. They thus establish a dynamic that
runs through horror comics of the era, where the source of horror is
always something external to white American masculinity. This is particularly pronounced in stories such as 'Corpse of the Jury' and 'Master
Race', where, even when the protagonist is, historically, the perpetrator
of violence, his Jewish victims are, through their erasure, denied access
to fear within the context of the story. As members of a marginalized
group they can only occupy the position of the monster.

Horror comics, then, depict a world that has been transformed, irrep-
arably, by the Second World War and its aftermath. They resist narratives of progress, attesting, instead, to the impossibility of peace either
for the individual or on the world stage. While these narratives represent
a challenge to dominant national scripts, they are articulated in such a
way as to restrict victimhood to white middle-class men. The suffering of women and people of colour – civilians, non-combat personnel,
and those who served in segregated units such as the men of the 442nd
infantry unit, remain absent and unacknowledged. The only place they
are granted is that of the monster. Each of the following two chapters,
accordingly, seeks to explore the ways in which access to fear is controlled, and the ways in which racial and gendered Otherness serves as
a primary source of fear.

## Notes

1 Anon., 'Hollow Horror', *Fantastic Fears* #6 (New York: Ajax-Farrell, March
  1954).
2 Gábor Klaniczay, *The Uses of Supernatural Power: The Transformation of
  Popular Religion in Medieval and Early Modern Europe* (Cambridge and
  Oxford: Polity Press, 1990), as cited in Nick Groom, *The Vampire: A New
  History* (New Haven, CT: Yale University Press, 2018), 88.
3 Trombetta, *The Horror! The Horror!*, 171.
4 *LIFE Magazine*, 22 May 1944, 35.
5 Robert Hierholzer, Jan Munson, Carol Peabody, and John Rosenberg, 'Clinical
  Presentation of PTSD in World War II Combat Veterans', *Hospital & Community
  Psychiatry* 43.8 (1992), 816–820.
6 Daniel Goleman, *Emotional Intelligence, Why It Can Matter More Than IQ*
  (New York: Bloomsbury, 1995), 201–202.
7 Reintegration was explored in a number of cultural artefacts, such as the film
  *The Best Years of Our Lives* (dir. William Wyler, 1946) with its cast of returning
  veterans, each of whom struggles to readjust to a peacetime existence for a range
  of different reasons. Al Stevenson (Fredric March), for example, is a sergeant
  who returns to a job and family, to the very framework that had been offered up

as a justification for the fight, yet he voices concerns related to their desires to 'rehabilitate me'.

8  Philip Roth, *American Pastoral* (Boston, MA and New York: Houghton Mifflin Company), 40

9  John Kenneth Galbraith, *The Affluent Society* (Boston, MA: Houghton Mifflin, 1958), 135.

10  Roger North, *The Life of the Honourable Sir Dudley North, Knt … and of the Honourable and Reverend Dr. John North …* (London, 1744), 125, as cited in Groom, *The Vampire: A New History*, 26.

11  Skal, *The Monster Show*, 186.

12  See Willard Waller, *The Veteran Comes Back* (New York: Dryden Press, 1944). Superhero fans were aware of this as a contemporary issue through the Superman radio show of 1946, which dramatized corruption in state government that led to returning veterans being denied jobs that instead went to members of Al Vincent's corrupt political machine. This came to the attention of the American Veterans' Committee and its president, Charles G. Bolte, appeared on the Superman radio show to praise the liberal trajectory of the series. The organization expanded rapidly until it was dragged into the Second Red Scare when it became apparent that communists rejected from the more conservative veterans groups had turned to the AVC. For more on this see Michael Goodrum, '"His Greatest Enemy – Intolerance!": The Superman Radio Show in 1946', *Scan: Journal of Media, Arts, & Culture* 5.2 (2008), retrieved from http://scan. net.au/scan/journal/display.php?journal_id=118 (accessed 16 June 2020).

13  For more on the AVC, see Charles G. Bolte, *The New Veteran* (New York: Reynal & Hitchcock, 1946).

14  Given the prominent role of race in the politics of trauma, this is discussed further in Chapter 3.

15  Quoted in Mark David Van Ells, *To Hear Only Thunder Again: America's World War II Veterans Come Home* (Lanham, MD: Lexington Books, 2001), 112.

16  Kaja Silverman, *Male Subjectivity at the Margins* (London: Routledge, 1992), 69.

17  Jonathan Rigby, *American Gothic: Sixty Years of Horror Cinema* (London: Reynolds and Hearn, 2007), 294

18  Stefan Dziemianowicz, 'Contemporary Horror Fiction 1950–1998', in Neil Barron (ed.), *Fantasy and Horror* (Lanham, MD: Scarecrow Press, 1999), 199–244 (200–1).

19  Beatrice M. Murphy, 'Horror Fiction from the Decline of Universal Horror to the Rise of the Psycho Killer', in Reyes (ed.), *Horror: A Literary History*, 131–158.

20  Roger Sabin, *Adult Comics: An Introduction* (London: Routledge, 1993), 48.

21  This does not mean that children did not read horror comics; rather than reading comics as exclusively for veterans or younger readers, it is more productive to read them as providing a simulation of war for both audiences simultaneously. While horror comics may have provided a means to contain and control violence for veterans, for younger readers they may have offered, as John Trevelyan, then

secretary of the British Board of Film Censors argued, 'a test of courage. Not having been in the last war [young people] wonder how they would stand up to another'. Quoted in Derick Hill, 'The Face of Horror', in Silver and Ursini (eds), *Horror Film Reader*, 51–61 (52).

22  Al Williamson, Larry Woromay, and King Ward (i), 'The Flapping Head', *Forbidden Worlds* #6 (New York: American Comics Group, 1952).

23  Several horror films stressed the fear of the new, with *The Black Cat* (1934) taking place in a stark modernist building, and *Son of Frankenstein* (1939) skilfully combining a Gothic castle aesthetic with modernist-inspired cinematography, lighting, and *mise en scène*.

24  Anon., 'Nightmare Merchant', *Strange Fantasy* #7 (New York: Farrell Comics, 1953).

25  Anon., 'Dirt of Death', *Ghost Comics* #4 (New York: Fiction House, 1952).

26  Murphy, 'Horror Fiction', in Reyes (ed.), *Horror: A Literary History*, 132. There is more discussion of the racialized nature of urban and suburban development in the chapters on race.

27  Anon., 'The Demon of Devonshire', *Ghost Comics* #7 (New York: Fiction House, 1953).

28  Owen Davies, *The Haunted: A Social History of Ghosts* (Basingstoke: Palgrave Macmillan, 2009), 82.
    To reinforce this, the ghosts, it transpires, are people whom the protagonist killed while in a fugue state, drawing on ideas around war trauma and horror raised as early as *The Cabinet of Dr. Caligari* (1920).

29  Drew Murdoch (w), 'The Ghost Gallery', *Ghost Comics* #2 (New York: Fiction House, 1952).

30  Darryl Jones, 'Introduction', in M. R. James, *Collected Ghost Stories*, ed. Darryl Jones (Oxford: Oxford University Press, 2017), ix–xxx (xvii).

31  In *If This Is a Man* Primo Levi describes a recurring dream in which he returns home from Auschwitz and tells his story only to meet indifference and incredulity. See Primo Levi, *If This Is A Man and The Truce*, trans. Stuart Woolf (London: Abacus, 1979). Elie Wiesel, similarly, was persuaded to write *Night* despite his fear of not being believed. See Victoria Nesfield and Philip Smith (eds), *The Struggle for Understanding: The Novels of Elie Wiesel* (New York: SUNY Press, 2019).

32  Trombetta. *The Horror! The Horror!*, 31–32

33  Korean War comics explored this terrain in detail. Some attempted to construct the same kind of gung-ho militaristic optimism in evidence in war comics of the Second World War; others were more thoughtful and acknowledged the malaise around Korea more generally. See Chapter 4, 'Korea', in William W. Savage Jr, *Commies, Cowboys, and Jungle Queens: Comic Books and America, 1945–1954* (Middletown, CT: Wesleyan University Press, 1990).

34  The term 'survivor' here is imprecise. One can state that not everyone who endured the ghettos, forced labour, and the death camps died, but to suggest that those who did not die 'survived' in the sense of being physically or psychologically unharmed would be inaccurate. Many of those who escaped or were liber-

ated from the death camps were profoundly affected by their experiences, and the loss of friends, families, and communities.

35 Art Spiegelman and Hillary Chute, *Metamaus* (New York: Pantheon, 2011), 60.

36 Robert Kraft, 'Archival Memory: Representations of the Holocaust in Oral Testimony', Holocaust Representations Since 1975, conference held at Chester University, 18 September 2009.

37 Art Spiegelman, *Comix, Essays, Graphics, and Scraps* (Selerrio: Editore-La Centrale dell'Arte, 1999), 80; Hillary Chute, *Disaster Drawn* (Cambridge, MA and London: Harvard University Press, 2016), 14.

38 Anon., 'Corpse of the Jury', *Voodoo #5* (New York: Four Star Publications/ Farrell Publications Inc, 1953). The story was likely inspired by the widely circulated claim that Ilse Koch, wife of Karl-Otto Koch, commandant of the Nazi concentration camp Buchenwald, possessed lampshades and purses made from human skin.

39 Not everyone who was killed in the death camps was Jewish, of course. This is true both in the sense that not everyone who the Nazis classified as a Jew would have considered themselves Jewish, and in the sense that the victims of the Holocaust also included homosexuals, political prisoners, Romani, disabled people, and prisoners of war. There is a case to be made, for example, for certain parts of Auschwitz, such as what has been called the 'death wall', being devoted to Polish memorialization.

40 Eugene Fisher and Leon Klenicki (eds), *Spiritual Pilgrimage: Texts on Jews and Judaism 1979–1995* (New York: The Crossroads Publishing Company, 1995), 151.

41 Bernard Krigstein, 'Master Race', *Impact* #1 (New York: EC Comics, 1955).

42 Spiegelman, *Comix*, 90

43 Iger Studio – Ruth Roche (w), Robert Webb, and David Heames (i), 'Corpses … Coast to Coast!', *Voodoo* #14 (New York: Four Star Publications/Farrell Publications Inc, 1954).

44 Hannah Arendt, *Eichmann in Jerusalem* (New York: Viking Press, 1963), 135.

45 Theodor Adorno and Max Horkheimer, *Dialectic of Enlightenment*, trans. Edmund Jephcott (Stanford, CT: Stanford University Press, 2002).

46 For further analysis of this comic, see Michael Goodrum, 'The Past That Will Not Die: Trauma, Race, and Zombie Empire in Horror Comics of the 1950s', in Dominic Davies and Candida Rifkind (eds), *Documenting Trauma in Comics: Traumatic Pasts, Embodied Histories, and Graphic Reportage* (London: Palgrave Macmillan, 2020), 69–84.

47 See, for instance, K. A. Cuordileone, '"Politics in an Age of Anxiety": Cold War Political Culture and the Crisis in American Masculinity, 1949–1960', *Journal of American History* 87.2 (2000), 515–545.

48 See Roger Luckhurst, *Zombies: A Cultural History* (London: Reaktion Books, 2015).

49 Roche, Webb, and Heames, 'Corpses … Coast to Coast!'. One might also consider the opening lyrical salvo of 'Kill the Poor' by the Dead Kennedys:

'Efficiency and progress is ours once more/Now that we have the neutron bomb/ It's nice and quick and clean and gets things done/Away with excess enemy/But no less value to property/No sense in war but perfect sense at home'. The cover of the 1980 single features a bulldozer burying bodies in front of a factory.

50 Helen Epstein, *Children of the Holocaust: Conversations with Sons and Daughters of Survivors* (New York: Bantam Books, 1980).

51 War comics, apart from those which contain horror tropes, are beyond the scope of this study. We recommend that readers consult Savage, *Commies, Cowboys, and Jungle Queens*.

52 For more on this see S. J. L. Gage, 'The Amerasian Problem: Blood, Duty, and Race', *International Relations* 21.1 (2007), 86–102.

53 Dennis Wainstock, *The Decision to Drop the Atomic Bomb* (Westport, CT: Praeger Publishers, 1996).

54 Luckhurst, 'Transitions: From Victorian Gothic to Modern Horror', in Reyes (ed.), *Horror: A Literary History*, 118.

55 For other contemporary stagings of blobs, see, fittingly, *The Blob* (1958). For fears of communism as homogeneity, see *The Invasion of the Body Snatchers* (1956). This is one reading of *Body Snatchers* – the other is of an anti-McCarthyism bent, though similarly, it is against homogeneity.

56 See, for instance, *Them!* (1954), dir. Gordon Douglas.

57 See, for instance, *The Thing From Another World* (1951), dir. Christian Nyby.

58 This is not, of course, to say that white male veterans did not suffer; it is clear that they did. The trauma of survival, however, was exacerbated for other communities of survivors as they were subjected to additional traumatic experiences, and an even greater marginalization of their service and experience, by the society to which they returned.

59 Silverman, *Male Subjectivity at the Margins*, 63–64.

# 2

## 'Men are beasts! Wild beasts! Wild beasts must be destroyed!' – gender in the 1940s and 1950s

In 'The Frenzy of Sheila Lord', from *Beyond* #5 (1951), a wealthy widow – the eponymous Sheila Lord – takes a new husband. Her new beau is, in every sense, different from the first. Harry was fat, Zack is muscular; Harry was bald, Zack has a full head of hair. Most notably, Harry was rich whereas Zack, an unemployed mechanic, is financially dependent on his new wife. Their fortunes change, however. Zack creates an invention that earns him a fortune, while Sheila loses her wealth. Sheila is uncomfortable with this change in household dynamics and laments her loss of power. Slowly, Zack begins to physically resemble the deceased Harry. Sheila finds herself trapped in the same marriage she had previously escaped. Eventually, she murders Zack in exactly the same way as she murdered Harry – by pushing him off a cliff. Things work out differently this time. She is caught and imprisoned.

For all the accusations later laid against the comics medium for undermining traditional American family values, 'The Frenzy of Sheila Lord' reads as a conservative treatise on man as the natural head of the household. Sheila Lord's sin, for which she is roundly and unironically punished, is that she wishes to hold financial power, with all of the privilege that entails, over her husband, and mocks his attempts to occupy a masculine role through his mechanical prowess. The dangers of female power are dramatized in the text. In one panel, Lord curses at her husband, demanding that he 'Stop this nonsense fooling around with your silly inventions' (Figure 19).[1] Later, when their fortunes are reversed, she demands that he give her five hundred dollars for a new gown and finds him far less compliant. Her husband looks on, delighted: 'Rave all you want, Sheila!', he says, 'It won't do you any good! No more dough this week!' (Figure 20).[2] The difference between the two panels, with Zack sunken and beaten in the first and glowing and satisfied (complete with pipe and a garish check coat) in the second, suggests that this change in household dynamics represents life as it should be, where a hard-working man is able to amass an honest fortune and enjoy

**19** Anon., 'The Frenzy of Sheila Lord', *Beyond* #5

**20** Anon., 'The Frenzy of Sheila Lord', *Beyond* #5

the benefits it brings, including power over his wife. This period of happiness is temporary, however; once a woman has had a taste of financial independence, the comic warns, a return to 'normal' is impossible. The plot is a familiar one from the horror genre, and from some postwar rhetoric about the wartime work of women. In the story, a woman is shown to exercise power – always ill-gotten – over men and is violently

**21** Anon., 'It', *Witches Tales* #10

punished for doing so; in reality, the 'punishment' took the form of an escalation of discourse aimed at getting women out of the workplace and into the home.

Even characters such as Sheila Lord fare better than most – the majority of women in horror comics meet violent, and often sexualized, deaths without even experiencing the momentary power afforded to the likes of Sheila Lord. In 'It', which appeared in *Witches Tales* #10, a female character appears in just two panels (Figure 21). In the first, she throws her hands up in defence when faced with a phallic lump of goo. In the second, she is enveloped in the goo, apparently naked. Her head is thrown back, her breasts are pushed forward, and she utters a prolonged wordless cry. She appears only to be horrified and then to die in a manner at once grotesque and erotic – which speaks, unmistakably, of rape. The reader, as voyeur, is directly incorporated into the image through the leering man who watches the woman's fate from the door. While the woman cannot return our gaze as hers is commanded by the phallic threat she faces, the man leers at both the woman and the reader, making them a partner in the scopophilic spectacle of her punishment. Through the gaze, the female body, and access to it, is presented as property at the disposal of white men; horror can be worked out on the female body and through the violence of the male gaze. Female agency – the representation of women as not just the property of men, but as agents in their own right – is presented as horrifying deviance.

In the previous chapter we argued that horror comics rejected the promise of American prosperity and a bright future, pointing, instead, to the continued relevance of the violence of the Second World War and the instability of international politics in the nuclear age. While rhetoric asserted that American society marched towards the future, in horror comics the past refused to remain in the past. While this theme reads against the dominant culture of the time, it should not necessarily be interpreted as counter-cultural in the sense of opposing the hegemonic conservativism and paranoia of the age; horror comics are interested primarily in the experience of white middle-class heterosexual men, all of whom are beset by various external threats. These threats are, in the majority, coded as Other in terms of gender and race. This, and the following, chapter examine those threats.

The treatment of women in horror comics mediated discourse of the time. Horror comics enjoyed their moment of greatest popularity at a time of significant disquiet around ideas of gender, sexuality, and the family unit. Wartime rhetoric regarding the empowerment of women required them to fill the spaces vacated by men. This social shift was contested even as it emerged; an early instance of such pushback against women can be found in Philip Wylie's *Generation of Vipers*, published in 1942, a book that forcefully urged men to renounce 'momism', the adoration of controlling mothers, and 'take back our dreams which, without the perfidious materialism of mom, were shaping up a new and braver world'.[3] Wylie was well-acquainted with the concept of creating apparently 'new' and 'braver' worlds. His co-authored apocalyptic science fiction novel, *When Worlds Collide* (1933) depicted the end of the world and the struggle of a small group of hand-picked specialists to fly to Bronson Beta, a rogue planet travelling through our solar system, in order to rebuild society. Marriage was forbidden among passengers as women were to bear the children of multiple male passengers in order to maximize the gene pool. Adapted into a film in 1951, concerns around the 'proper place' of women can be seen to resonate across the two decades since its initial publication. Wylie's concerns around the fragility of American masculinity recall Kristin Hoganson's approaches to American foreign policy of the 1890s as largely driven by anxieties regarding the impact of the closure of the frontier, the passing of the Civil War generation, and the impact of increasing political agitation by women on American masculinity.[4] After the Second World War, as many men returned to the workplace, anxiety over the fabric of American life in the wake of women working traditionally male jobs intensified, restaging fears of the 1890s about the threat of women to American masculinity. The impact of changing gender roles on both men and women, and the family units they constituted, was explicitly considered in Ferdinand Lundberg and Marynia F. Farnham's *Modern Woman: The Lost Sex*.[5] Lundberg and Farnham argued that it was precisely the empowerment of women that made both them and men unhappy, or 'neurotic', owing to the deviation from long-established gender roles in which both sexes allegedly found fulfilment.

Uncertainty around gender roles was also driven by contemporary investigations into American sexuality. The Kinsey reports of 1948 and 1953, which sought to bring a scientific understanding to the sex lives of ordinary Americans, documented accounts of homosexual activity. The two volumes of the report drove and drew upon anxieties concerning sexuality, reinforcing fears that an increasingly 'masculine' population of women would cause men to become feminized.[6] As Harry M. Benshoff states, 'queerness disrupts narrative equilibrium and sets in motion a questioning of the status quo', therefore positioning 'deviant' sexualities as a threat to projects of internal containment.[7] Attempts to contain perceived threats to white male hegemony in the postwar period were driven by anxiety of the apparent disruptive potential of these threats. The family, narrowly defined as a child-bearing union between a man and a woman, was at the centre of American society; competing notions of what it meant to be a man or woman, of how gender was performed, and the linked question of sexuality, constituted a major postwar concern. David K. Johnson states that 'in 1950, many politicians, journalists, and citizens thought that homosexuals posed more of a threat to national security than Communists', something frequently overlooked in the historiography on this period.[8] Miriam G. Reumann draws attention to the ways in which discussions of sexuality and gender, based on the two Kinsey reports, fed into 'analyses of America's class mobility and race relations, attitudes to work and leisure, and international political position'.[9] In short, the way in which anxieties around heteronormativity pervaded much wider considerations of what it meant to be American and what practices were compatible with that national(ist) identity. Horror comics engaged these fears directly, building on the idea of the femme fatale from hard-boiled fiction and her threat to the dominant fiction.

Horror served as an ideal medium for simultaneously exploring anxieties around gender and reinscribing gendered bodies and behaviours. The horror genre, particularly as it appears in comics, has often coupled an idealized female with a grotesque monster. Such trends can be traced from the virtuous Isabella in Walpole's *The Castle of Otranto* and Mina Harker in Stoker's *Dracula*, to the virginal survivor, the final girl, in the modern 'slasher' genre. As Judith Halberstam asserts, the Gothic inspires 'fear of and desire for the other'; the horror genre, and the comics considered in this chapter in particular, hinges on these opposing impulses.[10] This desire was intensified by changing expectations of female beauty during the mid-twentieth century. Increasing wealth and growth in the cosmetics industry, as well as the reactionary counter-momentum against female empowerment after the Second World War, led to changing expectations of women's appearance; the increasing availability of cosmetics and a greater understanding of diet meant that certain forms of beauty became achievable and, thus, expected. The juxtaposition of the feminine ideal and the monster were not necessarily opposed but served as two sides of the same societal shift. As Skal notes:

> A glimpse at the back pages of the fan magazine that published studio-canned features on the *Man of a Thousand Faces* is revealing; up front you discover [Lon] Chaney's latest gruelling disguise, and the agony he was enduring, Christ-like on your behalf; and when you finish reading about the actor's latest back-harness, you could peruse innumerable back-of-the-book advertisements for products to straighten your own spine, reduce or enlarge your body, or give yourself a 'round pretty' face instead of 'unsightly hollows'. Women especially would be expected, more and more, to become wizards of makeup in order to withstand the looming sexual rigours of the twentieth century.[11]

The fixation on the transformation of bodies into extremes – either of beauty or the grotesque – plays out not only in the stories of horror comics but in the advertising they contain. Horror comics carried advertisements for 'corsets (for men and women), pimple-removers, wigs, cosmetics, diets (to put weight on, as well as lose it), bodybuilding courses, books on courting and social etiquette, and so on'.[12] The comics not only presented images of bodies in extremes, but the means by which such bodies might be created.

The presence of the idealized female form in horror comics was a new fold in an established trope in American cartooning. Certain popular genres within the comics form have historically represented the female body in ways that indulge the male gaze; the comics form in America has been in continuous dialogue with pin-up art and photography. Histories of the pin-up generally begin with the work of Charles Dana Gibson during the late nineteenth century, with his pictures that were published in newspapers and magazines. The aesthetic quickly migrated to newspaper comics starring glamorous but adorably klutzy flappers such as *Fritzi Ritz* (1922–1929) and *Tillie the Toiler* (1921–1959). The pin-up genre was far larger than comics, but it is noteworthy that *Fritzi Ritz* cartoonist Ernie Bushmiller credited his senior colleagues in the art department at the New York *World* magazine for having invented pornography.[13] Other comics genres imported the Gibsonesque attractive woman archetype, none more so than *Wonder Woman*, who first appeared in 1941.[14] Horror, like Romance, Western, and Crime comics, followed the established tradition of idealized female bodies alongside cartoonish male peers. Where horror deviated from these other genres was in also subjecting this idealized woman to violence. In this sense they owe a debt not only to other comics genres but to Margaret Brundage's covers for *Weird Tales*, which typically depicted a nude or partially nude woman in a horror scenario. While *Wonder Woman* was often imperilled, and was tied up almost constantly, she always emerged as the victor. The women in horror comics remained victims.

The fear and hatred of women expressed through horror comics of the 1940s and 1950s, embodying as it does both a feminine ideal and misogynistic violence, does not invite charitable readings. Horror comics seem to delight in stripping women of power, dignity, and clothing. As standard fare, covers feature women, typically clad in a torn red dress, unconscious, held prisoner, or otherwise at the mercy of monsters. The portrayal of women in horror comics is almost uniformly aligned with what, in more modern terms, would be understood as an anti-feminist stance. They were a part of a postwar culture that, in the words of Ruth Rosen, 'suppressed dissent, glorified motherhood, celebrated women's biological difference, and sanctified the nuclear family'.[15] Women in horror comics often wield forms of unsanctioned power through involvement in crime, by manipulating men, or by access to supernatural powers. Over the course of horror narratives, these women are stripped of their power, humiliated, and subject to (often sexualized) violence. Indeed, while Gothic literature has often, George Haggerty argues, explored and made concrete desires 'which violate terms of conventional social intercourse', the sexuality on display in horror comics is, at first glance, entirely conventional: on almost every page of a given horror comic an attractive woman is offered up to the gaze in a state of powerlessness and distress/undress.[16] This process, in micro-narratives, represents one of rephallusization, whereby men are restored to their former position of power through executing violence on female bodies. The female characters who appear in horror comics therefore draw on a visual vocabulary learned from wartime propaganda and pin-up art. While the pin-up in Second World War popular culture exists in a world of fantasy, at once commenting on but separate to and protected from war, in horror comics she is afforded no such protection. At times the representations of violence against women seem to verge on the grotesque, satirizing the mythology of the pin-up as emblematic of the utopian space being offered to veterans after the war. By denying the female subject personhood, however, the genre closes off any possibility of complicating the reader's response to misogynistic violence. The bodies of pin-ups that line the pages of horror comics serve, instead, as part of the genre's recurring thesis of war as an insistent and traumatizing, but entirely male-centred, concern.

## Women and power

The first women's rights convention occurred in Seneca Falls, New York, in 1848 where the attendees discussed the role of women in society and how legal and social progress might be made.[17] During the late nineteenth and early twentieth century America saw the emergence of the New Woman and the American branch of the Suffragette movement. During this period, an increasing number of women were entering into post-secondary education. Many women sought not only greater legal autonomy including, most significantly, the vote, but models of respectability outside of marriage, including same-sex relationships and advocacy for birth control. Many members of the movement, such as Minnie Fisher Cunningham and Jeannette Rankin, had successful political careers.

During the Second World War, nine per cent of America's population served overseas, the majority of them able-bodied men aged eighteen to thirty-eight. Prior to the 1940s, men had, broadly, made up the majority of the American workforce while women tended to engage in housework and childrearing. In the vacuum of the Second World War, millions of women, recruited through campaigns such as the Rosie the Riveter posters, went to work, occupying traditionally male spaces such as offices, factories, and warehouses.[18] As transformative as these changes seemed, during the 1950s the threat of radical change to the social fabric was more theoretical than actual. As Ruth Rosen observes:

> [D]uring the 1950s, the president of Harvard University saw no reason to increase the number of female undergraduates because the university's mission was to 'train leaders', and Harvard's Lamont Library was off-limits to women for fear they would distract male students. Newspaper ads separated jobs by sex; employers paid women less than men for the same work. Bars often refused to serve women; banks routinely denied women credit or loans. Some states even excluded women from jury duty. Radio producers considered women's voices too abrasive to be on air; television executives

believed they didn't have enough credibility to anchor the news; no women ran big corporations or universities, worked as firefighters or police officers, sat on the Supreme Court, installed electric equipment, climbed telephone poles, or owned construction companies. All hurricanes bore female name, thanks to the widely-held view that women brought chaos and destruction to society. As late as 1970, Dr Edgar Berman, a well-known physician, proclaimed on television that women were too tortured by hormonal disturbances to assume the presidency of the nation. Few people knew more than a few women professors, doctors, or lawyers. Everyone addressed women as either Miss or Mrs, depending on her marital status, and if a woman wanted an abortion, legal nowhere in America, she risked her life, searching among quacks in back alleys for a competent and compassionate doctor. The public believed that rape victims had probably 'asked for it', most women felt too ashamed to report it, and no language existed to make sense of marital rape, date rape, domestic violence, or sexual harassment.[19]

The radical transformation of the American workforce during the Second World War, then, had yet to manifest in other arenas. Women continued to be treated as, in all respects, less than their male counterparts. As William Chafe notes:

> The hiring of millions of women did not itself signify that women had gained the right to be treated as equals with men in the job market. Economic equality could be achieved only through a substantial revision of social values and a lasting modification in the nature of male–female relationships.[20]

Change was, nonetheless, afoot. Women had shown that they were capable of performing roles traditionally reserved for men and a full return to pre-war gender dynamics was impossible. The entry of women into the workforce is, to use Weber's term, a moment of 'dephallusization'.[21] The historical trauma of the Second World War destabilized existing power structures, unsettling men's place as the 'breadwinner' of the family. Even when soldiers returned to American soil, many were, literally, dephallusized from war injuries or similarly rendered incapable of fulfilling their pre-war role in the family dynamic. In many families, women continued to go out to work as a result. While some women returned to their previous role as housewives (or took it up for the first time), the character of the American workforce had changed. The large-scale mobilization of women into wage-earning roles during the war, and then the socio-cultural pressure to disengage from those roles, worked towards the creation of a generation of women who, as Betty Friedan documented in *The Feminine Mystique* (1963), wanted their daughters to have options beyond housewifery.

The process of 'rephallusization' in media involved shifting representations of the female body, particularly through film. Horror, certainly, played a role in this regard; Raymond Durgnat argues, '[t]he only films whose erotic content is as open as that of musicals are horror films'.[22] The content of horror comics was informed and emboldened not only by horror cinema but the increasing acceptance of a genre that outdid even the musical in its overt eroticism. Pornography was hardly a new phenomenon and the pin-up, as discussed in more detail below, was a staple of wartime propaganda. The 1950s saw a transition, in the words of Joan Nicholson, towards 'the heavier side of sex – psychosexual themes illustrating fetishism, sadomasochism, masturbation, [...] lesbianism, and exhibitionism' as well as 'a more exploitative presentation of Hollywood's sex goddesses'.[23] During the 1940s, *Esquire* (launched 1933) had produced a series of cartoon pin-ups by George Petty and Alberto Vargas, all of which were, the editors argued, both artistic and patriotic. The postwar shift came in 1953 with the launch of *Playboy*, a publication that sought to become 'what *Esquire* had been before it de-emphasized sex'.[24] *Playboy*, taking advantage of the relaxation of censorship law, went further than *Esquire* in that it featured photographs of fully nude women with little pretence of artistry. The magazine normalized, and even added an air of sophistication to, the representation of women's bodies as subjects of male enjoyment in the US. It sparked many imitators (*Cabaret*, *Jem*, *Jaguar*, *Dude*, and *Escapade*, to name a few) and made the term 'playmate' a household word. Collectively, this form of media can be read as a reaction to the slow but visible shifts in women's role in American society. They present a fantasy of women as passive, unthreatening, and sexually available.

The horror genre, albeit obliquely, seeks to enact and extend this process of 'rephallusization', whereby women are removed from positions of power and rendered as sexual objects. Horror comics contain few images of women working in the occupations that American women entered during the 1940s. Instead, women are generally depicted in poses strongly reminiscent of the pin-up. When they do wield power, it is generally unsanctioned; in horror comics, women lead criminal groups, wield magical powers, or gain money and influence by seducing (and then generally killing) wealthy men. The nagging wife, too, was a recurring figure. One of the earliest stories to appear in a horror comic, 'The Strange Case of Hen-Pecked Harry', opens with the following:

From the moment Harry Horton slipped a marriage band on his wife's finger, he was at war with her! She gave him no peace, no rest, no mercy ... She mocked him, criticized him, nagged him, screamed at him, struck him.

**22** Anon., 'Payoff Blues', *Ghost Comics* #6

> He was a fool, a bungler, a failure, an imbecile! – Nothing he ever did was right. – So, is it any wonder that things turned out so wrong in 'The Strange Case of Hen-Pecked Harry'??[25]

In each case of a nagging wife, women's power represents a threat to the social order both within the home and in society as a whole and, as the comic tacitly posits, grounds for them to be both stripped of that power (and clothing) and punished in an often sexual manner.

One recurring figure, borrowed from the crime genre, is that of the female crime boss. This figure in turn draws from the femme fatale of hard-boiled fiction, the woman who uses her sexuality and femininity as a weapon against men. One such example can be found in 'Payoff Blues' in *Ghost Comics* #6 (Figure 22). The typical female crime boss, dressed in red and with black hair, exercises her will through the men under her command rather than taking action herself. She is a manipulative figure who uses her feminine charms, and apparent vulnerability, when it suits her, but has no qualms about switching to the language of the underworld when she issues orders to murder.

As well as influencing criminal activities, women are also shown to have access to otherworldly powers. Often, as is the case with 'Werewolf Hunter' from *Ghost Comics* #3, this otherworldly power is connected with Orientalist depictions of the East. In this comic, an Egyptian woman, Cephalia, Princess of the Web, is discovered to be 'practicing some strange sorcery' involving spiders (no doubt as much inspired by

the 1943 film *Spider Woman* as by terms such as Black Widow). Like a female crime boss, she acts through male underlings – in this case half-spider, half-men. She is coded in the language of the crime boss – black hair and a red dress – which here is also evocative of spiders. Cephalia is frequently depicted, as in Figure 23, in long, full-body panels and in poses that emphasize both power (being depicted from a low angle) and sensuality. The combination of spiders, eroticism, and female power recalls the act of a female spider eating her mate while in, or just after, copulation.

These images of sensuality and danger in a horror context preceded and were later informed by actress Maila Nurmi's persona Vampira. Skal describes the character as 'a landscape of cultural contradictions: simultaneously buxom and gaunt, well-fed yet skeletal [...] Drawing energy from the quintessentially fifties nexus of automotive styling and the female form, Vampira was a souped-up hearse ... with headlights'.[26] Nurmi, in her role as host of *The Vampira Show* (1954–1955) succeeded in combining the horror elements of the monster and his sexually available female victim into a singular seductive yet supernaturally powerful persona. Vampira engaged with the characterization of vampires as 'lustful, depraved,

**23** Anon., 'Werewolf Hunter',
*Ghost Comics* #3

and super-sexy: models of transgression, avatars of forbidden fantasies and fallen angels of the death drive', which drew on established representations.[27] Examples of eroticized female vampires include Joseph Sheridan Le Fanu's *Carmilla* (1872), the three Brides of Dracula from Stoker's novel and the film *Dracula's Daughter* (1936), a sequel to Tod Browning's 1931 *Dracula*. Perhaps the most direct inspiration for Vampira was *New Yorker* cartoonist Charles Addams' Morticia Addams. Nurmi's iconic performance, as captured in *Plan 9 From Outer Space* (1959), spawned many famous imitators including Vampirella,

Akasha, Elvira, and Gothic rock frontwomen such as Siouxsie Sioux and Amy Lee.

The possession of magical power in horror comics is generally a female trait. Indeed, witches often seek to recruit other women into their practices. Women, the comics suggest, wield dangerous powers, and these powers only increase when their numbers grow. The narrative broadly aligns (thematically if not stylistically) with what Richard Hofstadter and Timothy Melley describe as the 'paranoid style' of American art – the fear that other people may present a hidden threat. This relates, most obviously, to the rhetoric of vigilance against communists, but extends to a general sense of there being something to fear in the lives of one's neighbours or strangers in the street.[28]

Horror stories such as 'The Witch Who Wore White' from *Witches Tales* #8 corroborate fears of a lesbian conspiracy. In the comic, Abigail Sanders is married to Arthur, who is being nursed by the mysterious Miss Jessup. Through observing Miss Jessup, ultimately by sneaking into her room at night, Abigail discovers her secret: Miss Jessup is a witch. Rather than being horrified at Miss Jessup's declaration that she is 'dedicated to the destruction of man', Abigail Jessup instead asks to work with her (Figure 24).[29] After Miss Jessup orchestrates the death of Arthur Sanders, she tricks his nephew, Paul, into killing Abigail; this comes after Abigail, despite their earlier intimacy, refuses Miss Jessup's request to join her, become a witch, and reject her previous life. Given Abigail's earlier 'discovery' of Miss Jessup in her bedroom, and the relationship that subsequently develops between the two women, it is hard to read the comic as being about anything other than the fear of lesbian relationships and their potential impact on what was typically thought of as the American family unit. This point is driven home when Miss Jessup uses her magic to kill Paul, then burns down the house. The narrative ends with Miss Jessup appearing, as a nurse, at another house where, the reader is left to assume, she will repeat the same actions. More conventional narratives, such as a melodrama, might have the nurse threaten the marriage by vying for the husband's affections; the fact that it is the husband who is the first victim, and that there is an appeal to a form of union between the two women, inscribes homosexuality into this version of the narrative.

The ability of women to wield power, and particularly its connection to their sexuality, was a significant flashpoint for contemporary American society, and was deeply traumatizing to the white men who sought to shore up one potential interpretation of American life as the only viable one. The narrative suggests the fear of lesbianism in the

**24** Anon., 'The Witch Who Wore White', *Witches Tales* #8

1950s, a decade obsessed with sexuality and the nuclear family but at the same time increasingly aware of, and willing to fetishize, female homosexuality. These fears over lesbianism, where it occurred without the objectifying and disciplinary function of the male gaze, was directly tied to communism; as Elaine Tyler May asserts, '[m]any high-level government officials, along with individuals in positions of power and influence in fields ranging from industry to medicine and from science to psychology, believed wholeheartedly that there was a direct connection between communism and sexual depravity'.[30] As Johnson suggests, 'in the 1950s, congressional conservatives claimed to fear that homosexuals constituted a large, powerful cabal that threatened the security of the nation'.[31] The cure for this, as proposed in the comics, is for lesbianism to be brought within the purview of male sexuality, thereby removing the possibility of blackmail and conspiracy.

Questions of gender and sexuality served as sources of anxiety and had the potential to traumatize those who saw 'deviant' practices as threats to the contemporary construction of American society. Homosexuality, even female sexuality seen as 'too assertive' within the contexts of a heterosexual relationship, had the potential to begin unravelling the ideological binds that strained to hold together one particular construction of the US. These fears over the potential impact of homosexuality on the fabric of both the family and American society were tied to fears of communist influence.

As with communism, a single allegation of homosexual conduct could be enough to cost the accused their job and their respectability, as defined by the restrictive limits of the time. 'Morals squads' stalked known meeting areas for gay men, with officers eliciting contact with a suspected gay individual and then arresting them.[32] As with discussions of spaces becoming racialized (see Chapter 3 on race in the 1950s and Chapter 7 for the 1970s), Reumann notes how many 'men and women who had discovered or confirmed their homosexuality while in the service or while doing war work … congregated in urban areas where other homosexuals lived and worked', and these patterns of urban settlement, and their policing by white male forces of containment, created spaces that took on elements of horror for heterosexual white men.[33] As George Chauncey remarks of wartime service, soldiers were freed 'from the supervision of their families and small-town neighbourhoods … plac[ed] in a single sex environment', which meant that 'mobilisation increased the chances that they would meet gay men and explore their homosexual interests'.[34] Chauncey then highlights how 'many recruits saw the sort of gay life they could lead in large cities and chose to stay in those cities after the war', a move that took them from one means of supervision, the family, but only made them subject to the new, disciplinary, gaze of the morals squads.[35] The 'lavender scare' of the 1950s, during which homosexuals were publicly ousted from government positions, was enacted over fears that gay men were more liable to communist corruption. The figure of the lesbian appears, for example, in 'Vampires? Don't Make Me Laugh', in *The Clutching Hand* (1954).[36] In the story, Lisa, the protagonist, is a vampire who undergoes surgery in order to be 'normal' and marry a man, but subsequently reverts to her vampire nature. When she feeds upon female victims her body transforms to take on more masculine attributes, including hairy arms (Figure 25).

Lisa's hungers are beyond her control; when she attacks her first victim, she cries out 'Heaven help me – I can't – stop!' She experiences

**25** Anon. (w) and Harry Lazarus (a), 'Vampires? Don't Make Me Laugh', *The Clutching Hand*

urges that she is forced to keep secret from those around her. The
theme of vampirism as homosexual desire recurs elsewhere in the
horror genre; in 'Shadow of Death', which appeared in *Tomb of Terror*
#7, a homoerotic encounter is similarly coded as vampirism; the narra-
tor asserts: 'I stalked a pretty young thing who lived near the outskirts
of the village ... to blot out the temptation of killing desire ...'. All
of these narratives suggest that homosexuals represent a threat not
only to the American home, but to the nation; as Eric Butler argues,
'[t]he name "vampire" designates, above all a process of invasion'.[37]
The narrator of 'Vampires? Don't Make Me Laugh' concludes: 'so
there it is ... An authentic case that proves that vampires exist – and
shows that they're dangerous'. The narrative fits popular depictions
of homosexuality at the time, which presented gay men and lesbians
as morally weak and unable to control their desires. In accordance
with this, Lisa tries and fails to live a normal life, suggesting that, as
many argued at the time, her lesbianism represented at threat to the
American household.

Elsewhere, lesbianism is more coded, manifesting as a conspiracy
between women. Such stories recall long-standing associations of witchcraft with a female coven, of witchcraft as a threat to ongoing projects
of patriarchal order, as well as the sexualized accounts of witches and

their familiarity with the devil or his subordinates.[38] Many of the horror comics of the period embody the anti-feminist rhetoric of the time. One such example can be found in 'Crawling Evil' in *Journey into Fear* #10. It opens with a grandmother explaining to her granddaughter, Lorna, that men are 'foul beasts'.[39] When pressed to tell her story she agrees, stating 'you're old enough to start hating men now'. She relates how she was jilted at the altar and subsequently married 'a spineless fool who was glad to die! We had a son, your father, whom I hated! He died, too! I wish all men were dead!' Young Lorna takes the lesson to heart. She vows to hate men all her life, throws out her boy dolls, and prays to be kept safe from men. After granny dies (refusing to accept the help of a male doctor), Lorna discovers that she has been raised by a witch. She uses her grandmother's magic to turn men into worms, an effect she achieves by kissing them.

Lorna seduces a series of men, transforms them into worms and kills them. Eventually, however, she meets a man for whom she develops feelings (Figure 26). She makes him swear never to kiss her. Despite her warnings, he steals a kiss from her while she is asleep. She awakes, thinking that she dreamed the kiss, and steps on him. Overcome with grief and regret, Lorna drinks poison and, as she lies dying, worms descend upon her.

The comic serves as an example of the type of cautionary tale in which women are recruited into witchcraft, suggesting, as with 'The Witch in White', that women are dangerous in numbers. It understands the early feminist movement not as a process of female empowerment, but as a drive to destroy men. Lorna's training, the comic suggests, goes

**26** Iger Studio, 'Crawling Evil', *Journey into Fear* #10

against her natural instincts towards romance, embodying Lundberg and Farnham's arguments concerning what they saw as the dangers of female empowerment. Sexual difference wins out (notably, with Lorna's agency being taken from her) but the damage is already done. Lorna has adopted a lifestyle that has made heteronormative coupling and domesticity impossible.

Women who possess magical powers are not only sexualized within the narratives of the comics, but also in the advertisements those comics carry. *Witches Tales* #9 carried an advertisement for lingerie, promising 'black magic', 'oriental magic', and 'black sorcery' (Figure 27). The advertisement invites men to 'bewitch' their partners with these items, suggesting both that the buyer will possess power over the wearer, and that donning such garments will transform a woman into a (desirable) witch, in keeping with the increasingly public objectification of female bodies. While the advert speaks of the wearer as under the influence of its power, it is also clear that the wearer is able to exercise power over the presumably male buyer through conforming to or contesting her insertion into the fantasy offered by the advert. The purpose of these items is clearly sexual and suggests that while witches are figures of erotic fantasy, heterosexual narratives, imagery, and practice are a means to mitigate those powers.

## The male gaze

Sexualization, then, proves to be a common means for horror comics to destabilize female power. This is particularly evident in those comics that incorporate themes from the 'Jungle Queen' trope found in other genres.[40] In 'The Shelf of Skulls', which appeared in the first issue of *Voodoo*, a man recounts being rescued by a woman named Olane – a princess and leader of an unspecific Pacific Islander tribe. In one panel, in a reversal of the usual damsel-in-distress trope (a common theme of the jungle comic, commonly inverted in titles such as *Sheena, Queen of the Jungle*) the male protagonist is carried away while calling to a woman – Olane – to rescue him (Figure 28).

The presence of an emasculated male protagonist is standard for horror. As William K. Everson asserts: '[t]he hero, in fact, has always been unimportant in horror films. His usual role is that of a casual observer (often a newspaper reporter) and protective husband for the heroine at the fadeout'.[41] Phallic power, instead, lies with the monster. Even if her male counterpart is unremarkable, Olane reads as a reversal of many of the tropes found above. Her power is hereditary, non-magical,

**27** Advertisement from *Witches Tales* #9

**28** Anon., 'The Shelf of Skulls', *Voodoo* #1

and well-earned. Throughout the story, she puts herself at risk for the sake of others. She is fearless, loyal, and wields power with compassion. Her apparent power, however, is undercut by frequent moments of sexualization. She wears a tight-fitting, low-cut dress and is often depicted in full-body long panels facing away from, or at 90 degrees to, the reader. In the panel in Figure 29, rather than returning the reader's gaze, she is positioned to be looked at and, because she does not face us, the act of looking seems to be without danger. Her body is also framed by the light at the top of the panel and the big cat at the bottom, directing the reader's gaze to the space between: her breasts, her flat stomach, and the curve of her upper thigh.

The positioning of female bodies as objects to be acted upon, rather than as agents who take action, runs throughout the horror genre. The invitation to look at the female body is reinforced not only by the averted gaze of the women

**29** Anon., 'The Shelf of Skulls', *Voodoo* #1

ry...
I
:IND

I FEEL SO
MUCH SAFER
WITH DR. TRIMM
HERE...

WHICH WAY
DID HE GO,
ELLEN?

LL
>!

I
k
I
FRIGHT

**30** Anon., 'The Haunted One', *Voodoo* #1

in question, but by the presence of other observers within the pages of the comic. In 'The Haunted One' from *Voodoo* #1, for example, a woman (this time coded with the blonde hair of a victim) is depicted putting on stockings (Figure 30). Her leg dangles from the bottom of the frame, suggesting both that her body is of sufficient note to escape the confines of the page, and placing her in a position of unknowing peril. A space, unseen, exists below her into which she is, unwittingly, about to tumble. Indeed, her foot points, in an adjacent panel, to an image of herself crumpled into a heap. Behind her a shadowy male figure looms, watching as she clothes herself. Ironically, in a thought bubble, she tells herself, 'I feel so much safer with Dr. Trimm here ...'. The reader is implicated in this moment of voyeurism and, as above, our allegiance is tacitly not with the hero, but with the monster poised to attack.

The complicity between the reader and the monster who assaults women is powerfully illustrated on the cover of *Tomb of Terror* #7, in which a woman cowers, apparently, from the reader (Figure 31). Her body occupies the majority of the page. Her hand is raised but not so as to prevent the viewer from seeing her large, rounded breasts and slender waist. We see through the monster's eyes, so that all we see of it are two raised hands. We are poised to inflict violence on the woman before us.[42] Other horror narratives exploit similar devices, as in *Tales from the Crypt* #34 (1953), when the narrative repeatedly refers to 'you' as the source of terror, and the reader is therefore the agent of his wife's demise in the story. It does not require a significant logical leap to assert that the enactment of misogynistic violence through the horror genre spoke directly to certain reader's fantasies. Beverly Nichols, writing in *The New Statesman* during the 1950s, asserts: 'When I see a beetle the size of a bison inserting its plastic claws into the buttocks of some tedious Hollywood blonde, I heave a sigh of delight because that is just what I have been wanting to do for years'.[43]

**31** Cover, *Tomb of Terror* #7

The presentation of female bodies in horror comics is perhaps best illustrated in a panel from 'The Werewolf', which also featured in the first issue of *Voodoo* (Figure 32). In this speech-heavy panel, the artist, faced with the decision as to where to position dialogue, opted to cover the female character's face rather than her legs. The covering of her face both suggests that the reader's attention should be directed to her body and removes the possibility of her returning the reader's gaze. This panel speaks to the treatment of female characters as a whole in the genre – the problem is not simply that it indulges fantasies of misogynistic violence, but that it fails, in the words of Robin Wood, to endow the victims with 'any vivid personalized aliveness' that makes their suffering seem human or consequential.[44] They can be dismembered, either by monsters or the positioning of speech bubbles, without any sense of their wholeness having mattered.

The presentation of women as objects rather than agents undermines the possibility of their destabilizing male power. The deployment of the male gaze seeks to neutralize and resolve the threat which unsanc-

**32** Anon., 'The Werewolf', *Voodoo* #1

tioned female power represents to masculine power. They also evoke a familiar gender dynamic from Second World War popular culture. In its depiction of women as subjects of the male gaze, horror comics take their cue from the pin-up. Pin-ups were titillating, although typically not overtly pornographic, pictures – either photographs or paintings – of women. Pin-ups appeared on the noses of planes, in lockers, and on dashboards. Some, such as Alberta Vargas' *Target for Tonite*, contained indirect references to the military (in this case, the insignia for the US Army Air Force adapted into a hairpiece). The title equates the violence of war, the 'target', with the pursuit of heteronormative pleasure, in the process presenting sexual conquest as a battle to be won (Figure 33).

In many cases, pin-ups, such as those of Gil Elvgren's *Tail Wind*, catch a woman in a moment where she 'accidentally' reveals more of her leg and undergarments than she had intended (Figure 34). The billowing of her dress is caused, significantly, by the engines of a fighter-style aircraft behind her. She wears a warm smile, suggesting that while the moment of voyeurism being captured is unplanned, it is not unwelcome. The title refers to both a wind from behind while flying but could also double around the slang word for woman, tail.

Andre Bazin argues that the pin-up is a product of war, when images of absent femininity erred towards the mythic.[45] Despina Kakoudaki argues that the pin-up of the 1940s was the embodiment of 'sensual innocence' and 'patriotic values'.[46] She was mobilized as an embodiment

**33** Gil Elvgren, 'Target for Tonite', *Esquire* military edition

**34** Gil Elvgren, *Tail Wind*

of all that soldiers were fighting to protect and a tantalizing reward for
when the war was over. The pin-up is at once embedded within the
experience of warfare and separate from it – she exists as a fragment
from into another, better, world. The pin-up codified heterosexual coupling during wartime; as Robert B. Westbrook asserts: 'if men were
obliged to fight for their pin-up girls, women in turn were expected to
fashion themselves into pin-up girls worth fighting for'.[47] Once the war
was over, Bazin argues, the pin-up was replaced by images of domestic

**35** Anon., 'Gallows Curse', *Voodoo* #14

virtue and repurposed in advertising and cinema. She also found her way into comics.

Clearly, the horror comic has something of the pin-up in its gene-alogy. The genre represents part of a wave of increasing acceptance of the pin-up in US media – a phenomena found in the depiction of Hollywood actresses and in the pages of *Playboy*. It also shows a greater degree of explicit and fetishistic sexualization. Horror comics contain innumerable full-body images of women reclining in a state of undress. Figure 35, from *Voodoo* #14, for example, almost perfectly recalls Gil Elvgren's *Out on a Limb* (1937) (Figure 36). Such images call upon a visual vocabulary established by the pin-up artists of the Second World War era and before.

By presenting women using the codes of the pin-up, the horror genre evokes a familiar, if largely imagined, system of gender dynamics. The pin-up of the 1940s evoked a world where men went out to fight and women offered the promise of sexual reward and preserved the sanc-tity of home. The pin-up girl is not a threat to man's place in indus-try because she is not capable of work. Elvgren's *Is My Face Red?*, for example, shows a cartoonishly doll-like woman who has fallen down while attempting to lift a bowling ball (inevitably, revealing her upper thighs in the process). The pin-up is charmingly incompetent and in constant need of a man to offer her help. She issues no threat of dephallusization – instead, her sexualized incompetence operates as a clear indicator that she is wholly dependent on men.

**36** Gil Elvgren, *Out on a Limb*

### Violence towards women

The horror genre, then, enacted a process of rephallusization by rendering women in the language of the 1940s pin-up. It also articulated a world-view that appears, in some cases, to seek to naturalise the use of violence against women. In 'Hammer of Evil', a comic that featured in *Voodoo* #15, a man cohabitates with an unfrozen cave woman. While he is away at work, she kills and eats his dog (as cave women are wont to do). He reasons that, lacking a shared language, his best means to express his displeasure is to strike her. In what is, perhaps, the ugliest moment in all of horror comics, she responds enthusiastically, falling to his feet 'wriggling like a dog that has been whipped'. When he then pulls her by her hair she begins 'almost purring' (Figure 37). He admits, guiltily, that he also enjoyed the experience. The comic seems not only to condone domestic violence, but to suggest that violence is an essential and natural component of courtship, bequeathed to us by our 'savage' ancestors.

'Hammer of Evil' is certainly not the only comic of the genre to intermingle sex and violence. Almost inevitably, acts of violence towards women in horror comics tend to involve eroticism and penetration. Two examples are included below – 'Fatal Steps', which appeared in *Witches Tales* #9, includes an image of a woman, back-arched and breasts thrust forward, as a pair of scissors are rammed into her throat (Figure 38). In 'King of Hades', which appeared in *Voodoo* #11, Kiki, the former girl-friend of a deceased crime boss, is pictured half-fleeing the frame (Figure

**37** Anon., 'Hammer of Evil', *Voodoo* #15

39). As was the case in 'The Haunted One', described above, the architecture of the panel allows a full view of her leg as she steps, perilously,
out of the panel. As she does so, her former lover appears to penetrate
her with the prong of a pitchfork with sufficient force that, in the next
panel, he is able to fling her behind him.

In other instances, the violence against women makes even more
explicit reference to rape. 'Cavern of Doom' from *Tomb of Terror* #3
includes a panel in which the protagonist, who has sold her soul to
the devil in order to wield supernatural powers, is bound by one ghost
while others tear at her clothes (Figure 40). More disturbing still, in her
speech bubble she declares that rather than her clothes, it is her body
being ripped to pieces. Conveniently, the ghosts pull her hair and rip her
clothes in such a way as to push her breasts forward and render them
more visible, both through the removal of fabric and through pulling it
tight around their outline.

**38** Anon., 'Fatal Steps', *Witches Tales* #9

**39** Anon., 'King of Hades', *Voodoo* #11

   The trend of sexualized violence in the horror genre often reads not
only as titillating, but as grotesque. In 'Death Pact' from *Tomb of Terror*
#3, the protagonist forces his would-be killer to drink the poisoned
liquid she had prepared for him. As in the cases above, the position of the
figures is highly suggestive of rape and yet the composition of the image

**40** Anon., 'Cavern of Doom', *Tomb of Terror* #3

**41** Anon., 'Death Pact', *Tomb of Terror* #3

– the fine detail on the hands and the flared nostrils of the victim, is by design more disturbing than those encountered elsewhere (Figure 41).

Such images seem to invite revulsion as much as fascination. The narrative seems to, if not condone, then to at least complicate our response to the act of violence. These images invite us to consider over-lapping, and contested, historical contexts. Certainly, in part, the vio-lence towards women found in horror comics seeks to enact a process of rephallusization by showing female power to be unsanctioned, by presenting women as objects rather than agents, and through images of sexual and physical dominance. In certain instances, this violence also intersects with the trauma of the previous chapter, allowing readers who may have had direct experience of war to revisit those experiences in a controlled environment. In such instances, rather than reading comics as a response to the entry of women into the American workforce, we can productively read horror comics as problematizing the mythology of the pin-up.

As argued above, the pin-up existed in a world that was at once able to comment on but remained protected from the violence of war. The pin-up is a utopian vision of an America to which the soldier might one day return. The idea of women as somehow separate from war, however, did not match the reality that many American soldiers both witnessed and participated in during the Second World War. Rape was a common weapon of war practised, in the most-noted instances, by German soldiers in the Soviet Union, by Soviet soldiers as they entered Germany, and by Japanese soldiers who ransacked the Chinese city of Nanjing.[48] The Japanese military quasi-institutionalized the practice of keeping 'comfort women' – Chinese, Korean, Filipino, and other women who were kept as sex slaves. Women also died in large numbers as nurses on the battlefield, and as civilians, from bombs, bullets, starva-tion, disease, and at the hands of invading armies.

American soldiers, in almost all fields of battle, must have noted the incongruity between the wholesome pin-ups, simultaneously virginal and enticingly experienced, who adorned their lockers and airplane noses, compared with the women who were dead, dying, and subject to untold privations in Europe and the Pacific theatre. Indeed, the image of a woman's decapitated (and oddly bloodless) head left on display in a Pacific island in 'The Shelf of Skulls' seems to explicitly recall the heads hung for display by Japanese soldiers in Nanjing (Figure 42).[49] Challenges to patriarchy mounted through Olane's rule are also exter-nalized and associated with primitive societies, delegitimizing women's claims to rule; even though the challenge to Olane is the source of the horror in the narrative, the fact she is subject to continual agitation against her rule works to undermine its legitimacy.

Horror comics further satirized the pin-up not only by showing women to be victims of war, but by showing men to be incapable of serving as protectors. The pin-up, as argued above, presents a world

**42** Anon., 'The Shelf of Skulls', *Voodoo* #1

**43** Anon., 'Snow Beasts', *Tomb of Terror* #4

in which women are in constant need of help and infers that the (male) viewer should be the one to provide her with the assistance she so clearly needs – either by lifting a bowling ball or defeating Hitler. In the horror comic, however, men are often incapable of providing that help. In 'Snow Beasts', for example, a party of explorers watch helplessly as the female of their group is dragged away by snow monsters (Figure 43). When she next appears, she is naked and has frozen to death. The horror

**44** Anon., 'Dimension IV', *Witches Tales* #13

comic thus reads as a narrative of rephallusization deferred, wherein
the implied relationship between the pin-up and her saviour collapses.
Women are not immune from violence, men fail to act as rescuers, and
no one is able to withstand the impersonal will of war.

In 'Dimension IV', similarly, a couple find a cave. The man, timidly,
suggests that they should turn back and his partner teases him about
men being 'the weaker sex'. They find themselves trapped in the presence of a monster and both characters begin to call for help – help
that, of course, does not come. In the moment at which they find
themselves in peril, the man calls out 'I'm going crazy! This has to be a
nightmare! It has to be! The cave opening was just here a second ago!
Now there's nothing but a smooth wall! Help! Help!' (Figure 44). As
he vocalizes his panic, his partner gives him a look of utter disdain –
until now she had teased him for his cowardice, but now she sees it
fully articulated.

Such narratives would seem to run counter to the process of rephallusization described above. Rather than stripping women of power they
challenge the possibility of male heroism. Women in these stories are
victims, but men are incapable of serving as their saviours. Any challenge such narratives issue to gender norms, however, is undercut not
only by the genre's resistance to imbuing female characters with any
fully realized personhood, but by the centrality of the male experience.
As argued in the previous chapter, these narratives exclusively centre
upon the male protagonist; women may be victims, but we always

experience their victimhood through the eyes of the male characters. This is compounded by the tendency in such narratives to reduce female characters to types, robbing them of a sense of personhood and removing any significance from their suffering. Their deaths, however violent, serve primarily to drive the story of the male protagonist. As in the previous chapter, fear remains the domain of the hegemonic white male. Understood this way, the emasculation of male characters and the occasional moments that defamiliarize violence against women can be read, as with the last chapter, as playing out the anxieties of the white American male within a safe environment. The suffering of women, and the inability of men to prevent that suffering, thus becomes another facet of horror comics' attempts to process the cultural trauma of the Second World War as experienced by white men.

## Conclusion

This chapter has proposed two imbricated readings of the role of gender in horror comics. Horror comics can be seen as enacting a misogynistic response to the empowerment of women in Second World War America. They respond to this threat to patriarchal power by presenting female power as dangerous, by treating women as objects, and by proposing sexual violence as a reasonable means to maintain social order. Simultaneously, horror comics also explore violence against women as a symptom of war, and men as incapable of fulfilling their role as protector. On its surface, this reads as a contradictory impulse – one might expect horror comics to couple misogynistic violence exclusively with fantasies of male supremacy. One way to bring together these two readings is by way of Robin Wood's argument that because of the generic requirements of horror as reactionary or punitive, the genre struggles to maintain a sustained commitment to progressive politics – that even if we are to (charitably) read horror as recognizing women as victims of war, and emasculation as a consequence of trauma, the genre as a whole, with its unrelenting thirst for victims, undermines any potentially redemptive narratives.[50] The apparent gestures towards a feminist reading, then, are undercut by the focus on the male experience – the bodies of pin-ups that litter the pages of horror comics serve as both erotic titillation and part of the larger backdrop of war; their primary purpose is to inform the male experience of terror and fear. As in the previous chapter, the horror genre privileges the experience of white heterosexual males, sexualizing female suffering and subsuming it into narratives of male trauma.

The figurative and literal dismemberment of female characters enacted in the examples given here illustrates difference between the male victimhood described in the previous chapter and the female victimhood described here. Male victims are permitted humanity – their suffering may be grotesque and even humorous but it is always a cynical expression of a world upended, where the violence of war extends not simply to bodies but to the social fabric. Female victimhood, conversely, is an affirmation of male power – even when female bodies serve as evidence of the violence of war, the genre as a whole seeks to repress, contain, and marginalize female agency.

## Notes

1 Anon., 'The Frenzy of Sheila Lord', *Beyond*, 5 (New York: Ace Magazines Inc. 1951), 14.
2 Anon., 'The Frenzy of Sheila Lord', 15
3 Philip Wylie, *Generation of Vipers* (New York and Toronto: Muller, 1942), 203.
4 Kristin Hoganson, *Fighting for American Manhood: How Gender Politics Provoked the Spanish-American and Philippine-American Wars* (New Haven, CT: Yale University Press, 2000).
5 Ferdinand Lundberg and Marynia F. Farnham, *Modern Woman: The Lost Sex* (New York: Harper & Brothers, 1947).
6 See, for instance, Miriam G. Reumann, *American Sexual Character: Sex, Gender, and National Identity in the Kinsey Reports* (Berkeley, CA: University of California Press, 2005).
7 Harry M. Benshoff, *Monsters in the Closet: Homosexuality and the Horror Film* (Manchester: Manchester University Press, 1997), 5
8 David K. Johnson, *The Lavender Scare: The Cold War Persecution of Gays and Lesbians in the Federal Government* (Chicago, IL: University of Chicago Press, 2004), 2.
9 Reumann, *American Sexual Character*, 2.
10 Halberstam, *Skin Shows*, 13
11 Skal, *The Monster Show*, 71.
12 Sennitt, *Ghastly Terror!*, 47.
13 Karasik and Newgarden, *How to Read Nancy*, 33.
14 Sex in superhero comics has typically been treated, to borrow creator Howard Chaykin's words, either as images that evoke 'Sierra Club postcards'" or 'lustful sneering glances [from] Nazis'. Carolyn Cocca coined the term 'broke back' to describe the pose, often found in superhero comics, where a woman's breasts and buttocks both face the reader. Ed Bryant, 'Howard Chaykin: Heading for *Time*', in Brannon Costello (ed.), *Howard Chaykin: Conversations* (Jackson, MS: University Press of Mississippi, 2011), 57–78 (61); Carolyn Cocca, *Superwomen: Gender, Power, and Representation* (New York: Bloomsbury Academic 2016).

15 Ruth Rosen, *The World Split Open: How the Modern Women's Movement Changed America* (Old Saybrook, CT: Tantor Ebooks, 2012), iii.

16 Haggerty, 'Literature and Homosexuality in the Late Eighteenth Century', 350

17 Among the attendees was Frederic Douglass, demonstrating some understanding of the overlap between race and gender, and the need for collaboration in challenging social structures.

18 See, among others, Doris Weatherford, *American Women and World War II* (New York: Facts on File 1990).

19 Rosen, *The World Split Open*, 1.

20 William Chafe, *The Paradox of Change: American Women in the 20th Century* (Oxford: Oxford University Press, 1991), 152.

21 Cynthia Weber, *Faking It: U.S. Hegemony in a 'Post-Phallic' Era* (Minneapolis, MI: University of Minnesota Press: 1999).

22 Raymond Durgnat, 'The Subconscious: From Pleasure Castle to Libido Hotel', in Silver and Ursini (eds), *Horror Film Reader*, 39–49 (39).

23 Joan Nicholson, 'The Packaging of Rape: A Feminist Indictment', in Mark Gabor (ed.), *The Pinup: A Modest History* (New York: Evergreen, 1972), 13–16 (15).

24 Gabor (ed.), *The Pinup*, 78.

25 Kida, 'The Strange Case of Hen-Pecked Harry', *Eerie Comics* #1.

26 Skal, *The Monster Show*, 241.

27 Groom, *The Vampire: A New History*, 182.

28 Richard Hofstadter, *The Paranoid Style of American Politics* (New York: Alfred A. Knopf, 1968); Timothy Melley, *Empire of Conspiracy: The Culture of Paranoia in Postwar America* (Ithaca, NY: Cornell University Press, 2000).

29 Anon., 'The Witch Who Wore White', *Witches Tales* #8 (New York: Harvey Publications, 1952).

30 Elaine Tyler May, *Homeward Bound: American Families in the Cold War Era* (New York: Basic Books, 2008), 91.

31 He goes on to note that 'the policies meant to counter the power and influence of gay civil servants actually fostered the creation of an effective and influential gay pressure group'. As with so many other policies of the 1950s, attempts to marginalize and silence dissent only served to galvanize their targets to organize themselves and work towards overthrowing those policies in order to create a climate of greater inclusivity. Johnson, *The Lavender Scare*, 214

32 See Johnson, *The Lavender Scare*, Chapter 7, 'Interrogations and Disappearances'.

33 Reumann, *American Sexual Character*, 171.

34 George Chauncey, *Gay New York: Gender, Urban Culture, and the Making of the Gay World, 1890–1940* (New York: Basic Books, 1994), 10

35 Chauncey, *Gay New York*, 10

36 Anon. (w), and Harry Lazarus (a), 'Vampires? Don't Make Me Laugh', *The Clutching Hand* (New York: Best Syndicated Features Inc., 1954).

37 Eric Butler, *Metamorphoses of the Vampire in Literature and Film: Cultural Transformations in Europe, 1732–1933* (Rochester, NY: Random House, 2010), 2.

38 Alison Rowlands, 'Witchcraft and Old Women in Early Modern Germany', *Past & Present* 173.1 (2001), 50–89, interrogates the stereotypes around witchcraft, demonstrating that it was not only poor, old, women on the edges of society who were labelled witches, but also younger women capable of exercising social and economic power. Stacy Schiff is one among the many who have written on Salem, 1692, but her *The Witches: Salem, 1692* (New York: Little Brown and Co., 2015) is a readable account of the mass hysteria (used deliberately to convey the role of and reaction to women in this event) in New England and the responses to it by male colonial elites.

39 Iger Studio, 'Crawling Evil', *Journey into Fear* #10 (New York: Superior Publishers, 1952), 2.

40 For more on Jungle Queens, see Savage's *Cowboys, Commies and Jungle Queens*.

41 William K. Everson, 'Horror Films', in Silver and Ursini (eds), *Horror Film Reader*, 21–37 (32).

42 There is also a suggestion that the hands poised to undertake these actions are black, staging the conventional racial threat of black sexuality to white womanhood, but also placing the reader in the position of embodying a fantasy version of an African American subject position.

43 Quoted in Hill, 'The Face of Horror', in Silver and Ursini (eds), *Horror Film Reader*, 51–61 (57).

44 Robin Wood, 'Neglected Nightmares', in Silver and Ursini (eds), *Horror Film Reader*, 111–127.

45 Andre Bazin, 'Metamorphosis of the Pin-Up Girl', *What Is Cinema? Vol. 2* (Berkley, CA: University of California Press, 2005), 159–162.

46 Kakoudaki, Despina, 'Pinup: The American Secret Weapon in World War II', in Linda Williams (ed.), *Porn Studies* (Durham, NC and London: Duke University Press, 2004), 335–369 (335).

47 Robert B. Westbrook, *Why We Fought* (Washington, DC: Smithsonian Book, 2010), unpaginated.

48 See, for example, James W. Messerschmidt, 'The Forgotten Victims of World War II', *Violence Against Women* 12.7 (2006), 706–712; Iris Chang, *The Rape of Nanking: The Forgotten Holocaust of World War II* (New York: Basic Books, 2012).

49 It also perpetuates the notion of savagery, that the Pacific islanders are head-hunters, cannibals, and that their primitive Otherness constitutes a significant threat to Americans. In doing so, such representations mobilize racist and colonialist rhetoric from the Spanish-American-Cuban-Filipino War of 1898 and the Philippine-American War that followed American occupation. See Paul A. Kramer, *The Blood of Government: Race, Empire, the United States, and the Philippines* (Chapel Hill, NC: University of North Carolina Press, 2006).

50 Wood, *Hollywood from Vietnam to Regan*.

# 3

## 'Confusion turns to fear' – race in the 1940s and 1950s

In 1956, J. W. Milam told *Time* magazine that 'Niggers ain't gonna vote where I live. If they did, they'd control the government'.[1] Milam and those who shared his views used violence and intimidation to prevent the enfranchisement of black citizens; he was one of the two men who murdered fourteen-year-old Emmet Till in 1955 after Till interacted with a white woman.[2] Milam was not necessarily representative of white Americans at the time, but his assertion makes overt a recurring anxiety in national discussions around race; change seemed inevitable, and change required introspection. In order for America to fully recognize the violence and persecution to which people of colour, and those of African heritage in particular, had been subjected, change would mean providing historically disenfranchised groups with political capital. If white America were to accept the violence on which its economic, social, and political wealth had been built, in other words, then it would also need to accept the possibility of massive political change that would shape the future of the country. The inevitability of social change, and the buried truths it threatened to unearth, was, for men like Milam, a source of horror that needed to be violently suppressed.

In the previous two chapters, we have shown that horror comics of the 1950s presented a world profoundly affected by the Second World War. We have further demonstrated that, as a recurring theme, horror comics present white men as victims and women as a source of horror; women wield unsanctioned forms of power, are dangerous in numbers, actively seek to harm men and, the comics propose, must be stripped of their power through sexualized violence. This chapter looks to a different source of horror – that of the racialized Other. Horror comics of the 1940s and 1950s offer what, to a modern reader, can seem to be problematic and contradictory visions of race. The genre emerged during a pivotal moment in race relations in the United States, when the work of the National Association for the Advancement of Colored People (NAACP), the Double V Campaign, stepped towards greater legal protections for African Americans, and, among other landmark events, *Brown v. Board of Education* all brought the question of race in America into white public consciousness.

These cultural and political changes impacted on the practices and content of comics. In horror comics, questions of racism, colourism, segregation, and social stratification emerge in oblique, allegorical fashion, sometimes reinforcing racist conservatism, sometimes challenging it. Often, the comics do both simultaneously by promoting an apparently progressive agenda while at the same time maintaining an Orientalist framework that retains distinctions between 'Us' and 'Them'. Race is, as a recurring theme, linked to monstrosity through iconography and patterns of behaviour, both of the monster and of those it meets. The monstrous is also often located in familiar suburban locales, bringing horror firmly into American homes and mediating contemporary anxieties over racialized spaces. These stories generally recognize the violence to which minority groups are subjected and celebrate collaboration between different groups (albeit with little compromise on the part of whites), and yet they nonetheless present a series of scenarios in which the Other, driven mad by persecution, presents a threat to both white protagonists and the fabric of American society. Much of this fear is tied specifically to geography and property, with minority groups (re)occupying white spaces, and, as Milam feared, gaining 'control' of some kind, however tenuous and conditional that control might be.

**Historical background**

The place for people of colour in the American cultural landscape changed significantly during the early twentieth century. During the 1920s, the Harlem Renaissance produced a body of work termed, at the time, as the 'New Negro Movement'. African American writers, Paula T. Connolly asserts, 'shared a focus on racial pride as they explored black identity, recovered black heroes, and debated the nature of art, race, and politics'.[3] This body of cultural work, as well as the activities of the NAACP, opened a conversation around race and social justice. Bayard Rustin, one of the key strategists of the Civil Rights movement from the 1940s into the 1960s, defined the period from *Brown* in 1954 to the passage of the Voting Rights Act in 1965 as the 'classical phase' of the movement. The story that has come to be encapsulated by this definition is of a short, contained, period of peaceful mobilization that achieved its reasonable aims before fracturing into Black Power excess and anti-war agitation, offering the chance for the establishment of a 'conservative interregnum' that has subsequently dominated American civil rights discourse.[4] In contrast to this narrative, Jacquelyn Dowd Hall traces a continuous campaign (and simultaneous counter-movement) back into the 'liberal and radical milieu of the late 1930s', which takes into account the Popular Front, black socialist and communist agitation, and transnational activism as well as the Second World War and its impact on the trajectory of future racial policy.[5] The war itself was a moment of internal conflict and division as marginalized groups were enlisted to fight in support of a country that regarded them with, at best, uncertainty. Attempts to resolve these dilemmas took many forms, one of which was cultural. However, as Lauren Rebecca Sklaroff has noted, 'the use of culture to reduce wartime racial tensions became a subject of frequent debate, as officials questioned which individuals and which sectors of the media could best address black Americans without alarming white Americans', which posed difficulties for the Office of War Information (OWI), the agency charged with the regulation of American culture during the war.[6]

American experience of the Second World War was riven with conflict along lines of race. Almost one million African Americans saw active duty, in segregated units, during the Second World War and a further three million registered for service.[7] Despite being a war apparently fought for democracy and, at least in the European theatre, against virulent advocates of Aryan supremacy, demands by African Americans for equality of rights, access to jobs, and military opportunity were largely ignored. The sentiments of the American government were summed up in a letter from the War Department to Walter White, head of the NAACP, which stated that 'we must not indulge in social experimentation in time of war'.[8] The letter expresses a clear commitment to maintaining domestic relationships of power, even as the War Department sought to overthrow foreign ones. The Double V campaign was a direct response to this, an attempt by African Americans to bring about a 'double victory' over enemies 'at home and abroad'.[9] This campaign began in 1942 through the *Pittsburgh Courier*, an African American newspaper, when James G. Thompson wrote a letter questioning whether he should 'sacrifice my life to live half American'.[10] Double V was an attempt to show the sacrifices made by African Americans for a society that still refused to grant them equal status. This campaign built on the earlier March on Washington Movement of 1941, organized by Bayard Rustin and A. Philip Randolph, where civil rights groups had threatened a massive demonstration in Washington to protest against discriminatory hiring practices in highly paid defence industry jobs. Fearing the negative publicity of such a demonstration, President Roosevelt signed

Executive Order 8802, granting African Americans full access to the munitions jobs they had previously been denied. Just because African Americans could now make the weapons, however, did not mean that they could always use them. The Selective Training and Service Act of 1940 retained a segregated military, and African Americans generally found themselves in menial jobs and segregated units. The federal workforce and military were not desegregated until Executive Orders 9980 and 9981, respectively, in 1948 under President Truman. By that time, the Ku Klux Klan had been revived in a backlash against the perceived advances of people of colour.[11]

Events on US soil were informed by those occurring overseas. The Pan-African Conference first met in London in 1900 to discuss the decolonization of Africa. In 1955, several delegates gathered in Bandung, Indonesia to discuss the future of the 'third world'. The period from the end of the Second World War into the 1950s saw anti-colonial insurrections throughout the occupied territories of the European empires. This period saw the publication of works such as W. E. B. Du Bois' *Color and Democracy* (1945), Aimé Césaire's *Discours sur le colonialisme* (1950), George Padmore's *Pan-Africanism or Communism? The Coming Struggle for Africa* (1956), and Richard Wright's *White Man Listen!* (1957). In the US, these anti-imperialist movements were often associated, correctly or otherwise, with the threat of communism, though Mary L. Dudziak observes that the Cold War and racial issues have often been separated in the historiography of the period.[12] While domestic racial policy was not always seen as a 'Cold War' issue, scholars such as Dudziak have drawn attention to the ways in which the USSR mobilized American domestic affairs to delegitimize American geopolitical rhetoric around freedom and democracy. This is clear from contemporary documents, as 'US State Department files from the period are full of reports from the field that racial problems in the United States harmed US relations with particular nations and compromised the nation's Cold War objectives'.[13] This is evident from as early as 1936, long before the conventional origins of the Cold War, in the Soviet musical, *Circus* (1936), where Marion Dixon (Lyubov Orlova) faces racist discrimination in the US after giving birth to a biracial child. Unable to bear the discrimination in the US any longer, Dixon flees to the USSR, where both her and her child are embraced by a friendly multi-ethnic Soviet crowd.[14] Domestic actions also hampered cultural warfare when some prospective 'jazz ambassadors' recruited by the State Department refused to act in the name of the US, as in 1957 when Louis Armstrong cancelled his tour of the Soviet Union to protest the treatment of black schoolchildren in Little Rock, Arkansas.[15]

The most prominent race-related case of the 1950s was *Brown v. Board of Education of Topeka* in 1954, a significant legal victory for the NAACP, which ruled that the segregation of schools was unconstitutional. A significant plank supporting the legal notion of 'separate but equal' that meant African Americans would be provided with facilities that were separate from whites, but equal to them (equality of provision was never the goal, and never achieved), established in *Plessy v. Ferguson* of 1896, was therefore, at least in law, removed. Implementation of the law was a different matter. Just as communists had used domestic racial discrimination in the US as a propaganda weapon in their attempts to appeal to decolonizing territories in the early Cold War, the American government now ensured the *Brown* ruling was circulated globally, rooted in a narrative of the superiority of democratic gradualism over dictatorial rule in bringing about progressive reform and inclusive societies. Minorities had been weaponized during the war, and their apparent postwar inclusion in American society was itself weaponized; having helped to defeat the Nazis, minorities would now help to defeat the Soviets by demonstrating to people of colour around the world that the US could be trusted on issues of race. The intention was to increase international faith in American democracy and to deprive the communists of a specific weapon in their arsenal, or at least to diminish its effectiveness. Subsequent civil rights protests complicate this narrative and demonstrate the clear difference between *de jure* and *de facto* desegregation. However, *Brown* was far from the only 'moment' in 1954. First, the televised McCarthy hearings into communism in the US Army represent the final stage of the process that broke the increasingly fragmented and contested support for the communist witch-hunter in chief, Senator Joseph McCarthy; second, the Senate subcommittee hearings into juvenile delinquency, which ran chronologically parallel to the McCarthy hearings, resulted in the Comics Code Authority coming into being.[16] More than time and space connects these moments: Dr Fredric Wertham was a key figure in *Brown* and the Senate subcommittee hearings, running an experiment that demonstrated the negative psychological impact of segregation on children in the former and acting as key scholar for the prosecution, as it were, in the latter.[17] Wertham's involvement in *Brown*, a liberal victory, and the Senate subcommittee hearings, an apparent conservative triumph, demonstrate the political complexity of the period, which was concerned not only with these matters but also with the role of women, masculinity, sexuality, the organization of business, the family, science, the environment, and a whole host of other anxieties.[18]

African Americans, though, were not the only group to face

discrimination. Some communities marked as Other linguistically, such as Italian Americans, were also the target of nativist resentment.[19] The Japanese attack on Pearl Harbor on 7 December 1941 reactivated deep-seated and long-standing hatred of the Japanese that, during the war and beyond, extended to all Asian people. As far back as the Chinese Exclusion Act of 1882, and the Gentleman's Agreement of 1907 that regulated Japanese immigration, the American government had been working towards limiting migration to the US from Asia. A further Immigration Act in 1917 marked a significant step towards nativism and introduced an 'Asiatic Barred Zone', which while not including Japan, did include the rest of Asia, stretching from China to the Gulf of Suez and reaching as high as the base of Russia. At the peak of domestic nativism, the Immigration Act of 1924 took this even further by introducing measures so draconian that Hitler cited them approvingly as an inspiration for his own policies.[20] The most famous measure in regulating Japanese Americans, though, is Executive Order 9066, of 19 February 1942, which led to the internment in camps of Japanese Americans and the forced sale of their property and businesses. Despite OWI attempts to offer counter-narratives stressing the liberal war aims of the US, this pattern of domestic persecution gave rise to numerous racist depictions throughout the Second World War, establishing themes that continued in postwar comics.

Racism in comics was nothing new. As Fredrick Strömberg asserts, comics of the early twentieth century depicted black characters using seven recurring stereotypes: the native, the tom, the coon, the picka-ninny, the tragic mulatto, the mammy, and the buck.[21] These stereotypes were in no sense exclusive to comics but, with their focus on exaggeration and caricature, comics presented an ideal site for the propagation of racist imagery. The Second World War comics, similarly, depicted Japanese characters as cowardly, treacherous, and inhuman, often with exaggerated features, sallow skin and fangs. These overtly racist stereotypes largely vanished after the Second World War, at least in connection with Japan, which was occupied by the US until 1952. The rising visibility of minority groups in America's cultural landscape and the growth of the Civil Rights movement meant that comics creators had become aware that they risked offending minority readers with racist caricature – Steamboat, a racist caricature from *Captain Marvel Comics*, was removed from that publication after a campaign by schoolchildren.[22] Although aware of the possibility of offence, many lacked a means to represent people of colour without resorting to racist stereotypes. As a result, Strömberg argues, aside from those who appeared in jungle comics, black characters vanished completely from American comics.

Superheroes were almost exclusively white throughout the decade and into much of the 1960s. As with a great deal of other science fiction and fantasy of the time, visual markers of race, one of the defining issues of contemporary socio-political discourse, were largely absent.[23]

Horror comics carried this and other baggage into the 1950s. The central dilemmas of American society and politics played out in their pages, where writers and artists at once denounced the barbarity of racial discrimination while at the same time suggesting that the rapid political gains being made by minority groups represented a threat to those who held political and social capital. US rhetoric, as reflected in horror comics, was simultaneously progressive and regressive, pointing to a more inclusive future while (whether consciously or not) ignoring or trying to reinstate past inequalities.

## Race and horror comics

Race and horror were entwined, as in American society, from the very outset of the horror comics industry. *Eerie Comics* #1, a one-shot published by Avon in 1947, featured a story, 'Mystery of Murder Manor', which dramatizes many of the themes addressed by this book. The story features two white protagonists; an intellectual boy, Rupert, and an athlete, Johnny. They enter the eponymous Murder Manor in Louisiana, in search of shelter during a storm. Rupert, represented through image, speech, and naming practices as more intelligent and effeminate than his companion, is more superstitious and afraid, raising the spectre of debates around masculinity that refracted through hard-boiled fiction, horror, and wider debates of the 1940s and 1950s. These are not the only spectres raised by the comic. The narrative is replete with images of hanging, though only white bodies are hanged – including Rupert, who is saved by Johnny with the help of a bust of his 'favorite Confederate general, 'Bob Lee', here to help a son of the South!'[24] In this narrative, black traumas are appropriated and inscribed onto white bodies. It is the Southern man who saves the hanging bodies rather than puts them there in the first place. Lee literally strikes a blow for the South by knocking Johnny's assailant unconscious. While violence and sexuality increased in comics of the 1950s, the themes explored were, largely, already present.

The horror genre was a space in which contemporary tensions around race could be explored. By the time of the boom in the early 1950s, the vast majority of horror comics narratives and images were, at least superficially, in keeping with the more progressive culture of the Civil Rights era, and thus opposed to overt and violent manifestations of racism. 'Tusks of Terror', which appeared in *Voodoo* #10 (1953), for example, is a story set in 'Kipling's India' and concerns an interracial romance.[25] The villain of the story is Colonel Rankin, a white Englishman who first appears overseeing the torture of an Indian man. When his colleagues attempt to intervene, he chides them that they are 'all too soft with these natives'. He later declares that Indians are 'all thieves'. Rankin's daughter, Rose, it transpires, is having an illicit relationship with an Indian man named Ahmed, who belongs to Indian royalty and thus, he insists, is of heritage equal to Rankin's.[26] After Rankin discovers the affair, he orders that Ahmed be sown into the skin of a pig and shot. Ahmed, inevitably, returns as a boar and takes his revenge, not only on the colonel, but on British soldiers and even his former lover.

In its treatment of Ahmed, the comic recalls the urban myth that General Pershing ordered the execution of Muslim prisoners using bullets dipped in pigs' blood during the Philippine-American War.[27] It relocates the contemporary US debate over race to another locale, however, making a representative of the British Empire a more palatable stand-in for American racists. The translation of contemporary tensions into a different historical and geographical space serves a dual purpose. First, it provides a degree of distance – a relationship between an Indian man and an English woman in colonial India was far less provocative, for an American audience, than the depiction of a relationship between a black man and a white woman in contemporary America, or even within the American past. Second, the reinscription of contemporary concerns in a different space, in accordance with the propaganda war with the USSR, allows race relations in the US to appear progressive by comparison. The comic, then, seems to pursue a progressive agenda; it punishes Rankin's racism and the disgust he expresses at miscegenation. It depicts, and seems to approve of, an interracial romance roughly a decade before the first interracial kiss on US television. It also touches on an important, and often overlooked, aspect of British colonialism: that class frequently trumped race – the relationship is justified, Ahmed argues, because his class elevates him to the status of one of the colonial authorities; he presumably belongs to the class of English-educated collaborator/intermediaries drawn from Indian royalty.[28]

Even as it rejects overt and violent forms of racism, however, the comic falls into familiar patterns of Orientalist stereotyping. 'The Orient', the narrative voice that introduces the comic informs us, is a place where 'things happen that no white man can understand'. It is conceived of as a place of mystery and exoticism encoded in explicitly racial terms. When Ahmed returns as a pig, he, Othello-like, becomes a 'raging beast', killing his former lover as well as her father. The reversion to racial stereotypes is no doubt due, in part, to the writer's apparent ignorance of Indian cultures and religions. Ahmed's name suggests that he is Muslim, something corroborated by his aversion to pig flesh, and yet he wears a turban more commonly associated with Sikhs and, we are told, believes in reincarnation. He represents a homogenized version of an Oriental man in the Western imagination. He, and the land he comes from, is drawn primarily from popular depictions of the East, with little reference to the actual India. Even as the comic seems to pursue an anti-racist agenda, then, it appropriates aspects of various Asian cultures without seeking to engage with them in anything more than a superficial manner. In an echo of 'Corpse of the Jury', mentioned in Chapter 1 of this volume, it also presents the racialized Other as a source of horror – while the comic seems, at least in part, to represent Ahmed's revenge as justified, it also presents him as dangerous. Milam feared the political enfranchisement of African Americans would lead to dramatic changes in the American political landscape; in allegorical form here, the empowerment of a victim of racialized violence, albeit supernatural empowerment rather than democratic, leads to a massacre.

'Tusks of Terror' was not alone in presenting both critique and reinstatement of racism. Other comics seek to appear similarly progressive by suggesting collaboration between white characters and people of colour. One such example can be found in 'Death Is a Dream' – a comic set in Hong Kong in 1923 (once more, a relocation of US contradictions to a less immediate space) that appears in *Ghost Comics* #4 (1952) (Figure 45). The comic is replete with Orientalist images of China. Lili Shan, a Chinese woman (reminiscent of the Dragon Lady from *Terry and the Pirates* (1934–1973) and whose name recalls 'Shanghai Lil' from *Footlight Parade* (1933)) robed in a silk shirt with a mandarin collar and a cheongsam-style split skirt, is a double-agent, recruiting communist soldiers while selling secrets to the British. As with 'Tusks of Terror', the comic offers a flattened and stereotyped image of Asian cultures. The bottom of the first page shows the silhouettes of what seem to be Mongol warriors and a uni-browed, slit-eyed face peering at the reader. The communists are led by Yadin, who sports a Fu Manchu moustache. The ghost of Lili Shan has a wisp-like tail reminiscent of a genie from similarly Orientalized depictions of the Middle East found in, for example, the Looney Toons cartoon *A-Lad-In His Lamp* (1948).[29]

In the background, a man dressed in a mandarin collared shirt holds a jade Buddha. The dead of the China Sea, the reader is told, are 'looters ... the pirate horde ... conquerors of fire and blood'.[30] On the same page, slitted eyes stare at Lili Shan's brother, Kwang. As with 'Tusks

**45** Anon., 'Death Is a Dream', *Ghost Comics* #4

of Terror', the world evoked in the comic is primarily drawn from Orientalist depictions of Asia.

Where, in 'Tusks of Terror', the racialized Other represents a threat, 'Death Is a Dream' offers the possibility of assimilation. Over the course of the story, Lili Shan is killed. Kwang swears vengeance and joins the communist forces but Lili Shan's ghost dissuades him and sends a warning to the British. As a result, the British Navy capture the terrorists and save Kwang. In the final panel, a British officer stands by Kwang's bedside. 'Strange happenings brought us together and stranger ones kept us alive, Kwang ...', he asserts. 'Maybe it's a sign we belong together, working for peace between our people, eh?' Kwang's response is as spirited as it is servile: 'Yes, sir ... for peace and victory – Gung ho!'[31] But for his skin-tone, Kwang seems to become almost Western in the final panel, offering a fantasy of assimilation for 'honourable' Others, i.e. those who contribute to the reinforcement of Western power.[32] The comic thus proposes a redemptive role for those Others who collaborate with the white hegemony. If, as described above, white America feared that the march towards the enfranchisement of people of colour would mean (potentially violent) political change, and if narratives of civil rights were troubled by images of Soviet anti-racism, then 'Death Is a Dream' offers a counter-narrative in Lili Shan and Kwang – racialized Others who seek 'peace' rather than change.

Similar themes emerge in 'The Ghost Who Stole A Body', a story that features a prominent Indian surgeon, Dr. Rjee, who is able to enter trances and commune with the dead. As in the two comics discussed above and in the previous chapter, there is a clear connection between the gendered or racialized Other and the supernatural.[33] Like Kwang, Dr. Rjee is, in many ways, the hero of his story – despite being a surgeon, and therefore a skilled man of science, only Rjee is able to exorcise the titular ghost from its stolen body. In his acts of heroism, however, Dr. Rjee occupies the conventional trope of the ethnic sidekick to the white hero – one who is chastised earlier in the story by a white doctor for slipping into one of 'your yogi trances' during surgery.[34] His Otherness is, as with the other comics considered here, communicated through flattened racist signifiers; Rjee's non-Christian religion is marked by a turban-wearing, many-armed incense burner through which he is able to appeal to the 'great, thousand-eyed, all-seeing spirit of space', an entity more evocative of Lovecraft's weird fiction than any recognizable religion.[35] This, however, and his name are all that mark Rjee out from the other characters in the comic: in terms of skin colour and speech patterns, he is, like Kwang, indistinguishable from the white characters around him. Decisions such as this could result from laziness on the part of the creative team, or the art being coloured in a rush and therefore missing the cues (though *The Beyond* is a beautifully drawn series, so this seems unlikely), or, perhaps more likely, from a deliberate attempt to exclude visual representations of race. For white readers, Dr. Rjee's assumed whiteness may have seemed natural because he is a member of the elite, a surgeon in an American hospital, and while forever defined by his origins (he can, after all, talk to the dead), he has proven himself, like Kwang, 'worthy' of his place in the US. Although his surgical prowess is an ideological challenge to notions of white supremacy, his talents are put to use serving the white American community as an elite surgeon.

While Kwang and Dr. Rjee are granted limited access to whiteness and are generally presented as posing no real threat to the white hegemony (unlike Ahmed in 'Tusks of Terror') they seem uninterested in social or political change. They allow access to an uncomplicated and unthreatening form of civil rights that requires no introspection or change on the part of the white elite. Some characters occupying the same subject and narrative position, however, are presented as irredeemably Other. *Chamber of Chills* #22 (1951) features one such story that locates racial concerns within the US borders and dramatizes a significant point of tension in discussions of race in the 1950s: the right to travel on buses and to be served at a lunch counter.[36] In 'The Snake Man', 'Serpentine' is a member of a travelling freak show, a human born with green reptilian scales, a snake-like appearance, and a near-human intellect. The show is notified of the death of Serpentine's mother's, and that her final wish was for Serpentine to attend her funeral. Serpentine is put on a bus, resplendent with a sign announcing that he is the property of the show, recalling the signs or markers borne by slaves on errands outside plantations to prove they were not runaways. The other passengers on the bus resent his presence, and 'cringe at the sight of his ghastly face', leaving Serpentine to question 'Why do they hate me? I don't want to hurt anyone'.[37] Serpentine's face is 'ghastly' because it is drawn partly from racist depictions of African Americans, complete with a broad, flattened nose and exaggerated lips – features that the artists and editor presumably felt comfortable using because his blackness is inferred.

When the bus stops at a diner for lunch, Serpentine sits at the counter but is forced to flee the diner and the bus by the white American customers of both (Figure 46). As with 'Tusks of Terror', the comic offers a clear critique of the behaviour of those on the bus and in the diner. Only one man stands up for Serpentine, and he does not do this literally: he remains seated and his verbal intervention has no effect. Prior to this confrontation, Serpentine has been mild and cooperative, drawing on his characterization as African American through

**46** Anon', 'The Snake Man', *Chamber of Chills* #22

his docility and subservience. After the altercation at the lunch counter, Serpentine begins attacking and, invoking exotic accounts of black cannibalism, eating people, a project facilitated by his poisonous fangs. Like Ahmed, Serpentine is not initially violent, but embodies the monstrosity that others project onto him. While ostensibly a critique of racism, Serpentine's docility and desire to be liked is still problematic – as George Orwell famously states in his catalogue of racist stereotypes found in boy's fiction: 'Negro: Comic, very faithful'.[38] Serpentine's later lapse into violence and cannibalism, however – evoking, once again, the Othello trope – retrospectively justifies the behaviour of his persecutors, showing that by allowing the Other into 'their' space, they expose themselves to potential violence. Coded racism, in other words, diminishes the initial critique of white behaviour. In an attempt to find allies, Serpentine breaks into the zoo to free the snakes, which he expects will come to his aid against the humans. This draws on equally racist rhetoric (mirrored in 'Tusks of Terror' above), suggesting that the person of colour is closer to nature than the white man, and that the beast lingers just under the surface. However, in seeking the support of other reptiles, Serpentine's threat is contained when he is eaten by a boa constrictor: the narrative assures the reader that 'poisonous and non-poisonous snakes are deadly enemies and non-poisonous snakes are immune to venom!'[39] Serpentine is neither one thing nor the other: he is endangered by, and a danger to, both human and animal. This liminality makes him truly Other.

In these examples, difference is represented in a range of ways. Whereas Kwang and Dr. Rjee are capable of assimilation into dominant power structures, effectively becoming white in the process, and while Ahmed makes a contested claim to being equal to whites, Serpentine is defined by his Otherness. Homi K. Bhabha has theorized this as 'mimicry – a difference that is almost nothing but not quite – [and] menace – a difference that is almost total but not quite'.[40] Kwang and Rjee perform and affirm whiteness and are able to assimilate into the societies that privilege it. Kwang's performance attests to his desire to please his audience, both inside and outside the comic, while Serpentine's rejection of his humanity can never be complete because his body renders him a perpetual Other. Even Kwang and Dr. Rjee's mimicry, however, do not make them entirely safe. As Bhabha asserts:

Mimicry is also the sign of the inappropriate, however, a difference or recalcitrance which coheres the dominant strategic function of colonial power, intensifies surveillance, and poses an immanent threat to both 'normalized' knowledges and disciplinary powers.[41]

Kwang and Dr. Rjee's status as 'white' is contingent and subject to nego-
tiation. They are subject to the right of the white hegemony and Western
power to impose its own frameworks of ideology and systems of knowledge production and regulation on other territories. In Kwang's story,
communism is projected backwards in time as a threat to the colonial
authority of the British in Hong Kong, both acknowledging and disavow-
ing the escalation of ideological warfare in the 1950s in colonial spaces
and creating a heroic space populated by both colonizer and colonized.
Even if successfully performed, mimicry retains an element of threat; as
Bhabha asserts, 'the success of colonial appropriation depends on a proliferation of inappropriate objects that ensure its strategic failure, so that
mimicry is at once resemblance and menace', a testament both to power
and to the limits of power.[42] All of the characters considered here, then,
suggest imaginary solutions to an unsolvable problem of racialized difference; Ahmed and Serpentine have been subject to sustained discrimination to the point that any power they obtain they immediately turn to
violent ends. The threat they present to the white hegemony is resolved
through death – either their own or that of their persecutors. Kwang and
Rjee, by comparison, are assimilated Others who collaborate with and
work in service of the white characters. Even when reduced, however,
their difference, as Bhabha argues, is irreducible; at a fundamental level,
the Other remains a threat.

## Race and land

Asian and black characters are not the only racialized group to appear
in horror comics. Native American characters also make an appearance,
bringing with them similar anxieties around race and property to those
explored above – anxieties evident in Michael Rogin's resonant description of the US as 'a society built upon Indian graves'.[43] The process of,
to use Rogin's words, 'continually beginning again' is as applicable to
postwar resettlement as it is to the early processes of nation formation.[44]
Geopolitically, the nation was 'beginning again' as a legitimate global
superpower, not just economically but also militarily and culturally.
Horror comics incorporated and refracted the violence at the heart of
the American story. In 'Massacre of the Ghosts', in *Witches Tales* #2
(1951), the western town of Blood Creek is beset with earthquakes that
render the land almost uninhabitable. Worse, the local river occasionally turns to blood. A scientist, sent to investigate, interviews a local
chief, who tells him that when white settlers first came to the region
they lived peacefully alongside the native population. A panel shows a

**47** Anon., 'Massacre of the Ghosts', *Witches Tales* #2

white man and a Native American chief, both on horses, discussing a treaty. The white man says, 'There is no reason why the red man and the white man cannot live side by side in peace', to which his interlocutor replies, 'My people are glad to be at peace with our white brothers'.[45] Subsequent panels show white and Native American children playing together (Figure 47).

The treaty comes apart, however, when a Native American boy accidentally eats some poison and his death is blamed on the white settlers, leading the Native Americans to begin attacking white settlements in retaliation, culminating in a battle. The white settlers are presented, problematically, as a benign force; it is the ignorance and over-reaction of the Native Americans that leads to conflict. When the Native Americans become violent, much like Serpentine described above, their capacity for violence is immediate and horrific. They massacre a camp of white settlers, murdering women and children. The story presents a narrative of white continental expansion in which Native Americans are the aggressors. As with Serpentine and Ahmed in the comics described above, the comic suggests that, however regrettably, these violent racialized Others must be contained for the sake of society and order.[46]

'Indian Burial Mound' from *Tales from the Crypt* #26 (1951) also explores the tension between advancing modernity and Native American culture and history.[47] In this story, the white Roy Madison comes from the city to meet Hiram Becker, the owner of a farm that Madison wants to convert into an airfield. This project involves the levelling of the titular burial mound. Becker advises against such an action; Madison

laughs off what he sees as redneck superstition. After selling the farm
to Madison, Becker stays on to help for a time; until, that is, Madison
levels the mound. At this point, Becker flees, returning the next day
to find Madison in the farmhouse, scalped. This story restages myths
of Western settlement, with hostile Native Americans exacting vengeance for intrusion into their space, a space coded as pre-modern and
threatening to the white settlers and their displacement of the original inhabitants. Indigenous people, however, much like the nominally
Jewish characters in 'Corpse of the Jury' and 'Master Race' discussed
in Chapter 1, are only present in this story through the results of their
violent, racialized, actions; Jewish victims take blood and flesh and
Native Americans take scalps. Native Americans are only able to exact
vengeance from beyond the grave: they lay in the ground but cannot
lay claim to it. Becker's presence, like the white settlers of Blood Creek,
is coded as legitimate, or at least respectful, because, unlike Madison,
he did not seek to eradicate the traces of Native American society – a
society shown as a terrifying spectacle of the past without a place in the
modern world. As with the stories described above, the comic acknowledges the history of violence committed against people of colour and
condemns overt racism, while simultaneously presenting the racialized
Other as a danger to civilization. White American readers are assured
that, because they do not engage in the kind of overt acts of racism
embodied by Madison and (in the urban myth) Pershing, they are not
culpable for the systemic persecution of people of colour. Their claim to
the land is thus legitimate and any actions of resistance on the part of
people of colour is characterized as misplaced aggression. The comics,
in other words, ignore the ways in which white Americans continued
(and continue) to benefit from systemic racism while supporting racist
narratives that depict people of colour as a threat. Horror here serves,
as per Darryl Jones, Kendall Philips, and Noël Carroll's arguments, as
a conservative force, maintaining the status quo by depicting forces for
change as malevolent and the resolution of the horror narrative as a
cathartic return to normal.[48]

The return of the oppressed, in the form of vengeance enacted by the
former occupants of the land, is one way in which landscapes are rendered uncanny. Another is the cityscape in the context of 'white flight',
the movement of white families from urban centres to the suburban
margins, creating an urban vacuum that was then filled by people of
colour. Horror comics frequently dramatize this by staging the return
of white characters to an urban environment now rendered unfamiliar
and hostile to them. White flight was the departure; the return is *white
fright*. This engages with Carol J. Clover's concept of 'urbanoia', where

'people from the city are people like us. People from the country are
people not like us', only with a twist.[49] Here, the 'wrong' bodies in the
'wrong' spaces serve as an affront to the 'rules of civilization' which
order the urban spaces.[50] Marshall Berman notes that under the Federal
Housing Administration (FHA), cities were seen 'principally as obstruc-
tions to the flow of traffic, and of junkyards of substandard housing
and decaying neighbourhoods from which Americans should be given
every chance to escape', though filters were established to ensure that
only the 'right kind' of Americans could do so.[51] Robert Moses, the
architect of much of New York's road network in the first half of the
twentieth century, built his parkways in such a way that they 'could be
experienced only in cars: their underpasses were purposely built too low
for buses to clear them', so that, for instance, public transport could not
bring those without a car to the beach, putting into operation a principle of 'physical design as a means of social screening' that only ben-
efited those who already enjoyed privilege.[52] Processes of urban renewal
began with the passage of the Housing Act of 1949. This legislation was
intended to provide decent homes and 'a suitable living environment for
every American family'. The programmes put in place emphasized slum
clearance and the construction of new houses.

New houses were largely suburban; housing developments were
mostly urban. The difference was racially coded. As Kevin Fox Gotham
argues, urban policies were 'an exercise in the racialization of urban
space that linked race and culturally specific behaviour to place of
residence in the city', contributing to and reinforcing discourses of
black areas as ghettoes to be avoided, as spaces of deprivation and
danger caused by the actions of inhabitants rather than systemic
processes of oppression and marginalization.[53] Gotham goes on to
point out that 'from 1938 through the end of the 1950s, the Federal
Housing Administration insured mortgages on nearly one-third of all
new housing produced annually in the United States, the vast majority located in suburban areas and reserved for whites only', a period
during which the FHA's 'Underwriting manuals considered blacks
"adverse influences" on property values'.[54] Suburban life and attendant
notions of prosperity were promised to veterans as long as they were
in ' "racially homogenous" white neighbourhoods and covered with a
restrictive covenant'.[55] While the FHA removed overtly racist language
from their guidance in the 1950s, 'private appraisal associations, real
estate agents and firms, and banks continued to use such language
through the 1970s', demonstrating the persistence of structural and
institutional racism that dictated where and how people lived.[56] African
American veterans, having fought for a double victory, returned to a

double trauma: a nation built on their traumatic service that limited their access to space and services to support them.

In the urban settings that people of colour were able to access, construction was not synonymous with exercises of community construction. The clearance of old buildings and new housing projects did little to materially benefit marginalized communities. Regulations governing life there, too, were not conducive to the continuation of approaches that made subsistence on the verges of poverty endurable. Tenants could not take in boarders, or laundry, and residents of this new public housing were forbidden from using their dwellings for even minor commercial activities, such as repairs or reconditioning of broken-down items. Lee Rainwater describes these new spaces as 'fearful and forbidding', alienating those who formerly occupied them from the current occupants, who were themselves alienated from the practices developed in order to navigate life there.[57] In Berman's terms, 'millions of black and Hispanic people ... converge[d] on America's cities at precisely the moment when the jobs they sought, and the opportunities that earlier poor immigrants had found, were departing or disappearing', with employers shifting operations out of cities or out of the country altogether.[58] It is little wonder that urban communities, dissected by roads that explicitly set out to contain them, and deprived of the opportunities that had previously sustained them and provided opportunities for mobility on their own terms, became instead hostile spaces. As Robert Fredrick Burk notes, 'fundamental problems largely have remained unaddressed', particularly issues related to 'structural economic discrimination, the expansion of the white-collar suburban economy, inadequate supplies of affordable housing, and the perpetuating material and emotional miseries of the ghetto'.[59] Hindrances such as these mean that, no matter what legal protections were put in place for civil rights, many African Americans remained unable to reach them due to their material circumstances.

Pastoral visions of the city as found in Jane Jacobs' *The Death and Life of Great American Cities* depend on an older version of the city and the communities that underpinned its existence.[60] In Jacobs' account, 'the public peace [is] kept primarily by an intricate, almost unconscious, network of voluntary controls and standards among the people themselves, and enforced by the people themselves', implying that the fault for disorder depends on both design (Jacobs states that blocks are built in such a way as to facilitate easy crimes) but also on the breakdown of social fabrics and the inability of communities to police themselves.[61] By implication, the spaces now inhabited by recent arrivals are made hostile through personal and collective failures of their occupants. One such dramatization of newly hostile space is 'Dungeon of Doom' from

*Chamber of Chills* #6 (1952). While working on the subway, Larry Frost
bangs his head and starts seeing monsters all around him. Only Larry
and a girl, who banged her head at the same time as Larry, are able
to see these monsters: the blow lifts the 'hypnotic screen' the invading
Groundings have placed over the world.[62] Larry sees this girl captured
by these Groundings; the readers see her flesh melted from her bones,
while Larry runs back to his train to find the police. Instead of finding
help, however, Larry only finds another Grounding, initially disguised
as a white woman, who having fooled Larry with her disguise, reduces
him to a skeleton (Figure 48). Despite, or perhaps because of, the failure
of surveillance in the story, the narrative ends with a renewed appeal to
its readers for constant vigilance:

> You know what it means! So you be careful! Look carefully – scrutinize
> your neighbours, the people on the streets! Are they what they *seem* to be
> – or are they *monsters*? Perhaps, if you watch, there is still time to save the
> world from enslavement by *the monsters about you*!!

Appeals to monitor those around you recall Jacobs' accounts of the
role of 'kibitzers' in preventing street-level crime; this story provides a
warning against taking up that role in this newly hostile environment,
as the white man attempting it is killed.[63] The narrative also draws
on the constant vigilance associated with the recent past of European
fascism and contemporary McCarthyism, the notion that communists
were embedded throughout the USA and poised to overthrow it. The
pointing finger of the final panel certainly has a stylistic connection
to the First World War poster of Uncle Sam, and therefore a gloss of
patriotic fervour. However, the urban setting of the story suggests an
overdetermined space, one drawing on an archaeology of racialized
fears as well as more directly political ones. Linguistic choices reinforce
this, with talk of 'enslavement' directly referencing the lived experience
of the still recent past, as well as the popular American perception of life
under Soviet communism.[64] Both the term 'dungeon' and 'Grounding'
attest to a connection to the soil: to being kept below it, dungeon, or
kept on it, grounded. In the process, the language of the strip engages
with racist stereotypes of African Americans as rural farm workers.[65]
Discussions of soil may seem at odds with an urban setting but, when
combined with notions of invasion and defamiliarized space, it can be
seen to draw on the movement of African Americans into urban spaces
and white flight from them. While the idea of trains taking people to
death has connections to the Holocaust, the image also seems to suggest
suburban Americans riding peacefully towards death and the necessity
of the removal of the 'scales from their eyes', with said scales visibly

**48** Anon., 'Dungeon of Doom', *Chamber of Chills* #6

projected onto the monsters. The explicitly monstrous rendering of the 'enemy' works to maximize the threat, as does the means of murder: resistance is, literally, liquidated.

Trains also evoke the federal infrastructure projects to connect 'suburban commuters with downtown places of employment that destroyed already scarce housing in minority communities and often disrupted neighbourhood life as well', showing how white movement was not a singular departure from inner city areas, but a repeated movement between work and *de facto* segregated suburban communities.[66] The Federal Housing Act of 1934 made home ownership a reality for millions of Americans but money was allocated in a manner that privileged white people. Whiteness was a means of gaining access to funds and services that allowed an individual and a family to improve itself; whiteness, and its attendant privileges, therefore had to be, in the logic of the comics described above, defended. Non-whites had to be excluded in order to guarantee continued white access to (sub)urban spaces. Processes of urban 'renewal' underpinning this also more often targeted minority communities, clearing their housing and, instead of replacing it, making space for more commercial and industrial units, resulting in a loss of housing and taxation revenue and therefore increasing the burden on the minority communities who remained, making it hard to stay but even more difficult for them to leave.[67]

Shifts in perception of the modern city as somehow distinct from its iterations in the past are evident in both contemporary scholarship and horror. In 'He' (1926), based on his experiences of briefly living in New York, H. P. Lovecraft writes that modern New York:

> Is not a sentient perpetuation of Old New York as London is of Old London and Paris of Old Paris, but that it is in fact quite dead, its sprawling body imperfectly embalmed and infested with queer animate things which have nothing to do with it as it was in life.[68]

Oscar Handlin, for more complex reasons than Lovecraft, argued that 'the modern city is essentially different from its predecessors', drawing on considerations of how the city functions in, and relies on, the region in which it is located far more than cities of earlier periods.[69] Handlin goes on to set out how 'the men who now people the metropolis long for the security of isolation from the life about them. They strive to locate their families in space, with a minimum of connections to the hazards of the external world'.[70] In his use of the words 'security' and 'hazards', Handlin constructs the urban space as threatening, and fails to make the connection to the 'decline in urban creativity' with systems of public transportation.[71] As seen with 'Dungeon of Doom', public transportation is constructed as a threat to white users: it must cross space now seen as alien to white suburbanites and the reliance on private transportation, the car, has the result of marginalizing public transport, of coding it as for those who need to be kept separate from the suburbs: as Berman demonstrates, the means of facilitating private transportation, roads, were explicitly constructed to preclude public access, creating *de facto* segregated spaces.

Gender also emerges as a consideration in these spaces. It is telling that the final Grounding disguises itself as a white woman, feigning fear at finding herself trapped in this hostile space. In doing so, 'Dungeons of Doom' presents women and the spaces they inhabit as both threatened and threatening. White women are to be protected by ensuring they are kept in appropriate spaces, but those white women who actively seek out such dangerous places themselves become monstrous. This restages the idea of women, as discussed in the previous chapter, as a threat through associations of race and place; women can forfeit their investment in whiteness by making socially unacceptable choices about how they act, where, and with whom they associate themselves (recall, for example, the doomed interracial romance in 'Tusks of Terror'). In choosing (however that choice is defined) to step outside accepted norms, women partially risk their investment in whiteness and their ability to access its privileges, especially if they marry into minority communities. The revelation of the Grounding-as-woman is a reminder of woman-as-threat, especially given the close association of the final image with the direct address to the reader to be on guard against 'monsters about you'.

Women also play a role in another story where urban spaces are rendered uncanny and newly threatening. In 'Midnight Mess', Harold travels to visit his sister but finds the urban centre in which she lives strangely deserted after dark, potentially engaging with the existence of 'Sundown Towns', where minorities were kept out of white spaces through openly-made threats.[72] When he goes to investigate, he finds an open restaurant. It transpires that the town has been taken over by vampires, one of whom is his sister. Harold is then 'strung up ... head down' to form part of the vampires' dinner – the world, represented by the white man, is literally turned upside down.[73] The narrative and visual inversion, a sundown town in the literal sense that vampires cannot go out in the day, is cued by the verbal pun in the title, 'mess' instead of 'mass', which also plays on the long-standing associations between vampires as an inversion of some elements of Christianity (the blood is the life, an infernal sacrament, the ability to rise from the dead, and so on) while also making present the literal mess, the gore depicted in typical EC detail, and the more figurative mess, the lack of conventional racial and patriarchal order in Harold's demise.[74] There is also an inversion of racialized violence, here, as the language and imagery directed at Harold draws on lynching – but rather than a white mob lynching a monstrous figure, here a monstrous mob lynch a white man entering an urban space, and are specifically referred to as 'civilized' in the way they commit murder. One hears echoes, once again, of J. W. Milam's fear of what African Americans would do with power, as well as the invocation of the 'blood libel' myth of Jews sacrificing Christian children. As Nick Groom notes, vampires 'emerge from history to reveal more history in visions and transfused memories', disturbing 'territorial borders' and 'temporality' in the process.[75] Racist fears of the violence meted out by white men on people of colour being visited on white bodies informs these reconfigurations and refractions of vampiric visions, restaging the amorphous nature of the vampire as something between states, un/dead, and also something intangible, able to assume the form of smoke and to pass through boundaries by unconventional means. Refraction is also not staged singly: 'Midnight Mess' is consciously reprised as a metatextual act in later comics, transforming it, like the urban spaces and vampire history that inspire it, into an overdetermined space. The threat of contagion embodied in the vampire, so closely entwined with the nature of modernity, could transform any space into a site of potential vampiric violence.

In *Tales from the Crypt* #38 (1953), 'Midnight Mess' is reimagined as 'Mournin' Mess' and the vampires are replaced by ghouls. Action here revolves around a benevolent society established by a group of self-made men, the Grateful Hoboes, Outcasts and Unwanteds' Layaway Society, dedicated to providing for 'derelicts' who lack the means for a proper burial. The journalist invited to cover the establishment of the organization questions why they do not do anything to help these people while they are still alive, a line of questioning rebuffed by the assertion that, as those starting the group were able to make something of themselves, so should those who are ultimately helped by it. There is to be no private investment in schemes to ameliorate the worst excesses of modern capitalism. Seven years later, the journalist returns to cover the 1000th burial under the scheme and works out that the land obtained for the burials is insufficient to house 1000 graves. It is at this point that he discovers the truth of the society: 'we are what our initials stand for'.[76] The final reveal of the story is of the businessmen sitting around a table consuming the body of the 1000th person to be 'buried'. One way in which we could read this comic is by arguing that the acquisition of land in urban centres is depicted as a critique of predatory capitalism, the myth of the self-made man held up as a means of depriving assistance to those in greatest need, whose bodies are in turn quite literally fed to capitalists for their own ends. While no people of colour are represented, the space and its resonance with the earlier story about vampires draw attention to racialized practices, spaces, and the apathetic attitude of elite white men. While the comic could be read as a critique of systemic racism and thus a reversal of the trends above, it nonetheless continues the trend identified previously of externalizing racism – presenting it as a practice carried out by individuals who, in this case, through their monstrosity are rendered Other to the reader. As before, the ultimate message white readers can take from the story is that racism (defined as deliberate speech and action) is both produced by and produces monsters that then turn on a benign (in the terms of the comic, non-racist) white population.

## Horror abroad

If American social elites cannot be expected to show concern for the suffering of those in their own country, it comes as little surprise that horror comics represented them as even more indifferent to suffering abroad. Horror located outside the USA often draws on racist rhetoric that contributes to geopolitical narratives of marginalization and the institution and maintenance of hierarchies. A particularly clear example of this is the representation of zombies. At this point in the popular American history of the zombie, zombies both retained their links to popular depictions of Haitian voodoo but were increasingly being used as a convenient symbol for discussions of the Soviets.[77] Gary D. Rhodes remarks of 1930s horror films that 'the plot device of travel to a foreign land subtly revealed US xenophobia'; by the comics of the 1950s, the xenophobia was far from subtle.[78]

Racism and xenophobia occupied complex territory in *The Beyond*. For instance, on a trip to Spain in 'The Mystery of Lunablanca', the Spanish are referred to as 'superstitious … natives', suggesting the export of domestic attitudes towards Hispanic communities in the US to a European, Spanish-speaking, setting.[79] In the same comic, 'The Valley of the Scaly Monsters' prefigures much of the narrative thrust of *Creature from the Black Lagoon* (1954) as it concentrates on an American expedition down the Amazon, dismissive of native claims of 'a monster type that is supposedly part human and part lizard'.[80] The Gill-Man in *Creature* becomes fascinated by the bathing beauty, Kay Lawrence, and a strange symmetry between the two is explored before the film's violent climax. In the comic 'Scaly Monsters', the titular creatures develop a fascination with Diane, the narrative's interchangeable blonde, and, through forcing her to drink a potion, attempt to convert her into their queen.[81] In a development drawing on representational stereotypes of race and gender, the native guides who are captured by the creatures and fed the potion are transformed into scaly facsimiles of their captors; Diane, conversely, is presented in four over-sized panels explicitly for the male gaze. The racialized natives have their innate monstrosity rendered even more visible, while the threat Diane poses, moving from demure daughter to titillating temptress, suggests that the threat posed by women is, in part, their sexuality. As this suggests, Diane does not sprout scales like the men who are also captured; she is instead fitted out with a skin-tight, scanty outfit designed to accentuate her sexuality (Figure 49).

Race is explicitly associated here with monstrosity and located as a threat to white womanhood. The initial representation of Diane, who is forced to drink a potion, suggests sexual coercion, drawing on racist stereotypes of the man of colour as a threat to white femininity; that Diane is somehow damaged or cheapened by her association with men of colour is underlined in the narration by the fact that while she is under their control, she is only referred as 'the girl' or 'she'. It is only after she has been freed by Roy, the white male hero, that she can once again become Diane. Her identity is bound up in her whiteness and status as property – while she is 'stolen' by the scaly monsters, her identity is also lost.

Elsewhere in the horror genre, zombies represent the most monstrous of all attempts by people of colour to wield control over white bodies. Prior to the Second World War, zombies were typically depicted as 'a lone figure or a gang of pitiful slaves under a single master', whereas the Cold War ushered in zombies as 'an anonymous, overwhelming mass' that threatened the world as a whole.[82] Early versions of the zombie dramatized anxieties and fears around slavery and, once again, the ability of those who had been subject to the institution to invert its hierarchies through black magic. In this, it draws on historical realities rooted in the Haitian Revolution (1791–1804), the overthrow of French colonial authority, and the establishment of the first republic in the Western hemisphere led by people of colour. This independence led to the marginalization of Haiti from Atlantic flows of trade as a deliberate tactic to impede its development and thus prevent it from serving as an inspiration for other enslaved people. In more recent history, US Marines occupied Haiti in 1915 during a period of political instability to ensure that debts to the US were paid (and also to limit growing German influence on the island). The American occupation did not end until 1934 and, while it was ongoing, a system of enforced

**49** Anon., 'The Valley of the Scaly Monsters', *The Beyond* #2

labour was in place. American forces brutally suppressed resistance to the occupation, known as the Caco Wars. Zombie narratives, which first emerged in US popular culture during the occupation, were therefore an overdetermined space in the early Cold War period. Although zombies retained the links in the semiotic chain that kept them attached to their Franco-Caribbean origins, they took on additional relevance through the dominant American interpretation of communism as that of millions enslaved by conformist ideology. Fears of a racialized threat therefore took on additional connotations of ideology, tying the figure of the zombie into ideological conflict between the superpowers but also standing in as a space for working through anxieties around decolonizing spaces. American imperial policy also played a role with the shift from formal to informal empire, territorial control to economic and cultural influence with the ever-present threat of military intervention to keep other countries 'on the right track'.[83]

The zombie embodied fears around issues of both the exercise of and resistance to control. In 'Cult of the Undead' from *The Beyond* #4 (1951), anxieties around empire were displaced on to 'Pizarro, the bloody Spanish conquistador' and his 'swordpoint empire' in the Andes.[84] Here, the American Gerald Knowlton is lured to Peru in search of gold, and chooses a 'soldier of fortune', Rick Brawson, to lead his expedition, despite concerns over Brawson's conduct. When Knowlton disappears, his daughter, Pat, and her fiancé, Gordon, travel in search of him. They find Brawson in charge of an army of zombies, established as the head of 'Rick Brawson's empire', exploiting the zombies to mine gold from the mountains thanks to his voice control over them.[85] Brawson takes advantage of existing zombie labour, killing the 'Inca chief' who had previously controlled them rather than creating his own zombie labour through Voodoo. Brawson therefore mimics the Spanish usurpation of *mit'a*, Incan tribute labour, into their *repartimiento* system during their period of imperial rule. Gordon, a professional ventriloquist, is able to mimic Brawson and, after donning the ceremonial robes of the murdered chief, destroys the zombie empire and its leader. As with *White Zombie* (1932) and a number of other successor narratives, the elimination of the master tends to also lead to the eradication of the zombies. In keeping with the narratives explored above, the enslavement and its end are the result of the actions of 'outsiders', with white American men acting as saviour to people of colour. Gordon is not only able to free his own party but to end the barbarism of zombie labour, in the process positioning the US as a source of freedom and enlightenment. The comic therefore overwrites the competing narrative of Rick Brawson as a soldier of fortune intent on exploiting natural resources and indigenous labour for his own profit, and even Gerald Knowlton, cast as the hapless victim here, who set off to extract resources from another country as part of 'an old claim' that the 'natives' would not pursue because 'thees [sic] mountain is filled with evil spirits!'[86] The comic offers a critique of American empire but only when it 'gets out of hand' – benevolent imperialism still seems to be the best course of action, and it is still the noble heteronormative pair of Pat and Gordon who know what is best for everyone. The comic, echoing the themes we have encountered above, suggests that the practice of slavery and colonialist exploitation are an aberration, and casts people of colour as dangerous and incapable of self-governance. The comic thus, once again, exempts the average white American citizen from culpability in the racist and neo-colonial systems of which he or she is a beneficiary.

In 'Cult of the Undead', empire is projected onto another power in the relatively distant past, the Spanish, while implicitly acknowledged through the presence of an American 'soldier of fortune' in South America, a space frequently subject to American interventions in the name of a democratic order managed and mandated by the USA. Although there is a white American at fault, Brawson is flagged as a criminal from the beginning, establishing Pat and Gordon as the ultimate moral arbiters of the story. Through Gordon's vocal abilities, he is also able to assume the role of an 'Inca chief'; this, alongside Pat's greater sympathy for the local community, is, we presume, intended to establish them as more likeable characters and exemplars of non-racist and culturally empathetic Americans. Contemporary readers might, however, see both the assumption of tribal costume and the story itself as an exercise in cultural imperialism, the exportation of American culture, and cultural appropriation, the forced claiming of an external culture by Americans. Culture becomes a piece of property that can be picked up and discarded, used and abused as necessary – provided the user occupies the privileged position of a white American, someone able to own, rather than be, property.

## Conclusion

American comic book horror of the 1950s oscillated around the connected notions of property and space, of who was able to own things and places. In so doing, horror comics resonated with contemporary upheavals around the question of race both domestically and internationally. Engagement with those struggles, however, was not without its own issues. As this chapter has demonstrated, even as horror comics made explicitly anti-racist overtures, they often reinstated, or failed to fully unpack, the racism and power differentials attendant in existing political and social structures. This is especially evident in international affairs, where people of colour are presented either as superstitious natives or practitioners of hostile black magic. Hostility on the part of residents of countries outside the US has specific functions. First, it manifests the resentment regarding American intervention in the affairs of other countries, whether under the guise of the imposition of global economic structures through initiatives such as those codified at Bretton Woods, or through Cold War covert military operations. The former, with its privileging of the 'developed' world of the Global North, continued a form of imperial relationship with the 'undeveloped' Global South that developed and extended processes of marginalization that entrenched poverty and resentment; the latter, often used as a means of bringing about regime change, was connected to the former as it was invariably used to undermine regimes hostile to American interests and overarching global patterns of trade and socio-political organization. Entrenching poverty and marginalization is a form of insidious horror, clearly evident in the international treatment of Haiti since its revolution.

As we have found throughout the examples offered here, horror comics offered several recurring themes on the question of race; they acknowledge the realities of racism and (neo)colonial exploitation, but they present the agents of such actions as either literal or figurative monsters. The comics, in contrast to the images of emasculation discussed in the second chapter of this volume, almost always offer a heroic white male who opposes racist practices and it is generally this figure with whom the audience is expected to sympathize. People of colour are exclusively shown as either a superstitious mass or a source of danger and while the comics often present the monsters born of racism as inherently benign beings, driven mad by persecution, their responses are typically represented as misplaced aggression that must, unfortunately, be neutralized through violence. The reading we offer here runs counter to some of the existent scholarship on EC, which has typically characterized the company as pursuing a progressive agenda.[87] One of the most famous instances can be found in *Weird Fantasy* #18 (1953), in the story 'Judgment Day!'[88] In this story, an astronaut (Tarlton) travels to Cybrinia, 'the planet of mechanical life', to inspect it and determine whether it is ready to receive 'all of the wonders and greatness of Earth'.[89] Tarlton's inspection discovers that the robots, placed there thousands of years previously by a team from Earth to build a new society, have constructed a segregated system. The only way difference is introduced, and the resultant two-tier system maintained, is through 'the Educator', 'the parents and relatives and the environment and the school all rolled into one'. Tarlton concludes that Cybrinia is not yet ready to receive the wonders of Earth that were unlocked after its peoples began to work together.[90] Throughout the story, the astronaut from Earth has remained concealed by the visor of his helmet; the final panel reveals him to be black.

'Judgment Day!' has been championed, particularly among fans, as an example of the racially progressive and politically subversive content of 1950s comics.[91] This is partly due to a confrontation between Bill Gaines and the Comics Code Authority; when EC sought to republish the story in 1956 the CCA deemed the astronaut's ethnicity to be unacceptable. There are, however, other elements worthy of critical consideration. First, Tarlton is an emissary of 'Earth Colonization', an agency with the authority to establish, monitor, and instruct new civilizations if they meet certain appointed criteria. While the product of apparent enlightenment on Earth, Tarlton's inspection, and the mission it follows, remains a project of colonization. Tarlton remarks that the robots of Cybrinia were placed there with 'the know-how to build more of you', which implies not just a technological body of knowledge but the social and cultural underpinnings that cannot be disentangled from it.[92] As such, the story suggests that segregationist practice is intrinsic to human development; the fact that the story is set thousands of years in the future also suggests that it may take considerable time for humans to overcome such drives, which may in turn see their reinstatement through other hierarchical forms of governance, education, and organization. This is not to say that the story is racist; it was certainly more progressive in its engagement with the question of civil rights than the CCA, who objected to its positive representation of race. Its focus on the systems that inculcate division through education, housing, and so on is, if heavy-handed, at least making a productive and powerful political point. However, as with other stories discussed in this chapter, it positions 'less advanced' societies as incapable of equitable self-governance and suggests that the only solution to systemic racism is the intervention of a benevolent colonizing force.

Nick Groom states that 'the return of the dead is a primaeval fear … Black magic, demonic possession, or simply a terrifying intensity of will can drag lifeless corpses back into some macabre form of animation to wreak havoc', with actions often directed against those who had wronged them.[93] Dead bodies are stacked remarkably high in American history; it is no wonder that American society is periodically gripped by fears of the reanimated dead. One key factor in driving the death of many victims of American violence was (alas, is) race. As a result of a legacy of wrongs, and the continued perpetuation of those wrongs in Cold War America, race was a source of horror. The violence of both America's past and present, both at home and overseas, threatened to erupt – indeed, was erupting – into public consciousness. Horror comics sought to engage with narratives of racist and imperialist violence, not to corroborate them but to disrupt them, reworking their themes so that white Americans are, in the majority, recast as victims rather than aggressors and so that the system of US social structure and intervention overseas remains unchallenged. Our argument here, then, runs counter to many of the narratives of genre fiction from the time. Judith Merril, one of the key editors and authors of science fiction in this era, argues, for example, that in the 1950s science fiction was 'virtually the only vehicle of political dissent', one of the few spaces in which critical narratives of McCarthyism, Cold War policy, and the reassertion of patriarchal values could be contested.[94] Science fiction certainly did mount a critique of contemporary America, especially in the hands of authors such as Merril, but even at its most progressive, as Malisa Kurtz notes, 'SF can embrace a form of multi-culturalism while hiding its own colonialist attitude', a practice seen in 'Judgment Day!' above.[95] Horror comics plumbed similar waters, offering critiques that both challenged and reinforced oppressive elements of American society. Race was all too often a subject mined for monsters, rather than a question to be interrogated. When it came to race, the genre dealt in binaries of villains and victims. Such configurations did not lend themselves to nuanced critiques of systemic racism or neo-colonialism. The resulting texts acknowledged some of the issues raised by the growing Civil Rights movement, the systemic racism of urban planning, and US imperialism, yet sought to configure this material so as to assuage any guilt on the part of its readers. This is aided by occasional heroic roles for black characters, such as Tarlton the astronaut. As we have seen in the previous chapters, however, horror comics overwhelmingly preferred scenarios in which white men served as victim to the racialized or gendered Other, and where racist practices are shown as aberrations rather than the norm.

The Senate subcommittee hearings of 1954 dealt a damaging blow to the horror comics industry on the eve of a period of heightened Civil Rights activism. It is possible that, had the genre continued to develop, it may have been able to respond with more nuance and sensitivity to shifting discourse around race. The near-destruction of the horror comics industry in 1954, however, removed the possibility of such developments. Horror, instead, migrated to film. The rise of Hammer studios from 1957 onwards gave horror a new visibility, and a perceived new role as a force for cultural criticism. The scene was set for horror comics' gradual return.

## Notes

1 Quoted in William Bradford Huie, 'The Shocking Story of Approved Killing in Mississippi', *Look* (24 January 1956), 46–50 (50). Available at 'Killers' Confession', *American Experience: The Murder of Emmett Till*, www.pbs.org/wgbh/amex/till/sfeature/sf_look_confession.html (accessed 29 July 2019).

2 An all-white jury found Milam and his accomplice Roy Bryant not guilty, despite overwhelming evidence to the contrary. Carolyn Bryant has subsequently stated that she made up part of her story. See Rory Carroll 'Woman at Center of Emmett Till Case Tells Author She Fabricated Testimony', *The Guardian* (27 January 2017), retrieved from www.theguardian.com/us-news/2017/jan/27/emmett-till-book-carolyn-bryant-confession (accessed 29 July 2019). Milam and Bryant confessed to the murder months after they were acquitted of it, Huie 'The Shocking Story of Approved Killing in Mississippi'.

3 Paula T. Connolly, *Slavery in American Children's Literature 1790–2010* (Iowa City, IA: University of Iowa Press, 2013), 135.

4 Jacquelyn Dowd Hall, 'The Long Civil Rights Movement and the Political Uses of the Past', *Journal of American History* (2005), 1233–1263 (1234).

5 Hall, 'The Long Civil Rights Movement', 1235.

6 Lauren Rebecca Sklaroff, 'Constructing GI Joe Louis: Cultural Solutions to the "Negro Problem" During World War II', *Journal of American History* 89.3 (2002), 958–983 (959). For a further discussion of the OWI, see Clayton R. Koppes and Gregory D. Black, *Hollywood Goes to War: Patriotism, Movies and the Second World War, from 'Ninotchka' to 'Mrs. Miniver'* (London and New York: Tauris Parke, 2000) and Allan M. Winkler, *The Politics of Propaganda: The Office of War Information 1942–1945* (New Haven, CT: Yale University Press, 1978). For an example of how comics sought to tackle racial issues, see Michael Goodrum, '"Friend of the People of Many Lands": Johnny Everyman, "critical internationalism", and liberal postwar US heroism', *Social History* 38.2 (2013), 203–219.

7 Ron Eyerman, *Cultural Trauma: Slavery and the Formation of African American Identity* (Cambridge: Cambridge University Press, 2001), 163.

8 Letter from the War Department to Walter White, as cited in Walter White, *A Man Called White* (New York: Viking Press, 1948), 222.

9 For the best account of all the American racial movements in the Second World War, see Ronald Takaki, *Double Victory: A Multicultural History of American in World War II* (New York: Back Bay Books, 2001).

10 See Neil A. Wynn, *The African American Experience during World War II* (New York: Rowman & Littlefield 2010), 110.

11 The 1946 resurrection of the Ku Klux Klan, however, is now better remembered for Superman's anti-Klan storyline and the information-gathering efforts

of Stetson Kennedy that prompted it rather than any of its own successes. For more on this, see Stetson Kennedy, *I Rode with the Ku Klux Klan* (London: Arco, 1954); Steven D. Levitt and Stephen J. Dubner, *Freakonomics: A Rogue Economist Explores the Hidden Side of Everything* (London: Penguin, 2007), which features a chapter on Kennedy; and Goodrum, '"His Greatest Enemy – Intolerance!"'.

12  Mary L. Dudziak, '*Brown* as a Cold War Case', *Journal of American History* 91.1 (2004), 32–42.

13  Dudziak, '*Brown* as a Cold War Case', 34.

14  Additional authenticity is provided by the fact that the black child in the film, James Lloydovich Patterson, really was the son of an American immigrant, albeit an African American man rather than a white woman.

15  See, for more information, Penny M. von Eschen, *Satchmo Blows Up the World: Jazz Ambassadors Play the Cold War* (Cambridge, MA: Harvard University Press, 2006).

16  For more on McCarthy, see David M. Oshinsky, *A Conspiracy So Immense: The World of Joe McCarthy* (Oxford: Oxford University Press, 2005). For a detailed analysis of the Senate subcommittee hearings on juvenile delinquency, see Nyberg, *Seal of Approval*.

17  Fredric Wertham has often been demonized in comics criticism for the role he played in the anti-comics movement. His views on comics were, indeed, largely negative and, as Carol Tilley has demonstrated, poorly researched. Far less has been made, however, of his advocacy for civil rights and interventions he made in improving the lives of African Americans. For more on Wertham, see Bart Beaty, *Fredric Wertham and the Critique of Mass Culture: A Re-examination of the Critic Whose Congressional Testimony Sparked the Comics Code* (Jackson, MS: University Press of Mississippi, 2005). Tilley, 'Seducing the Innocent', 383–413. Wertham's work is also worthy of consultation, particularly *Seduction of the Innocent*.

18  For a discussion of many of these issues, see Lori May (ed.), *Recasting America: Culture and Politics in the Age of Cold War* (Chicago, IL and London: University of Chicago Press, 1989), and Julie Hughes and Nathan Abrams (eds), *Containing America: Cultural Consumption and Production in 50s America* (London: Bloomsbury, 2000).

19  For a discussion of this, see Nancy C. Carnevale, '"No Italian Spoken for the Duration of the War": Language, Italian American Identity, and Cultural Pluralism in the World War II Years', *Journal of American Ethnic History* 22.3 (2003), 3–33.

20  For a complete discussion of this, see Mae M. Ngai, 'The Architecture of Race in American Immigration Law: A Reexamination of the Immigration Act of 1924', *The Journal of American History* 86.1 (1999), 67–92.

21  Fredrick Strömberg, *Black Images in the Comics: A Visual History* (Seattle, WA: Fantagraphics, 2003).

22  See Michael Goodrum, *Superheroes and American Self Image: From War to Watergate* (Farnham: Ashgate, 2016), 48–50.

23  This phenomena was not limited to comics. Tod Browning worked on a film script in the 1930s titled 'Witch of Timbuctoo' in which a black voodoo practitioner and her son are involved in a revenge plot. The Production Code Agency in the US and their counterparts in the UK demanded significant changes to the script. The UK office, headed by Joseph Breen, were concerned that the plot might inspire revolts among black people across the British Empire. As a result, all black characters were removed from the story, as were references to voodoo. The film would eventually become *The Devil Doll* (1936). See Madeline F Norden and Madeline Cahill, 'Violence, Women, and Disability in Tod Browning's *Freaks* and *The Devil Doll*', in Silver and Ursini (eds), *Horror Film Reader*, 151–165.

24  Edward Bellin (w), Fred Kida, George Roussos and Joe Kubert (a), *Eerie Comics* #1 (New York: Avon, 1947). I (Mitch) am indebted to Jordan Newton for bringing this comic to my attention as part of his presentation in 2016 for my third year comics module at Canterbury Christ Church University.

25  Iger Studio, 'Tusks of Terror', *Voodoo* #10 (New York: Four Star Publications, 1953).

26  This recalls arguments around the case of Bhagat Singh Thind in the 1920s, who sought naturalization as an American citizen on the basis of being a 'high caste Hindu of Caucasian origin'. Thind was denied on the grounds that he did not meet the constitutional definition of 'free white persons'.

27  This story has such currency that it is still circulating. Donald Trump cited it in 2016 during his presidential campaign: Tom Embury-Dennis, 'Trump Tells Fake Story About US General Slaughtering 49 Muslims Using Bullets Dipped in Pig's Blood, in Resurfaced Video', *The Independent* (19 March 2019), retrieved from www.independent.co.uk/news/world/americas/us-politics/trump-muslims-general-pershing-pigs-blood-video-a8829676.html (accessed 28 January 2020).

28  David Cannadine, *Ornamentalism: How the British Saw Their Empire* (London: Penguin, 2002).

29  Anon., 'Death Is a Dream', *Ghost Comics* #4 (New York: Fiction House, 1952), 3

30  Anon., 'Death Is a Dream', 4.

31  Anon., 'Death Is a Dream', 8.

32  Anon., 'Death Is a Dream', 5.

33  Ken Rice, 'The Ghost Who Stole a Body', *The Beyond* #2 (New York: Ace Magazines, 1951). A similar logic re-emerges in Brother Voodoo in *Strange Tales* from the 1970s. See Chapter 7 for a full discussion.

34  Rice, 'The Ghost Who Stole a Body'.

35  Rice, 'The Ghost Who Stole a Body'.

36  The numbering carried over from the previous magazine *Blondie Comics*, reverting to its own numbering system at #5 in February 1952. *Chamber of Chills* features more than its fair share of Orientalist horror, containing at least one story in an exotic setting in each issue of its run (1951–1954). Such stories were often supported by short sections on myths, legends, or ancient practices of far-flung places for the 'education' of its readers.

37  Anon., 'The Snake Man', *Chamber of Chills* #22 (New York: Harvey Publications, 1951).
38  George Orwell, 'Boy's Weeklies', in *George Orwell Essays* (London: Penguin Classics, 2000), 88.
39  Anon., 'The Snake Man'.
40  Homi K. Bhabha, 'Of Mimicry and Man: The Ambivalence of Colonial Discourse', *October* 28 (Spring 1984), 125–133 (132).
41  Bhabha, 'Of Mimicry and Man', 126.
42  Bhabha, 'Of Mimicry and Man', 127.
43  Michael Rogin, 'Liberal Society and the Indian Question', *Politics and Society* 1.3 (1971), 269–312 (273).
44  Rogin, 'Liberal Society', 271.
45  Anon., 'Massacre of the Ghosts', *Witches Tales* #2 (New York: Witches Tales Inc., 1951), 22.
46  This story can also be seen as an example of the horror trope of the Native American burial ground as a site that visits vengeance on those who meddle with these ancient imagined practices. One famous example is *Pet Sematary* (New York: Doubleday), the 1983 novel by Stephen King subsequently adapted into a film in 1989. There are several other such stories in horror comics of the 1950s, and H. P. Lovecraft's short story of 1926, 'He', in *Weird Tales*, explores similar territory.
47  Bill Gaines (w), Al Feldstein (w), and George Roussos (a), 'Indian Burial Mound', *Tales from the Crypt* #26 (1951).
48  Jones, *Horror Stories*; Phillips, *Projected Fears*; Carroll, *The Philosophy of Horror*. See the introduction for an overview of these arguments.
49  Carol J. Clover, *Men, Women, and Chain Saws: Gender in the Modern Horror Film* (Princeton, NJ: Princeton University Press, 2015), 124.
50  Clover, *Men, Women, and Chain Saws*, 124.
51  Marshall Berman, *All That Is Solid Melts Into Air: The Experience of Modernity* (London: Penguin Books, 1988), 307.
52  Berman, *All That Is Solid*, 299.
53  Kevin Fox Gotham, 'Urban Space, Restrictive Covenants, and the Origins of Racial Residential Segregation in a US City, 1900–1950', *International Journal of Urban and Regional Research* 24.3 (2000), 616–633 (617).
54  Gotham, 'Urban Space', 625–626.
55  Gotham, 'Urban Space', 626.
56  Gotham, 'Urban Space', 626.
57  See Lee Rainwater, *Behind Ghetto Walls: Black Families in a Federal Slum* (Abingdon: Routledge, 2017).
58  Berman, *All That Is Solid*, 324–325.
59  Robert Fredrick Burk, *The Eisenhower Administration and Black Civil Rights* (Knoxville, TN: University of Tennessee Press, 1984), 4.
60  See Jane Jacobs, *The Death and Life of Great American Cities* (New York: Vintage, 1961).
61  Jacobs, *The Death and Life of Great American Cities*, 32.

62  Anon., 'Dungeon of Doom', *Chamber of Chills* #6 (New York: Harvey Publications, 1952).

63  Jacobs, *The Death and Life of Great American Cities*, 33–34. 'Kibitzer' is a Yiddish term for a spectator who engages verbally with the events they are watching.

64  While the Emancipation Proclamation declared an end to slavery in 1863, and the defeat of the Confederacy in 1865 finally brought the 'peculiar institution' to a close, the Federal Writers' Project collected slave narratives between 1936 and 1938. More about this can be found in the Library of Congress catalogue, 'Born in Slavery: Slave Narratives from the Federal Writers' Project, 1936 to 1938', retrieved from: www.loc.gov/collections/slave-narratives-from-the-federal-writers-project-1936-to-1938/about-this-collection/ (accessed 5 June 2020).

65  The term 'dungeon' also recalls Gothic tropes: that which is hidden, kept secret, as well as a space of punishment.

66  George Lipsitz, 'The Possessive Investment in Whiteness: Racialized Social Democracy and the "White" Problem in American Studies', *American Quarterly* 47.3 (1995), 369–387 (374).

67  See Lipsitz, 'The Possessive Investment in Whiteness', 373–375.

68  Lovecraft, 'He'.

69  Oscar Handlin, 'The Modern City as a Field of Historical Study', in Alexander B. Callow Jr (ed.), *American Urban History: An Interpretive Reader with Commentaries* (Oxford: Oxford University Press, 1973), 17–36 (18).

70  Handlin, 'The Modern City', 32.

71  Handlin, 'The Modern City', 32.

72  See, for instance, James W. Loewen, *Sundown Towns: A Hidden Dimension of American Racism* (New York: New Press, 2005).

73  Bill Gaines (w), Al Feldstein (w), and Joe Orlando (a), 'Midnight Mess', *Tales from the Crypt* #35 (New York: EC, 1953).

74  For all such plays on words, I am indebted to Kevin Ruane for instructing me in the dark arts of cryptic crosswords. Useful in research, on buses, and in dull meetings.

75  Groom, *The Vampire: A New History*, 125.

76  Bill Gaines (w), Albert B. Feldstein (w), and Graham Ingels (a), 'Mournin' Mess', *Tales from the Crypt* #38 (New York: EC Comics, 1953). The initials, for convenience, are GHOULS.

77  For more on this see Goodrum, 'The Past That Will Not Die', in Davies and Rifkind (eds), *Documenting Trauma in Comics*.

78  Gary D. Rhodes, *White Zombie: Anatomy of a Horror Film* (Jefferson, NC: McFarland, 2001), 19.

79  Maurice Gutwirth and George Appel, 'The Mystery of Lunablanca', *The Beyond* #2 (New York: Ace Magazines, 1951). It also reproduces some language of eighteenth-century Gothic fiction, with 'superstition' being used there in connection to a significant Other of the time, Catholicism.

80  Anon., 'The Valley of the Scaly Monsters', *The Beyond* #2 (New York: Ace Magazines, 1951).

81  For further discussion of the interchangeability of blonde women in horror comics, see Chapter 1 in this book.

82  Luckhurst, *Zombies: A Cultural History*, 109.

83  This is not to say that the US moved entirely away from formal empire in the wake of the Second World War but that it certainly started telling different stories, to itself and to others, about the way it interacted with the world.

84  Jim McLaughlin, 'Cult of the Undead', *The Beyond* #4 (New York: Ace Magazines, 1951).

85  McLaughlin, 'Cult of the Undead'.

86  McLaughlin, 'Cult of the Undead'.

87  See, for example, Frances Gateward and John Jennings (eds), *The Blacker the Ink: Constructions of Black Identity in Comics and Sequential Art* (New Brunswick NJ: Rutgers University Press 2015).

88  Al Feldstein (w), Joe Orlando (a), *Weird Fantasy* #18 (New York: EC Comics, 1953). While 'Judgment Day!' is not a horror story, 'Zero Hour' (in the same issue) is an adaptation of a Ray Bradbury story where the largely ignored children of a near-future summon a Martian invasion intent on wiping out all adults; similarly, 'Counter-Clockwise' features a body horror story about another near future where Ron, while still a child, and his father kill a hideous humanoid alien and capture its craft. It is subsequently revealed that the 'alien' is the product of the exposure of Ron's body (by then a grown man and flying the 'captured' ship) to the atmosphere of another planet. As we discuss in the introduction, the boundaries between horror and other genres were far from rigid.

89  Feldstein and Orlando, *Weird Fantasy* #18.

90  Feldstein and Orlando, *Weird Fantasy* #18.

91  See, for instance, Hubert Motley Jr, 'Black History in Comics: EC Comics "Judgment Day" the Anvil that Needed to be Dropped', *Groonk[dot]Net ಠ_ಠ* (n.d.), retrieved from www.groonk.net/blog/2010/02/black-history-in-comics-ec-comics-judgment-day-the-anvil-that-needed-to-be-dropped/ (accessed 30 July 2019), and Whitted, *EC Comics*.

92  Feldstein (w), Orlando (a), *Weird Fantasy* #18.

93  Groom, *The Vampire: A New History*, 4.

94  Judith Merril, 'What Do You Mean: Science? Fiction?', in Thomas Clareson (ed.), *SF: The Other Side of Realism* (Bowling Green, OH: Bowling Green University Press), 53–95, as cited in Malisa Kurtz, 'After the War, 1945–65', in Roger Luckhurst (ed.), *Science Fiction: A Literary History* (London: British Library, 2017), 130–156 (138).

95  Kurtz, 'After the War, 1945–65', in Luckhurst (ed.), *Science Fiction*, 152.

# 4

## Monster kids –
## bridging the pre- and post-CCA eras

In 1954, in the fallout of the Senate Subcommittee Hearings, comics publishers agreed to adopt the Comics Code Authority. Any comic that carried the CCA stamp offered a promise to potential buyers that the contents therein would be entirely wholesome and appropriate for a young audience. The CCA was a blow from which the horror comics industry would never fully recover. The end of the horror comic did not, of course, mean the end of horror (indeed, it did not even mean a complete end to horror comics). From the late 1950s onward, film was the driving force behind changes in the American horror genre. It is telling that when, in 1969, the horror magazine *Vampirella* ran a story that followed the classic formula of a horror writer's creation coming to life, the medium in which the writer works is no longer comics, but film.[1] Movies, the story suggests, had superseded comics as America's primary source of horror; worse than that, for horror comics at least, film had superseded comics even within comics. Unlike comics, film had recovered from the dip in production of horror titles that followed the Second World War. As horror comic production slumped, film spiked: nine major horror films were released in 1955, nineteen in 1956, and thirty-five in 1957.[2]

A key element in the changing face of horror was the rise of what Skal calls 'Monster Culture', a key part of which we will term here (borrowing a phrase from Aaron AuBuchon) as 'monster kids' – a group of individuals, mostly children and adolescents, who consumed classic and new horror films and were avid purchasers of Warren's magazines, toys, and other paraphernalia. The appearance of a horror subculture in the late 1950s existed in dialogue with this new cinematic interest in the genre. The successful release of Universal horror films from the 1930s on American television in 1957 sparked a monster craze among a certain subculture of adolescents; testimony from an earlier generation suggested these 1930s films had already served a similar function, with Ray Bradbury numbering among the young enthusiasts.[3] The engagement with horror seemed to continue to divide between revulsion and empathy, and along similar age lines. Publisher James Warren recalls of the era that '[k]ids were watching these [horror] shows, not adults; and these kids were rooting for the monster – not for the townspeople with the pitchforks and crude torches'.[4] Monster kids set themselves against mainstream culture through their patterns of consumption.

Central to the monster kid subculture was the phenomenon of the horror magazine. In February 1958, publisher James Warren and editor Forrest James Ackerman launched *Famous Monsters of Filmland*, which included articles on and images from the horror movie industry. Ackerman had been involved in fandom and fanzines since the 1930s but *Famous Monsters of Filmland* represented a significant new fold in his work. The publication was highly successful, selling 90 per cent of its initial run.[5] *Famous Monsters*, as well as the many imitators it spawned, was instrumental, if not in creating, then at least in coalescing, a horror fan culture. Director Joe Dante asserts that reading *Famous Monsters* made him and his friends realize that 'there were other people out there like us'.[6] The magazine's 'Fang Mail' section printed letters by readers, creating the possibility of dialogue and developing a sense of shared identity among horror enthusiasts that had in some senses lapsed since the demise of the horror comics industry of the 1940s and 1950s, when titles had carried their own letter pages.

The existence of the monster kid subculture is evident in an advert for the toy company Aurora, taken from the DC title *The House of Secrets* #92 (1971). The advertised toy collection brings together a mad scientist, Vampirella, and Frankenstein's monster, but makes the child the agent entrusted with deciding what the experiments are, and whether they succeed. This suggests something about the presumed readership of horror comics in the 1970s – there are eight kits to collect in this series, and Aurora made a number of other kits throughout the 1960s. Rather than being standalone figures, like these earlier kits, the Monster Scenes were explicitly toys to play with. The type of play, the kit suggests, centres on the monster – any hero to thwart the sinister schemes is conspicuously absent. The inclusion of the 'girl victim', whose various potential fates were detailed in a comic that accompanied the sets, caused outcry, and the sets were quickly recalled.[7]

## The megamonster

One of the most direct manifestations of the monster kid subculture in comics was the emergence of the city-destroying megamonster. During

the 1940s and 1950s, horror comics, as we have seen, explored the consequences of nuclear war either literally or through allegory. Stories that
featured scientific apocalypses did not wholly vanish during the 1960s
and 1970s. In 'Beware Small Evils!' in *Nightmare* #3, for example, 'an
immense creeping carpet of death', born of a government experiment,
consumes most of Southern California.[8] Such narratives were far less
common than they had been during the 1950s, however. As noted in
the previous chapter, the CCA had ruled out most kinds of horror.
Specifically, it asserts:

> (1) No comic magazine shall use the word 'horror' or 'terror' in its title.
> (2) All scenes of horror, excessive bloodshed, gory or gruesome crimes,
> depravity, lust, sadism, masochism shall not be permitted.
> (3) All lurid, unsavory, gruesome illustrations shall be eliminated.
> (4) Inclusion of stories dealing with evil shall be used or shall be published
> only where the intent is to illustrate a moral issue and in no case shall evil
> be presented alluringly, nor so as to injure the sensibilities of the reader.
> (5) Scenes dealing with, or instruments associated with walking dead,
> torture, vampires and vampirism, ghouls, cannibalism, and werewolfism
> are prohibited.[9]

As noted previously in this volume, and at length in other literature
on the subject, horror comics as they had once existed could no longer
operate after the CCA was established. Unlike his supernatural breth-
ren, however, the megamonster thrived under the CCA. Atlas/Marvel's
*Strange Tales* and several of Charlton's comics featured creatures with
names such as Konga (Charlton, *Konga*, 1960–1965), Taboo (Atlas/
Marvel, *Strange Tales* #75 and #77, 1960), and Gorgolla (Marvel,
*Strange Tales* #74, 1960). These monsters were all depicted toppling
buildings, throwing cars, and otherwise destroying all that lay in their
path. Such monsters did not engage with any of the supernatural horror
tropes outlined by the CCA and scenes of mass destruction (of buildings
being toppled and people running in fear) were bloodless enough to
avoid the prohibitions of the Code (indeed, if knocking over a building
constituted horror, then the superhero genre would not have survived
the CCA, either).

The megamonster was a transmedia phenomenon not limited
to comics. Perhaps the most iconic megamonster (and certainly the
inspiration for *Konga*), was King Kong, who made his film debut in
1933 and was reprised in a more domesticated form in *Mighty Joe
Young* in 1949. A more recent intervention was the hugely influential
Japanese film, *Godzilla* (1954). In an unsubtle reference to the bombing
of Nagasaki and Hiroshima, and the Lucky Dragon incident of 1954

when a Japanese fishing boat was caught in an American nuclear test, American science produces a monster that destroys a Japanese city.[10] In the redemptive retelling of the bombing in the film, a Japanese scientist is able to stop the monster, destroying himself and his new superweapon in the process. The film was released with new footage in America under the title *Godzilla, King of the Monsters!* in 1956. The Godzilla brand was hugely influential in both Japan and America, spawning, to use Mark I. West's term, a 'Godzilla industry' with numerous further films (including *Godzilla vs Kong*, 1963) and incarnations in various media.[11] Godzilla featured in Japanese comics from the 1950s onward and in American comics from 1976. He went on to fight various Marvel superheroes in a 24-issue arc from 1977 to 1979. King Kong appeared in another film in 1967, *King Kong Escapes*, and an animated TV series, *The King Kong Show*, from 1966–1969 – with character designs by EC veteran, Jack Davis.

The widespread adoption of the city-destroying megamonster in comics during the 1960s was a new development in the horror genre. It was more explicitly gleeful in its depictions of mass destruction. While the horror comics of the 1950s sought, at least in part, to give shape to anxieties about the instability of global politics after the bomb, the monster craze of the 1960s and 1970s meant a different kind of engagement with the horror genre. Where before monsters had, historically, represented various external threats, during the 1960s and 1970s a subculture of monster kids openly revelled in the destruction and violence embedded in the horror genre, often empathizing with the monster rather than its victims. Nuclear scenarios during the 1940s and 1950s engaged with some of the politics of nuclear proliferation, but the megamonsters of the 1960s offered counter-histories. Here, the US military-industrial complex is positioned as the target of nuclear threat rather than the aggressor, and subsequently offers a means by which nuclear war might be averted.

Scholarship on megamonsters has tended to emphasize their cathartic qualities, both in the joy of the spectacle of destruction and in the sense of the reader/viewer having vicariously survived. Sharon Diane King, writing about megamonsters in film, argues that such creatures 'exist to entertain. They do so by shoring up the audience's tottering matrix of confidence in the future. The very presence of monsters that threaten gives confidence to spectators. That they can defend themselves staves off the terror that they perhaps cannot ultimately be master'.[12] Daniel Yezbick, similarly, describes these works as presenting 'cathartic visions of enormous, prehistoric monsters that crushed every emblem of civilized progress in orgies of postnuclear terror and Cold War angst'.[13]

Indeed, the megamonster seemed to epitomise the 'monster culture' of the era – they were loud, epic, and camp celebrations of destruction.

The pure and joyful excess of the megamonster can make it an unyielding subject of critical and social readings; its uncomplicated affect can be seen to make it unsuitable for nuanced political commentary. What we can argue, however, is that destruction can be read more explicitly from the narrative position of the monster – the outsider who seeks to destroy society based on their marginalization from it. Many of the monster kids were white, affluent boys who, for whatever reason, felt that they did not fit the privileged definitions of normality then in circulation. While the monster contains the potential for audiences more forcefully constructed as marginal, whether queer, of colour, or otherwise Othered, to identify with the monster as it destroys the hegemony, it also offered a screen on to which white, heterosexual, male anxieties could be projected. The megamonster's simplicity thus renders it an effective vehicle for anyone who feels (justifiably or otherwise) that they have been left out of the political system. The megamonster, in other words, is an echo chamber, giving the viewer back their own politics. It was adopted by monster kids of various stripes and became a key feature of mid-twentieth century horror.

## Horror cinema

One company to capitalise on the horror craze, in a large part through high-profile girl victims, was Hammer Horror. The British studio had first launched in the 1930s and turned to horror from the mid-1950s onward. They became one of the premier creators of low-budget, but widely consumed, horror films. While the Gothic, unlike other forms of horror, was otherwise marginalized and mined for parody, Hammer Horror kept the sub-genre alive with violent Gothic titles such as *The Curse of Frankenstein* (1957), *Dracula* (1958), and *The Mummy* (1959). As these titles demonstrate, much of Hammer's content followed the paths worn by Universal from the 1930s to the 1940s.[14] From the late 1950s to the 1970s, Hammer was a highly successful studio, turning profits to rival major US companies with its gory, melodramatic, sexualized shlock horror.

*The Curse of Frankenstein* (1957) was Hammer's first major international success. Its writer, Jimmy Sangster, argued that it offered something different from other contemporary horror films:

The whole concept of horror is different. The public is more hard-boiled since the Frankenstein pictures of the thirties. So many horrible things have happened since then that a film has to be really tough to get the desired reaction. But that doesn't mean that you have to use a bludgeon. There is, now, the horror of implication.[15]

*The Curse of Frankenstein* is largely positioned as a break with previous practice, partly due to its approach as outlined above, and partly due to the increased levels of gore it brought to the screen. While Hammer has been praised for its innovation, the basic approach had already been set out in the horror comics boom that preceded it.[16] High-profile debates in both the US and the UK, home of Hammer, on the nature of the horror comics and their impact on those who read them did not escape the attention of either horror producers or the teenage demographic increasingly being targeted by the film industry. Kevin Heffernan asserts that 'the growing sophistication of this young audience is underscored by its ability to maintain an ironic distance from the horrific content of the films: the social ritual of horror movie attendance was often an occasion for laughter'.[17] The same approach can be seen in many horror comics of the period, which included a satirical, anarchic humour that was as much part of the appeal as the horrific content. Although this style was most often associated with EC, *Chamber of Chills* (published by Harvey Comics) had a regular feature called 'Chilly Chamber Music – Songs from the Spook Box!', which parodied popular songs and narrative tropes in rhyming, 'spooky' verse.[18] As a consequence of the turn towards humour, the icons of Gothic horror descended into parody and camp re-creation. The success of the song 'Monster Mash' in 1962, comedian Lenny Bruce's Bela Lugosi impression on his album *Lenny Bruce Is Out Again* (1964), and the television shows *The Munsters* and *The Addams Family* (both 1964–1966) all turned Dracula and Frankenstein into comedic figures.[19]

The presence of humour was also a defining feature of the appeal of the new wave of films that followed *The Curse of Frankenstein*. Terence Fisher (director of *The Curse*) said:

> Humour, of course, is important in horror, both the intentional and the accidental kinds. We have found quite ordinary lines can become unintentionally funny in a horror setting ... By and large, though, a few giggles during a horror film can be taken as a compliment – it shows the picture is really doing its work, that the audience is really gripped.[20]

The combination of excessive gore and anarchic humour worked towards alienating older audiences. *The Curse* followed comics in another way by having 'images of bourgeois splendour juxtaposed with those of madness, decay, and death', a practice that suggested flaws in the ideological project of postwar suburbanism.[21] With the odd exception, however, Hammer films were period pieces, aligned with a generally backward-looking approach to horror in Britain. A good example of this is *The Plague of the Zombies* (1966), a Hammer film set in a remote Cornish village in the nineteenth century. The new squire, recently returned from Haiti, uses zombies as labour in his tin mine; in this, the squire is ably supported by a group of huntsmen, making this a particularly British indictment of class structures and the nature of the labour that underpins the 'bourgeois splendour' its beneficiaries enjoy.

While fans of the classic and neo-classic horror film continued to revel in Gothic themes, another branch of horror cinema was becoming increasingly invested in psychological and non-supernatural horror. One watershed contribution to the genre, quite different from the Gothic horror of Hammer, was Alfred Hitchcock's *Psycho* (1960). Despite its later admission into the canon of great cinema, early critical responses to *Psycho* were unfavourable and the film was broadly regarded as a mis-step by Hitchcock (the *New York Times* described it as a 'blot on an honorable career').[22] As the decade progressed, however, *Psycho* came to serve as a model for other horror narratives, both in the trope of the 'killer next door' and in its formal elements such as the use of high strings at moments of dramatic tension. Phillips contends that *Psycho* 'changed the way Americans understood horror', in that it located suburbia as the primary site of horror and the lone murderer as its source.[23] He asserts: 'Hitchcock meticulously laid out the American dream of prosperous, suburban family dwellings and liberating mobility – a dream disseminated in movies and television – and then proceeded to savagely tear it in half'.[24] Hill, similarly, argues that *Psycho* 'is not just a sick and a sad joke, it is a derisive misuse of the key-images of the American way of life'.[25] This approach, in itself, was not particularly original; horror comics, as the previous chapters have shown, had cast suburban America as a potential site of violence throughout the 1940s and 1950s. Even earlier, Poe and Lovecraft had both written stories centred on an encounter with a killer in a domestic setting. What *Psycho* achieved, however, was a level of artistry the horror genre had rarely attained previously. As Phillips notes, *Psycho* attacks not just suburbia but also, crucially for the rhetoric of middle-class prosperity, the car that enables mobility and the flight of the middle classes to suburban developments. More prosaically, cars also became the means for a whole generation of adolescents to engage with cinema through the advent of the 'drive-in' movie, a means of consumption originating in 1933 and peaking in 1958 with 4,063 drive-ins across the United States.[26] *Psycho* spawned many immediate imitators and, arguably, went on to create the 'slasher' genre of the 1970s and 1980s, typified by the films of directors such as Brian De Palma and John Carpenter. *Psycho* was eventually adopted as a staple of Film Studies classrooms as cinema criticism shifted from newspaper and magazine reviews to the academy during the 1960s.[27]

As the decade progressed, the relocation of horror to the American home gave rise to a series of films that, following the new horror tradition of *Psycho*, provoked new forms of disgust and unease. One recurring theme was of children and childbirth; films such as *The Village of the Damned* (1960), and (most profoundly) *Rosemary's Baby* (1968) proliferated throughout the decade. Skal, among others, has argued that these films were a collective response to the introduction of the birth control pill and the Thalidomide tragedy. In horror films of the 1960s, Skal asserts, 'Women would become pregnant by machines or computers, tinkered with by genetic engineers. Pregnancy was an act of war, a violent invasion by the enemy. These fearful images were rarely part of the debate over reproduction technology and abortion rights, but they provided a persistent subtext worth examination'.[28] The themes of gynaecological horror and demon children became a recurring theme in cinema that followed, from *It's Alive* (1974), to *Demon Seed* (1977), to *The Brood* and *Alien* (both 1979).

Another key moment in horror cinema was the low-budget but highly successful *Night of the Living Dead* (1968), a film set in a rural farmhouse where a small group of survivors seek refuge from a zombie hoard. These are not the zombies of the Haitian past, however: Romero's ghouls (as they are known in the film) are dead bodies, reactivated by radiation and driven to consume the flesh of the living. While there might be a crossover in terms of the representation of the zombies as proletarian revolution, *Night of the Living Dead* made *The Plague of the Zombies* appear crushingly outdated only two years after its release. Jon Towlson notes that when Barbra flees the graveyard at the beginning of the film, 'she runs out of a classic horror movie and into a modern one', issuing in a new age of horror cinema in the process.[29] While other films and texts had explored issues around the survival of apocalyptic outbreaks, *Night of the Living Dead* ushered in the zombie survival sub-genre, which became a staple of future horror cinema, fiction, television, and comics. Despite being made independently for an estimated $114,000, *Night of the Living Dead* became a breakout success, earning widespread acclaim in the US and becoming the top-grossing film in Europe in 1969. In part, the film generated such commercial and critical acclaim because its cynicism and focus on social dynamics engaged in dialogue with the politics of the age. The film's release came a few months after the assassinations of Martin Luther King and Senator Robert Kennedy and as the

Vietnam War began to look like a longer, more difficult, conflict than the American public had been led to believe.

It was not just the dominant culture that was losing an abiding sense of consensus; during the late 1960s, the counter-culture also seemed to be splintering into groups that differed in terms of aims and methods. As critics such as Reynolds Humphreys have argued, *Night of the Living Dead* seemed to encapsulate a crisis in national identity. Phillips reinforces this, contending that 'Romero's zombies slowly and disturbingly shredded the last vestiges of American hope and optimism'.[30] The final scene, in which the sole survivor, Ben (Duane Jones) – an African American man – is shot by a posse of white zombie hunters spoke powerfully to the growing tensions around race in America at the time. The series of stills under the credits, where Ben's body is recovered from the house and burned, establishes a point of continuity with contemporary civil rights photography, while also evoking the images circulated by the NAACP's campaign against spectacle lynching in the 1930s.

*Night of the Living Dead* also belonged, alongside *Bonnie and Clyde* (1967) and campy horror such as *Blood Fest* and *Straight Jacket* (both 1963), to the first wave of violent filmmaking that would come to characterize the cinema of the 1970s. As a sign of the times, Hammer Horror made three versions of each of their films depending on the severity of censorship: English cinemas received the least explicitly violent cut and Japan the most, with America somewhere in the middle.[31] The turn towards explicit violence that began in the 1950s, but reached a peak during the late 1960s, was no doubt exacerbated by reporting on the Vietnam War. Even from the first year of American troops on the ground in Vietnam, embedded reporters began sending home footage of the victims of war – both the wounded and deceased – from both sides of the conflict. Televised violence thus crept into the American home. Perhaps most profoundly, American viewers were not only aware that violence was taking place, but that American soldiers, the government, and even the public were culpable. It was perhaps the greatest achievement of horror cinema at the time to explore, develop, and create narratives from that revelation. As Robin Wood argues, the ultra-violent film *The Last House on the Left* (1972) served to prove that 'Mỹ Lai was not an unfortunate occurrence out there; it was created within the American home', with the graphic violence of the film meted out not only by the 'villains', but also by the bourgeois American family.[32]

Some of the most important developments for horror film during the 1970s came from outside the genre. *A Clockwork Orange* and *Straw Dogs* (both 1971), while not necessarily classified as horror, represented a new benchmark in this era of provocative and violent filmmaking.

These films inarguably shaped the horror genre and, coupled with rising special effects technologies, gave rise to films such as *The Texas Chainsaw Massacre* (1974), which combined the gore of 1970s cinema with the serial killer trope that had become a popular theme since *Psycho*. *The Texas Chainsaw Massacre* was significant because it was adopted within the trend of horror fandom. Phillips argues that it 'became a kind of taboo film – horrifying and condemned for its graphic brutality and, of course, irresistible to young audiences seeking to break taboos'.[33] Darryl Jones regards it as 'the greatest of all modern horror movies'.[34] It is, at least in part, about forces of marginalization and the breakdown of national narratives. Linnie Blake argues that the representation of the 'poor white rural south' in films such as *The Texas Chainsaw Massacre* 'enables a potent critique of the nation-state, its modes of political organisation and its representation and its pretensions to occupy the civilised pole of a static Orientalist binarism'.[35] The film not only embodied the national mood during Vietnam but the 'leaving behind' of portions of the South such that its inhabitants became not fellow American citizens, but Othered sources of horror.

Another film that both contains horror themes and dramatizes the conflict between wealthy urban and poor rural areas is *Deliverance* (1972). As with *The Texas Chainsaw Massacre*, in *Deliverance* it is the rich who travel and the poor who are stationary, left behind in an area from which they cannot escape. Both films literalize the statement often attributed to Jean-Jacques Rousseau: 'when the people have nothing more to eat, they will eat the rich'. As with *The Last House on the Left*, and in keeping with the disillusionment that accompanied Vietnam, the horror is not entirely externalized; an encounter with the Other brings out the barbarity of the conventional bourgeois family man; in fact, in both films it is ultimately the middle-class urban male who is shown to be capable of the most violence and the greatest deceit. The heart of darkness was not only in Vietnam; it also beat steadily at home, a tell-tale rhythm of cruelty and violence beneath the façade of a modern bourgeois state.

Another significant intervention in horror of this era was *The Exorcist* (1973), a film that reportedly caused vomiting and claims of 'supernatural' experiences among audience members.[36] The film was also significant for, like *Psycho,* its ability to attract respectability to horror cinema. Phillips asserts, '[t]he technical skill and excellent pacing of the film attracted not only enormous popularity but unprecedented critical acclaim'.[37] Following in the wake of *The Exorcist* and *The Texas Chainsaw Massacre*, the 1970s saw a series of cult horror films including *The Omen, Carrie* (both 1976), *The Hills Have Eyes, Halloween, The*

*Fury* (all 1978), *The Brood*, and *The Amityville Horror* (both 1979). Horror had reached a position of both critical acclaim and box office success.

## Horror beyond cinema

Horror was not only successful in cinemas: it also found its way into other sub-cultures, such as rock music, which began taking on the trappings of the genre. In 1960 The Frantics, a Washington instrumental outfit, received acclaim among audiences with 'Werewolf', a song that quotes the film *The Wolf Man* (1941). The term 'Gothic Rock' was first used in 1967 to describe the musical style of The Doors, although it was perhaps best summed up in Alice Cooper's 1971 tour, which featured horror-themed glam rock outfits by designer Cindy Dunaway, and simulated torture on stage. From the mid-1970s, the band Kiss adopted a similar aesthetic, with Gene Simmons projecting simulated blood before fans. These early adopters of horror aesthetics paved the way for the Gothic rock movement, a trend that reached full fruition in the early 1980s.[38] The trappings of sensual horror found in Anne Rice's *Interview with the Vampire* (1976), a text very much in keeping with the glam-rock horror images found in popular music, too, contributed to the burgeoning Goth subculture, while once again conjuring the spectre of same-sex attraction in vampire stories. While the Gothic movement had its first stirrings during the 1970s, music historian Simon Reynolds identifies Bauhaus' 'Bela Lugosi's Dead' (1979) as 'the ground zero of goth proper'.[39] Its cover image was a still from *The Sorrows of Satan*, a silent D. W. Griffiths film of 1926, suggesting (and encouraging on the part of the viewer) an affinity with horror fandom.[40]

In addition to Anne Rice's seductive vampires, Stephen King's *Carrie* (1974) transformed the landscape for genre fiction for a different audience. King's success was due, in part, to his accessible writing style, and was buoyed by the appearance of chain bookstores in the late 1970s. King spoke to a reading public, Skal contends, who otherwise eschewed the printed word as a source of entertainment. Brian De Palma's 1976 adaptation of *Carrie*, too, was a huge commercial success, capitalizing on the immense popularity of King's horror fiction, which in itself fed back into his childhood as a monster kid and his love of EC horror comics.

Horror, or at least the Gothic, also found its way onto television with the long-running success of *Dark Shadows* (1966–1971), a series that extended to 1,225 episodes and a host of tie-in marketing opportunities.[41] As Rick Worland remarks:

The near-surreal tension between gothic horror and the soap opera format was central to the show's style. Although the latter concentrates on the upper-middle-class home and family threatened by disruptions of domestic, sexual, and social propriety, the gothic is defined by the dark house as the decaying remnant of unresolved traumas and guilty secrets that have already ravaged these same institutions in the past.[42]

Normality is difficult to locate within *Dark Shadows*; monsters and the Gothic take centre stage and every situation reads as in some sense macabre. As Worland suggests, 'for the world of *Dark Shadows*, a permanent state of strained, hysterical crisis was its daily mode', establishing a thematic resonance with its climate of reception, even if it was one that did not deliberately tease out specific connections to the war in Vietnam or domestic unrest.[43] Although the series transitioned into film in 1970, its days were numbered, partly due to the shifting nature of horror in the period and the rise of new, more contemporary, narratives such as *Night of the Living Dead* and *Rosemary's Baby*, both of which came out in 1968. These films, and those that followed, shifted horror out of the Gothic and into new terrain; although they did not end the appeal of the Gothic, which still persists, new films and the chance to feature spectacles both more horrifying and titillating than the film cycle of the 1950s and 1960s, created stiff competition.[44]

## Warren Publishing

Although most of the trappings of horror were expressly forbidden by the self-regulatory Comics Code Authority, horror comics did not entirely die after the introduction of the CCA. The majority of publishers put an end to their horror titles, but some, such as *Adventures into the Unknown*, continued as tamer versions of their former selves, working within the strict confines of the Code. There were also various unsuccessful attempts to circumvent the Code with 'picto-fiction' magazines such as Hastings' *Eerie Tales* (1959), which closed after a single issue, and EC's *Terror Illustrated* (1955–1956), which lasted two issues. New forms of horror comics arose, however; while the Code forbade most forms of horror, the megamonster thrived during the 1960s in the form of various city-destroying beasts such as Fin Fang Foom, who first appeared in Atlas/Marvel's *Strange Tales* #89 (1961) and eventually became a part of the superhero genre. Charlton continued to publish horror comics and anthologies for several decades after the introduction of the CCA, selling a brand of horror founded upon both megamonsters and existential dread.[45] A handful of new titles joined the infernal legions when in 1962, Dell launched *Ghost Stories* and *Tales from the Tomb* – horror comics adapted from literature and film. Dell never submitted work for CCA approval, arguing that it already had a reputation for wholesome content, and their horror comics bore out this claim, presenting restrained horror stories drawn from respectable media. *Classics Illustrated*, which adapted works of literature to the comics format, similarly, did not carry the CCA stamp and continued to publish horror stories.

Other undead horror comics changed form, moving from four-colour comics to black and white magazines. During the early 1960s, writer and artist Russ Jones approached William Gaines with the project of relaunching a horror comic franchise, but Gaines was unenthusiastic about fighting the same battles he had faced in the 1950s. Instead, Gaines introduced Jones and fellow creators Larry Ivie, Archie Goodwin, and Al Williams to some former EC artists. The team eventually persuaded James Warren, publisher of *Famous Monsters of Filmland*, to launch *Creepy*.[46] The first issue featured the work of a host of former EC writers and artists such as Jack Davis, Al Williamson, Joe Orlando, Frank Frazetta, Angelo Torres, Reed Crandall, and Gray Morrow. A decade after the introduction of the Code, *Creepy* was, Sennitt asserts, 'the first full-blooded ongoing horror comic'.[47] It was followed by two other publications from Warren: *Eerie* (launched 1965) and *Vampirella* (launched 1969).

In addition to championing talents of the 1950s, Warren made space for new writers and editors such as Archie Goodwin, who was responsible for most of the stories in both *Eerie* and *Creepy*. Warren's line was, in many ways, a resurrection of the horror comics tradition; the first issue of *Creepy* features a story in which a team of comics creators kill a lazy collaborator. Richard J. Arndt states that the 'first issue [of *Eerie*] was originally intended to be an "all EC artists" effort', although ultimately one artist with only minor ties to EC, Gray Morrow, was included.[48] Arndt suggests that the early success of *Eerie* and *Creepy* provided 'a writing template for other comics writers and for many future writers of horror prose'.[49] The Warren style evolved to allow more individual style and less text-heavy stories than had typically featured in EC's horror lines.[50] Horror comics from major companies such as Marvel, which started to publish horror titles from 1969 onwards, drew more from the Warren tradition than that of EC. Such developments can be explained by shifts in personnel as, from 1968, Archie Goodwin was working at Marvel, and undertook some foundational work on their titles in the 1970s horror comics boom, such as *Tomb of Dracula*. For horror, as for so many other things, the 1960s was a decade of change and development that looked backwards as much as forwards.[51]

Warren's success meant that the 1960s saw a range of reprints of golden age horror comics mixed with some original stories in a similar style. Titles included *Weird* (Eerie Publications, 1966–1976), *Chilling Tales of Horror* (Stanley Publications, 1969–1971), *Nightmare* (Skywald Magazines, 1970–1975), and *Web of Horror* (Major Magazines, 1969–1970). Many of these magazines not only reprinted stories from the 1940s and 1950s but followed a similar format, eschewing the editorials and letters pages that had become standard by the 1960s. Sennitt describes Eerie Publications' line as 'some of the most consistently weird, disgusting, gory and truly horrific comics ever seen [...] it was as though they emerged out of a dark realm where the Comics Code had never existed'.[52]

The (re)appearance of horror-comic-inflected magazines can be traced to two factors: the gradual return to health of the comics industry, and the development of specific fan cultures around horror. Both *Eerie* and *Creepy* can be seen to come out of the same reader base as *Famous Monsters of Filmland*. These publications helped to create and facilitate a network of readers and viewers around horror.[53] *Eerie*, *Creepy*, and *Vampirella* were read primarily by a different (although often overlapping) sub-culture than those who were readers of DC or Marvel comics. Monster kids were just as fervent as other comics readers but were less numerous – each issue of *Vampirella* sold an average of 93,750 copies from 1974 to 1979.[54] *Amazing Spider-Man,* by comparison, sold an average of 266,500 copies of each issue during the same period.[55] Warren's publications were marketed as magazines and priced at 50 cents (35 cents higher than a DC or Marvel comic at the time), suggesting that they sought to appeal to a different audience, one more invested in the horror genre (and thus prepared to invest more in it).

Comics also seemed to appeal to the early Gothic subculture; the fourth issue of *Vampirella*, in April of 1970, for example, features a letter by Jane Church who asserts, 'Most of us who read your magazine are also rock music fans'.[56] She asks that the magazine feature more rock-related stories. While *Vampirella* may have offered some thematic connections to contemporary rock music, Church would have to wait until 2003, when the relaunched magazine featured Vampirella and Kiss's Gene Simmons on the cover, and 2017, when Kiss and Vampirella appeared in a comic together. Marvel were quicker to capitalize on the connection; the fifth issue of *Monster of Frankenstein* opens with lyrics from John Fogerty of Creedence Clearwater Revival (CCR).[57]

**50** Don Glut (w) and Mike Royer (a), 'Last Act: October', *Vampirella* #1

Even as these new horror comics seem to gleefully reject the CCA, they are haunted by its presence; the first issue of *Vampirella*, for example, includes a story in which a puritanical babysitter expresses the kind of sentiment that led to the CCA while brandishing a copy of *Creepy* (Figure 50).

## Marvel horror

Just as horror changed during the 1960s, so too did comics. The CCA, the collapse of distribution networks, and the widespread adoption of television did significant damage to comics sales. Supermarkets, which rapidly replaced grocery stores throughout this period, were less inclined to devote shelf space to low-margin items such as comics and so availability also suffered. All of these factors led, by the end of the decade, to plummeting sales and the erosion of comics as a mass medium. Many publishers closed their doors and those who held on faced difficult decisions as to which titles to continue. By the late 1960s, it became increasingly obvious that comics publishers were not attracting new, young readers at the rate they once had, and that their existing readers, many of whom were old enough to be enrolled in higher education, were at risk of losing interest. Despite these challenges, Nyberg argues that publishers were 'generally content with the status quo and unwilling to risk [their] economic health on experimentation that would challenge the public's perception of comic-books'.[58]

Whether publishers wanted it or not, comics were changing, and the change was being led by the readers. Comics readership experienced what Glen Weldon calls the 'Great Inward Turn' – comics ceased to be a mass medium consumed by all and became associated with a subculture of adolescents and young adults who met with one another at the earliest comics conventions and argued over their chosen medium in letter columns and fanzines.[59] The price of entry, the currency of insider knowledge, skyrocketed; during the 1960s, Weldon asserts, comics readers began 'mapping and policing the fictive universes of these heroes and villains, vigilant for any new piece of information that enriched or – especially – contradicted what had previously been established'.[60] Book stores began to appear with boxes of past issues, allowing readers to fill the gaps in their collections and their knowledge. An important change in the comic book format during this time was the habitual inclusion of a letters page, where readers could discuss comics with the creators and one another.

The Great Inward Turn shaped comics content. While comics of the 1950s were largely regarded as disposable entertainment made up of single stories, comics of the 1960s became parts of a whole, to be reread and collected. In the 1960s, comics increasingly began to feature recurring characters and ongoing storylines that covered multiple titles in a shared universe. By the 1970s, the 'silver age' of comics saw far more emotionally complex heroes tackling more complex, human problems. This not only spoke to readers' desires for more developed narrative universes, but the emotional focus of a readership who were discovering themselves and their place in the world. The Great Inward Turn and the development of emotionally complex characters were not enough to return the comics industry to pre-CCA level of sales, but it was enough to sustain a thriving community of committed readers in a shifting industrial landscape.

Comics and comics readership had changed. Until 1971, however, the Code had not. Marvel made some tentative steps into horror during the late 1960s with *Tower of Shadows* and *Chamber of Darkness* in 1969. They did not, indeed could not, fully embrace the return of the horror genre as seen in Warren's magazines and their imitators for as long as the Code was in effect. Adjustment to the scope of comics content began in 1970 when the United States Department of Health, Education and Welfare commissioned Marvel to create a comic that dealt with the theme of drug abuse. Any discussion of narcotics was explicitly banned by the CCA. Marvel accepted the commission anyway and the three-issue arc *The Amazing Spider-Man* #96-98 (all 1971) was published without CCA approval. In part, this change mediated, as discussed above, the aging readership; the Department of Health, Education and Welfare had correctly identified comics as a medium consumed by teenagers and these were exactly the individuals they wished to target with an anti-drugs message as part of the opening shots in the Republican War on Drugs. The arbiters of the CCA took note of the success and in 1971, alongside changes concerning engagement with social issues, the Code was revised. The revisions included the following: 'vampires, ghouls and werewolves shall be permitted to be used when handled in the classic tradition'.[61] The revision did not permit every form of horror

– rules concerning the 'walking dead, torture [and] cannibalism' from the 1954 Code remained in effect.[62] A complete return of the horror genre remained impossible, but certain forms, particularly those relating to the Gothic tradition, were allowed once again.

Marvel wasted no time. Morbius, the living vampire, was introduced as an antagonist for Spider-Man in 1971. Marvel then set about launching a series of horror titles in 1972, with reprints of pre-Code Atlas titles. These reprints appeared in various magazines, the longest-running being *Chamber of Chills* (no connection to the Harvey title of the 1950s), which ran mostly new material until #7 (1973), after which it reverted to reprints of 1950s Atlas material, its run lasting until #25 in 1976. Rather than seeking a complete return to the horror of the 1950s, however, these titles also acknowledged that the terrain they traversed had changed. In this, it is worth considering the concepts of *mouvance* and *variance*, techniques developed for the analysis of the copying and reproduction of medieval manuscripts. *Mouvance* concerns the fact that 'no matter how many times a text derived from oral traditions is written down, it will change or move'; *variance* is the same idea but applied to the ways in which the re-creation of physical texts also introduces slippages and shifts in meaning.[63] Such an approach to the nature of reprinting issues from the past, and indeed of the restaging of narratives and images of the past in new contexts, is profitable for exploring the nostalgia-inflected restagings of the 1960s, as well as the industrial processes that gave rise to both the original and its repackaging. It is tempting to consider the decision to reprint as driven purely by a remorseless capitalist logic – trying to get paid for the same product twice. While this no doubt plays a part, the choice of material to be reprinted, its relationship to other stories in the same issue and, more than anything else, its relationship to the new context in which it is consumed, mean that the 'same' material can both lose and acquire meaning. Editorial decisions about what and when to reprint, much like artistic decisions as to which stories should be redrawn or rewritten, also create patterns of meaning. The concern here is not with a quest for authenticity, the task with which some medievalists deploying these strategies concern themselves; rather, *variance* provides comics scholars with a lens for considering the intervention of individual comics, or stories, in a larger overarching metatext. A metatext of this nature consists not just of the texts, but also of the fan practices around them and the industrial developments that work towards or against their acceptance and appearance. This inclusion of the monster kid phenomenon within the structures of horror comics begins to explain the forms they took, as well as where and when they took them.[64]

A further explanation for the nature of horror comics can be found in the industrial context to which they returned. In the 1950s, superhero titles had sought to imitate horror thanks to its tremendous success; horror comics of the 1970s, conversely, absorbed characteristics of the then-popular superhero genre. When Marvel returned to the horror genre, then, unlike Warren they did so accustomed to creating stories that ran over several instalments and with emotionally complex recurring characters who belonged to a larger, interconnected universe. The lengthening of arcs necessitated recognizable characters, such as the titular hero of *Frankenstein's Monster* (1973–1975), Jack Russell, the werewolf protagonist of *Werewolf by Night* (1972–1979), and descendent of Dracula turned vampire-hunter, Frank Drake in *Tomb of Dracula* (1972–1979). These characters were part of a larger shared universe – in order to find every appearance of a character, readers had to purchase multiple stories spread across various titles. *Marvel Team-Up* #36–37 (1975), for example, had Frankenstein's monster fighting alongside Man-Wolf and Spider-Man. Multiple appearances in a shared universe, as well as a strategy to drive consumption, also attest to the fact that horror could erupt anywhere; appearances outside their host publication could also mean slippages in art and narrative style that introduce or tease out new layers of meaning from existing characters, as could the juxtaposition between a horror character and, as in the example above, Spider-Man (though on reflection, a man-spider hybrid is body horror at its best, something the series often plays with). Serial narratives and emotional complexity might not have been solely derived from the training of the creative team in superhero narratives: the shared universe of Universal horror films of the 1940s could be read as instalments in a narrative centred on Larry Talbot, the Wolf Man, who regards his werewolfism as a curse and, in each of the films, seeks a cure or an end to his suffering.

The comics detailed above did not represent a complete return of the horror genre, but publishers found creative ways to circumvent what remained of the Code. The representation of zombies in comics, for example, was still subject to Comics Code restrictions; even though the revisions to the Code of 1971 made a space for the return of the undead, they (along with vampires, werewolves, and so on) had to be treated in a way that corresponded with established literary conventions. Nonetheless, *Tales of the Zombie*, a black and white magazine, appeared without CCA approval. When 'zombies' appeared in *Strange Tales*, which was published subject to Code approval, Marvel used the term 'zuvembies' instead. Zuvembies was derived from a Robert E. Howard story, 'Pigeons from Hell', which was published in *Weird Tales*

(May, 1938) and drew on tropes of Louisiana voodoo and the historic home of the zombie in the Caribbean for narrative content and affect.[65] This background in the pulps provided sufficient literary justification for the Comics Code Authority, though it did get rather confusing for readers: as narratives shifted between Code-approved and unapproved publications, the walking dead had different labels attached to them.

The following three chapters examine the horror comics of the 1960s to the mid-1970s. Many things had changed from the pre-Code era; the wave of 1950s optimism, as encoded in white middle-class movement to the suburbs and rising standards of living for those white enough and rich enough to access them, had broken and was replaced by divisions over the Vietnam War, Civil Rights campaigns, and women's liberation, all of which challenged the simplistic narratives of American triumphalism that had previously characterized mainstream discourse. Horror comics continued to revolve around themes of trauma, gender, and race, but the space in which those debates occurred had changed. The following chapter examines the portrayal of war in horror comics, documenting the ways in which the horror genre worked through the violence of Vietnam. As an evolution of the genre, many of the comics suggest scenarios in which trauma occurs through, as well as to, white male bodies. The genre nonetheless offers something of a redemption for white male protagonists, constructing them as figures of sympathy, despite their capacity for violence. Such narrative strategies subsequently play out through the Vietnam films of the 1970s and 1980s, drawing more attention to the suffering of white male minds and bodies than those people of colour who were disproportionately deployed in the most dangerous areas and assignments, or even of the people of Vietnam and the surrounding nations who were dragged into the conflict.

Chapter 6 examines the representation of gender, arguing that while horror comics absorbed some of the language and ideals of the feminist movement, they continued to show women as wielding unsanctioned power. The genre continued to undermine female agency through sexualization, introducing the trope of the idealized girlfriend. The seventh chapter concerns the representation of race. In it, we seek to show that, as with the representation of gender, horror comics acknowledged contemporary debates around race while representing the rhetoric of civil rights in a manner that made no requirement for white America to change. Fear, we argue, continued to remain the exclusive property of white men. Women and people of colour continued to serve as an ever-encroaching source of fear, symptomatic of conflicts at home that sought to decentre white male privilege. New attitudes to old fears therefore permeated the horror comics industry of the 1970s.

## Notes

1 Don Glut (w) and Dick Piscopo (a), 'Queen of Horror', *Vampirella* #2 (New York: Warren Publishing, 1969), 31–39.

2 Hill, 'The Face of Horror', in Silver and Ursini (eds), *Horror Film Reader*, 51–61.

3 Ray Bradbury remarks in a documentary that 'I wouldn't be the kind of writer I am today without the early horror films, especially those of Universal'. *Universal Horror* (1998), dir. Kevin Brownlow.

4 David Roach and Jon B. Cooke, *The Warren Companion: The Definitive Compendium to the Great Comics of Warren Publishing* (Raleigh, NC: TwoMorrows Publishing, 2001), 22.

5 Skal, *The Monster Show*, 271

6 Quoted in Skal, *The Monster Show*, 273

7 For more on this see Dennis L. Prince and Andrew P. Yanchus, *Aurora Monster Scenes: The Most Controversial Toys of a Generation* (Drexel Hill, PA: StarComm, 2014).

8 Frank Voltaire (w), Jack Katz (a), and Frank Giacoia (i), 'Beware Small Evils', *Nightmare* #3 (New York: Skywald Magazines, 1971).

9 From the Code of the Comics Magazine Association of America, reprinted in Nyberg, *Seal of Approval*, 172.

10 See Susan J. Napier, 'Panic Sites: The Japanese Imagination of Disaster from Godzilla to Akira', *Journal of Japanese Studies* 19.2 (Summer, 1993), 327–351

11 Mark I. West, *The Japanification of Children's Popular Culture: From Godzilla to Miyazaki* (Lanham, MD: Scarecrow Press, 2009), 2.

12 Sharon Diane King, 'The Apocalypse Will Not Take Place', in Leisa A. Clark, Amanda Firestone, and Mary F. Pharr (eds), *The Last Midnight: Essays on Apocalyptic Narratives in Millennial Media* (Jefferson, NC: McFarland, 2016), 165–173 (172).

13 Yezbick, 'Horror', in Booker (ed.), *Comics Through Time*, 624.

14 For more on the deal between Hammer and Universal, see Vincent L. Barnett, 'Hammering Out a Deal: The Contractual and Commercial Contexts of *The Curse of Frankenstein* (1957) and *Dracula* (1958)', *Historical Journal of Film, Radio and Television* 34.2 (2014), 231–252.

15 Quoted in Heffernan, *Ghouls, Gimmicks, and Gold*, 49.

16 Indeed, if mention is being made of the horror of implication, then Hammer was preceded by the brilliantly atmospheric RKO films produced by Val Lewton in the 1940s.

17 Heffernan, *Ghouls, Gimmicks, and Gold*, 68.

18 One of these songs was read at humourless face value by presenter Paul Coates in the 1955 documentary about comics that aired as part of the series *Confidential File*.

19 My particular favourite is 'Monster Holiday' (1964), a novelty Christmas single by former Universal star Lon Chaney Jr, which reframed 'Monster Mash' and 'The Night Before Christmas'.

20  See '"I Don't Make Horror Films" says Fisher', *Kinematograph Weekly* (26 March 1959), 17, as cited in Heffernan, *Ghouls, Gimmicks, and Gold*, 50.

21  In this sense, Hammer can be seen as a continuation of many of the themes found in horror comics from a decade before such as the *Chamber of Chills* comic 'Happy Anniversary', a story told from the perspective of a wife on her tenth anniversary. She narrates the many infidelities and insults she suffered at the hands of her fiancé while walking around their beautiful suburban home, and then points out how he has been faithful throughout their marriage. The horror is in the final reveal, where she tells how she killed him on the wedding night and kept his body in the house, carrying on as if he were still alive. In an era of unprecedented concern about marriage and the American family, this story plays on a range of contemporary fears and specifically renders the home, the foundation of American society, as a horrific space. The series often explored such themes, so it is little wonder that it was cited by Dr Fredric Wertham in *Seduction of the Innocent*. Elsewhere the series features a story in which giant crabs kill a man's wife and then turn him into a crab so he can join them in eating her body; a short text story in which a man kills a werewolf only to discover it was his wife; and a story where a man turns the garden of his house into a killing ground to which he invites people, before he is ultimately killed by the reanimated corpses of those he sent to their death. Two of these stories are about couples being broken up through monstrous means, and 'Garden of Horror' suggests the threats that lurk in the apparently tamed spaces of suburban greenery – or, more obliquely, the horrifyingly banal labour of teenagers in tending to those spaces at the behest of their parents, or in order to raise some money to buy comics and watch films. *The Curse of Frankenstein* and the wave of films that followed cashed in on this, but comics had already shown the way.

22  Quoted in Phillips, *Projected Fears*, 62.

23  Phillips, *Projected Fears*, 64

24  Phillips, *Projected Fears*, 80.

25  Hill, 'The Face of Horror', in Silver and Ursini (eds), *Horror Film Reader*, 58.

26  Robin T. Reid, 'The History of the Drive-In Movie Theater', *Smithsonian Magazine* (27 May 2008), retrieved from www.smithsonianmag.com/arts-cul ture/the-history-of-the-drive-in-movie-theater-51331221/ (accessed 4 December 2018).

27  We can see a similar journey in the critical reception of *Peeping Tom* (1960), dir. Michael Powell, which seriously damaged Powell's career and is now regarded rather more favourably. He now has a building named after him at Canterbury Christ Church University.

28  Skal, *The Monster Show*, 294.

29  Jon Towlson, 'Why *Night of the Living Dead* Was a Big-Band Moment for Horror Movies', *BFI* (29 October 2018), retrieved from www.bfi.org.uk/news- opinion/news-bfi/features/night-living-dead-george-romero (accessed 8 March 2019).

30  Reynolds Humphreys, *The American Horror Film: An Introduction* (Edinburgh: Edinburgh University Press, 2002); Phillips, *Projected Fears*, 83.

31  Hill, 'The Face of Horror', in Silver and Ursini (eds), *Horror Film Reader*, 57.

32  Wood, 'Neglected Nightmares', in Silver and Ursini (eds), *Horror Film Reader*, 111–127. We discuss depictions of the Mỹ Lai massacre in horror comics in the next chapter.

33  Phillips, *Projected Fears*, 106.

34  Darryl Jones, *Horror: A Thematic History in Fiction and Film* (London: Arnold Publishers, 2002).

35  Linnie Blake, *The Wounds of Nations: Horror Cinema, Historical Trauma, and National Identity* (Manchester: Manchester University Press, 2008), 12.

36  Its taboo status was such that, when it was finally released on home video in the UK, my friends and I (Mitch) took advantage of the fact that one of us had an older brother, and made him rent it for us.

37  Phillips, *Projected Fears*, 105.

38  John Stickney, 'Four Doors to the Future: Gothic Rock Is Their Thing', *The Williams Record* (24 October 1967).

39  Simon Reynolds, *Rip It Up and Start Again: Postpunk 1978–1984* (London: Faber and Faber, 2005), n.p.

40  Bauhaus continued to mine Gothic imagery and horror history throughout their career, with their name directing fans back to the 1920s and 1930s and the first flowering of horror cinema. Perhaps more unconventionally, their track 'Party of the First Part' (1982) is an unsettlingly repetitive score to an animated Halloween special of 1978, *The Devil and Daniel Mouse*, itself an adaptation of 'The Devil and Daniel Webster', a short story by Stephen Vincent Benét. White Zombie, formed in 1985, took a similar approach, borrowing their name from the 1932 film starring Bela Lugosi and also incorporating samples of dialogue from films in their songs.

41  The reach of the series into horror comics is indicated by an advert for a poster of Barnabas, the vampire star of the series, in *Psycho* #1 (New York: Skywald Publications, 1971).

42  Rick Worland, 'Dark Shadows 1970: Industry, Anxiety, and Adaptation', *Journal of Popular Film and Television* 40.4 (2012), 169–180 (171). For more on *Dark Shadows*, see Harry M. Benshoff, *Dark Shadows* (Detroit, MI: Wayne State University Press, 2011).

43  Worland, 'Dark Shadows 1970', 176.

44  The allure of the Gothic certainly persists for the authors.

45  Yezbick, 'Horror', in Booker (ed.), *Comics Through Time*, 624.

46  Sennitt, *Ghastly Terror!*, 64.

47  Sennitt, *Ghastly Terror!*, 64

48  Richard J. Arndt, *Horror Comics in Black and White: A History and Catalogue, 1964–2004* (Jefferson, NC: McFarland, 2013), 17. Morrow worked on one of the early black and white horror comic/magazines, *Eerie Tales* (which ran for one issue in 1959, and may well have been the second issue of another series that only made it to one issue in 1959, *Weird Mysteries*).

49  Arndt, *Horror Comics*, 14.

50  Wandtke, *The Comics Scare Returns*, 56.

51  The stable of creators from EC lasted until *Creepy* #18 (1968), when, following proposed wage cuts from Warren, Angelo Torres, Joe Orlando, Gray Morrow, Steve Ditko, Frank Frazetta, Reed Crandall, Neal Adams, Alex Toth, Al Williamson, and Archie Goodwin all ceased to submit work. They were replaced by newcomers such as Ron White and Spanish artists such as Sanjulian and José M. Bea, who began to draw for Warren following a deal with José Toutan Publishing. Some of the EC veterans eventually returned, but by the late 1960s Warren Publications was a resurrection of EC's horror work more in spirit than in personnel.

52  Sennitt, *Ghastly Terror!*, 123.

53  These magazines featured stories that also had something of the horror comic in their lineage. Like horror comics, they included short prose fiction. Forest J. Ackerman, the editor of *Famous Monsters*, reports that he received a story submission from then fourteen-year-old Stephen King of Maine, who was 'basically lifting story ideas from old copies of E.C. comics', quoted in Skal, *The Monster Show*, 271.

54  John Jackson Miller, '*Vampirella* Sales Figures', *Comichron.com* (n.d.), retrieved from www.comichron.com/titlespotlights/vampirella.html (accessed 26 May 2020).

55  John Jackson Miller, '*Amazing Spider-Man* Sales Figures', *Chomichron.com* (n.d.), retrieved from www.comichron.com/titlespotlights/amazingspiderman.html (accessed 26 May 2020).

56  Jane Church, 'Whatever Turns You On', *Vampirella* #4 (New York: Warren Publishing, 1970), 5.

57  Gary Friedrich (w), Mike Ploog (a), John Verpoorten (i), Artie Simek (l), and Glynis Wien (c), *Monster of Frankenstein* #5 (New York: Marvel, 1973), 1. While in no way Gothic, CCR tracks often included topical references and they played at Woodstock in 1969, giving them counter-cultural capital.

58  Nyberg, *Seal of Approval*, 142.

59  Weldon, *The Caped Crusade*, 105.

60  Weldon, *The Caped Crusade*, 104.

61  1971 Code, reproduced in Nyberg, *Seal of Approval*, 172.

62  1954 Code, reproduced in Nyberg, *Seal of Approval*, 167.

63  Olga M. Davidson and Ferdowsi, 'The Text of Ferdowsi's Shahnama and the Burden of the Past', *Journal of the American Oriental Society* 118.1 (1998), 63–68 (64). I (Mitch) am indebted to Mara Keire for an enlightening conversation on this topic.

64  Film also engaged in practices of nostalgic restaging in 1971. *Dracula vs. Frankenstein* (1971) harks back to the Universal shared universe of the 1940s and features veterans of those films, Lon Chaney Jr and J. Carrol Naish, and attempts to update their appeal through the introduction of a more graphic sexual element, as seen in the strapline, 'Yesterday they were cold and dead – today they're hot and bothered!'

65 Howard was a writer already very familiar to Marvel through their adaptations of his most famous character, Conan of Cimmeria; *Conan the Barbarian* began its run in 1970, so Howard was a very current concern for Marvel. 'Pigeons from Hell' is an excellent example of Southern Gothic and is freely available online from a number of different sources.

# 5

## 'The war has done strange things to you' – trauma in the 1960s and 1970s

As medic, Rat Kiley carried a canvas satchel filled with morphine and plasma and malaria tablets and surgical tape and comic books. (Tim O'Brien, *The Things They Carried*, 1990)

America was both a source and subject of traumatic violence in the 1960s and 1970s. The violence of these decades was such that Adam Lowenstein positions contemporary discourse as indicative of a nation verging on 'tearing itself in half' over a series of increasingly polarized and contested divisions.[1] The prime mover in much of this was the war in Vietnam. In the spring of 1965, the US escalated its military intervention in the civil war. This was not the first war experienced by the generation who came of age after the Second World War; between 1945 and 1965, the US dispatched troops to Korea, Lebanon, and Santo Domingo. The threat of war with the Soviet Union, too, had loomed since the end of the Second World War. War, then, was never too distant from public consciousness, but the Vietnam War was nonetheless an unprecedented development in American military history in both its nature and the public reaction it provoked. The re-emergence of the horror genre occurred at a time when, once again, the figure of the veteran loomed large in America's social and political landscape.

Horror comics of this era obliquely engage with the war in Vietnam and the political turmoil at home. While horror comics often appear to express distrust in the state, however, this does not necessarily mean that they express unambiguous support for feminism, civil rights, LGBT issues, or other left-leaning elements of the counter-culture. Instead they offer token appearances by, and gestures of sympathy and support towards, women and people of colour while remaining fundamentally invested in preserving existing networks of property and privilege. Horror comics in this sense remain apolitical, either keeping the war at a distance or offering equal condemnation to both the state and those who oppose it. The one overtly political horror sub-genre, the megamonster, leans heavily to the right, playing out a series of fantasy scenarios wherein, rather than deploying nuclear weapons as an aggressor, the US engages in justified retaliation against a foreign nuclear threat. This genre reimagines nuclear war so as to celebrate the primacy of an erstwhile white male hegemony.[2] Elsewhere, we find examples of comics that seem to acknowledge the violence performed by white American men on behalf of the state, and the first sustained depiction of such men as monsters. This occurs alongside the simultaneous turn towards longer episodic narratives, which explore the experience of monsterdom and offer paths to redemption. While these narratives ostensibly reverse previous trends of white male victimhood, they nonetheless suggest that, as we have seen in previous chapters, white men are made subject to circumstances beyond their control. White male fear is again presented as a response to the perceived inability of the hegemony to exert untrammelled control over people and places.

The central event in shaping the horror genre during this decade was the American intervention in Vietnam. American troops were present in Vietnam in large numbers from 1965 to 1975. Over that period, 2.5 million American GIs served in Vietnam, one third of whom were drafted. One in ten were wounded or killed and in total, 58,214 American soldiers never returned home. Vietnam was a divisive war. While many Americans at least initially believed that military intervention was necessary to prevent the spread of communism in Southeast Asia, others argued that the US was supporting a corrupt regime, that the war was unconstitutional, and that Vietnamese civilians were paying the cost of Cold War geopolitical strategies. The anti-war cause was taken up by various branches of the counter-culture movement of the 1960s and 1970s. Just two weeks after American soldiers first arrived in Denang, the University of Michigan hosted an all-night debate featuring professors and 3,000 students. This was the first of a series of teach-ins and protests on university campuses that only grew in intensity as the war continued. In 1965, 25,000 people, many of them students and professors, gathered in Washington to protest against the war. In October 1967, their number grew to 35,000.[3]

The anti-war movement was further fuelled by media coverage. The conflict in Vietnam has been popularly referred to as the first 'living room' war, where images of military operations and their effects appeared directly on televisions in American households.[4] Lowenstein, drawing on the work on Daniel C. Hallin, makes it clear that the footage that reached audiences was still curated by the Nixon administration. This led to audiences seeing the war as an error and a tragedy, but not a crime, as its more radical opponents alleged.[5] Early in the conflict, reporters tended to follow the state narrative, emphasizing national security and the necessity of military intervention to prevent the spread of communism. Even from the beginning, however, reporters also documented the costs of war. In 1965, CBS showed footage of American soldiers burning a Vietnamese village, shocking many viewers at home. This was the first of many such broadcasts. The Tet Offensive of 1968, when the North Vietnamese forces made a coordinated attack on multiple cities in the South, disproved General Westmoreland's assertions of 1967 that victory was just around the corner. It also made clear that his statement that the Vietnamese were incapable of mounting large-scale operations was based on prejudice rather than reality. After this moment, reporters overwhelmingly focused on the violence and the cost of war including, in November of 1969, reports of American soldiers having murdered 400 civilians in the town of Mỹ Lai. The rising tension between journalists and the state exacerbated an already sizeable anti-war movement and, in 1969, 250,000 protestors came to Washington to oppose the war.

As the war continued and its underpinning narrative crumbled, a growing number of Americans began to question their faith not only in the justification of the war but in the state and its grand project of intervention overseas. As with the return of the repressed past in Gothic fiction, the present was beset by the past as the attention of historians turned back to the Spanish-American War of 1898 (as it was then known) as a means of addressing the contemporary situation in Vietnam. The conventional notion of the war being fought on humanitarian grounds was attacked by Philip S. Foner's assertion that 'the Spanish-American War was indeed an imperialist war'.[6] By 1969, then, according to Matthew J. Costello, 'the enemy was no longer an external entity threatening American security, but the internal problems besetting the richest society in the world'.[7]

The Watergate scandal, which ended with President Nixon resigning from office, was in some ways the culmination of the erosion of ideological investment in a government that was already crumbling following American failures internationally, in Vietnam, and domestically, in relation to the Civil Rights movement, the women's movement, and the LGBT movement. The visual representation of this was John Filo's Pulitzer Prize-winning photograph of a horror-struck Mary Vecchio standing by a dead body at the Kent State University shooting of 4 May, 1970. The use of fatal violence by the Ohio National Guard against student protestors attested not only to the unbridgeable divisions in American society, but also the extent to which the use of violence by the state upon citizens, already established as an official practice through responses to the Civil Rights movement and LGBT protests such as the Stonewall riots of 1969, had become normalized as a method of containment.

Ian Tyrrell characterizes the US of the early 1970s as 'a beleaguered nation' with 'strong impulses to turn inward'.[8] The war, compounded by the reckoning over race relations brought about by the Civil Rights movement, and the crisis of confidence in the political system precipitated by the Watergate scandal, caused a permanent shift in the relationship between American citizens, regardless of their political affiliation, and the state. Narratives of the time communicate a confusion over national identity and the future of the nation. There seemed to be no peaceful option; the state had shown its willingness to use violence, but so too had those who opposed the state. In some cases, this violence was more rhetorical than actual; the Black Panthers, for example, used the threat of violence, if not the practice, in their rhetoric of resistance. In other cases, however, forces on the political left used terrorism to further their goals. Organized across lines of race and gender, but united by a common interest in communism, the Weather Underground sought to use violence to challenge what they saw as the greater violence being enacted by the American military. In their own words, 'the main struggle going on in the world today is between US imperialism and the national liberation struggles against it'.[9] The Weathermen advocated bloody revolution, decrying the inability of non-violent protest to enact significant change. Similar rhetoric appeared in superhero comics through the character Firebrand, who stated in 1970 that 'this country doesn't want to be changed! The only way to build anything decent is to tear down what's here and start over'.[10] After the death of several leading Weathermen in 1970 in an accidental explosion, the organization shifted to symbolic acts of violence, most notably the repeated destruction of a monument to the police killed in the 1886 Haymarket bombing in Chicago.[11] The monument to fallen police officers, in the eyes of the Weather Underground, paid tribute to a history of state violence against workers. They believed that the American government depended on violence to sustain itself; the domestication of violence during Vietnam was not a new development, in other words, just another slippage of the mask. The violence practised on both sides of the political spectrum led to a sense of escalating conflict and a vanishing middle-ground.

The major success of the horror genre in the 1970s, and horror film in particular, was its ability to mediate the tensions of the time. Lowenstein contends that horror film in this period blurred 'the distinctions between the counterculture and the bourgeois family [resulting] in a complex and disturbing depiction of violence's relation to the social', which, in the process, refused any escapist project.[12] American horror cinema of the 1970s gazed into the abyss and dramatized what it saw. In his investigation of this development, Noël Carroll notes the political acuity, commercial success, and lasting impact of the film cycle that began in the 1970s, coincident with these struggles over American identity and prestige. Carroll remarks that film has 'remained so obsessed with horror since the box office triumph of *The Exorcist* that it is difficult to visit your local multiplex theatre without meeting at least one monster', a trend that only seems to have accelerated throughout the three decades since Carroll wrote those words.[13]

The late 1960s and 1970s, broadly speaking, gave us the kind of horror that we recognise today. The horror films of the 1970s spawned sequels and their continuing popularity has driven the creation of new monsters in the decades that followed. This can partly be seen as an instance of, fittingly, capitalism eating itself. The long, drawn-out wars of Vietnam and later the Gulf Wars and the conflicts they have spawned also offer clear parallels, with horror images of violence received and dealt out by Americans through the later twentieth century and beyond; horror is a capitalist enterprise, but it is also well-suited to political critique. Similarly, arguments around rights for, and representation of women, people of colour, and LGBT communities are prominent in both 1970s film and in popular culture at the time of writing.[14] Ultimately, the fascination with the films of the 1970s can also be read as a fascination with the decade, with the monsters that lurk in the shadows of Vietnam and the broader political malaise around the war, the political crisis of Watergate, and the failure of domestic reform programmes initiated by President Johnson in the 1960s. A simplistic but nonetheless accurate reading of horror cinema during this period argues that the violence that appeared on American televisions each evening informed the excessively bloody horror films that appeared in cinemas during the 1960s and 1970s.

Horror was also taken up in comics. Rather than directly mimicking contemporary horror cinema, however, many mainstream horror comics turned towards episodic storylines and, in accordance with the expanded CCA rules, evocation of the Gothic – an outdated but nonetheless prescient sub-genre. Skal describes the genre as follows; '[o]ut of those things we believed we had left behind comes some thing to haunt our present and remind us that our confidence in our knowledge of the world is unfounded. Out of this distant past comes the chaos and savagery that we believed ourselves beyond'.[15] Such generic conventions, while less overtly political than the violent cinema of the time, seemed obliquely fitting for a nation that was reckoning not only with the state-sponsored actions of its citizens overseas, but with an ugly past of racial and sexual discrimination. As Wandtke asserts, Marvel's ongoing horror stories 'suggest that genuine horror doesn't end at dawn; instead they argue that the terror of America as a post-industrial superpower may be never-ending'.[16] It was an era when American history as remembered by the oppressed began to surface, and where new revelations as to the truth of warfare invited a reassessment of the past.

## The nation in crisis

As established in Chapter 1, horror comics of the 1950s describe a nation unwittingly in crisis as it failed to resolve the traumatic social upheavals of the Second World War. These same themes were resonant during the 1970s, to the point that we find 1950s horror comics repurposed to reflect the Vietnam era. *Psycho* #1 (1971), for example, features a reprint of 'The Thing in the Mirror', which originally appeared in *Phantom Witch Doctor* #1 (1952).[17] The choice to reprint this story involves a conscious selection from the material available; despite the story being twenty years old, its reproduction in the context of 1971 serves as an invitation to read the story afresh. As Cynthia Erb asserts, 'the production of textual meanings is shaped by contextual factors'.[18] The story centres on James Crawford, an orphan adopted by a wealthy couple. Crawford is handsome, young, and talented, but refuses to 'play fair' in any enterprise. At nineteen, his adoptive parents are killed in a plane crash, and Crawford inherits their estate. At twenty-five, Crawford sees Barbara, the girl he wants to marry. Unfortunately for him, she is engaged to George Dana, an older, less attractive man, albeit one deemed to be an 'electrical genius' by his scientific co-workers. Crawford is unable to prise Barbara away from George through any romantic overtures. He therefore murders his rival and covers up the crime. Crawford is, however, unable to take advantage of George's absence to try to win Barbara because he is stalked by the titular 'thing'; a small green monster he sees every time he looks in a mirror. One night, Crawford decides it is time to banish the monster by confronting it directly. When he looks into the mirror, he sees both the monster and the ghost of George Dana, who taunts him about how ugly he is about to become. As Crawford's servants watch, he metamorphoses into the monster, runs out of his house, and is captured by a travelling freak show (Figure 51).[19]

Crawford's descent, where a wealthy and talented individual kills

**51** Sol Cohen (w) and Everett Raymond Kinstler (a), 'The Thing in the Mirror', *Psycho* #1

to claim for himself things he could not otherwise possess and is transformed to a freakish monster in the process, can be repositioned as a narrative of national decline. This is a particularly attractive reading given the ways in which the trauma experienced by the US over the Vietnam War and mass protests became televisual spectacle as it occurred.

Crawford's actions cause his transformation from an outwardly attractive, though inwardly repellent man, to a diminutive abomination. His decline is then staged for the public through a freakshow. On viewing 'the gibbering thing', as Crawford is now known, a word balloon with its origin outside the panel states that 'you'd swear it was trying to communicate something!' This line can be read as both inside and outside the narrative – the 'gibbering' is Crawford's attempt to communicate, and also the moral that the story seeks to express. This moral could be as simple as the 'boomerang' morality of horror comics wherein actions projected by an individual return to hurt them, reinforcing the status quo and policing conventional morality in the process. Alternatively, the shift from an attractive exterior, coupled with wealth, to a monstrous exterior, with severely reduced stature, can be read as a commentary on the contemporary standing of the US.

When 'The Thing in the Mirror' was first published in 1952, cultural imperialism was a significant arm of American Cold War policy.[20] When it was reprinted, Civil Rights protests, student protests, and women's rights protests, or more precisely the violence meted out against them, disrupted the appeal of the US as a domestic space; the Vietnam War and its international representation via television and photography exacerbated that damage, diminishing the cultural appeal of the US in the process. The connection between the freak show and the news cycle has been discussed by Gary Hoppenstand, who makes the case that, like the news, 'the grotesquery of the circus freak is not mitigated by the audience's understanding of the fundamental difference between story and fact'.[21] The image of the US, for many (but by no means all), metamorphosed from statuesque and attractive to stunted and malformed as the result of violent interventions at home and abroad. The cultural performance morphed from the powerful appeal of 1950s American culture, with its concomitant meanings of democracy and affluence, to the confusion and malaise of the 1970s. From peak show to freak show, as it were.

Another commentary on the trauma embedded in contemporary American life manifests in 'I Am Dead: I Am Buried' in *Nightmare* #12 (1973).[22] It begins in 1931 with Ed Warton trying to escape from a brutal prison in Arkansas, which is surrounded by a cypress swamp. Warton is captured in the swamp and returned to the prison, where he is whipped and thrown into a pit, where he dies. When the guards come to check on him two days later, Warton's corpse, reanimated by the desire for freedom, kills the guards and walks into the swamp, where he wanders for days. At this point, the story cuts to the writer, sat in a café, wondering how to finally kill off the character. When he resolves to leave him wandering the swamp forever, Warton breaks the fourth wall and attacks the writer. A child reader at a newsstand, reading about Warton attacking the writer, then posits a solution that is unsatisfactory to Warton – so he bursts through the page to attack the child, bringing the writer with him, attesting to the ways in which past trauma can erupt within the present, and how fiction can play a part in that. The action then returns to the discovery of Warton's corpse in the prison pit; this time, the dead bodies of the boy and the writer are with him. Walking away, one guard orders the other to bury the bodies, providing a sense of closure, but not the freedom desired by Warton, therefore leaving the trauma open and unresolved.

In this narrative, the restless corpse desirous of freedom suggests historical injustice – the lingering presence of historical trauma in the present. The choice of date, 1931, might therefore be incidental or (though none of the characters are black), it might refer back to the arrest of the Scottsboro Boys, nine young African American men who were arrested in Alabama in 1931 for the alleged rape of two young white women.[23] Dan Carter's book on Scottsboro was first published in 1969 and interest in the case proved sufficiently enduring that a television documentary aired in 1976. As discussed in earlier chapters, the theme of the monster created by the artists in the comics coming alive to torment their creator was well established; this trope was expanded here, though, by including the reader both inside and outside the text. The final lines of the story state that 'since you entered here too ... that means you too are dead', showing that both the offered image of the reader and the actual reader are implicated in this exposure to trauma. One potential reading of this is that all Americans are imprisoned by the history of the nation, the walls of which 'are alive and grip and grab' them as they move around, whether consciously or not, within this prison.[24] The writer, who has created this narrative world, is powerless to control it; the child reader, while adopting a critical stance towards the narrative, does not offer solutions agreeable to Warton, its victim. The story suggests that, for all the textual interventions and the adoption of appropriate stances, Americans remain bound together by a shared history of violence. Whether they have been victims, active participants, or bystanders, the traumatic legacies of national violence are inescapable. Neither of the 'solutions' offered in the present effect change; they both leave Warton wandering the swamp, locked in his own trauma. His perpetual imprisonment, though, means closure for the writer and reader; in short, struggle is acknowledged, but not acted upon. To move beyond the historical trauma embedded in this narrative, the narrative has to be changed.

There is, however, no desire for change on the part of what, following Althusser, we might term the Repressive State Apparatus. Althusser distinguishes between the Repressive State Apparatus, a singular construction that functions by violence in the public domain, and Ideological State Apparatuses, which are multiple and largely private.[25] 'I Am Dead: I Am Buried' engages with both, dramatizing the attempts of the penal system to literally bury dissent through its treatment of Warton. In terms of Ideological State Apparatuses, through its metatextual treatment of the writer and reader of the text, and Warton's attempts not to be buried, the narrative shows how culture can work to inculcate an acceptance of both historical injustice, and the traumatic legacies for those subject to it; it also, however, represents the same texts as capable of mounting critiques of that system, encouraging readers to follow Warton and contest the confining structures with which they are presented. To seek freedom rather than burial. The narrative tries to reincorporate this more radical reading by subjecting the body of the reader, both diegetically and non-diegetically, to violence.

## Political (non-)engagement

Horror comics of the 1970s, as with horror comics of the 1950s, attested to a society in crisis. While comics of this era seemed to mediate a general spirit of social conflict, they faced something of a crisis regarding direct representation of Vietnam. The war was too large a part of the ambient culture to be ignored, and yet it was too politically divisive, its violence too visceral, to be contained in the traditional confines of a thirty-page story that had to conform to the prohibitions of the CCA. Comics readers, many of whom were students, often wanted to engage in debate around the war; figures such as Spider-Man and the Incredible Hulk were adopted as icons of the anti-war movement and comics letters pages often played host to debates concerning the morality of war and the danger of communism. Despite this, the comics and editors of Marvel and DC tended to avoid the topic. Superman had a brief storyline set in Vietnam (in *Superman* #216, 1969),[26] Captain America visited the country only twice during the war and once in 1963, before the escalation that followed the Gulf of Tonkin. Iron Man found his beginning there. None of these storylines offered the same patriotic fervour for war as the superhero stories of the Second World War, and instead of showing the characters engaged in combat, focused on less partisan issues such as the rescue of captured American soldiers. In his analysis of letters pages in superhero comics during the war, Michael Goodrum concludes that editors tended to avoid direct discussion of Vietnam. They espoused a philosophy that discouraged partisanship, was broadly liberal, and expressed faith in America's capacity to fix its own problems, suggesting that no fundamental change in the status quo was desirable or necessary. In 1969, Stan Lee responded to one letter-writer as follows: 'maybe every party will have to give in a little to get a little', suggesting that, Goodrum states, '[t]he main source of political engagement was therefore coming from readers, not writers, editors and artists'.[27]

The politics of the companies changed behind the scenes during the 1960s, even if the editorial policy did not (indeed, under the terms of the CCA, could not). During the late 1960s, many of the writers and artistic staff at Marvel were augmented by younger creators with more progressive views; if the old guard were not all replaced, they were at least joined by, and ultimately outnumbered by, newer recruits. Dennis O'Neil, who was hired to write for Marvel in 1965, describes himself as a 'rebel, hippie, peacenik kind of guy'.[28] Until the late 1960s, the perception among many fans was that 'DC writers were old farts, hopelessly out of touch with the youth culture that Marvel embraced'.[29] These older writers at DC were subject to a mass-firing in 1968 when they campaigned for health insurance – when they, in other words, embraced the protest culture from which they were apparently so distant. They were replaced overnight by 'fresh young writers with a modern sensibility'.[30] While the editorial policy of Marvel and DC remained steadfastly apolitical (or, when comment was unavoidable, as centrist as possible), the politics of its staff were evident in, for example, the use of a Peace symbol on the cover of *Sgt Fury and His Howling Commandos* #64 in 1969, and changing character appearances to reflect youth culture.[31]

In comparison with Marvel and DC, Warren Publishing was far more vocal concerning the war. The seventh issue of *Vampirella* begins with an open letter from James Warren to the President and Congress, asserting that 'the Viet Nam war is not only hell, its absolute insanity for your country'.[32] Warren asserts that his company has consistently printed controversial material because they believe it to be right. As evidence, he cites *Blazing Combat Magazine*, a short-lived publication that sought to depict the true horrors of war. The magazine, he reports, received so many complaints that it became economically unsustainable. His commitment to the anti-war movement remained, however: '[W]e are angry with you adults, Mr. President and Members of Congress'. He asserts, 'You adults have let this drag on for half our lives. We've tried to tell you this at our demonstrations. We tried to tell you at Kent State. Were you listening?'[33] Despite the strong editorial stance, however, the magazine does not include any stories that explicitly engage with the war and the letters pages continued to print commentary on the comics with no mention of world events. It seems as if comic reading itself was assumed to stand in for a counter-cultural position in Warren's editorial, meaning that the stories did not have to undertake explicit critique.

Actual commentary on Vietnam, then, is oblique. In part, the politics of the time appear in the narratives as a general distrust of authority that ran throughout comics of the era in all genres. Despite the edicts of the CCA, the protagonists of horror comics often found themselves at odds with the state. The November 1972 issue of *Werewolf by Night*, for example, opens with the comic's protagonist, Jack Russell, in werewolf form, being pursued by the police.[34] The culture of protests, too, bled into horror comics; the same issue of *Werewolf by Night*, for example, takes place against the backdrop of a rally against 'United Fruit Growers Association', led by an academic and populated mainly by college students. The name seems a clear reference to 'United Fruit', which had become 'United Brands' in 1970, and was accused by several governments of host nations throughout South America of undertaking neo-colonial practices. For instance, United Fruit had lobbied the

Eisenhower administration in 1954 to take action against Jacobo Arbenz Guzman, the democratically elected leader of Guatemala, because his administration proposed to introduce land reforms and new codes to govern labour.[35] So soon after the deaths at Kent State in 1970, and with the violence of the 1960s protests still a recent memory, protest as a backdrop for a werewolf narrative constructs resistance to government and capitalist authority as a space of horror, just as the werewolf erupting from within Jack Russell attests to the savagery that lies inside American men.

Protests against United Fruit also suggest a broader affinity with protest cultures of the 1960s, extending beyond the US to labour agitation against exploitative neo-colonial practices of the 1950s and 1960s – to economic, as well as physical, violence. *Werewolf by Night* therefore demonstrates its creative team's awareness of contemporary geopolitical struggle, of the multitude of forms American violence could take. It also hints at less overt forms of critique than those offered by Firebrand, with the crucial difference being that Russell has reader sympathy, while Firebrand, at least in preferred narrative terms, loses and never commands that support. *Werewolf by Night* nonetheless continues to centre its narratives around a white heterosexual male protagonist, thus simultaneously engaging in indirect critique of the state while positioning its beneficiary in (somewhat tepid) opposition to such changes. The actions of politically and financially powerful white men, in other words, may be the problem but, Marvel assures its white heterosexual male readers, they are also the solution. We can understand this unresolved tension in terms of 'urbanoia', or the conflict between representatives of prosperous and poor spaces, as propounded by Carol J. Clover. Clover positions 'economic guilt' as a key driver of much of horror cinema.[36] Here, prosperity based on exploitation makes the protest both possible and necessary. Whereas Clover's discussion of urbanoia focuses on a town/country split, or north/south, it is possible to extrapolate from this to Global North/Global South (a problematic label but one that gives a sense of the argument deployed here), exposing the guilt and attendant anxiety in the exploitative neo-colonial relationships forged by the US in the name of anti-colonialism. While the comic attests to such guilt, however, it positions its protagonist outside of these concerns.

Protagonists were overtly involved, however, in the narrative events of 'Beware Small Evils', a story in the Skywald title, *Nightmare* #3 (1971). As with the Marvel plotlines described above, 'Beware Small Evils' engages indirectly with protest culture without aligning with or endorsing its advocates.[37] Set in the year 1983, the comic addresses the environment and counter-cultural movements. It expresses a lack of faith in both sides of the political divide; politicians and scientists fail to adequately address a global crisis, but the counter-culture shares the blame for precipitating the demise of human society. In the comic, a scientist and a senator try to find a solution to the environmental crisis that facilitated the earlier partial collapse of the US. As part of this process, Spacey's Spitfires, a 'huge multi-ethnic terrorist hoodlum gang', have taken over Southern California. As the biker gang gather for the funeral of the (implied) pornographic actress, Spacey Jaglin, who gave them their name, the senator and scientist accidentally unleash a microbial experiment intended to restore the world's oxygen to acceptable levels when one of the bikers breaks into the facility, demanding to be treated for an injury. When the released microbes make contact with the chemicals in Spacey's body, however, they grow and mutate into monstrously large things and begin consuming all in their path. The senator calls Washington, ordering them to napalm the entire state of California in an attempt to save the world (Figure 52).

Although the strike is completed, the scientist suggests that the spread of spores is now such that the world only has about four days of oxygen remaining. The story ends with the scientist and his female assistant typing up a record, in case anyone should survive, while threatening the senator with a large knife: 'it's getting hard to breathe, nurse! Slash the senator's stomach open!' he commands. 'Any scientist knows – politicians are full of hot air!'[38]

**52** Frank Voltaire (w), Jack Katz (a), and Frank Giacoia (i), 'Beware Small Evils', *Nightmare* #3

No one really escapes the 'horror-mood' of this Skywald story. For Skywald:

> Horror is people and emotion and expression ... fiends, monsters, and your fear of the unknown are secondary horrors ... the real horror is you ... and the unbridled, brutal alter ego madman inside you who is capable of horrors far more evil than the world now knows ... what is horror? You are![39]

This approach is apparent in 'Beware Small Evils', which combines the horror of napalm in Vietnam – a different iteration of the chickens of American policy coming home to roost – with humankind's destruction of the environment, the self-destructive excesses of science, and the dark underside of the hippies and biker gangs. Spacey's Spitfires are a fusion of hippies and Hell's Angels, a biker gang who pollute the atmosphere yet are visually coded in some ways as hippies, commit acts of violence, and worship an actress from pornographic films. Had this been a 1950s science fiction film, the collaboration between science and the military might have saved the day and converted many of the young bikers to the cause of American society. Here, it ends the world.

This story activates a nexus of contemporary resonance. Vietnam looms large, most prominently in the image in Figure 52 of napalm being dropped from planes. The relocation of the Vietnamese struggle against American incursion to monstrous microbes that could end the world is problematic but, if considered as comparative in an ideological rather than literal sense, potentially highly instructive. Napalm might deal with the problem in the immediate locale, but it does not prevent it spreading elsewhere: the spores of ideology take to the wind, as it were. If Vietnam was meant as a war of containment, it did not work – communism in Vietnam was not defeated, and the conflict spilled over into Laos and Cambodia, destabilizing those countries and helping to bring about the exact opposite outcome to that desired by the US. The spilling over was not accidental: from 1969 to 1970, US forces undertook huge bombing campaigns in Laos and Cambodia. It was not only war that spread; opposition to it also built across the world, harming US relations with other nations, both allies and enemies. Hippies formed part of the resistance to the war, yet here, fused with biker gangs, they are presented as part of the problem, rather than the solution.

This era witnessed the breakdown of the New Left as a coherent faction. Hunter S. Thompson, writing in 1971, famously states that 'you can go up on a steep hill in Las Vegas and look West, and with the right kind of eyes you can almost see the high-water mark – that place where the wave finally broke and rolled back', ending the coherent progressive 'sense of inevitable victory over the forces of Old and Evil'.[40] Hegemonic Evil survived the counter-culture, as in 'Beware Small Evils', and the representation of the Spitfires makes it clear, in the terms of the narrative, that the counter-culture could never have triumphed. Indeed, the comic not only suggests a failure of protest culture, but a culpability in social and environmental collapse. Spacey's Spitfires draw on the Manson 'Family', a group drawn to Charles Manson, who presented as a hippie guru of sorts in the late 1960s. Manson expounded the benefits of communal living; he also prophesied a race war, after which the 'Family' would rule. Manson was not a complete outlier. He was an associate of Dennis Wilson, a member of the Beach Boys, and through him met a number of high-profile people in the entertainment industry – Manson, for instance, is listed as co-writer, with Dennis Wilson, on the 1969 Beach Boys track 'Never Learn Not to Love'. Manson therefore occupied a visible, if not prominent, position in Californian life. Throughout 1969, Manson and his followers became increasingly violent. Eventually his followers committed a series of gruesome murders. This led to their arrest in late 1969. They stood trial in 1970, and were ultimately convicted in 1971. They were initially sentenced to death, though these were commuted to life imprisonment in 1972. Associates of Manson committed more murders in 1972, meaning that the group and its legacy was still prominent at the time this story was being created. Importantly, for the bleak atmosphere of this narrative, the hippie advocacy of love and 'flower power' results in violence and the destruction of nature.

Biker gangs, most notably the Hell's Angels, were also prominent in the late 1960s. Hunter S. Thompson first made his name as a journalist with his 1967 book, *Hell's Angels: The Strange and Terrible Saga of the Outlaw Motorcycle Gangs*, which narrated his experience of a year with the gang. Thompson ended his relationship with the Hell's Angels after he was 'stomped', or badly beaten, by gang members following his criticism of a biker for beating his wife.[41] This was not an isolated incidence of violence by the gang. It was, however, the Altamont Free Concert, at which the Hell's Angels were advertised as providing security, where their violence attained national and international prominence. The event, a one-day concert featuring high-profile acts, spiralled out of control, culminating in a murder committed by one of the bikers. Many of the bands at Altamont had also been at Woodstock, the cultural pinnacle of the hippie project, and two aspects of the supposed counter-culture clashing in this way led to an apparent break in faith in its potential to reshape American society. Controversy around the Hell's Angels continued into the 1970s, with high-profile stories around the group connecting them to murder and organized crime.[42]

The description of the Spitfires as multi-ethnic also draws on continuing anxieties around race. Despite the fact that everyone depicted in the comic is white, the text promotes and dramatizes fears around the threat of expanding civil rights to existing political structures; while the Spitfires are, at least in terms of their description, multi-ethnic, all of those in positions of power – the senator, the scientist, gang leaders, Spacey Jaglin – are white. The hedonism of the hippies and Angels, evident in references to drug use and pornography, is combined to create a greater threat: an organized, mobile, and aggressive force, capable of taking and holding territory. While it is the white elite who undertake the experiment that ultimately causes the end of human civilization, it is a biker who unleashes it. 'Things fall apart, the centre cannot hold': the ideological forces set in motion by the bikers begin by stripping away racial hierarchies, and end with the destruction of life on Earth.

'Beware Small Evils' therefore mediates trauma from both domestic and international contexts. In its narrative confines, trauma erupts from both the dominant and the counter cultures, with both offering solutions to contemporary problems that ultimately unleash yet greater violence. The narrative and images suggest a society locked in a death spiral with no hope of escape. The political vision it presents is not quite as vapid as Stan Lee's pronouncement that pro- and anti-war factions should find common ground but nonetheless refuses to commit to either side. For all its apparent condemnation of the state and invocation of protest culture, the comic remains, as with *Werewolf by Night*, resoundingly apolitical and thus opposed to meaningful structural change.


### Rewriting nuclear history

Horror comics of the 1970s, then, unlike film, largely avoided direct political comment. They are evasive and, where they do engage with protest culture, are equally sceptical of the state and its critics. Their protagonists and, implicitly, the imagined reader, exist outside of and separate to political factions. In the megamonster sub-genre, however, we find a far more hawkish rhetoric, which belies the apparent sympathy expressed for protest culture found in other manifestations of the genre. As noted in the previous chapter, the megamonster can be seen as resistant to nuanced readings. We can nonetheless detect in these comics a recurring fantasy of white American supremacy, where America is reimagined as the victim of nuclear threat and external (i.e. foreign, non-white) threats are resolved through American ingenuity.

The threat of nuclear war haunts the megamonster sub-genre, trading as it does in destroyed cityscapes and existential threats. Despite their preoccupation with the possibility of nuclear destruction, and despite the more immediate manifestations of war erupting on American television screens, megamonsters came at a time of relatively low anxiety concerning nuclear war. The 1960s and 1970s were a period of détente – cooling tensions – between the US and the Soviet Union. In 1963, the US and the Soviets reached an arms control agreement following the Cuban missile crisis and the brinksmanship that had brought the prospect of nuclear conflict too close for comfort. Throughout the 1960s, the Sino-Soviet split also became increasingly apparent, reducing the perceived threat of a global communist movement directed from Moscow and working in concert against the US.[43] Communism in the American imaginary was no longer monolithic; the means of opposing and containing it had to be similarly diverse. This is not to say that causes of tension between the US and the USSR were not also alleviated through conventional means, to some extent, or that equally conventional animosities did not remain. In 1972, Richard Nixon and Leonid Brezhnev signed treaties limiting both countries' build-up of weaponry. The perceived need to contain communism – most obvious during the Vietnam War – was still apparent but had become one of several perspectives that existed within the ecosystem of American political and social discourse. The possibility of nuclear war had not evaporated, but it seemed less pressing than a decade before; anxieties over warfare largely concerned napalm, bullets, and tear gas rather than nuclear warheads. Given the US's economic slump in the 1970s, a legacy in part of the war in Vietnam, shifts in the nature of capitalist development, and economic dislocation wrought by attempting to pursue expensive programmes of social reform while also waging war, there was also a need to save money – averting an arms race while maintaining American supremacy offered a way out with dignity.

The relative distance from nuclear war allowed space for previous narratives of the use of the bomb to be rewritten with America as victim. Where American science is unambiguously responsible for birthing a monster – such as *Godzilla*, 'Beware Small Evils', and the various narratives described in the first chapter of this volume – megamonsters are presented as external threats that are resolved through American intervention. A sample of four issues of *Strange Tales* can serve as an illustrative example.[44] The eponymous Colossus from 'I Fought the Colossus' that ran in *Strange Tales* #72 (1959) is the creation of a super-computer (and, it transpires, no threat to man). The giant ant Grottu, King of the Insects, which featured in the next issue, was the result of Soviet nuclear tests and both Gorgolla and Taboo, from issues 74 and 75 respectively, belong to a race of aliens. While the US bears no responsibility for creating such monsters, these threats are invariably resolved through American scientific and military-industrial ingenuity – a computer engineer arranges for Colossus to fall into the sea, for example, and an American explorer buries Grottu in sugar. Rather than causing the creation of Taboo, the American-built H-Bomb leads to his destruction – Taboo demands to be given all human scientific knowledge (represented in the strip as a large metal box) and flies into space. As he does so, the H-Bomb inside the metal box detonates, killing him. Naming practices are of interest here as while the others seem to be riffs on existing names, Taboo, which deals explicitly with the H-Bomb, draws on questions of what should and should not be done or known.

We can see further evidence of the reinscription of the nuclear narrative with America as victim in the two-part tale of Fin Fang Foom, which featured in *Strange Tales* #89 (1961). In the story Chan Liuchow, a young man from Taiwan (then called the Republic of Formosa) of dual Taiwanese-American heritage learns of a dragon-demon named Fin Fang Foom living beneath the ground in China. Liuchow learns an incantation that will make the monster sleep, then creeps to the mainland to awaken it. Over the subsequent pages he encourages the monster to chase him, leading it into the path of the Red Army and a Chinese warship. The monster destroys both the soldiers and the ship, derailing a planned Chinese invasion of Taiwan, a narrative development that draws on the Taiwan Straits Crises of 1954–1955 and 1958, where the People's Republic of China (PRC) applied pressure to Chiang Kai-shek's Nationalist government in Taiwan. Relations between the PRC, Taiwan, and its backer, the US, were strained, and the Eisenhower administration feared that Chinese moves were the precursor to a full invasion. In 'Fin Fang Foom!', the US have no need to worry: Liuchow leads the monster back underground and delivers the necessary words to return it to sleep, its work in derailing the Chinese invasion being satisfactorily complete. The comic suggests American interventionism – manifest in both Liuchow's dual heritage and the allegory of the bomb – as a necessary means to curb the spread of communism in Asia. The fact that the weapon is appropriated from the Chinese by an American ally (recalling, of course, Kwang and other 'good' foreigners from the 1950s) removes any possibility of guilt – Liuchow is turning the weapons of a powerful enemy against them. Despite this, anxiety around the potentially monstrous power of the PRC persists, with Liuchow's ability to turn a Chinese monster against China seemingly demonstrating faith, albeit tentative, in the ability of a Nationalist Taiwan, when allied with the US, to hold its own against the larger power.

The megamonster genre, then, allows a narrative of nuclear destruction without any need for introspection and with the promise that humanity (and the US specifically) can overcome any threat, be it monsters from space or an encroaching Chinese Army. The genre offers both the spectacle of large-scale destruction and a sense of having survived. This represents something of a departure from horror comics of the 1950s in that these megamonster comics offer unabashed faith in the American military industrial complex and present nuclear war as eminently avoidable. Rather than opposing the dominant culture of progress (that brought with it threats of female emancipation and civil rights for LGBT communities and people of colour), these narratives reimagine the postwar era as one where white American men represent an unambiguous force for good. Horror remains, in a reversal of history, something that happens to white men that is enacted by gendered, sexualized, or racialized Others.

## Trauma

Horror comics, then, were either apolitical, apportioning equal blame to both sides of the divide between the state and its critics, or, in the case of much of the megamonster genre, frequently espoused a hawkish rhetoric. All of the manifestations of the genre we have considered thus far, however, avoid the figure of the veteran. It is through the depiction of the veteran that horror comics offer their most direct engagement with the trauma of Vietnam. The average soldier in Vietnam saw more combat than his predecessor who fought in the Second World War. As a consequence, a significant number of soldiers returned home suffering from PTSD, with associated alcoholism, drug abuse, insomnia, divorce, homelessness, an oppressive sense of guilt, and a propensity for violence.[45] Weiss et al. report that around 830,000 returning veterans, roughly one in four, suffered from chronic combat-related PTSD.[46] Where narratives of the Second World War, described in Chapter 1, tended to emphasize a return to suburbia and the building of a new life, popular depictions of Vietnam veterans such as *Taxi Driver* (1976) emphasized their instability and violent outbursts.[47] Unlike their predecessors, then, soldiers returning from Vietnam often met with fear and hostility from the civilian population. Veterans of Vietnam suggested dislocation and rupture at both the individual and national level, raising issues around reintegration quite different from those experienced by veterans after the Second World War. Former marine, Karl Marlantes, reports that returning home from Vietnam was, for him, as traumatic as the war itself.[48]

Horror comics absorbed and mediated the various traumas affecting veterans. In *Vampirella* #3, for example, the story 'I Wake Up Screaming' includes a return to the trope of insomnia, nightmares, and the pervasive presence of past violence. The experience of trauma that opens the story is both symbolic of the ongoing violence on American soil, and specific to the experience of the veteran. *Vampirella* included GIs among its readership – the fourth issue features a letter from Specialist Stephen Fritte, who asserts that the magazine was popular among those stationed in Vietnam (although perhaps more for its softcore erotic content than its therapeutic potential) and the thirteenth issue includes a letter from Specialist John Putt, who asserts that the magazine provides a source of escapism for the troops.

The image from *Vampirella* shows a scene of violence, with partially clad and naked women either dead or in states of grief. A demonic figure flies overhead and an inset image shows a face screaming (Figure 53). The text reads:

> Far away somewhere in the caverns of my mind, an anguished murmur turned the silence into a shriek of warning! My eyes unable to unclench themselves, could feel the movement of some monstrous phantasm approaching. I could hear the beat of wings struggling to seize the wind, and when at last no sound escapes the panic in my throat ...[49]

The image appeared just a few months after the news of the Mỹ Lai Massacre, where American soldiers murdered between 347 and 504 Vietnamese civilians. The strewn bodies in Figure 53 echo the famous photograph by Ronald L. Haeberle, which shows the bodies of women and children, many in a state of undress, lying in a road (Figure 54). Figure 53 attests, more broadly, to the violence of Vietnam, with the 'beat of wings' resembling the sound of a helicopter, and the description echoing the experience of many veterans, whose sleep was troubled by the disruptive presence of the past.

Other stories engage more directly with the veteran's experience. The story 'Out of the Fog ... Into the Mist', for example, includes a Second World War veteran who struggles with his memories of combat (Figure 55). In a half-page spread the character remembers 'the war ... the mud we used to march through ... the killing and the waste'.[50] The accompanying image shows him charging into two German soldiers, killing them. All three of the faces in the image are contorted. The storyteller seems to have grown fangs – a trope typically used in American superhero comics during the 1940s to depict Japanese soldiers. The story is reminiscent in tone to *Blazing Combat Magazine* and its focus on the horrors, rather than the glory, of war. In a subsequent

**53** Billy Graham (w, a), 'I Wake Up Screaming!', *Vampirella* #3

**54** Photograph by Ronald L. Haeberle, taken on 16 March 1968 showing victims of the Mỹ Lai Massacre

panel, a woman asserts, 'the war has done strange things to you. You are very unhappy!' The veteran responds, 'You don't know the half of it'.[51] The woman leads him to her home, promising to make him feel 'happy again'. Once they are alone, the man transforms into a monster and, in the final panel, he descends on her as she screams. Here, then, trauma is not just the effect of war on the men returning from battle, but the effects of the effects, as it were, on the communities to which they return.[52]

Past violence, the veteran's experience of PTSD, and the impact of living with someone who has suffered trauma, is, similarly, reflected in the origin of Swamp Thing, who first appeared in DC's long-running *The House of Secrets* series (1956–1966, 1969–1978, and then sporadic publication after that as it was incorporated into Neil Gaiman's *Sandman* universe). Swamp Thing debuted in *The House of Secrets* #92 (1971), in a story that dwelt on body horror, the pain of memory, and violence.[53] In this origin story, narrative perspective moves between two characters, Alex Olsen and Linda Olsen. Both discourse at relative length on the nature of memory and its impact on the present. The first line of the story, 'I cannot remember the morning any more – but I know the evening well!', aligns the fragmented, monstrous body of the narrative's first protagonist with the night, with an inability to wake from the

**55** Steve Skeates (w) and Ken Barr (a), 'Out of the Fog … Into the Mist', *Vampirella* #8

traumatic nightmare in which he lives, and to enjoy the sense of hope symbolized by the morning.[54] As the narrative cuts from the swamp to the Gothic house that sits at its edge, the stream of consciousness shifts to Linda Olsen. The shift from external to internal monologue is facilitated by the line 'your name is Linda Olsen Ridge – and your mind is a raging river this night – carrying your thoughts along a surging stream of consciousness – sending memories crashing like waves upon some distant shore'.[55] Here, memory is presented as an assault, something that is not easily contained and that can easily overwhelm the individual involved in the act of remembering. This is reinforced in the wonderfully melodramatic line, 'memories fall with the tears', where a series of vignettes are arranged in a hazy, misty style, in teardrop shapes.

Successive definitions of memory then overlap on a single page, taking the reader from Linda's memories of her wedding anniversary party with Alex, her pride in his scientific achievements – and then a sudden explosion, where a memory is defined as 'the searing sound of devastation', which is followed with further delicious melodrama, of memory as 'the gaping wound that once had been your heart'.[56]

A final definition of memory is offered on the next page as 'a fleeting fantasy far too painful to long remain – that carries you back through the portal of the past to the harsh reality of now'.[57] With the departure from Linda's memories into the narrative present, there is another shift to the monster standing outside the house, in the rain. As it begins to move, Linda's new husband, Damian, then offers a third perspective on memory, setting out his part in the 'accident' that led to Alex's death, after which Damian buried Alex's body in the swamp. As Swamp Thing takes one last look at Linda, he realises Damian is about to kill her. Swamp Thing breaks into the room and kills Damian, but is unable to communicate with Linda and leaves, noting that 'only the swamp is kind to me now'.[58] In its long and very detailed consideration of memory, then, 'Swamp Thing' draws on contemporary histories of PTSD found in Vietnam veterans and the threat they pose to the communities that house them.[59] In line with this, Swamp Thing, a monstrous being who cannot leave wet terrain akin to that where much of the war in Vietnam was fought, and whose wife is routinely overcome by both happy memories of life before exposure to traumatic violence, and of memories of the violence itself, can be seen to refract legacies of Vietnam.

American horror comics during this era contained a range of such monsters. Swamp Thing first appeared in July 1971; Man-Thing, a Marvel character, was another story about a very similar monster, which appeared in March 1971 and was allegedly a revival of a Hillman character, The Heap, who first appeared in 1942. The cross-company pollination can partly be explained as the result of a conversation between Roy Thomas at Marvel and Sol Brodsky at Skywald.[60] Environmental concerns were increasingly prominent through the 1960s and into the 1970s, and may have contributed to the creation of creatures where the Earth struck back. As an indication of the visibility of environmental movements, the inaugural Earth Day took place on 22 April 1970, a crystallization of a range of concerns; these was particularly evident in the high-profile work of Paul Ehrlich, such as *The Population Bomb* (1968), who argued that the Earth would be unable to support growing populations and there would, of necessity, therefore be a Malthusian crisis. Of Earth Day in 1970, David Lowenthal of the American Geographical Society remarked that 'activities throughout the United States cast this nation in the role of the prime destroyer, and by extension, potential saviour, of the entire planet', fears that can be seen to refract through a fusion of science and swamp to create monstrous beings who want to live in harmony with the planet and humankind.[61] Swamp Thing's inability to communicate can be seen as the inability of the veteran to communicate with those around him, with the monstrous body he occupies standing as testament to humans' abuse of the planet, and each other. The Gothic stylings of the house and the narrative style – stories within stories that gradually unfold dark secrets – also engage with the question of Gothic form, where landscape is particularly important. As Chloe Chard notes, 'landscape description is of importance within the Gothic novel's mechanisms of self-definition', with landscape serving both a narrative and theoretical function.[62] In Gothic fiction of the late eighteenth and early nineteenth century, the morality of characters can often be derived through their 'responsiveness towards the visual delights of the landscape', and this is inverted in these Gothic-infused images of the 1970s.[63] Here, the horror of humankind in the landscape, and of responses to that, provide a means of reading environmental trauma. This connects back to the issue of Vietnam already raised in connection with Swamp Thing through the devastating effects of the war on the Vietnamese landscape.

All of these representations take the white male as their focus. During the 1950s, the returning veteran was typically cast as the victim beset by an external (gendered and racialized) threat. Victims of horror narratives – who were, as we have argued, exclusively white men – were presented as being haunted by the ghosts of their past, representing psychological wounds, or bearing bodily disfigurement. While these ghosts represented internal struggles with trauma and guilt, they were depicted as external monsters – the violence of war happened *to* the white male body rather than *through* it. During the 1970s, conversely, as the stories above demonstrate, the veteran had become the monster. The experience of war has transformed the soldier into a killer and, in a thinly veiled metaphor in 'Out of the Fog ... Into the Mist', a rapist. The loss of control in the Vietnam War is refracted through a loss of bodily control on the part of those who fought in it; the failure of executive morality in the Watergate scandal becomes a failure of American morality more generally. The promise of the pin-up to restore domestic harmony through sexuality, a vain hope clung to excessively in the 1950s, is literally savaged in 'Out of the Fog ... Into the Mist' and is threatened with violence in *Swamp Thing*. Women are presented as a failed solution, a broken promise, and punished for their inability to fix that which war had damaged.

Elsewhere in the genre, however, the veteran is offered a form of redemption through focalization and complications in the horror dynamic. We find in Marvel comics during this era a series of misunderstood protagonists who grapple with their own monstrosity, trying to reconcile with their pasts and find a safe place in a world that regards them with fear. The titular protagonist of *Monster of Frankenstein*, for example, is drawn from Shelley's novel, with a heavy emphasis on the monster's humanity. The first three issues are devoted to a retelling of *Frankenstein*. The story is introduced through a framing narrative during which a team of Arctic explorers discover the monster frozen in ice. In a recurring theme from Shelley's novel, many of the explorers fear the monster, and some attempt to destroy it. The monster turns on them, accusing them of trying to kill him 'for no reason'.[64] One explorer, the man who told the monster's story, pleads with them to 'Look at its face man ... Can't you see its eyes [...] it means us no harm'.

The explorers do have good reason to fear and hate the monster – he is responsible for, and readily admits to having committed, multiple murders. Rather than being malevolent, however, he appears to be tortured by his past. He asks, 'what right have *I* to hope – in view of what I've done?' As his narrative continues beyond Shelley's, the monster recounts being trapped in a war between two Arctic tribes. The first tribe accept him because they are 'creatures so grotesque as to make even me appear human!'[65] He is softened by their kindness and learns to participate in their cultural practices. His hosts are then massacred by another tribe. While the first group seem to resemble Native Americans, the second are decidedly more Asiatic, resembling popular depictions of Mongols and suggesting the Viet Cong. Despite the monster's best efforts, he is beaten into unconsciousness and, when he awakes, he finds that all of his friends are dead. This reproduces reductive notions of Native Americans as a homogenous people living peacefully and in harmony with nature and similarly reductive, racist notions of an Asiatic

'Yellow Peril' who kill for no reason.[66] As Lowenstein notes, some contemporary radicals 'fetishized' the reductive idea of the Native American as a revolutionary force, potentially engaging with the revolutionary idea of the *tiers monde*, the decolonizing world, as capable of offering a path of development outside the confines of capitalism.[67] In this, even as war is critiqued, specific wars – those against foes who only understand violence – are implicitly justified.

While the monster's narrative does not map perfectly onto that of a Vietnam veteran, there are certainly resonances; he is an individual drawn, unwillingly, into a civil war; he witnesses, and participates in, mass violence; and he finds that those with whom he interacts regard him as a monster. The monster's presence is only destructive – although a failed agent of violence, his presence leads to, or at least fails to prevent, the death of his sympathisers. In a recurring theme from the horror genre, many react to the monster based on his disfigurement. As Skal notes, the fixation on body horror during the early twentieth century coincided with the presence of veterans of the First World War who had sustained irreparable physical damage, particularly facial injuries.[68] We find a continuation and development of that theme here; in addition to his physical disfigurement, the monster carries a burden of guilt. He describes himself as having known nothing 'save hate and misery', and he narrates a failed attempt to end his own life.[69] His narrative no doubt resonated with many of those who had returned to the US having witnessed and participated in violence and found themselves regarded with revulsion and fear. The narrative does not wholly exempt the veteran from responsibility for his actions but understands him as a victim of circumstances. He is a monster, but he is a monster deserving of sympathy.

While the monster's Otherness is physically obvious, other horror characters find themselves leading something of a double-life, hiding their true nature from others. Jack Russell, the protagonist of *Werewolf by Night*, is one such character. Russell inherited the curse of lycanthropy, a condition that turns him into an uncontrollable monster every full moon. Like many Americans at the time, he was thrust into a role, and became a killer, when he was a teenager – the minimum age for a draftee was eighteen. Russell resembles the Vietnam veteran in popular fiction in that his condition makes him dangerous to those around him. Unlike Frankenstein's monster he can pass as a civilian, but his monstrous nature and violent history present a never-ending source of anxiety and self-doubt. He spends the majority of the comic seeking redemption by battling against those who present a threat to others. In this, Jack Russell follows in the tradition of the werewolf curse as established in the Universal horror cycle of the 1930s and 1940s, harking back to a time when, at least in dominant American discourse, the violence meted out by Americans was done so with noble intentions, to bring 'freedom' to the world.

## Conclusion

In the horror comics of the 1950s, fear is an experience to which only white male characters have access. As a recurring theme, the genre presented monsters as either female or ambiguously gendered, or racially Other. The violence perpetrated against civilian populations in Vietnam during the 1960s and 1970s, however, and by agents of the state on American soil made it difficult to maintain that the monster was always Other. The megamonster narrative resisted this by upholding the idea of white America as resistant to external threats, or rather as able to experience them and emerge bloody yet triumphant on the other side, as an opportunity to demonstrate American might and in the process affirm values traditionally associated with masculine heroism. Later manifestations of the genre recognized the white male body as capable of containing, or rather as failing to adequately contain, monstrosity. Nonetheless, the genre remained invested in white male subjectivity, representing the monster as a figure of sympathy who battles with and seeks to come to terms with his own capacity for violence.

As with horror comics of the 1950s, horror comics of the 1960s and 1970s are critical of the state, of science, and of authority. They suggest that there is something fundamentally broken at the heart of American life and yet they fail to connect social disintegration with fundamental inequalities along lines of gender and race. They retain, instead, the recurring narrative of white American men as observers or victims of social forces beyond their control. Their monstrosity, while a vehicle for violence, also becomes a means of enacting change. Female and racialized characters, as the following two chapters will show, were offered no such introspection or capacity for redemption – they remain a source of horror.

## Notes

1 Lowenstein, *Shocking Representation*, 112.
2 Other readings of the megamonster genre are possible, and are offered in this book. What we refer to here is what might be termed as the dominant or preferred reading, however problematic that might be.
3 See, for instance, Mark Kurlansky, *1968: The Year That Rocked the World*

(London: Vintage, 2005); David Maraniss, *They Marched into Sunlight: War and Peace, Vietnam and America, October 1967* (New York: Simon & Schuster, 2004); and for some of the contemporary debate on this and other matters in the student body, see George Kennan, *Democracy and the Student Left* (London: Hutchinson & Co., 1968).

4  See Philip Smith, 'Living Room War', in Paul Joseph (ed.), *The SAGE Encyclopedia of War: Social Science Perspectives* (Thousand Oaks, CA: Sage Publications, 2016), 989.

5  Lowenstein, *Shocking Representation*, 129.

6  Philip S. Foner, 'Why the United States Went to War with Spain in 1898', *Science & Society* 32.1 (1968), 39–65 (65).

7  Matthew J. Costello, *Secret Identity Crisis: Comic Books & the Unmasking of Cold War America* (London and New York: Continuum, 2009), 88.

8  Ian Tyrrell, *Transnational Nation: United States History in Global Perspective Since 1789* (London: Palgrave Macmillan, 2015), 221.

9  Karin Asbley, Bill Ayers, Bernadine Dohrn, John Jacobs, Jeff Jones, Gerry Long, Home Machtinger, Jim Mellen, Terry Robbins, Mark Rudd, and Steve Tappis, 'You Don't Need a Weatherman to Know Which Way the Wind Blows', *New Left Notes* (18 June 1969), retrieved from https://archive.org/details/YouDontNeedAWeathermanToKnowWhichWayTheWindBlows_925 (accessed 13 August 2019).

10  Archie Goodwin (w) and Don Heck (a), *The Invincible Iron Man* #27 (New York: Marvel, 1970).

11  See Richard M. Sommer and Glenn Forley, 'Dyn-o-Mite Fiends: The Weather Underground at Chicago's Haymarket', *Journal of Architectural Education* 61.3 (2008), 13–24.

12  Lowenstein, *Shocking Representation*, 120.

13  Carroll, *The Philosophy of Horror*, 1. *The Hills Have Eyes* (1977) was remade in 2006; *Halloween* (1978) was remade in 2007, a film that spawned a sequel while the original franchise still continues to produce sequels; *I Spit On Your Grave* (1978) was remade in 2010; *It's Alive* (1974) was remade in 2009; *The Amityville Horror* (1979) was remade in 2005; *The Crazies* (1973) was remade in 2010; *The Last House on the Left* (1972) was remade in 2009; *The Texas Chainsaw Massacre* (1974) was remade in 2003; and so on. No list of 1970s remakes, however, is complete without the glorious Nicolas Cage version of *The Wicker Man* (original 1973, remake 2006).

14  The lingering trauma of Vietnam is also evident in, for example, *Kong: Skull Island* (2017), which is set in the Vietnam era and draws heavily on both imagery and tropes of the war.

15  Skal, *The Monster Show*, 31–32.

16  Wandtke, *The Comics Scare Returns*, 71.

17  Sol Cohen (w) and Everett Raymond Kinstler (a), 'The Thing in the Mirror', *Psycho* #1 (New York: Skywald Publications, 1971).

18  Cynthia Erb, *Tracking King Kong: A Hollywood Icon in World Culture*, 2nd edn (Detroit, MI: Wayne State University Press, 2009), 7.

19  For more on freak shows, see Adams, *Sideshow USA*.

20  See, for instance, Frances Stonor Saunders, *Who Paid the Piper? The CIA and the Cultural Cold War* (New York: Granta, 2000); von Eschen, *Satchmo Blows Up the World*, and for a cultural critique of the same policy, see Louis Armstrong, Dave Brubeck, and Iola Brubeck, *The Real Ambassadors* (Monterey Jazz Festival, 1962).

21  Gary Hoppenstand, 'Editorial: Today's Televised Circus', *Journal of Popular Culture* 40.3 (2007), 407–408 (408).

22  Al Hewetson (w) and Francisco Javier Gonzalez (a), 'I Am Dead: I Am Buried', *Nightmare* #12 (New York: Skywald Publications, 1973).

23  Dan Carter, *Scottsboro: A Tragedy of the American South* (Baton Rouge, LA: Louisiana State University Press, 2007).

24  Hewetson and Gonzalez, 'I Am Dead'.

25  For his discussion of this, see Louis Althusser, 'Ideology and Ideological State Apparatuses', in *Lenin and Philosophy and Other Essays* (New York: Monthly Review Press, 2001), 127–188.

26  Robert Kanigher (w), and Ross Andru (a), *Superman* #216 (New York: DC Comics, 1969).

27  Stan Lee, 'The Spider's Web', *The Amazing Spider-Man* #76 (New York: Marvel, 1963); Goodrum, *Superheroes and American Self Image*, 139.

28  Quoted in Phoenix, *Comics' Second City*, 23.

29  Phoenix, *Comics' Second City*, 52.

30  Phoenix, *Comics' Second City*, 27.

31  Gary Friedrich (w) and Dick Ayers (a), *Sgt Fury and His Howling Commandos* #64 (New York: Marvel, 1969).

32  James Warren, 'An Editorial to the President of the United States and all the Members of Congress – on behalf of our readers, most of whom are from 10 to 18 years old', *Vampirella* #7 (New York: Warren Publishing, 1970), 1

33  The pronoun 'we' is interesting here given that Warren sides with youth against 'you adults', yet he was forty when he composed this editorial.

34  Gerry Conway (w) and Mike Ploog (a), *Werewolf by Night* #2 (New York: Marvel, 1972).

35  See, for instance, Stephen Schlesinger and Stephen Kinzer, *Bitter Fruit: The Story of the American Coup in Guatemala, Revised and Expanded* (Cambridge, MA: Harvard University Press, 2005).

36  Clover, *Men, Women, and Chain Saws*, 134.

37  Voltaire, Katz, and Giacoia, 'Beware Small Evils'.

38  Voltaire, Katz, and Giacoia, 'Beware Small Evils'.

39  Alan Hewetson, *Psycho* #13 (New York: Skywald Publications, 1973).

40  Hunter S. Thompson, *Fear and Loathing in Las Vegas* (London: HarperCollins, 2005), 68.

41  Hunter S. Thompson, *Hell's Angels: The Strange and Terrible Saga of the Outlaw Motorcycle Gangs* (New York: Random House, 1967).

42  See, for instance, the timeline of stories in the *New York Times* here: https://archive.nytimes.com/www.nytimes.com/interactive/2013/02/13/us/hellsangels-timeline.html#/#time235_7127 (accessed 8 June 2020).

43 Images of China were also undergoing cultural revision to go with the international politics of the Cold War. The Kung Fu craze of the early 1970s coincided
with both international concerns around exacerbating the Sino-Soviet split and
an economic boom in Hong Kong. Centred around Bruce Lee, particularly the
phenomenally successful *Way of the Dragon* (1972), the Kung Fu craze emerged
from the colonial context of Hong Kong, then occupied by the British.

44 The briefest of surveys of covers (here: https://marvel.fandom.com/wiki/Strange_
Tales_Vol_1, accessed 8 June 2020) demonstrate the extent to which the series,
from 1959 to 1962, was dominated by megamonsters. In 1962, *Strange Tales*
became an outlet for more of Marvel's superhero fare, then rapidly gaining in
popularity.

45 D. Michael Glenn, Jean C. Beckham, Michelle E. Feldman, Angela C. Kirby,
Michael A. Hertzberg, and Scott D. Moore, 'Violence and Hostility Among
Families of Vietnam Veterans with Combat-Related Posttraumatic Stress
Disorder', *Violence and Victims* 17.4 (2002), 473–489.

46 Daniel S. Weiss, Charles R. Marmar, William E. Schlenger, John A. Fairbank,
B. Kathleen Jordan, Richard L. Hough, and Richard A. Kulka, 'The Prevalence of
Lifetime and Partial Posttraumatic Stress Disorder in Vietnam Theater Veterans',
*Journal of Traumatic Stress* 5 (1992), 365–376.

47 Kathleen McClancy, *Back in the World: Vietnam Veterans through Popular
Culture* (unpublished dissertation, 2009). https://dukespace.lib.duke.edu/dspace/
handle/10161/1658 (accessed 26 May 2020).

48 *The Vietnam War* (2017), dir. Ken Burns and Lynn Novick S1E1.

49 Billy Graham (w, a), 'I Wake Up Screaming!', *Vampirella* #3 (New York: Warren
Publishing, 1970), 34.

50 Steve Skeates (w) and Ken Barr (a), 'Out of the Fog… Into the Mist', *Vampirella*
#8 (New York: Warren Publishing, 1970), 36.

51 Skeates and Barr, 'Out of the Fog … Into the Mist', 36.

52 The most famous example of the veteran in popular culture can be found in the
spectacular violence of John Rambo in the *Rambo* films (1982–present) and
the lesser-known original 1972 novel by David Morrell. In brief, Rambo is a
veteran who becomes a vagrant as the result of his combat trauma and enters
into violent conflict with an unsympathetic police force in a small town. Not all
veterans laid siege to towns – but many experienced violent outbursts, which
means that those living with and around them were placed in danger. As *Rambo*
suggests, the trauma of veterans was not individual, but collective. (The original
film is far more restrained and politically nuanced than the subsequent films,
which feature the eponymous character. The 2019 film *Rambo: Last Blood* is, in
our scholarly opinion, a mess of xenophobia and pointless violence.)

53 Len Wein (w) and Berni Wrightson (a), 'Swamp Thing', *The House of Secrets* #92
(New York: DC Comics, 1971). Between 1956 and 1966, the series did not have
the definite article in its title.

54 Wein and Wrightson, 'Swamp Thing'.

55 Wein and Wrightson, 'Swamp Thing'.

56 Wein and Wrightson, 'Swamp Thing'.

57  Wein and Wrightson, 'Swamp Thing'.
58  Wein and Wrightson, 'Swamp Thing'.
59  See, for example, Erika M. Roberge, Nathaniel J. Allen, Judith W. Taylor, and Craig J. Bryan, 'Relationship Functioning in Vietnam Veteran Couples: The Roles of PTSD and Anger', *Journal of Clinical Psychology* 72.9 (2016), 966–974.
60  See George Khoury, 'The Thing About Man-Thing', *Alter-Ego* #81 (Raleigh, NC: TwoMorrows Publishing, 2008), 26–28.
61  David Lowenthal, 'Earth Day', *Area: Institute of British Geographers* 4 (1970), 1–10 (10).
62  Chloe Chard, 'Introduction', in Ann Radcliffe, *The Romance of the Forest* (Oxford: Oxford University Press, 1999), xviii.
63  Chard, 'Introduction', xxi.
64  Gary Friedrich (w), Mike Ploog (p), John Verpoorten (i), Artie Simek (l), Glynis Wein (c), *Monster of Frankenstein* #4 (New York: Marvel, 1973), 3.
65  Friedrich et al., *Monster of Frankenstein* #4, 10.
66  The Native American characters are nonetheless depicted with somewhat exaggerated features, emphasizing their Otherness and undercutting their naturalism and innocence.
67  Lowenstein, *Shocking Representation*, 131.
68  Skal, *The Monster Show*.
69  Friedrich et al., *Monster of Frankenstein* #4, 7.

# 6

## 'This isn't a dream! This is really happening!' – gender in the 1960s and 1970s

During the 1950s, the presence of women in both blue- and white-collar jobs, coupled with the trauma inflicted on male bodies and psyches during the Second World War, disrupted privileged models of the American household. The seeds sown during this time slowly blossomed in the following decades. The 1960s and 1970s gave rise to a widescale movement that sought to challenge entrenched views of gender in US culture. Those who fought for women's rights during the early twentieth century (sometimes referred to, somewhat problematically, as the 'first wave') had, broadly, sought enfranchisement, focusing on legal issues such as voting and property rights. The various manifestations of the 'second wave', from the 1960s to the early 1990s, campaigned for further legal progress, while also drawing attention to cultural inequalities, engaging with issues such as reproductive rights, domestic violence, and the underrepresentation of women in public office. The late 1960s and 1970s saw the formation of groups such as the National Organization for Women (formed 1966) and the Women's Equity Action League (formed 1968), and publications such as Helen Gurley Brown's *Sex and the Single Girl* (1962), Betty Friedan's *The Feminine Mystique* (1963), *Voice of the Women's Liberation Movement* (first published 1968), Germaine Greer's *The Female Eunuch* (1971), and *Ms.* magazine (first published 1972).

The feminist movement, like the Civil Rights movement with which its concerns intertwined and overlapped, employed strategies of visibility. Activists were aware of the value of the image, a strategy previously seen in the picketing of the White House in 1917 by ten suffragists seeking to pressure President Wilson into supporting the Anthony amendment that would have given women the vote. Alice Paul, one of the orchestrators of that protest, was still active in the 1960s, and received plaudits for her work with Howard W. Smith (a Virginian Democratic Congressman), the Chair of the House Rules Committee, to add women's rights to the Civil Rights Act of 1964.[1] Developing the strategy of this previous generation, women's rights advocates gathered in New York on 15 January 1968, to bury a model of 'Traditional Womanhood'. On 9 September of the same year, activists gathered again to protest against the Miss America pageant. 1970 saw demonstrations across North America, including a sit-in at the offices of *Ladies Home Journal*, marches, protests, and demonstrations. In Boston Commons, women distributed contraceptive foam and in New York, women gathered in large numbers, smashed tea cups, and draped a banner reading 'Women of the World Unite' over the Statue of Liberty. Women in New York also distributed medals at advertising agencies reading 'This ad insults women'.[2] By the early 1970s, the image of the feminist rally was firmly established in popular consciousness.[3]

The feminisms of the 1970s, then, took several forms, with various branches gathering around key issues and at key moments. The feminist movement was by no means a coherent group; Friedan, for example, rejected much of Brown's approach even as they shared some common goals, such as furthering women's careers.[4] There were, nonetheless, certain through-lines that connected different aspects of the movement, one central concept being 'sisterhood' – a term that became popular in the late 1960s and expressed the need for women to build networks of support and solidarity. Various branches of the women's liberation movement sought to engage a policy of 'consciousness raising' – drawing attention to systemic inequalities and challenging the dominant order. Certain manifestations of the movement advocated for a reordering of society to work towards the elimination, in the words of Shulamith Firestone, not only 'male privilege but of the sex distinction itself'.[5]

There was, inevitably, a backlash. In *Prisoner of Sex* (1971), Norman Mailer, while conceding that society is unequal, expressed concern over the loss of 'polarity' between the genders, which the societal changes advocated by feminist groups sought to bring about.[6] Mailer casts feminists as militant and humourless, and laments the possibility of male sexual desire becoming taboo or of sexual difference – as he sees it, the driver of sexual desire – being annihilated. Mailer was not alone in opposing the feminist movement. Many anti-feminist groups came from conservative Christian backgrounds. In *The Total Woman* (1973), Marabel Morgan, for example, asserts that 'God ordained man to be the head of the family, its president', and tells female readers, '[y]our husband is what he is. Accept him as that ... A Total Woman caters to her man's special quirks, whether it be in salads, sex, or sports'.[7] One of the central battlegrounds between feminist and anti-feminist organizations was the Equal Rights Amendment (ERA), which promised equal rights to every individual regardless of sex. The ERA passed Congress in 1972 but was never ratified, falling three states short of the thirty-eight needed to bring about an amendment to the constitution. This was largely due to a campaign launched by conservative groups. Françoise Coste argues that anti-feminists did not see women as oppressed, but privileged:

> According to feminists, the ERA was necessary because it would change a status quo defined by the inferior position of women in society; whereas according to anti-feminist women, the ERA would alter a status quo defined by the superior position of women. For feminists, passing from inferiority to equality would be an extraordinary progress, but for anti-feminists, passing from superiority to equality would actually be a regression.[8]

Conservative writers and activists, such as Phyllis Schlafly, were afraid that the ERA would remove men's obligations to provide for women, and that a radical change in gender dynamics would remove many of the privileges that she believed women enjoyed. Such rhetoric around protective legislation being set against equality had characterized discussion of the ERA ever since it was first drafted by Alice Paul in 1923.

Many of the conflicts of this era played out in the representation of female bodies in popular culture. Some popular culture texts presented a superficial form of feminism with the trappings and language of female empowerment, while celebrating the polarity espoused by Mailer and, crucially, presenting a version of feminism that did not require change on either a societal or individual level. During the 1960s and 1970s, *Playboy* gained several successful competitors including *Penthouse* (launched 1965), *Mayfair* (launched 1966), and *Men Only* (launched 1971). These magazines used a larger format, firmer covers, and a higher price tag to suggest an air of sophistication. *Penthouse*, in particular, sought to appeal to, Gabor contends, 'slightly older, less conventional, more liberal, intellectual' men.[9] The women featured, unlike those of *Playboy*, were 'less servile [...] not so ready to please her man, [...] more spirited looking, unconventional, and independent [...] she seems more oriented to pop culture than to cabaret life, to natural womanhood (but not yet to Women's Liberation) than to idealized femininity – distinctions that suggest a generation gap between Playmate and Pet'.[10] The pin-up of the second half of the twentieth century, then, was often aligned, awkwardly and superficially, with the feminist movement. One *Penthouse* centrefold from 1971, Miss Josee Troyat, for example, is represented with her back to the camera and her torso turned so that one of her breasts is visible. She wears an ammo belt around her waist. The caption reads, 'In these days of Women's Liberation, when beauty contestants get picketed and gibes of "male chauvinism" are hurled at magazines for men, it takes a defiant spirit among females, and a mind not easily intimidated, to proclaim Petdom as a pinnacle of women's rights'.[11] The language and ideals of second-wave feminism had penetrated popular culture, even if its message had been wilfully lost.

Feminist thinkers were understandably sceptical of superficial gestures of empowerment. Organizations such as Women Against Pornography (WAP) argued that pornography was founded on exploitation and promoted the mistreatment of women.[12] During the 1970s, the WAP led tours of sex shops, engaging in discussions concerning the representation of women in pornography. These consciousness-raising activities affected comics in the form of empowered and independent female characters in heroic roles. *Wonder Woman* #203 (1972), for example, describes itself as a 'Women's Lib' issue, with the heroine taking on wage discrimination and working with a member of a women's liberation group. Written by Samuel R. Delany, who was already a well-regarded science fiction author at this time, the issue features rallies where women discuss their employment issues at Grandee's department store, foreshadowing the strike organized by the National Organization for Women against Sears, Roebuck, & Co., in 1975.[13] The issue ends with 250 disgruntled women storming a celebration in honour of Wonder Woman's success through strike action because the reforms enacted by the group led to the closure of Grandee's store. It is not possible to discover how this would have played out, however, as Delany's run on the title came to an end with that issue; he was replaced by the returning Robert Kanigher, writer of the series from 1948–1968, whose first narrative action was to kill off the female editor of a women's magazine, Dottie Cottonman. This is a very clear reference to Dorothy Woolfolk, who took over *Superman's Girl Friend, Lois Lane* in 1972, having become editor of DC's entire romance line in 1971 and taken it in a more feminist direction.[14] Wonder Woman, though, was not done for 1972: she also appeared, on the cover of the inaugural issue of the feminist publication *Ms.* as part of encouraging a return to the character's feminist origins, albeit as reconstructed along the lines of the liberal feminism espoused by Gloria Steinem and her staff. Sexualization, however, remained a perennial problem in the superhero genre and elsewhere in mainstream comics. The apparent independence afforded to certain characters was often undercut through storylines, with many female characters depicted in similar ways to their predecessors from the 1950s.[15]

Horror recapitulated and refracted many of these discussions and preoccupations, though through existing lenses. We begin to find examples of female characters who exist beyond the bounds of either malevolent monster or passive victim. One such character is Rachel

**56** Gardner Fox (w),
Eugene Colan (a), Tom
Palmer (i), Artie Simek (l),
Roy Thomas (e), *Tomb of
Dracula* #5

van Helsing, a recurring character in *Tomb of Dracula* (Figure 56). Van Helsing, great-granddaughter of Abraham van Helsing and a capable vampire hunter in her own right, teams up with Frank Drake and Blade to kill Dracula. This is in stark contrast to the women of the original novel, who offer little in the way of agency beyond Mina stitching together the composite body of research gathered by the Crew of Light and her savant's knowledge of train timetables – until, that is, her 'man-brain' develops after Dracula drinks her blood, and forces her to drink his.[16]

In comparison to the scantily clad, shrieking, or comatose victims of 1950s horror, Rachel van Helsing neither required rescue nor was represented in such a way as to invite the male gaze – she typically wears a large form-less cloak with a hood. Her appearance was of sufficient note to provoke one letter writer, Clint Higgenbotham, to ask that she be made 'more ladylike' in order to serve a more credible love interest for Drake. Higgenbotham writes: 'Frank needs someone more than just a mere friend, and he would fight Dracula with more fury than ever before, if he loved Rachel and knew the evil Count would destroy her'.[17] Editor Roy Thomas defended her representation, however, arguing that 'the great-granddaughter of a vampire-slayer, much less a woman who's taken up the profession herself, would tend to be the self-reliant type Archie [Goodwin] portrayed in that story'.[18] The response suggests that certain branches of feminist thought had sufficient impact to, at least, change the way in which Archie Goodwin and Roy Thomas approached female characters.

While she represented a new fold in horror comics, Rachel Van Helsing was hardly the realization of a feminist ideal. She represents the uplift of an individual rather than a change to society as a whole. Her agency is derived from her own abilities but also from her relationship to a privileged white man. As shall be discussed in more detail below, the series otherwise explored the same territory as Hammer films by filling its pages with buxom women who easily fall under Dracula's spell. As a woman who is able to fight alongside men, Rachel still privileges traditionally masculine traits, such as a capacity for violence, even as she uses those to enact her own agency. Her existence does not require that men change; she is allowed in the treehouse, as it were, but she neither disrupts male privilege nor demands introspection on the part of male characters. Indeed, as a vampire hunter, she seeks to protect society from external threats and thereby maintain the status quo. Rachel is therefore similar to Blade, considered in the next chapter, as both characters draw on contemporary protest movements but, instead of fighting for societal change, are a token inclusion in a pre-existing story formula that reinscribes pre-existing socio-political relations in an apparently progressive way.

## The ideal girlfriend

The exchange in the letters page columns described above is symptomatic of larger changes occurring in the industry at the time. Comics, which had once been consumed by virtually all young people (and a significant proportion of adults into their thirties), were becoming an increasingly gendered cultural form. As Tim Hanley demonstrates, by 1972 just 10 per cent of letters printed by DC and 8 per cent of letters printed by Marvel were signed with a female name.[19] This represents a significant drop from the 20 per cent average found in 1960. Comics had ceased to be a medium consumed by all and were becoming something read by a predominantly white male readership, many of whom, like Higgenbotham, were uncomfortable with images of female empowerment.[20]

Given their readership – and the persistence of many artists and writers who had been working twenty years previously – it is perhaps unsurprising that horror comics of the 1970s returned to some of the imagery of the 1950s. The September 1973 cover of *Monster of Frankenstein #5*, for example, features an image of the monster apparently menacing an imperilled woman in a red dress (Figure 57).

The title, 'The Monster Walks Among Us!', is in itself another 1950s reference: the third film in the Gill-man trilogy, *The Creature Walks Among Us*, came out in 1956.[21] In the comic itself, a different story unfolds from that suggested on the cover, albeit one in which, as with 1950s horror, the empowered (and therefore monstrous) woman represents a threat to both a community and the heroic male protagonist. The monster, adrift in the world, discovers a woman tied to a burning boat. He is moved to save her and leaps aboard. He is momentarily

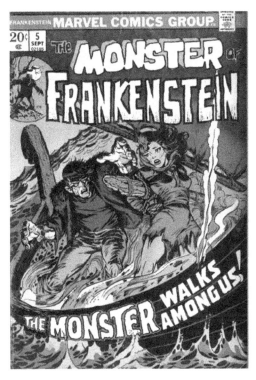

**57** Gary Friedrich (w), Mike Ploog (a) John Verpoorten (i), Glynis Wein (c), Artie Simek (l), Roy Thomas (e), *Monster of Frankenstein* #5

shocked by her beauty and his 'realization that, for the first time, he is holding a woman'.[22] Having saved her from the blaze, he takes her to a nearby village. The villagers, however, turn on him and he realizes, to his horror, that they were the ones who had tried to kill her. The monster, 'amazed by man's inhumanity to fellow man', rescues her once more.[23] When she regains consciousness, the woman tells the monster that the villagers are in the thrall of a demon. The monster returns to the village and, after some fighting, returns with medical supplies. He nurses the woman back to health, and she tells him that her name is Lenore; throughout this time the monster takes on domestic responsibilities, cooking for Lenore and feeding her. Lenore tells the monster that she could grow to love him, and the monster experiences an, albeit fleeting, moment of domestic bliss. He awakens one night and finds her gone. As he searches for her, he is attacked by a werewolf. He eventually kills the beast, only for it to return to its human form – Lenore. She, it transpires, was the one possessed by a demon and the villagers, the comic suggests, were right to have tried to burn her alive. 'He'd known a woman for the first time', the narrative informs us, 'and paid a terrible price for it'.[24]

The comic recycles many of the themes discussed in the chapter concerning the representation of gender in the 1950s; a female character is shown to be in possession of unnatural power, which makes her a threat to the hero and, by extension, the patriarchal society of which he is emblematic. That threat is resolved through violence and through the reduction of women to sexual objects – it is significant, for example, that in the last panel in which Lenore appears, having been killed by the monster, she is naked. The comic also includes an additional development not prevalent in comics of the 1940s and 1950s in that it offers a female character as girlfriend-proxy. As Gabriel Gianola and Janine Coleman argue of Gwen Stacy, the sometime girlfriend of Peter Parker and contemporary of the monster and Lenore, many readers often formed strong attachments to female characters.[25] As Arnold T. Blumberg argues, Gwen Stacy 'became the first "girlfriend" for many comic book fans'.[26] Gwen Stacy had been created as a perfect girlfriend and her death in 1973 created a huge fan backlash, quite out of proportion to Marvel's expectations. Lenore offers a microcosm of the Gwen Stacy effect, appearing (at first) as the idealized woman of 1950s horror – beautiful, inept, and in constant need of rescue – only to finally invert that by using the monster for as long as she needed, then turning on him. A key difference here is in the characterization of the protagonist, who here is a monstrous outcast; though fundamentally good, he is capable of terrific acts of violence, and exists on the margins of society. This could stand in for both the increasingly niche state of comic readership in this period, and the more contested position of the US as the result of domestic and international political developments.

Throughout the story, Lenore is represented in ways that emphasize her passivity and sexual availability. On page 15, for example, the monster carries her over his shoulder. Her skirt rides almost to the top of her legs and her buttocks, rendered with careful shading, are positioned in the centre of the image (Figure 58). Despite appearing on almost every page of the comic, she is almost always lying down or being carried – she is always acted upon rather than participating in or controlling the action.

When Lenore becomes capable of moving under her own power, even before she becomes a werewolf, she is visually coded as a threat. Her ability to act of her own accord creates a shift in the dynamics between her and the male protagonist such that she ceases to serve as an ideal girlfriend and, instead, becomes a dangerous and disruptive force. On page 18, when she is first able to stand unaided, she is positioned behind the monster, mostly hidden by shadow (Figure 59).

**58** Gary Friedrich (w), Mike Ploog (a), John Verpoorten (i), Artie Simek (l), and Glynis Wein (c), *Monster of Frankenstein* #5

**59** Gary Friedrich (w), Mike Ploog (a), John Verpoorten (i), Artie Simek (l), and Glynis Wein (c), *Monster of Frankenstein* #5

As with the horror comics of the 1950s, women are presented here as untrustworthy and capable of wielding unsanctioned power. The community that had attempted to kill Lenore recognizes the threat she poses and tries to kill her. She lies to the monster and, in her wolf form, tries to kill him. Ultimately, he kills her in self-defence. This old refrain is combined with a new theme of the girlfriend fantasy where, like many comics readers of the time, the monster, who has had little to no previous interaction with women, is allowed to play out a fantasy of romance. While these two impulses may seem to pull in opposite directions – with the desire to protect the female character on one hand, and the perceived need to inflict violence on her on the other – we should note that misogyny and the girlfriend proxy were far from incompatible; as Goodrum notes, a debate raged in the pages of *Superman's Girl Friend, Lois Lane* from 1960 to 1962 where readers frequently expressed a desire to see Superman spank Lois for what they perceived to be her misdemeanours.[27]

The protagonist of *Monster of Frankenstein* is a well-meaning creature who only wants the comfort of romance, which remediates and restages some of the themes of the novel *Frankenstein*. This is in keeping with the shift in emphasis, described in the previous chapter, which places the monster at the emotional centre of the narrative. *Tomb of Dracula*, another series drawing on a classic of horror literature, offers quite a different, and more overtly misogynistic, form of fantasy fulfilment. As with the other horror titles, the comic follows the adventures of its titular character. *Tomb of Dracula* contains a rotating cast of characters with Dracula as the only constant. Unlike Frankenstein's monster and Jack Russell, in *Werewolf by Night*, however, Dracula is the villain of his comic, and the plot documents various unsuccessful attempts to kill him. Among Dracula's powers, in keeping with the original source material, is his ability to hypnotize women. In the first issue, Dracula's first action on awakening is to draw Jeanie, fiancée to sometime protagonist Frank Drake, to him. 'There's something – about his eyes!' Jeanie says, breaking from Drake's arms, 'I must go to him'.[28] Drake's response is to strike her, delivering a blow that, implausibly, causes her shirt to fall open (Figure 60).

The theme of Dracula preying upon women is lifted directly from Bram Stoker's novel; Dracula transforms Lucy Westenra into a vampire and attempts to do the same to Mina Harker. The novel is often read as an unsubtle allegory for anxieties over the perceived threat that immigrants allegedly posed to English women (one hears echoes here of the fear of miscegenation discussed in Chapter 3.[29] Read in such a context, Drake's attempt to awaken Jeanie from Dracula's influence is a white

**60** Gerry Conway (w), Gene Colan (a, i), John Costanza (l), and Stan Lee (e), *Tomb of Dracula* #1

man using violence to control a woman's sexuality and to prevent her from having any romantic contact with men of colour and/or any other marker of Otherness.

Dracula preys on women throughout the series, using his power of hypnosis not only to draw them to him but to express love for him. The July 1973 issue of the comic places Dracula on a luxury boat to which he has been invited as a guest of honour. He expresses his disgust for 'weaklings, effeminate fops and mindless women' and proceeds to hypnotize one of the women there.[30] She leads him to her cabin 'for a nightcap'. He feeds on her and instructs a servant to watch over her so that he can return later. She later awakens and renders the servant unconscious so that she can be with Dracula, whom she claims to love (Figure 61).

Dracula is positioned as the villain of the comic but the image of the woman, comatose, seductive, declaring her love, and always available for the male gaze, no doubt satisfies certain fantasies held by some members of the comic's readership. The placement of the third word balloon in the Figure 61 seems to make a direct reference to sexualized violence, with the words 'to my love' apparently issuing from her genitals, while the arrow of the balloon directs the reader's gaze to her crotch. The shading on her stomach and breasts guides the eye down to

the balloon, but the act of reading the text directs the eye to scale that shading back to her breasts, encouraging the viewer to take in her body as spectacle. While *Monster of Frankenstein*, like *Spider-Man*, offered a fantasy of an ideal girlfriend, *Tomb of Dracula* offers a cruder but perhaps equally appealing fantasy of dominating women and receiving their unconditional adoration.[31]

## Vampirella

A recurring manifestation of the idealized girlfriend trope first appeared when, in 1969, Warren Publications put the first issue of *Vampirella* on sale. The comic was published by James Warren and featured stories by Forrest James Ackerman – the duo behind the hugely successful movie magazine, *Famous Monsters of Filmland*. The comic features many of Ackerman's characteristic horror puns – in the opening issue the titular protagonist describes the publication as 'the coolest girl-meet-ghoul mag on the market'.[32] It also featured early work by now-famous artists such as Neal Adams and Ernie Colón. Unlike the Marvel titles discussed above, *Vampirella* followed the horror

**61** Marv Wolfman (w), Gene Colan (a), Jack Abel (i), Denise Vladimer (l), and Roy Thomas (e), *Tomb of Dracula* #10

formula from the 1950s, offering a series of self-contained stories albeit in black and white and for a higher price-tag.[33]

Vampirella was not the first horror host. She follows in the footsteps of the Crypt Keeper, the Old Witch, and so on, from EC and Uncle Creepy of *Creepy*. *Vampirella*, like *Creepy*, *Eerie*, and *Famous Monsters of Filmland*, were all Warren Publishing titles and the latter three, in particular, derived their appeal from stock horror tropes. While previous horror hosts, at least in comics, were generally monstrous, Vampirella combined the violence of the monster with the appearance of the idealized woman. In presenting a sexualized, monstrously empowered woman, *Vampirella* draws on unthreatening and wilfully misunderstood elements of contemporary second-wave feminism while looking back-wards to Vampira, Maila Nurmi's late night horror host of the 1950s. The internal logic behind the comic is explained in a story in the second issue, one that teases out precisely this conflict between the past, present, and future: a horror film director's previous five films have been flops and his studio is threatening to cancel his upcoming feature. An actor offers him a suggestion; 'The old monsters are still good', he asserts, 'but you need a new face! A girl! That's it! A "Queen of Horror!" A Barbarella type actress, but one who could portray a werewolf or a vampire or some other classic fiend of, say, the 1930s or 40s!'[34] Vampirella's titular protagonist, accordingly, comes from a planet where water has the same molecular constitution as blood. She has many of the characteristics one would typically associate with vampirism; flight, the ability to turn into a bat, fangs, and a thirst for blood. She almost exclusively appears either naked or barely clothed; the first two pages of the inaugural issue, for example, are of the comic's protagonist taking a shower and making facial expressions that suggest sexual climax. Indeed, over the course of its run, *Vampirella* was far more explicitly sexual than the comics of the 1940s and 1950s; as well as a high proportion of women in sexual-ized poses, the comics featured occasional instances of partial nudity such as Lucy Fuhr's bare breasts in the third issue.[35] In keeping with its title character, every story in the comic uniformly features similarly buxom and under-dressed female characters, so much so that the fifth issue features a letter in which a reader reports that a newspaper vendor chastised him for buying pornography. In the subsequent issue, another reader asked that *Vampirella* be the first comic to feature a centrefold.[36] The tenth issue even featured a story with 'Rachel Walsh' – a transpar-ent reference to perhaps the most famous actress and pin-up model of the 1960s, Raquel Welch. It is worth noting through this, though, that the comic genders itself as female; in the fifth issue, Vampirella describes *Eerie* and *Creepy* (hosted by male characters) as, 'As good as men can get', implying that *Vampirella*, their feminine counterpart, is better.[37]

Despite the fact that the unifying feature of *Vampirella* was its high proportion of female protagonists, its female mascot, and a prepon-derance of concupiscent art, it was the work of an all-male creative team. It was certainly not the case that Warren could not have hired female writers and artists; there were several women working in comics during the 1960s and 1970s including, to name just three, Marie Severin at Marvel, Marcia Snyder at Fiction House, and Linda Fite at DC.[38] Indeed, many readers assumed that *Vampirella* must have included women on its staff; the fourth issue includes a letter asking for Nicola Cuti's picture, asserting, '[t]here aren't many girls who can write that

well in the science fiction field'.[39] In her reply, Vampirella explains that
Nicola is a man and will, no doubt, find the mistake hilarious (in the
same pages as, apparently without irony 'she' flirts with readers).[40] In
understanding the image of femininity projected by *Vampirella*, then, we
can usefully employ Art Spiegelman's observation of 'Tijuana Bibles' –
pornographic comics produced during the 1940s and 1950s: 'there actually are no women in these books. This is a genre drawn primarily, if not
entirely by men for an audience of men, depicting women with omnivo-
rous male libidos'.[41] Despite its ostensibly feminine veneer, *Vampirella* is
constructed without the presence of or input from women, beyond Trina
Robbins' work on Vampirella's costume. It is made entirely of the stuff
of heterosexual male fantasy, designed for an audience who were, in the
words of Jerry Boyd, 'far too unsophisticated for *Esquire*, and a bit too
young for *Playboy*'.[42]

The monster-as-beautiful-woman trope was relatively new to horror
comics but was not original to the genre as a whole. Even before
*Dracula*, Joseph Sheridan le Fanu depicted a female vampire with
lesbian desires in his novella, *Carmilla* (1872). More famously, early
in Bram Stoker's *Dracula*, Jonathan Harker narrowly avoids being fed
upon by three women who are described as 'both thrilling and repulsive'.[43] *Dracula's Daughter* (1936), the first sequel to 1931's *Dracula*,
follows Countess Marya Zaleska, the daughter of Dracula, as she seeks
to destroy the body of her father in a bid to live free of the curse of
vampirism; part of that quest involves the implied seduction of Lili,
a beautiful young girl from London, in the Countess' art studio. The
three 'sisters' featured in *Dracula* were reimagined in the Hammer
Horror film, *Brides of Dracula* (1960).[44] Vampirella also undoubtedly owes something of her genealogy to the character who would
eventually be known as Morticia Addams; a character created by the
*New Yorker* cartoonist Charles Addams and later played by Carolyn
Jones and Anjelica Huston in television and film adaptations. Addams'
work inspired television actress Maila Nurmi's Vampira, which also
likely informed the creation of Vampirella.[45] From 1954 to 1955, as
discussed previously, Nurmi appeared in *The Vampira Show*, clad in
a low-cut black gown with a pinched waist. She appeared in various
horror-inspired scenarios, bathing in a cauldron, petting a tarantula,
and emerging from foreboding woods. Vampira became something of
a household name during the late 1950s; she was nominated for an
Emmy in 1954 for Most Outstanding Female Personality and was a
friend and possible lover to actor James Dean.

Like Vampira, Vampirella appears at the start and end of each story to
address the reader. This use of direct address creates a sense of intimacy

**62** Jack Sparling (a), Vampirella Fan Club Advertisement, *Vampirella* #3

between the character and reader. On the back cover of the first issue she asserts, 'If you're my kinda bird or boyfriend you'll lose your mind over me anyway ...'. The use of 'bird' suggests a lingering representation of lesbian vampire titillation made safe by the presence of the male gaze. Similarly, in the third issue, a page advertising Vampirella's fan club shows Vampirella in a seductive pose beside the words, 'This space is reserved for you!' (Figure 62).

The idea of Vampirella as girlfriend was reinforced in the letters pages, where responses were written in character. This resulted in a steady stream of declarations of love from readers. In the third issue, the first to feature letters, one writer, Don Doering, opens his letter, 'Yes! I'm your kind of boyfriend Vampi. I got latched onto your magazine the minute I started to read it [...] I wish I could be the first human to clutch on to you'.[46] He asks if Vampirella has heard of a 'blood bribe', to which she responds coquettishly, 'No, but it sounds like fun!' Vampirella did not only flirt with male readers, flagging the issues raised above around lesbian representation; the same letters page prints a script from Lynda Rothman who requests a signed photo from Vampirella, delivered in person. Vampirella responds, 'Love to. What's your blood type?' Later issues seemed to encourage the idea of Vampirella as the subject of sapphic fantasy. In the seventh issue, in response to a letter, she writes, 'Girls appreciate me too [...] Not in the same way but in their own way, just as much'.[47]

Like Lenore in *Monster of Frankenstein*, Vampirella is (at least initially) a monster – the first story shows her gleefully murdering a group of stranded astronauts.[48] This made her something of a new development in horror comics – while, as discussed previously, 1950s horror had tended to juxtapose the idealized female and the monster, the two had rarely existed as a single figure. Whenever a female character transpired to be monstrous, the revelation of her monstrosity would coincide with the loss of her beauty. In 'Vampires? Don't Make Me Laugh' (considered in Chapter 2), for example, the archetypally beautiful woman sprouts hair and develops exaggerated facial features when she becomes a vampire.[49] Vampirella, conversely, is drawn using the aesthetics of the pin-up even as she engages in monstrous acts. This discordant imagery caused some confusion among some readers – the fourth issue of the magazine features a letter by Greg Morgan who asserts that Vampirella is 'particularly bloodthirsty' and that '[t]his particular little fault of yours doesn't very much enhance your image with male readers'.[50] Vampirella seems unphased: 'I am no average vampire', she asserts, 'I thought you knew that'. Vampirella, then, was intended to embody some of the same pseudo-feminist principals as the playmate – she is a coquettishly independent and unapologetic object of male desire.

In developing the idealized girlfriend trope, the editorial philosophy of the *Vampirella* team included a commitment to write more convincingly human female characters. A one-page overview of the writing team in issue seven asserts: 'Witches are women, and as women they are usually complex. It would be a great injustice to limit them to a mere two dimensions. The off-beat heroines of these tales are innocent, vindictive, jealous, protective, romantic, everything that a woman is'.[51] Read charitably, this passage can be understood as a commitment by the writers and editors to create female characters with enough complexity that they avoid the phenomenon, described in Chapter 2, of their experiences having no consequence. The problem is that all of the characteristics ascribed to women in the passage are those that often exist in relation to a man – these female characters may be more complex, but their complexity is understood exclusively in terms of their status and relationship to sexual and romantic partners.

The representation of women in *Vampirella*, then, is problematic, but nonetheless shows some evidence that James Warren and Billy Graham maintained a (clumsily executed) editorial commitment to presenting independent and complex female protagonists. Trina Robbins, similarly, defends her role in creating the character by describing her as a 'strong female lead'.[52] The editorial team at Warren do not, however, go so far as to align themselves with the feminist movement. The fifteenth issue of

*Vampirella* includes the story 'Welcome to the Witches' Coven', which, Vampirella promises, is 'from the witches' cauldron flavored with a contemporary theme'.[53] The story opens with an argument between a husband, Brad, and wife, Jennifer. Brad complains that Jennifer has been negligent in her duties at home while she responds: 'I'm no more than an object to you! Someone to kiss on the cheek, call for in the night and cook your meals!' Brad meets with a friend to lament that his wife has been influenced by the women's liberation movement. His friend opines that, echoing Mailer and similar opponents of the feminist movement, societal change will come at the cost of 'femininity … the art of being a woman'.[54] Meanwhile, Jennifer visits her own friends – those who encouraged her to stand up to her husband – and is invited to join a coven of witches who are committed to the 'downfall of male domination'.[55] Her induction first involves her disrobing to partake in an 'exotic ritual' – an erotic reimagining of political lesbianism performed, in this reimagining, for the titillation of the heterosexual male reader – and then requires her to kidnap a man so that, she learns, he can be sacrificed in a ritual to summon the goddess Diana. She has second thoughts, but the priestesses summon Diana regardless. Diana asserts that the coven's mission is to unite 'all women, all sisters, all enslaved females together in a total assault for freedom!'[56] Jennifer realizes, all too late, that she has been used – 'you're no more my masters than Brad is!' she declares, before being chased and destroyed.

We find in this story similar themes to those found in 'The Witch Who Wore White' and 'Crawling Evil', described previously – women are shown to possess unnatural power, and this power is amplified when they work together. While the stories of the 1940s and 1950s express anxiety over shifts in gender norms they do not engage explicitly with the feminist movement. 'Welcome to the Witches' Coven', conversely, is an unambiguously and directly anti-feminist story. It casts the feminist movement as malevolent, dangerous, and as a source of horror. It accuses feminist thinkers and leaders of manipulating impressionable women, forcing them to engage in homosexual activities and acts of violence, and of defacing those attributes that make women appealing to men. The priestesses in the story are dishonest and cruel – they are willing to lie to and murder other women in order to wreak violence on men.

The comic's anti-feminism also manifests elsewhere in *Vampirella* in the representation of superficially empowered women as sexual objects and as dependent on men. There seems to be little consistency in Vampirella's character between stories, with Vampirella as a blood-thirsty monster in the first issue, an innocent would-be starlet in issue

**63** Archie Goodwin (w) and Jose Gonzales (a), *Vampirella* #12

two, and a simpering romantic lead who loses her vampiric powers and stumbles upon a cult in issue eight. She is given a potion by a male scientist to control her craving for human blood and temporarily restore her powers. She falls in love with the scientist and vows to help humankind. Her status as empowered woman, then, is dependent upon the support of a man, and she proves willing to abandon her entire *raison d'être* following a short speech from her new lover. The use of the potion to control desire also raises connections between Vampirella and Blade, discussed in the next chapter, who must also use a serum to stave off his own insatiable desire for human blood. Women and African Americans, these comics suggest, are the locus of powerful desires and anxieties, which might destabilize existing relations of power. The serum that controls those desires defers but does not eliminate the threat which they pose. Both remain inherently dangerous, standing as warnings of what might happen if individual uplift is replaced with a broader social programme.

Subsequent issues contain images of Vampirella fighting against various monsters and would-be vampire killers but, drawing on *Wonder Woman* and erotic series of the 1950s such as *Nights of Horror*, an equal number of images show her bound, defeated, or subject to violence. The image of Vampirella chained in issue twelve is accompanied by the presence of male observers who encourage the reader to look at her (Figure 63).

To understand these images, we can usefully turn to criticism of *Wonder Woman* comics. During the 1940s, as many as 27 per cent of *Wonder Woman* panels featured the titular character either tying someone up or being tied up.[57] The comic was a platform for creator William Moulton Marston's philosophy of human sexuality where bondage is understood as a normal and necessary part of both erotic practices and socialization. Marston famously believed that men needed to learn submission from women and that bondage was a key means to achieve this. As Berlatsky argues, Wonder Woman's imprisonment can be read in a multitude of ways; she always breaks free of her bonds, enacting a process of liberation that metaphorically plays out the political and social quest for female emancipation, and yet, for readers who enjoy images of women being bound and humiliated, the comic offered much to enjoy.[58] It is likely that *Vampirella* comics, similarly, offered at least two conflicting readings – she always overcomes whatever adversity she encounters, evoking as she does the imagery of breaking free from chains that appeared as a recurring metaphor in feminist rhetoric and imagery, and yet the individual panels, to which the reader can return, offer her as erotic spectacle (Figure 64).

Elsewhere in *Vampirella* we find, as with horror comics from the 1940s and 1950s, frequent images of sexualized violence without the redemptive potential of a female character overcoming her enemies. The full-page spread in Figure 65 features in *Vampirella* #3, where a group of settlers on an alien world are assaulted by monsters. The majority of those under attack are attractive young women. The individual in the foreground is topless (although oddly without nipples), with tentacles encircling her breasts and hips. While the men struggle against their attackers, the women seem to either express surprise or sexual arousal.

The same issue contains a re-enactment of the image, previously discussed in Chapter 2, that appeared in 'King of Hades' from *Voodoo*

**64** Archie Goodwin (w) and Jose Gonzales (a), *Vampirella* #12

**65** Jack Sparling (a), '4… 3… 2… 1… Blast off! To a Nightmare!', *Vampirella* #3

#11, where a woman – once again, one who has taken advantage of men – is punished by being penetrated with a pitchfork. The thrust of the male character's hips makes the image unmistakably sexual (Figure 66).

The depiction of women as sexual objects robbed of agency extends beyond the imagery to the rhetoric of the stories. In 'Spaced-out Girls' in *Vampirella* #1, for example, a human male is tempted onto a spaceship by voluptuous women clad in bikinis who tell him that they need him to help them repopulate their planet. During the journey he learns that he will only breed with the queen, a being who, it transpires, is hideous. 'There are two lessons to learn from this!!' asserts Vampirella. 'Don't trust chicks that are too far out! And don't get sucked in by marriage to the wrong girl despite social position! Some wives can be possessive …'.[59] A woman's value lies entirely in her appearance, the comic suggests. They are emotionally unstable and marriage is a trap.

The same issue contains 'A Slimy Situation'. The story opens with a one-page prologue in which a young girl, Amy, demands that two of her male classmates allow her to copy their homework. When they refuse,

**66** Terri Abrahams (w) and Ed Robbins (a), 'Eleven Footsteps to Lucy Fuhr', *Vampirella* #3

she lies to the teacher, claiming that the boys bullied her. Vampirella describes her as 'a little snake' and a 'twisted miss'.[60] As an adult, Amy marries a scientist. 'He's brilliant, respected, and soon he'll be rich and famous! And handsome too! What a husband he'll make once I make up his mind for him to marry me!'[61] She becomes frustrated that he refuses to sell his 'devolution' formula – a serum that causes animals to transform into their prehistoric ancestors. Amy steals the formula, planning to sell it and divorce her husband. She breaks into a part of the lab she has never entered before, trying to gather more things to steal. Instead, she finds a creature she cannot control; the final panel shows her naked, about to be eaten by a dragon (Figure 67). The story covers familiar ground; marriage is a trap, women are manipulative, they achieve power through nefarious means and are rightly punished through sexualized violence. Little, it seems, had changed from the 1940s and 1950s.

Women in *Vampirella* do not necessarily need to be manipulative or evil to be subject to sexualized violence. In 'Forgotten Kingdom', in issue four, a male astronaut crashes on a planet populated entirely by women. He is imprisoned and told that he will be used to repopulate the planet. The woman who found him helps him to escape and, on the final page, she states, 'You'll always be mine, Keifer! Promise!' He responds, 'It's not possible, Zodi. My superiors would never permit it!' He draws close to her in the final panel as she attempts to pull away from him as he says, '... on my world there are no women!!!' The ending suggests, we can

**67** R. Michael Rosen (w) and Jack Sparling (a), 'A Slimy Situation', *Vampirella* #3

only assume, that she is going to be raped and made to bear children for the rest of her life. Vampirella closes the story with the equally troubling assertion, 'How lucky can one girl get? Just think of all the date mates she'll meet once Mr. Keifer introduces her to ... the boys!'[62]

In addition to sexualization, *Vampirella* undercuts the apparent agency of strong women by consistently having them outwitted by men. The presence of female vampires, for example, offers a reversal of the hypnotism trope described above, where female vampires bring male victims under their spell. Such a scenario plays out in 'Rhapsody in Red' in *Vampirella* #2. In this story, a couple are driven from the road while driving through Transylvania. They take refuge in a castle that is, predictably, occupied by a female vampire. During the night the man awakens and is drawn to the vampire in much the same way as Dracula's victims described above (Figure 68).

In this scenario, however, the man turns the tables. 'You shall be my husband in death', the vampire asserts and then, as the man runs from her, 'Wait! To where do you run?' She follows him to the bedroom

**68** Don Glut (w) and Billy Graham (a), 'Rhapsody in Red', *Vampirella* #2

where his partner sleeps, calling after him. Where she previously acted from a position of power, she is suddenly pleading: 'Wait! Do not do the thing I suspect! Do not act foolishly Richard! Come back we must stay together!' She arrives to discover that he has passed on vampirism to his human partner. He then stabs the pleading vampire with a sword, reducing her to a pile of bones. 'I said I'd always love you, dear', he says, 'Now I can give you something a travelling insurance man couldn't! Eternal life!' While the story engages with the trope of vampiric seduction, it does so in a way that continues to privilege masculine agency.[63]

## Conclusion

The horror genre of the 1960s and 1970s, then, seems to have absorbed some of the language and rhetoric of second-wave feminism; it presented a range of independent and powerful female characters, many of whom wield power in a way endorsed by the story. In rare cases, such as that of Rachel Van Helsing, these characters are not presented as direct objects of the male gaze, despite the protests of male readers. Such representational strategies were rendered in stark relief by the women around them. Women such as Rachel Van Helsing are staged as 'resistant texts'; they simultaneously promote a message of empowerment but, through their proximity to other, less resistant, bodies, are nonetheless subject to the diegetic and extradiegetic male gaze. Letters do not praise Rachel for her resistance; they condemn her for sartorial choices and present her as something to be decoded – or de-clothed. While there are, as this indicates, divergent reading strategies, the male readers who wrote to complain about Rachel's dress sense, whether consciously or not, aligned themselves with Dracula in seeking to use their gaze to change the behaviour of the women at whom they look. In most cases, any power these female characters are seen to possess is undercut by their representation, as the explicit subject of male desire both in the visual rhetoric on the page and in the idealized girlfriend trope. In this sense, these comics resemble contemporary pin-ups found in the pages of *Penthouse* – they borrow the language of female empowerment while reinscribing familiar tropes of objectification.

In the majority of stories, too, female power is either presented in such a way as to be contingent on male authority or an endorsement of male power; Rachel Van Helsing is allowed to wield a stake only as long as her doing so does not require any change on the part of her male allies, and Vampirella's ability to control her monstrosity is contingent on her relationship with a man. While these female characters act with a greater degree of agency than their predecessors in the 1940s and 1950s, they nonetheless ultimately serve to assure male readers of their own power. Women are empowered within existing structures, provided it is at the behest of, and to the benefit of, male characters who remain in a position of unchallenged authority. Critical projects on the nature of women and their social role therefore seem to have passed by creative teams of this period; instead of a deconstruction of practice and representation, contemporary discourse on the place of women seems to have mostly led to the inclusion of 'powerful' women who are narratively capable of very little.

More troubling still, comics of this era contain storylines and images that both demonize the feminist movement and depict women as manipulative, evil, and deserving of sexualized violence. Lenore makes Frankenstein's monster fall in love with her, only to betray him; Amy in 'A Slimy Situation' meets a sexualized and violent end after she attempts to steal from her husband; and the vampire in 'Rhapsody in Red' turns the male protagonist into a vampire only to die at his hands. In this sense, little had changed since the 1940s and 1950s; women continued to play the role of the monster, to be subject to seemingly well-deserved misogynistic violence, or to be so divested of personality that the violence to which they are subjected serves only as the background to male victimhood.

Anxieties around the role of women in American society mapped clearly onto contemporary comics, though in refracted and mediated ways. Comics exist in dialogue with not just social, political, and economic histories, but also their own institutional histories. Horror narratives crafted in the wake of the revision of the Comics Code in 1971, amid a crisis of readership as sales figures declined right across the industry, show awareness of contemporary events, but also look back to the 1950s – sometimes because they are, in fact, reprinted stories from the 1950s. Many comics creators working in the 1970s had lived and worked through the horror boom of the 1950s. Given the growth in popularity of horror films in the late 1960s and early 1970s, having precipitated one crisis, horror comics seemed to offer the solution to another. This meant a remediation of past narratives, imagery, and techniques, within an increasingly complex matrix of unrest, industrially and contextually. The continuing strictures of the Code, even after revision, meant that horror comics could not compete with the innovations in horror cinema by directors such as George Romero (*Night of the Living Dead*, 1968), Wes Craven (*The Last House on the Left*, 1972), and Tobe Hooper (*The Texas Chainsaw Massacre*, 1974). Similarly, films such as *Rosemary's Baby* (1968) documented fears of and about women in ways that comics could not match, not only due to the Code but the formal limitations that, even in continuing series, tended to work against complexity and depth in narrative and representation. Another factor working against the nuanced representation of women was the preponderance of male writers and artists working in comics. Character development and the exploration of contemporary issues leant characters more depth during this era, but a lack of diversity among writers did little to ameliorate the continued adoption of stereotypes and conventional representational practices that were more often restrictive of, or harmful to, women. All too often, women were under attack in, and by, the horror comic.

## Notes

1 Paul had been working with Smith since 1945 on ways to advance women's rights. Despite the overlap of the Civil Rights and women's rights movements, Smith supported equal rights for women but was opposed to equality for African Americans. Many of the concerns in the two movements might have been similar (and certainly appear similar to some contemporary and more modern eyes) but by no means did supporting one cause mean that support for the other logically followed. The passage of the Civil Rights Act of 1964 was, clearly, also not the end for either movement.

2 Rosen, *The World Split Open*, 66

3 While Miss America came under criticism for its objectification and commodification of women, it also came under fire for the beauty conventions it offered as models. The first Miss Black America pageant took place in 1968 to 'champion the beauty of Black women and protest racial exclusion in the Miss America pageant' and in the process demonstrated 'radical feminism's failure to be a multiracial and intersectional political movement'. While this period marked a high point in feminist activism, it does not mean that all of those involved in the various branches of feminism were attuned to, or willing to challenge, intersecting axes of oppression.

4 See, for instance, Julie Berebitsky, 'The Joy of Work: Helen Gurley Brown, Gender, and Sexuality in the White-Collar Office', *Journal of the History of Sexuality* 15.1 (2006), 89–127, and Jennifer Scanlon, 'Sexy from the Start: Anticipatory Elements of Second Wave Feminism', *Women's Studies* 38.2 (2009), 127–150.

5 Shulamith Firestone, *The Dialectic of Sex: The Case for Feminist Revolution* (New York: William Morrow and Company, 1970), 11.

6 Norman Mailer, *Prisoner of Sex* (New York: Little Brown, 1971), 128.

7 Marabel Morgan, *The Total Woman* (Old Tappan, NJ: Spire Books, 1973), 60, 57.

8 Françoise Coste, 'Conservative Women and Feminism in the United States:

Between Hatred and Appropriation', *Caliban: French Journal of English Studies* 27 (2017), 167–176 (167).

9  Gabor (ed.), *The Pinup*, 79.

10  Gabor (ed.), *The Pinup*, 79.

11  Quoted in Gabor (ed.), *The Pinup*, 118.

12  See also, for instance, Andrea Dworkin, *Pornography: Men Possessing Women* (New York: Penguin, 1989).

13  See, for instance, Katherine Turk, 'Out of the Revolution, into the Mainstream: Employment Activism in the NOW Sears Campaign and the Growing Pains of Liberal Feminism', *Journal of American History* 97.2 (2010), 399–423.

14  For more on the Kanigher/Woolfolk incident, see Michael Goodrum, '"Superman Believes that a Wife's Place is in the Home": *Superman's Girl Friend, Lois Lane* and the Representation of Women', *Gender & History* 30.2 (2018), 442–464, and Tim Hanley, *Investigating Lois Lane: The Turbulent History of the Daily Planet's Ace Reporter* (Chicago, IL: Chicago Review Press, 2016).

15  Even in the twenty-first century, the representation of female bodies in super-hero comics remains problematic. See, for example, Cocca, *Superwomen*; Mike Madrid, *The Supergirls: Fashion, Feminism, Fantasy, and the History of Comic Book Heroines* (Minneapolis, MN: Exterminating Angel Press, 2009); Michael Goodrum, Tara Prescott, and Philip Smith (eds), *Gender and the Superhero Narrative* (Jackson, MS: University Press of Mississippi, 2018).

16  Admittedly, all we have done with this book is stitch together research using our 'man-brains'. While some of this was done on trains, Mina's knowledge would certainly make her our superior – and have averted, if nothing else, two hours on a rail replacement bus between Ashford and Hastings. For a more considered take on Mina's research and its meaning, and the role of work and productivity in the novel, see Eric Kwan-Wai Yu, 'Productive Fear: Labour, Sexuality and, Mimicry in Bram Stoker's *Dracula*', *Texas Studies in Literature and Language* 48.2 (2006), 145–170.

17  Clint Higgenbotham in Gardner F. Fox (w), Eugene Colan (a), Tom Palmer (i), Artie Simek (l), and Roy Thomas (e), 'Death to a Vampire-Slayer!', *Tomb of Dracula* #5 (New York: Marvel, 1972), 30.

18  Fox et al., 'Death to a Vampire-Slayer!', 30.

19  Tim Hanley 'The Evolution of Female Readership', in Goodrum, Prescott, and Smith (eds), *Gender and the Superhero Narrative*, 221–250.

20  Hanley acknowledges that letters columns are a curated space and so are not necessarily reflective of readership. It is significant, nonetheless, that comics editors saw less of a need to represent female voices in letters pages as they had a decade previously.

21  The notion of something horrifying walking 'among us' most likely stems from scripture, with similar sentiments in Job 1:7 with Satan 'roaming through the Earth' and 1 Peter 5:8, where the Devil 'walketh about, seeking whom he may devour'.

22  Friedrich et al., *Monster of Frankenstein* #5, 3. This assertion is arguably untrue to the source material, where the monster murders Elizabeth, Frankenstein's

fiancée, presumably with his hands (although we could debate whether or not this constitutes 'holding' a woman).

23 Friedrich et al., *Monster of Frankenstein #5*, 6.
24 Friedrich et al., *Monster of Frankenstein #5*, 28.
25 Gabriel Gianola and Janine Coleman, 'Gwen Stacy and the Progression of Women in Comics', in Goodrum, Prescott, and Smith (eds), *Gender and the Superhero Narrative*, 251–295.
26 Arnold T. Blumberg, '"The Night Gwen Stacy Died": The End of Innocence and the "Last Gasp of the Silver Age"', *International Journal of Comic Art* 8.1 (2006), 197–211 (198).
27 Goodrum, '"Superman Believes that a Wife's Place is in the Home"'.
28 Gerry Conway (w), Gene Colan (a, i), John Costanza (l), and Stan Lee (e), *Tomb of Dracula #1* (New York: Marvel, 1972), 17.
29 See, for example, Stephen D. Arata, '"The Occidental Tourist": *Dracula* and the Anxiety of Reverse Colonization', *Victorian Studies* 33.4 (1990), 621–645; John Allen Stevenson, 'A Vampire in the Mirror: The Sexuality of Dracula', *Publications of the Modern Language Association of America* (1988), 139–149.
30 Gerry Conway (w), Gene Colan (a), Tom Palmer (i), John Costanza (l), and Stan Lee (e), *Tomb of Dracula #10* (New York: Marvel, 1973), 11.
31 Writer Gerry Conway was a mere twenty years old at the time, which perhaps partly explains, though not excuses, the presence of immature attitudes to women and relationships in his work.
32 Forrest J. Ackerman, *Vampirella #1* (New York: Warren Publishing, 1969).
33 Much like the horror comics of the 1950s, *Vampirella* presented horror in combination with a range of other genres. The first issue makes the following proposal: 'Interested in vampire stories reader bleeders?' asks Vampirella, 'But sick of the same old rot about red clotted cloaks and crumbling crypts? Looking for something disgustingly new and cute?' The stories which follow deliver on the promise, providing a rage of sub-genres within horror from science fiction to pirates.
34 Glut and Piscopo, 'Queen of Horror', 33. *Barbarella* was a (mildly) sexually explicit French comic book created by Jean-Claude Forest and first published in 1962. It served as inspiration for a film of the same name in 1968.
35 The number of instances of female nudity increase significantly after issue twelve. Sales figures for *Vampirella* are only available after 1974. We might speculate that the anti-war letter from the editor which opened issue seven in September 1970 might have damaged sales although youth opinion was overwhelmingly against the war by this stage and so it is unlikely that many readers would have taken offence. The higher instances of nudity are more likely to be due to changes in the artistic duties from a rotating group of veterans to several Spanish artists drafted in for their professionalism and speed. These Spanish artists radically altered the look of Warren's magazines. See Richard J. Arndt's foreword to *Creepy Archives* vol. 9 (New York: Dark Horse, 2011) for more information.
36 Michael P. Paumgardhen, 'Third Degree', *Vampirella #5* (New York: Warren Publishing, 1970), 4; Gary Charwin, Letter, *Vampirella #6* (New York: Warren Publishing, 1970), 4.

37  Vampirella, 'Around the Edges', *Vampirella* #5 (New York: Warren Publishing, 1970), 4.

38  For more on the history of women in comics see Betsy Gomez (ed.), *She Changed Comics: The Untold Story of the Women Who Changed Free Expression in Comics* (Berkley, CA: Image Comics, 2001).

39  Pete Shaeffer, 'Cuti Pie', *Vampirella* #4 (New York: Warren Publishing, 1970), 5.

40  The letters pages of each issue typically featured fifteen letters, of which one would be written by someone with a female name. This proportion is lower than those from DC titles at the same time, and far below the industry average from the 1960s. See Hanley, 'The Evolution of Female Readership', in Goodrum, Prescott, and Smith (eds), *Gender and the Superhero Narrative.*

41  Art Spiegelman, 'Those Dirty Little Comics', in Bob Aldeman (ed.), *The Tijuana Bibles* (New York: Simon & Schuster, 2006), 9.

42  Jerry Boyd, 'Taste the Blood of Vampirella: A 40th Anniversary Tribute', *Back Issue* 36 (2009) 20–27 (20). Readership figures for *Vampirella* do not include a breakdown by gender, but a 1970 survey revealed that readers of Skywald Publications' *Scream*, *Nightmare*, and *Psycho* were 90 per cent male and predominantly thirteen to sixteen years old, see Mike Benton, *Horror Comics: The Illustrated History* (Dallas, TX: Taylor Publishing, 1991) 68.

43  Bram Stoker, *Dracula*, ed. Roger Luckhurst (Oxford: Oxford University Press, 2011), 39.

44  Stoker, *Dracula*, 343.

45  The only surviving footage of Nurmi as Vampira is in Ed Wood's *Plan 9 From Outer Space* (1959). This was also the last film to feature Bela Lugosi.

46  Don Doering, Letter, *Vampirella* #3 (New York: Warren Publishing, 1970), 4.

47  Vampirella, Letter, *Vampirella* #7 (New York: Warren Publishing, 1970), 4.

48  As Wandtke observes, Vampirella's status as monster does not last long. By the eighth issue she 'mostly wants to do good' and becomes 'a superhero with powers tied to her monstrous nature'. Wandtke, *The Comics Scare Returns*, 60.

49  Anon. and Lazarus, 'Vampires? Don't Make Me Laugh'.

50  Greg Morgan, 'Too Blood Thirsty', *Vampirella* #4 (New York: Warren Publishing, 1970), 2.

51  Vampirella, 'Why a Witch Trilogy?', *Vampirella* #7 (New York: Warren Publishing, 1970), 6

52  Quoted in Roach and Cooke, *The Warren Companion*, 96.

53  Donald F. McGregor (w) and Luis Garcia (a), 'Welcome to the Witches' Coven', *Vampirella* #15 (New York: Warren Publishing, 1972), 57.

54  McGregor and Garcia, 'Welcome to the Witches' Coven', 60

55  McGregor and Garcia, 'Welcome to the Witches' Coven', 58

56  McGregor and Garcia, 'Welcome to the Witches' Coven', 65

57  Tim Hanley, *Wonder Woman Unbound* (Chicago, IL: Chicago Review Press, 2014).

58  Noah Berlatsky, *Wonder Woman: Bondage and Feminism in the Marston/Peter Comics* (New Brunswick, NJ: Rutgers University Press, 2015).

59  Don Glut (w) and Tony Tallarigo (a), 'Spaced-out Girls!', *Vampirella* #1 (New York: Warren Publishing, 1969), 45.

60  R. Michael Rosen (w) and Jack Sparling (a), 'A Slimy Situation', *Vampirella* #3 (New York: Warren Publishing 1970), 58

61  Rosen and Sparling, 'A Slimy Situation'.

62  Bill Parente (w) and David Sinclair (a), 'Forgotten Kingdom', *Vampirella* #2 (New York: Warren Publishing, 1970), 15. The narrative overlooks the simpler solution of bringing the two planets together, resolving the problems of each through less forcible means.

63  This obliquely references Universal's 1943 film *Son of Dracula*, where the male object of female vampiric sexual desire appears to succumb to her advances, only to later exercise male agency over and above the power of the female supernatural.

# 7

## 'We are a species that fears itself most of all' – race in the 1960s and 1970s

During the 1940s and 1950s, as previously established, people of colour were underrepresented in comics. In the 1970s, publishers, who had once readily evoked racist stereotypes, were now cautious of causing offence but uncertain as to how to reach new, and retain old, markets. They thus tended either to approach the question of race through allegory or simply to omit people of colour from their works. While many comics publishers were broadly opposed to overt racism, they nonetheless contributed to both the erasure of minority identities and a sense of white America as under threat from encroaching multiculturalism. By the 1970s, the public conversation around race and representation had changed. This is not to say that the problem of structural and direct racism had, in any sense, been resolved, or that there were distinctive new challenges, but rather that the question of civil rights in the US had reached a level of such political and social import that it penetrated popular culture – the minority experience could no longer simply be ignored.

As successors to EC, comics by Warren Publications inevitably featured many of the same types of story as their predecessor and while the context around race had changed, the types of storyline and implicit assumptions around race had not. As before, these comics often addressed overt forms of racism while reinforcing racist stereotypes. In 'Freedom's Just Another Word', which appeared in *Creepy* #53 (1973), for example, a white community harass and eventually murder a black family who move into their neighbourhood. The one survivor, the grandmother of the family, then uses voodoo to enact her revenge, suggesting, at least in part, that the fears of the white characters in the story were justified. While there was no shift away from people of colour as a source of horror, progress in civil rights can nonetheless be measured by the situations in which racism is shown to occur. The comic 'Snake Eyes', for example, which appears in *Vampirella* #8, is a reworking of 'The Snake Man' published in *Chamber of Chills* twenty years

**69** Nicola Cuti (w) and Jack Sparling (w), 'Snake Eyes', *Vampirella* #8

previously. While the metaphorical African American, Serpentine, was a carnival freak who is abused on a bus and at a lunch counter, Sara, the snake-like protagonist of 'Snake Eyes', is a third-generation Egyptian immigrant who is attacked and made to feel unwelcome on a university campus. In one scene, two white students approach Sara and mock her appearance; 'Hi there, SSSSara', says the girl. 'My but your fangs looks esssspecially ssssharp today!' The boy asks, 'Do you like my gloves Sara? They're made of genuine snakeskin!' (Figure 69).[1]

If 'The Snake Man' was a (problematic) depiction of 1950s racism, then 'Snake Eyes' is the same story for the 1970s. The events are a somewhat transparent reference to the tensions around increased number of African Americans attending institutions of higher education. Riots and protests had erupted during the 1960s at the University of Georgia and the University of Mississippi over the arrival of the first black students. When, in 1963, Vivian Malone and James Hood arrived at the University of Alabama in Tuscaloosa, they did so under the watch of guards, sent for their protection. In 1970, as the story 'Snake Eyes' was being written, protests by students at Ohio State University, who demanded greater enrolment opportunities for black students, were met by the National Guard. In 'Snake Eyes', Sara's protector, her white friend Charlie, leaps to Sara's aid, infantilizing people of colour and subsuming their story into that of a white hero.[2] More problematically still, Charlie's kindness and access to education are not enough to civilize Sara and, like Serpentine before her, she reverts to savagery by the end of the story, validating stereotypes and justifying the prejudice that the story seems, on its surface, to oppose.

The 1970s also saw a return of anxieties over racialized spaces in the US, as well as a reconfiguration and refraction of anxieties around urban development and redevelopment. While the 1950s was characterized by the movement of middle-class white families into the suburbs, the late 1960s and 1970s were characterized by transregional migration. Between 1968 and 1978, the US Bureau of Labor Statistics recorded net migration in the four major regions of the US as follows: Northeast -2,284,000; North Central -2,034,000; South 2,655,000; and West 1,763,000.[3] This reversal of the trend of postbellum migration and patterns of development (apart from the continued expansion of the West) drove changing patterns of federal funding, leading to relative job losses in the developed industrial heartlands of the frostbelt as new industries moved to, or were established in, the South. Debates about the effects of this led *Business Week* to refer to a 'Second War Between the States', demonstrating both the level of tension reached in national discourse and drawing on the racialized language embedded in discussions of the Civil War by adopting one of the Southern names for the conflict.[4] Such concerns filtered into horror comics in stories such as 'New Girl in Town', where a woman walks through an unfamiliar neighbourhood. The horror host Vampirella introduces the story: 'You stand in the recessed doorway of the little store staring down the main street of this odd town. Everything seems so different from the pleasant hills where you used to live. But your parents moved away from there'.[5] The following panels show a woman (the 'you' whom Vampirella addresses) walking through a neighbourhood filled with broken windows and tenement blocks. She is afraid of the residents, commenting that 'These folks give me the heebie-jeebies! They're trying to be friendly, I guess – But they sure go about it in a funny way!' (Figure 70).[6]

One resident wears an open shirt and a medallion. Others wear dark glasses. They are not coded explicitly as people of colour (although they could be read as Latino), but they are presented as a source of horror: 'What a pair of goofballs', the protagonist says to herself, 'They sure were scary'.[7] As with the comics of the 1950s, here monstrosity is substituted for race, and is tied to a specific urban space. The protagonist can be read as having moved from a white suburban neighbourhood to an inner-city, or from one region to another. This is partially supported by the fact that she regards the people around her, whose ways are unlike those to which she is accustomed, with revulsion and fear. At its close, the story corroborates those fears; she discovers that, like her new

**70** Gardner Fox (w) and Dan Dakins (a), 'New Girl in Town', *Vampirella* #5

**71** Gardner Fox (w) and Dan Dakins (a), 'New Girl in Town', *Vampirella* #5

neighbours, she is living in the land of the dead. In the final panel the monsters lunge at her, telling her 'Your [sic] one of us now! This is your home!' (Figure 71).[8]

The comic, as with those of the 1950s, communicates a fear of people of colour entering white spaces, and of white people (and women in particular) being harmed in neighbourhoods primarily populated by minorities. The continuity of concerns can partly be attributed to continuity in writers: Gardner Fox, who wrote 'New Girl in Town', for example, had been working in comics since the 1930s. The danger in the story transforms from fear of being assaulted or robbed, to a fear over a loss of identity – that when the racial profile of a neighbourhood's residents changes, so too does the neighbourhood. While urban centres may have been formerly desirable to white Americans, demographic shifts rendered them not just undesirable, but threatening and uncanny. This is relevant to the construction of new communities in the sunbelt as affluent migrants moved into still-developing, or redeveloping, spaces. The context for the stories, then, had changed, but the underlying themes (in the majority of Warren Publications' horror magazines, at least) had not. Both 'Snake Eyes' and 'New Girl in Town' recycled racist tropes from the 1950s. They depict people of colour, and the spaces they inhabit, as dangerous. The two decades of vocal and visible Civil Rights agitation had done little to change horror writers' perspective – they were critical of overt racism, yet perpetuated its more subtle, but no less toxic, manifestations.

## Black power

While some themes endured, comics creators were not entirely insulated from debates around race. As the previous chapter established, horror comics did not develop in isolation from cultural shifts occurring during the 1960s and 1970s. They continued to promote a phallocentric world-view while incorporating pseudo-feminist messages that were, at best, superficial and unthreatening to the white male hegemony. Just as the Women's Liberation movement informed the horror genre, so too did the Civil Rights movement. While white characters were still overwhelmingly the norm, the changing public conversation around race gave rise to characters of colour in horror comics who (like parallel figures in the superhero genre) occupy roles of heroes and protagonists. 'The Black Witch', which appeared in *Vampirella* #7, for example, features an African American protagonist who educates himself in the supernatural and successfully outsmarts a witch.[9]

The growing visibility of black characters was a symptom of cultural changes. Following the gains made during the Second World War, an organized movement in support of legal and cultural shifts around racial issues developed during the 1950s. In 1954, the landmark *Brown v. Board of Education* case made segregation in public schools illegal, and in 1955 a group of black ministers, most famously Dr Martin Luther King Jr, formed the thousand-strong Montgomery Improvement Association. They were followed, during the early 1960s by the Student Non-Violent Coordinating Committee (SNCC), which sought to represent the interests of younger African Americans and accelerate the pace of change. In 1963, 200,000 people marched on Washington in support of equal rights. The Civil Rights Act, which followed in 1964, outlawed discrimination based on race, colour, sex, religion, or country of birth.

Major comics publishers such as Marvel and DC were broadly aligned with the more moderate advocates of civil rights but were opposed to any kind of dramatic shifts in the social order. Goodrum argues that 'Marvel had consistently argued for a liberal agenda throughout the 1960s on points of inclusion, but it had never advocated any change to the system'.[10] During the 1960s and early 1970s, various superhero comics not only introduced black characters but acknowledged the challenges facing black communities in the US. In *Green Lantern co-starring Green Arrow* #76 (1970), for example, the titular hero is confronted by an elderly black man who accuses him of saving 'blue skins ... orange skins ...[and] purple skins' but never 'black skins'.[11] His companion, Green Arrow, continues the harangue, declaring, 'On the streets of Memphis a good black man died, and in Los Angeles, a good white man fell. Something is wrong! Something is killing us all! Some hideous moral cancer is rotting our very souls'.[12] A similar plot plays out in *Superman's Girl Friend, Lois Lane* #106, when Lois is turned into a black woman for a day. She experiences racism and is witness to life in an economically disadvantaged black community.[13] Lois gives a blood transfusion to Dave Stevens, an individual who is, the comic heavily suggests, a member of, or at least ideologically aligned with, the Black Panther party. On discovering that his life has been saved by a white woman, Stevens overcomes his own prejudice against whites and agrees to work with Lois. No change is necessary on the part of Lois or Superman, both of whom, the comic suggests, are already sufficiently educated on matters of race relations. Creative teams, then, were clearly interested in addressing social issues around race to a far greater extent than their predecessors two decades before.[14] Their delivery was clumsy, however – for all of his rhetoric, the Green Lantern did little to follow through on his vow to protect black communities on Earth, and Lois Lane's plotline fails to differentiate between types of prejudice, suggesting that a member of the Black Panther party who (quite reasonably) distrusts white authority is equally at fault as a white racist who hates blacks. In the Lois Lane story, black gangsters are shown luring children out of school and into a life of crime, and the only direct victim of prejudice in the story is Lois (while she is both white and black). Both stories are written from a position of self-congratulatory white superiority and seem to suggest that African Americans are incapable of improving their own lives. Instead, the best solution to endemic poverty and systematic racism, the comics suggest, is intervention by well-meaning white people on an individual basis of uplift rather than systemic reform and the empowerment of marginalized communities. In this sense, comics had failed to move on from the paternalistic liberalism of the 1940s and 1950s, best exemplified in the series of 'public announcements' found in DC comics and the series Johnny Everyman.[15]

The increasing visibility of people of colour in the pages of horror comics mediates the growing Black Power movement of the time and the cultural trend of Blaxploitation that grew out of it. During the mid-1960s, the division between different branches of the Civil Rights movement became pronounced, with Stokely Carmichael, then-head of the SNCC, popularizing the concept of Black Power and arguing, unlike others in the movement, that violence was an appropriate and necessary means to protect African American lives. The Black Panther Party for Self-Defense, which formed in 1966, organized armed citizen patrols, marches, and community social programmes providing food and education for disenfranchised black communities. One premise that informed the Black Power movement was that the white hegemony would never give up power willingly – that any significant social change could only be achieved if supported by the threat of force. The image of armed black men marching in support of radical social change was horrifying to many white Americans. J. Edgar Hoover, then-director of the FBI, famously described the Black Panther Party as 'the greatest threat to the internal security of the country'.[16] One figure who engages with this trend is Blade, a vampire hunter who made his debut in *Tomb of Dracula* #10 (1973). While Blade's origin speaks directly to the experience of African Americans, he nonetheless embodies certain toxic stereotypes of black masculinity and engages with the history of race in America in such a way as to alleviate any sense of responsibility on the part of white readers.

Blade is dramatically different from the black characters who appeared in the pages of *Green Lantern co-starring Green Arrow* and *Superman's Girl Friend, Lois Lane*. Rather than serving as motivation for an existing white character to intervene in the lives of others, Blade is a hero in his own right. He was not the first black hero to appear in a comic – the Black Panther first appeared in 1966, and the Falcon made his debut three years later in 1969. Blade was the first character, however, to be visually coded as a member of the Black Power movement (Figure 72).

Blade lacks a beret and lapel pin, and his green leather jacket is somewhat more stylized than those worn by members of the Black Panther Party, but he has clearly been modelled on their aesthetics (Figure 73). This includes not only his clothing but also his willingness to wield weapons; no sooner has he appeared, than he launches himself into combat with a group of vampires, killing all of them. Indeed, the rhetoric (if not, typically, the practice) of the Black Power movement seems well-suited to the comics medium at the time – in superhero (and superhero-inflected horror) comics problems are generally resolved through combat rather than dialogue, peaceful protest, and legal reforms.

The representation of a black character as a hero was an improvement on the representation of black characters during the 1950s, but it nonetheless needs to be carefully unpacked. It is problematic, for example, that Blade is presented as physically tough and never fearful. Instead, he presents the problematic archetype of the tough black man – a heroic and perhaps admirable figure who is always nonetheless required to present a hypermasculine demeanour.[17] To choose one of numerous examples, in *Tomb of Dracula* #12, Blade smashes through a wooden door to confront Dracula, emerging entirely unscathed. Such actions were part of the standard fare of the superhero genre and yet the image of the black male as emotionally and physically stronger than his white

**72** Marv Wolfman (w), Gene Colan (a), Jack Abel (i), Denise Vladimer (l), and Roy Thomas (e), *Tomb of Dracula* #10

counterpart (an attribute that Blade shares, in a more codified form, with Luke Cage) supports racist assumptions with roots in the antebellum period that black people are less sensitive to pain than white people. The strong black archetype, Angelica Jade Bastién argues, 'operates as another way for our pain to go unheard and the institutions that wreak havoc on our communities to go unchecked'.[18] That Blade is also more physical than cerebral, another racist trope, is present in the fact that his initial actions disturb the plan of attack laid out by the white characters; Blade's violence is less carefully directed and is therefore, unlike representations of white violence, destructive rather than regenerative.[19]

Despite the invocation of certain racist stereotypes, Blade is made to speak to specifically African American concerns. In *Tomb of Dracula* #13, Blade gives his origin story. He describes how his was a difficult birth; his mother 'was cryin' out in agony 'cause I was proving I was a tough one – even then'.[20] When it became apparent that she would need medical care, her friends called for a doctor. Finding one proved

**73** Members of the Black Panther Party gathered at the Free Huey Rally in Oakland California, 1969 ©, Stephen Shames

difficult: 'it took forever 'fore they got one who'd come to them an' even then it was hours 'fore he finally came'. What is heavily suggested here is that African Americans were (and, indeed, are) under-served by health-care providers. As Angela K. Woods demonstrates, African Americans have historically experienced worse healthcare outcomes than those of white European heritage.[21] Enslaved Africans and their descend-ants living in the Southern US, Woods asserts, were generally denied access to healthcare and so tended to rely upon more traditional home medical practices. Enslaved black people were also subject to medical experimentation, as in the work of Dr J. Marion Sims, who carried out experimental procedures on enslaved women between 1845 and 1849.[22] After the end of the antebellum period and Northern migration, many African Americans continued (and still continue) to be more likely to turn to self-treatment over care received from a doctor than those who identify as belonging to other racial groups. This arises not only from a culture of self-care, but from racist practices in the medical profession. During the famous Tuskegee Syphilis study, which ran from 1930 to 1972, the United States Public Health Service withheld treatment from 400 black men. The failure of the US government to provide for the medical needs of African American citizens was one of the causes taken up by the Black Panther Party, which ran free screenings for Sickle Cell

Anaemia and advocated for free healthcare for all black and oppressed people.[23] The ramifications of this history continue to be felt today; Spector reports that, even in the twenty-first century, African Americans continue to find the experience of receiving health care degrading, are less trustful of doctors, and feel that the healthcare system privileges white patients over those of colour.[24] Blade's mother's experience, then, is tied directly to her status as a black woman, and the scene as a whole plays out a history, and critique, of discriminatory and exploitative medical practices.

By giving birth at home, under the care of friends and family, Blade's mother, faced with an emergency beyond the capacity of those attending to her, is forced to open her doors to a predator. The doctor who comes to visit her is a white man. In the panel in which he first appears, he is depicted from below, emphasizing his power. In the background, one of Blade's mother's friends, an African American woman, raises her hands to her face in horror (Figure 74).

The man, it transpires, is a vampire, and, when the others have left the room, he begins to feed on Blade's mother. Blade asserts, 'He smiled at her and said something softly in her ear, and whatever that something was made her break … and scream!'[25] The accompanying panel shows the vampire drawing close and enveloping her as she attempts to pull away from him, her mouth open in horror (Figure 75). The scene speaks to a long history of sexual violence inflicted by white men on African and African American women, beginning during the antebellum period, with white slave owners assaulting black women, and continuing as

**74** Marv Wolfman (w), Gene Colan (a), Tom Palmer (i, c), John Costanza (l), and Roy Thomas (e), *Tomb of Dracula* #13

**75** Marv Wolfman (w), Gene Colan (a), Tom Palmer (i, c), John Costanza (l), and Roy Thomas (e), *Tomb of Dracula* #13

a weapon used by racist groups. It also draws on Florence Marryat's novel of 1897, *Blood of the Vampire*, which features a child conceived by a white slave-owner with his black slave who, while pregnant, is bitten by a vampire bat. She subsequently dies in childbirth, like Blade's mother, and the vampiric taint is passed through the blood to the child.[26] Discussions of 'tainted' blood also inevitably draw on racist discussions of miscegenation. Historically, discourse around rape in America has tended to focus on the white woman's experience and has underplayed or ignored the rape of black women.[27] That black women were frequently subject to rape under slavery is well documented: in the case of Celia in 1855, a slave in Missouri killed her master as he was trying to rape her. Although state law decreed that any woman who killed a man in such circumstances was acting in self-defence, state law also refused to acknowledge Celia as a woman; she was, instead, property, and as such it was decided that her master had been acting within his legal rights. Celia was sentenced to death but not until she had delivered the pregnancy that resulted from sexual abuse.

Blade's origin story thus recasts vampirism as an allegory for systemic racism, with white vampires preying on African Americans, and Blade as an emblem of black power, resisting this oppression through militant means. This is made perhaps most apparent when Dracula is an invited guest of honour on a cruise ship in *Tomb of Dracula* #10, a move that aligns him with those who hold economic and social capital. This is not a new characterization for vampires; there is a long history of the representation of the vampire as an aristocrat, codified as early as John Polidori's *The Vampyre* (1819).[28] In challenging vampires here, Blade challenges a wider system of social and economic subjugation. *Tomb of Dracula* is noteworthy for drawing attention to African American concerns, specifically the ways in which healthcare and the law have failed to serve African American communities. It also inverts many of the tropes of the 1950s horror comics, with a white body in a black space as threatening rather than threatened. Black fear is therefore presented as empathetic, as a position for the reader to occupy, rather than as spectacle, as a representational strategy to emphasise the threat to the white protagonists. Blade's origin story advocates a philosophy of both individual and community self-defence, where a group of young black women are capable of confronting a vampire and, later, a black man takes up arms against a foe who has subjected him and the generations who came before him to violence.

By making vampires the symbol of a white hegemony, however, the comic effectively exonerates the white protagonists with whom the reader is expected to empathise. In Blade's first appearance, the characters he rescues are white, suggesting that people of all backgrounds are equally at risk of falling prey to a vampire. Just as Lois Lane and Green Lantern present themselves as the white saviours of African American communities, Frank Drake, the recurring hero of the *Tomb of Dracula* stories, fights alongside Blade in an effort to kill Dracula without recognizing that, if Blade is to be understood as a member of the Black Power movement, then Drake, a white man who has inherited wealth and property and is invested in preserving the status quo, is part of the problem. The comic thus presents racism as an external problem, the solution to which just requires the elimination of overt racists rather than introspection, reparation, and societal reform. A white reader can easily read the comic and, even if he or she recognizes the metaphors at play, congratulate him or herself for not being the kind of predator who killed Blade's mother and thus feel exonerated. The version of Black Power embodied by Blade neither threatens the social fabric nor requires any change on the part of white readers on either a societal or individual level. Just as Vampirella is a superficial embodiment of the feminist movement presented primarily for titillation, Blade appropriates the aesthetics of Black Power while robbing it of its philosophical underpinnings and attendant critique of white America.

## Brother voodoo

Another black character who was able to make something of himself, as it were, yet never fully escape his blackness, is Jericho Drumm. Much of the voodoo imagery that appeared in horror comics of the 1970s recycled tropes from comics of the 1950s and, indeed, Jericho Drumm was first imagined during the 1950s.[29] Drumm, however, was not only a nostalgic figure, but was redesigned to engage with the voodoo craze of the era. Drumm's introduction by Tony Isabella in *Tales of the Zombie* #2 (1973) declared that voodoo was 'the current rage ... Paperbacks on the subject litter newsstands throughout the world [and] voodoo cults are reportedly springing up in major cities throughout the United States'.[30] Examples of voodoo abound in popular culture of the period: *Live and Let Die* (1973), the first Bond film to star Roger Moore, for example, drew on popular images of Louisiana voodoo and contemporary American racial politics. Voodoo also became a popular touchstone in music; Dr. John brought Louisiana voodoo to a wider audience through his debut album, *Gris-Gris* (1968).[31] More famously in 1968, Jimi Hendrix described himself (or rather, the speaker in his song) as a 'Voodoo Child'.[32] Film also produced an interest in zombies: George A. Romero's seminal *Night of the Living Dead* (1968), discussed previously, redefined the zombie (without ever using the word) as the flesh-eating undead, removing the figure from its historical, cultural, and political context in colonial Caribbean spaces. In the process, the film engaged with more contemporary concerns, still around race, through the death of the black protagonist, Ben, who having survived the nocturnal zombie assault is killed by a white posse he is preparing to welcome as his rescuers.[33] Romero writes that 'when observers began to write about the film, calling it "important", it was almost uniformly regarded as such because a black man gets gunned down in the end by a posse of white, redneck, good-ole-boys', an event given extra resonance by the assassination of Martin Luther King Jr just before the film's release.[34] Similarly, the fragmented photographs of the white posse dragging Ben's body to a fire recalls earlier cases of spectacle lynching and civil rights photography; the interviews with the police and the posse interspersed through the film also seem to draw on coverage of white resistance to civil rights protests.

Such concerns, though, were absent from Brother Voodoo. In the early form imagined by Roy Thomas in the 1950s, the character was a 'more-inclined-to-physical-violence version of the present-day Dr. Strange', engaging once again with the stereotype that the black male body is more predisposed to violence than that of white men.[35] In the 1970s version of Drumm's origin story, though, he is an 'author, scholar, [and] noted psychologist', returning to his home on Haiti at his younger brother's request, having spent nearly twenty years in the US.[36] In that time, his brother Daniel has become the main *houngan*, or voodoo priest, on Haiti. When Jericho returns, he finds Daniel dying from a curse issued by Damballah, a *Zobop* (an alleged Haitian group practising voodoo and cannibalism) who claims to be a *loa*, a spirit given human form – in this case, the spirit of the snake god. Damballah curses Daniel to die, which he does, and at the moment of his death, Damballah arrives to confront Jericho. Damballah defeats Jericho in hand-to-hand combat and mocks him for rejecting his 'birth right' – the role of chief *houngan* on Haiti. Jericho subsequently travels into the jungle to find Papa Jambo, an elderly voodoo priest who can teach him how to defeat Damballah, avenge his brother, and break Damballah's hold on the island. As this summary suggests, the narrative is awash with exotic references to the popular American reimagining of Haitian voodoo.[37] Many of these references go unexplained, either presupposing familiarity with the popular zombie genre on the part of the reader or attempting to create a sense of dislocation, of Otherness, which renders the events more frightening because these linguistic choices work with the images to create an unfamiliar space.[38] Like Jericho Drumm, the reader must venture into the unknown. Except this was not really 'the unknown': Haiti was brought back to the attention of the US in 1970 as some of its inhabitants began to flee to the US from the nation's dictator, Papa Doc Duvalier, and his increasing political oppression. Duvalier, who died in 1971, was an advocate of Haitian Vodou, even going so far as to expel the Catholic Church from the island during his time in office. In this context, American intervention, in the form of Drumm, against an aggressive force seeking to disrupt the tacitly approved state of affairs in Haiti, can be read as Cold War interventionism.[39] In some ways, it doubles as a fantasy of a successful version of the failed invasion of Cuba, with the US-trained expat, Drumm, able to overthrow the Caribbean dictator. If the political situation seems familiar, so too does the narrative structure: Jericho Drumm's training montage takes up much of the next issue of *Strange Tales*, building to his second bout with Damballah, who has recently established himself as the voodoo leader of the world, as acknowledged by 'all de leaders of all de cults of de world', with the specific regions mentioned being 'Russia, New Orleans, [and] the Middle East'; Chinese voodoo is also present, and it is Damballah's destruction of its representative, Fong Lee, by conjuring a dragon to prove his power, which convinces those present to accept him as their leader.[40] Haitian resistance to the Chinese works towards positioning this as a Cold War narrative, with Damballah's invitation of the Chinese to Haiti presenting the threat (albeit unrealized) of further communist penetration of the Caribbean.

While Blade is primarily a refraction of domestic concerns, Brother Voodoo channels anxieties over world events. As the first black nation to gain independence, Haiti has historically presented a problem to neo-colonial and white-supremacist world-views and, as such, has historically been presented as a source of horror. China was also a geopolitically sensitive region in 1973. President Nixon made a sustained attempt to engage with China from early on in his presidency as part of a Cold War strategy to exacerbate the Sino-Soviet split.[41] Nixon visited China himself in 1972 as part of this process.[42] Nixon, however, was beaten to China by Huey P. Newton, founder of the Black Panther Party, whose espousal of Maoist internationalism saw him well-received there.[43] Russia also has obvious Cold War connections, linking back to the overdetermination of the zombie as an allegory for communism in the 1950s.[44] The Middle East, meanwhile, was a major concern in US foreign policy in 1973 with the outbreak of the Yom Kippur War, a defining moment in Arab–Israeli relations and the cause of the 1973 energy crisis following the implementation of an oil embargo by the Arab members of the Organization of Petroleum Exporting Countries against the US and other allies of Israel.[45] Damballah's global alliance of voodoo practitioners, then, reads as a collective of America's enemies, a monstrous alliance against the heroic Americans.

Brother Voodoo, despite his ability to project his brother's spirit on the astral plane, remains tied to the 'superstitious Caribbean isle' of Haiti. He chooses to have his home, however, in a 'sprawling old mansion on the outskirts of New Orleans' exotic French Quarter', suggesting a continuing affiliation with the US – and indeed Louisiana voodoo – and also maintaining tropes of US interventions in the 'Third World' as desirable for global order, and even as welcomed by citizens of the nation in question.[46] Indeed, Haitians in *Strange Tales* #171 explicitly state that they have appealed to the UN for a 'clinical pathologist' to help them deal with an outbreak of zombies.[47] The zombies in question turn out to be the result of a collaboration between Baron Samedi, 'the lord of the dead', and Advanced Idea Mechanics (AIM), one of the criminal organizations of the Marvel universe. As the story progresses, the horror elements give way to a conventional superhero narrative; not even the three-part story in *Strange Tales* #172–173, concluding in *Tales of the Zombie* #6, which gave the creative team more room to craft a specifically 'horror' story in a black and white magazine outside the oversight of the CCA, broke from the pattern of introducing a threat to the hero, then having him physically fight it before finally emerging triumphant.[48]

As with Blade, Brother Voodoo found his way into more conventional superhero comics – something made possible by the fact that, in form and content, new horror comics perfectly resembled superhero comics. In *Marvel Team-Up* #24 (1974), Brother Voodoo works alongside Spider-Man. Even though Drumm saves Spider-Man, he is introduced as 'Jericho Drumm ... once he was an author, a scholar, a noted psychologist ... now he is merely Brother Voodoo', with the linguistic choice of 'merely' implying a decline in status, a decline demonstrated through the space he occupies, moving from the political centre of the US to its margins. Drumm has embraced a position more clearly aligned with Othered racial and geopolitical identities that apparently exists on the other side of a cultural divide, with his old life left behind him as he returns to Haiti and its concerns. This is also evident in the way Brother Voodoo approaches his final battle alongside Spider-Man against Moondog, a voodoo priest trying to establish a cult in New York. In a clear departure from superhero practice, Brother Voodoo states that he 'will have to kill him', before throwing Moondog to his apparent death – a fate from which the villain is only saved by Spider-Man.[49] It is not clear whether Brother Voodoo did this to cause the *loa* possessing that body to flee, or whether he truly intended to kill Moondog. While Brother Voodoo is capable of saving Spider-Man from physical harm on more than one occasion, Spider-Man is the guardian of what might be construed as proper superhero practice. Relationships of power and morality are therefore perpetuated through this narrative, as are stereotypes of racialized savagery. The white character, who presents as weaker than the black, ultimately retains the guardianship of what constitutes heroism.[50]

## Race and foreign policy

Any consideration of the violence of anti-colonial struggles in the 1970s must also be understood in relation to the war in Vietnam. African Americans supplied a disproportionate number of combat troops; 12.5 per cent of American soldiers sent to fight in Vietnam were black compared to just 11 per cent of the general population. Early in the war, black soldiers made up 14.9 per cent of casualties, leading Dr Martin Luther King Jr to describe the conflict as 'a white man's war, a black man's fight'.[51] In 1967, Muhammed Ali famously refused the draft, asserting that he had no quarrel with the Viet Cong and that, in America, the black man's true enemy was much closer to home.

In his analysis of *Deathdream* (1974), a film drawing on themes from the story of 'The Monkey's Paw' in its narrative of the horrific return of an undead soldier killed in Vietnam due to the wish of his mother, Adam Lowenstein proposes the notion of an 'allegorical moment'.[52] Such a moment is a 'shocking collision of film, spectator, and history where registers of bodily space and historical time are disrupted, confronted, and intertwined' in such a way as to elicit connection to, and commentary on, their moment of production and consumption.[53] The war in Vietnam, from its inception as colonial resistance to French rule, was a war of national liberation that took on Cold War connotations through the presence of, and therefore resistance to, communism.[54] In practice, the American presence in Vietnam and neighbouring countries did tremendous violence to the landscape, the political fabric, and the economy of Vietnam. Vietnam was rarely directly represented in horror comics, or indeed horror films, of the 1970s. Lowenstein, however, persuasively argues that the domestication of violence exported to Vietnam became a dominant theme of American horror films in the 1970s. The trauma of events such as the Kent State shooting of 4 May 1970, discussed in detail in Chapter 5, were horrifying both as human tragedies and as examples of the violence the government was prepared to use against its own citizens.

For the purposes of this chapter, however, we shall take as our focus the ways in which race and colonial narratives of Vietnam were displaced onto other arenas. One such location was Haiti, a long term anti-colonial thorn in the side of the US. Representational strategies, such as placing families in huts rather than houses, and the nature of Haitian struggles against imperialism and modernity, suggested clear thematic and visual links. In *Tales of the Zombie* #10, Brother Voodoo returns to Haiti to assist an old friend but finds her dead – killed by her dead husband, resurrected as a zombie by Dramabu, a new voodoo *houngan* on the island. In a graveyard ritual, Dramabu rails against 'the incursions of modern society' into Haiti, stating that he:

Went to the school, my brothers, to learn what modern society offers – to try to help our land. But I found that modern society offers nothing but death. So I have returned to the old ways and rescued you from death that together we may fight the new ways – fight the new death![55]

Dramabu's resistance can be read as an anti-colonial struggle, a rejection of the modern international capitalism that exploits colonial spaces to advance imperial metropoles. In the process, it can be read as a continuation of the Haitian Revolution and its rejection of European exploitation. Problematically, however, Dramabu does not rally the living to act through positive action, nor does he harness the potential revolutionary power of the 'Third World' to effect systemic change, but instead raises the dead and sacrifices the living in acts of horrifying violence that undermine his own position as a revolutionary leader. This is especially true as Dramabu's acts of violence are directed against his own people and, graphically, children – acts that create literal death rather than the figurative death he describes.[56] While this can be seen to undermine anti-colonial initiatives on the part of the colonized, it also perpetuates racist assumptions regarding Haiti as a space unable to govern itself, one inextricably entangled in histories of bloody violence, revolution, and civil war.[57] As such, the actions and images in this narrative derive their power from a longer, larger, narrative of Haiti as a dark and dangerous space, where not even Haitians can be safe. In fact, safety can only be achieved, as a clearly interim measure, through the intervention of Brother Voodoo, someone who through his position as an enlightened and Americanized Haitian is shown as able to occupy both 'old' and 'new' worlds.

The mindless conformity of Haitian zombie hordes also cannot help but raise the spectre of Vietnam and the attendant forces of communism deployed there against the US. In the increasingly blurred division between life and death, right and wrong, and superhero narratives and horror in Brother Voodoo stories, the political confusion and malaise of the 1970s confronts the reader at every turn. As Lowenstein remarks, the allegorical moment produces 'forms of knowing not easily described by conventional delineations of bodily space and historical time',[58] knowledge dramatized in Brother Voodoo through the presence of astral bodies that exist inside and outside physical ones, of the explicitly Othered power to reach beyond the realm of life and explore death.[59]

Further struggles of resistance appear in *Supernatural Thrillers #5* (1973).[60] In an instance of nominative determinism, Doctor Skarab, a prominent Egyptologist, discovers some ancient papyrus that fills gaps in the history of Ancient Egypt. The notion of gaps in the history of Egypt being filled was current at the time of publication, with the small-scale tours of exhibits from the tomb of Tutankhamun (chiefly in the US, 1962–1964) leading to a far larger touring exhibition beginning in 1972.[61] The papyrus narrates how an African tribe, the Swarilis, were enslaved by the Egyptians but had their own version of Moses to lead them to freedom. N'Kantu, the Swarili chief, led a revolt and killed the pharaoh but not his high priest, Nephrus. Nephrus outwitted N'Kantu and condemned him to an eternal life, paralysed within a coffin. There N'Kantu remains until 1973 and the outbreak of the Arab–Israeli War, which forms the backdrop to his awakening in the Gaza strip. The mummified body of N'Kantu manifests several racist stereotypes; Jeffrey A. Brown, echoing the imagery in *Tomb of Dracula*, describes the black male body as 'being too hard, too physical, too bodily'.[62] This is clearly apparent in N'Kantu's 'hellish strength' and his Blade-like invulnerability. Bullets, tear gas, and electric shocks fail to 'kill' him. Although 'Israeli-occupied Egypt' only forms the backdrop to the origin story, the spectre of African revolt against Israel is raised and, through the black African body of N'Kantu, taps into the historical fear of similar revolts in Haiti, Vietnam, and, potentially, the American South.

The comic engages fears over rebellious bodies of colour in the US when N'Kantu is transported to a New York museum, from which he promptly escapes. However, N'Kantu quickly ends up enslaved once again, this time by the Elementals, a name that establishes links back to Ancient Egypt.[63] The Elementals in question here are four Atlantean gods who seek to restore their power over the world, which had been broken thousands of years before by a warrior and a priest from Ancient Egypt. N'Kantu manages to break free of their control, stating that while 'the Swarilis were enslaved, at least they died free!'[64]

Such frequent returns to, and escapes from, slavery dramatize the struggle for emancipation, while also positioning slavery as an institution never far from African experience. As part of his struggle with the Elementals, N'Kantu is returned to Egypt, raising the spectre of the American Colonization Society and attempts to take freed slaves from the US 'back to Africa', to the American settlement of Liberia. More sympathetically, it could also draw on the attempts of African American activists to involve themselves more fully in African issues, particularly from the 1930s to the 1960s.[65] In a more contemporary, and more direct, reference, however, N'Kantu uses his recovered freedom in Africa to save a female Israeli soldier, Racha Meyer, who, while on foot, is being pursued by an armoured car manned by several Egyptian soldiers who laugh as they fire at her.

Thanks to N'Kantu's intervention, Meyer is able to destroy the armoured car in a splash page, restaging N'Kantu's warrior initiation ritual (Figure 76). In the process, the Israeli side in the conflict, already shown to be more virtuous through the ugly, laughing faces of the Egyptians and the beautiful, capable body of Meyer, is glorified. Association with the heroic protagonist, N'Kantu, and his struggle for

**76** Full page from Len Wein (w), Tony Isabella (w), and Val Mayerick (w/a), *Supernatural Thrillers* #10

freedom against Egyptian oppressors, gives this an extra biblical gloss, abstracting the contemporary Arab–Israeli conflict from geopolitical concerns and making it a clash of absolute binary moral opposites.

Although N'Kantu shook off the control of the Elementals, his escape from them does not, in itself, end their campaign. The next stage of this conquest sees the Elementals reach Earth in *Supernatural Thrillers* #12 (1974), with their arrival described as 'instant holy war'; the main combatants standing against the Elementals are N'Kantu and the African American anthropologist, Ron McAllister, who in N'Kantu sees 'the face of a man, a man who successfully led his people from slavery against the wishes of an entire nation'.[66] N'Kantu and those who rally around him, notably Ron and Doctor Skarab, defeat the Elementals. The bold claim that 'the war that shook the world is, at long last, over', which must be part of an allegorical moment drawing on the Arab–Israeli War, is sadly far from true. Given the location of the story, and the fuel crisis precipitated by the actions of the Organization of Arab Petroleum Exporting Countries as an economic arm of the war, this regional conflict did take on global significance. Part of its importance is inevitably the role of the global in the local, the fact that this struggle was, and is, facilitated and fostered through global actions and concerns.[67] However, *Supernatural Thrillers* avoids more nuanced commentary as N'Kantu's biblical struggle against Egyptian slavery is explicitly mapped on to Israel's struggle against the Arab states, with Israel once again aligned by the narrative and images with the forces of right. Through its support for Israel, the US is placed, literally, on the side of the angels, at least in the narrative's own terms.

Networks of power and race intersect to great effect in these stories of Haiti and the Middle East. As with narratives of Vietnam, American intervention is written into both, and in both instances is the deciding factor in victory for the forces of righteousness: Ron McAllister, the African American academic, is essential to N'Kantu's success, just as Jericho Drumm's time in, and embrace of, American modernity is vital to his ability to occupy two worlds, the past and the future, and successfully use his knowledge of both to overcome those allied to the former alone. N'Kantu's status as a freedom fighter, a rebel leader against two regimes who sought to enslave him, occupies a problematic position in a narrative celebrating Israeli military violence against a coalition of Arab states; Ron's contact with N'Kantu radicalizes him, leading him into acts of violence he had previously regarded himself as incapable of committing. An international coalition of anti-imperial forces is therefore forged between an African and an African American at a crucial moment of Black Power agitation, but its political significance is diminished by its direction towards allegorical, and literal, intervention in a war directly supported by the US. Discussions around Black Power, civil rights and Palestine had been ongoing since at least 1967, and Keith Feldman argues that the position adopted by the Student Non-violent Coordinating Committee in 1967 demonstrates the 'formal limitations of the civil rights movement and the deep entrenchment of U.S. popular, ideological, and material support for Palestine's colonial occupation'.[68] The conflicting positions inherent in US support for Israel and Black Power support for Palestine play out in Ron McAllister, whose radicalization binds him to the ideological position, shared by the US government, of supporting Israel, rather than the view of Black Power activists who saw the oppression of fellow people of colour in this practice. Ron therefore becomes, like Blade, what we might see as a 'safely radicalized' African American, whose activism upholds rather than challenges contemporary US policy. Reductive attempts to position the Arab–Israeli War of 1973 as a biblical struggle frame, rather than contain, attempts to read the narrative as an endorsement of wider freedom struggles, co-opting racialized movements into narratives that affirm white American values.

Just as both Brother Voodoo and N'Kantu depend on existing iterations of American policy, they also rely on earlier superhero and horror stories. Brother Voodoo operates in the context of the explicitly colonial acts of the US in Haiti, whereas N'Kantu draws on a range of Egyptological anxieties reaching back into the nineteenth century. These anxieties also link back to the Civil War and freedom struggles. Louisa May Alcott's 'Lost in a Pyramid; or, the Mummy's Curse' was the first narrative to draw on an ancient Egyptian curse, and was published in 1869, four years after the conclusion of the Civil War. Alcott briefly served as a nurse in the war, and published about her experiences in Boston's anti-slavery paper, *Commonwealth*. Although the imperial anxiety manifest in Egyptology is usually associated with the late nineteenth and early twentieth century, as evident in Bram Stoker's *The Jewel of Seven Stars* (1903) and more famously, Universal's *The Mummy* (1932) and its subsequent sequels and remakes, this is largely European in focus. The US had its own reasons for anxiety around Egypt: chief of these was cotton. The Civil War had disrupted cotton production in the South, previously the world's chief exporter of this valuable commodity, and as such a global race to discover alternatives began. Britain increased production in India, though the cotton grown there was of inferior quality.[69] The real solution was found in Egypt, where, 'by 1864, 40 percent of all fertile land in Lower Egypt had been converted to cotton cultivation', leading to a 500 per cent increase in exports during the war and the acceleration of a modernization process through the economic boost provided by cotton production.[70] The economic plight of the South in the postbellum era can therefore be seen as a mummy's curse, something also evident in rumours of a cholera panic attributed to the importation of Egyptian cotton and contaminated mummy rags.[71] The sickly state of the economy in the South was reimagined as a literal sickness. Early American mummy fiction therefore drew on and dramatized new agricultural trade relations. In Alcott's story, the wife of the American who was 'lost in a pyramid' is killed by the mummy's curse when she grows some seeds taken from the mummy.[72] Just as Egyptian intervention in cotton production proved damaging to the US in the 1860s, its intervention in oil production and distribution, through the actions of OAPEC, proved damaging in the 1970s. Horror comics of the 1970s were created during a period of anxiety around Egypt; they operate as overdetermined spaces that refract and restage imperial and economic tensions, both contemporary and over a century old, celebrating the resistance of the enslaved while also situating their ability to resist slavery in a horrifying space – as something intended to scare an imagined audience of white readers. In so doing, they restage Marx's notion of the commodity as a 'social hieroglyphic' and 'put in play centuries of discursive production of Egypt as enigmatic', therefore staging the comic in which they appear as captivating and in need of decoding, yet also inextricably Other, never fully reduceable to something that can be wholly known in its new or original context.[73] Similar tensions play out in Haiti, where narratives of occupation and successful revolt generate simultaneous narratives of unknowable non-Western power.[74]

## Conclusion

Horror comics of the 1970s showed evidence of the influence of world events. Where people of colour had once either been absent from comics or presented, allegorically or otherwise, as a source of horror, the 1970s, influenced by the Civil Rights movement and Blaxploitation, featured some black characters in heroic roles. While these figures represent a significant improvement on what had come before in terms of the representation of people of colour as agents (or as present at all), they nonetheless continued to reinforce racist stereotypes. In the case of Blade, Marvel appropriated the imagery of the Black Power movement while reinforcing the archetype of the 'tough' black male and removing any requirement for social change. Brother Voodoo played out various anxieties over foreign relations while tying black identities to a reductive and misrepresentative imagining of Haitian spiritual practices. N'Kantu resisted slavery, yet found himself repeatedly drawn back into it, in the process suggesting that African bodies might be more susceptible to falling into subjugation than others.

A unifying theme in these stories is a sense that America, both as a society and a political actor, is inherently healthy and blameless. Threats to black lives are consistently presented as rogue individuals on US soil or monsters from the 'old world' beyond US borders. An illustration of this problem can be found in its obverse. One narrative that opens up a way of, as Nick Groom suggests, 'thinking with vampires', can be found in a short story by Ronald Chetwynd-Hayes.[75] In 'The Labyrinth', Rosemary and Brian, a couple wandering through the English country-side, stumble upon an isolated rural house where an old woman, Mrs Brown, lives with her domestic servant, Carlo. The house, it transpires, has grown from the grave of a vampire who has only been incapacitated, not destroyed. This vampire's body-as-house first traps and then con-sumes those fed into it by Mrs Brown and Carlo, shifting the vampire from an individual threat, a sexualized predator, to a structural menace that slowly consumes those who cannot escape. Chetwynd-Hayes sug-gests structures larger than the house when he writes that 'the entire set-up is a nightmare produced by a monstrous intelligence'.[76] By con-trast, although the comics under consideration in this book routinely show the destruction of the monster, the environment in which that destruction takes place is inherently healthy; the demon of systemic racism is never acknowledged or exorcised. There is no recognition of the improperly destroyed vampire below the soil of American society. These characters remain, effectively, in 'The Labyrinth'; the very build-ings and environments in which the socially and politically marginalized live suck the life and hope out of them. The violence is in the architec-ture. And not just the architecture of the built environment, but the political fabric, the 'monstrous intelligence' that allowed, even worked towards, the construction and perpetuation of such areas and attitudes.

To return to one of the major recurring themes of this volume, these comics come close to, but never fully realise, the possibility of people of colour having access to fear. The apparent invulnerability of Blade and N'Kantu make them protectors and allies of white characters. Instead, these comics continue to be primarily interested in resolving threats to the white hegemony, whether they issue from Black Panthers, Russian communists, Vietnamese guerrilla fighters, Haitian voodoo, or Egyptian militants. Given the apparent advances, at least in *de jure* terms, of the Civil Rights movement, the horror of the comics and the situations on which they drew became increasingly insidious. One such development in the late 1960s was the shift towards a concern with housing – with access to the urban spaces discussed most prominently in this chapter and its counterpart on race in the 1950s. The Fair Housing Act of 1968, signed during riots over the assassination of Martin Luther King Jr, toughened provisions in the 1866 Civil Rights Act by specifying that race, among other factors, could no longer be used as a barrier to deny groups access to housing. The same act also made what would now be termed 'hate crimes' federal crimes and extended a number of rights to Native Americans. However, it also conflated legitimate political protest and illegitimate political violence by making it a felony to use interstate transport to engage in a riot, with the issue of the definition of 'riot' being left to the accuser. These changes in law demonstrate the same concerns we have found in comics – of growing acknowledgement of people of colour as agents who are embroiled in a struggle for civil liberties, while at the same time never quite abandoning the sense of people of colour as a threat to white lives or property and the white hegemony.

Given our preoccupation with property, it is worth considering houses as a finishing point for this chapter. Houses have long had a deep and complex relationship with horror. Part of this is undoubtedly the unsettling inversion of the home as a safe space into the home as threatening. The house, however, can also stand in for the nation: when one buys a house, to some extent one buys into the nation, both economically and ideologically. As Owen Davies argues, 'the house can be understood as an expression of the human body with its entrances open to spiritual and physical pollution, assault, and intrusion', with 'thresholds, both physical and symbolic [as] weak points', meaning that action has to be taken to contain the threat at those specific junctures.[77] Houses can also stand as, in the words of Jason Dittmer, a 'rescaling icon', or smaller units through which individuals and communities can make sense of national issues and, indeed, nations.[78] If the act of buying a house is taken as belonging, of the owner becoming increasingly bound up in the national fabric, then that national fabric itself is subject to change. Ghettoes, and the nature of the economic and physical infrastructure that perpetuates them, operate as makeshift containment units; increasing Civil Rights legislation led to white fears that those units might be about to fail, releasing 'pollutants', whether people, ideas, or products such as drugs, into the wider body politic. And, if people of colour were moving out, perhaps white people would get sucked back into the transformed urban spaces they had sought to vacate. This chapter has therefore concerned access to physical property and access to fear as emotional property. Even N'Kantu's struggles against the Egyptians essentially concern property; the racialized Egyptians who he fights threaten the vulnerable white body of Racha Meyer and, by extension, the integrity of Israel. N'Kantu enables her to defend herself and her homeland, but by operating largely as an object to be manipulated and mobilized. Despite N'Kantu being the eponymous protagonist of the comic, in this instance, agency rests with Meyer. Everything had changed, and yet nothing had changed: horror comics of the 1970s were, despite or because of the seismic changes ongoing around them, as concerned as ever with the wrong bodies in the wrong spaces.

## Notes

1 Nicola Cuti (w) and Jack Sparling (w), 'Snake Eyes' *Vampirella* #8 (New York: Warren Publishing 1970), 40.
2 This conforms to the narrative strategy found in other films of the time such as *Guess Who's Coming to Dinner* (1967), dir. Stanley Kramer, where the liberal white protagonist, Matt Drayton, is forced to confront his own, previously unconscious, racism when his young daughter announces her intention to marry John Prentice (Sidney Poitier), an (intentionally) almost impossibly perfect young doctor.
3 Philip L. Rones, 'Moving to the Sun: Job Growth in the Sunbelt (1968–1978)', *Monthly Labor Review* 103.3 (1980), 12–19.
4 For a discussion of this, see Richard M. Bernard and Bradley R. Rice (eds), *Sunbelt Cities: Politics and Growth Since World War II* (Austin, TX: University of Texas Press, 1983).
5 Gardner Fox (w) and Dan Dakins (a), 'New Girl in Town', *Vampirella* #5 (New York: Warren Publishing, 1970), 28.
6 Fox and Dakins, 'New Girl in Town', 29
7 Fox and Dakins, 'New Girl in Town', 29.
8 Fox and Dakins, 'New Girl in Town', 31.
9 Nick Cuti (w) and Billy Graham (a), 'The Black Witch', *Vampirella* #7 (New York: Warren Publishing, 1970), 22–28. See the concluding chapter for an analysis of this comic.
    This trend follows the superhero genre where characters such as Black Panther (first appeared July 1966), The Falcon (first appeared September 1969), and Luke Cage (first appeared June 1972) fought alongside established white characters. This did not mean, however, that the comics medium was free of earlier problems concerning the representation of race. In the superhero genre powers are often derived and exercised thanks to a moment of transgression: Luke Cage acquires his powers as the result of medical experimentation while (wrongly) imprisoned and the Falcon is revealed to be the result of a plan by the Red Skull to create a sleeper agent who would appeal to Captain America's "snivelling liberalism"; he is a plot to undermine Captain America, as a means rather than an end in himself (Steve Englehart and Frank Robbins, et al., *Captain America and the Falcon* #185 (New York: Marvel, 1975)). While the Falcon is still a hero,

the basis of his identity is attacked in ways white heroes do not experience, see Goodrum, *Superheroes and American Self Image*, 211–214.

10 Goodrum, *Superheroes and American Self Image*, 140.

11 Dennis O'Neil and Neal Adams, *Green Lantern co-starring Green Arrow* #76 (New York: DC Comics, 1970).

12 O'Neil and Adams, *Green Lantern co-starring Green Arrow* #76.

13 Robert Kanigher (w) and Werner Roth (a), *Superman's Girl Friend, Lois Lane* #106 (New York: DC Comics, 1970).

14 Lois' story was almost certainly inspired by John Howard Griffin's *Black Like Me*, a 1961 book detailing his experiences as a white man passing as African American in the South. A film was produced in 1964. Ray Sprigle had attempted a similar project in 1948, published in 1949 as *In the Land of Jim Crow*, but it did not have the same impact as Griffin's account. Kanigher was a DC veteran who had been writing comics since the 1950s. The plotline suggests that, while his execution was problematic, he was conscious of shifts in the public conversation concerning race in America.

15 For an analysis of Johnny Everyman, see Goodrum, '"Friend of the People of Many Lands"'.

16 'Hoover Calls Panthers Top Threat to Security', *The Washington Post* (WP Company LLC, 16 July 1969).

17 For analysis of this, see Rob Lendrum, 'The Super Black Macho, One Baaad Mutha: Black Superhero Masculinity in 1970s Mainstream Comic Books', *Extrapolation* 46.3 (2005), 360–372; Adilifu Nama, *Super Black: American Pop Culture and Black Superheroes* (Austin, TX: University of Texas Press, 2011); the introduction to Jeffrey A. Brown, *Black Superheroes, Milestone Comics, and Their Fans* (Jackson, MS: University Press of Mississippi, 2001) and his article 'Comic Book Masculinity and the New Black Superhero', *African American Review* 33.1 (2000), 25–42.

18 Angelica Jade Bastién, 'Vulnerability and the Strong Black Female Archetype', in Kelly Sue Deconnick (w), Valentine De Landro (a), and Kelly Fitzpatrick (i), *Bitch Planet* #7 (Berkeley, CA: Image Comics, 2016), n.p.

19 See, for one of the defining studies of the trope, Richard Slotkin, *Regeneration Through Violence: The Mythology of the American Frontier, 1600–1860* (Middletown, CT: Wesleyan University Press, 1973).

20 Marv Wolfman (w), Gene Colan (a), Tom Palmer (i, c), John Costanza (l), and Roy Thomas (e), *Tomb of Dracula* #13 (New York: Marvel, 1973).

21 Angela K. Wood, 'African Americans and Their Distrust of the Health Care System: Health Care for Diverse Populations', *Journal of Cultural Diversity* 14.2 (2007), 56–60.

22 L. L. Wall argues that, while the women who Sims experimented upon were members of a vulnerable population, there is some evidence to suggest that they were in some pain from fistulas and were willing participants. They were nonetheless part of a total institution, making questions of consent somewhat problematic. There are also numerous ethical oversights in Sims' work concerning, among other things, his decision to withhold anaesthetic. See L. L. Wall, 'The

Medical Ethics of Dr J Marion Sims: A Fresh Look at the Historical Record', *Journal of Medical Ethics* 32.6 (2006), 346–350.

23  Mary T. Bassett, 'Beyond Berets: The Black Panthers as Health Activists', *American Journal of Public Health* 106.10 (2016), 1741–1743.

24  Rachel E. Spector, *Cultural Diversity in Heath and Illness*, 6th edn (Upper Saddle River, NJ: Pearson Prentice Hall, 2004).

25  Wolfman, Colan, Palmer, Costanza, and Thomas, *Tomb of Dracula* #13, 12.

26  Florence Marryat was the daughter of Captain Frederick Marryat, an English officer in the Royal Navy and prolific author. Frederick Marryat's father, the Member of Parliament Joseph Marryat, was a prominent campaigner against the abolition of slavery.

27  Jennifer Wriggins, 'Rape, Racism, and the Law', *Harvard Women's Law Journal* 6 (1983), 103–141.

28  Vampires are famously connected to wealth in the work of Marx, and rather less famously in the splendidly bizarre *Vampire City* by Paul Féval (1867).

29  Tony Isabella states the Roy Thomas 'had an idea for a superhero he called Dr. Voodoo … back in the '50s', establishing explicit connections between the two periods. See Tony Isabella, 'Introducing Brother Voodoo: The Creation of Marvel's Most Mysterious Superhero', *Tales of the Zombie* #2 (New York: Marvel, 1973).

30  Isabella, 'Introducing Brother Voodoo'.

31  Dr. John might not have reached that audience straight away as the record failed to chart – but subsequent reception has confirmed it as a classic.

32  'Voodoo Chile' and 'Voodoo Child (Slight Return)' both feature on the double album, *Electric Ladyland* by the Jimi Hendrix Experience. It was the band's last, and most commercially successful, album, reaching number 1 in the US and number 6 in the UK. Readers interested in other musical engagements with voodoo might be interested in *Juju* (1981) by Siouxsie and the Banshees.

33  See Jones, *Horror*, 160–164.

34  George A. Romero, 'Introduction', in William B. Seabrook, *The Magic Island* (New York: Dover Publications, 2016), xv–xxiii (xix).

35  Romero, 'Introduction', in Seabrook, *The Magic Island*.

36  Len Wein (w) and Gene Colan (a), 'Brother Voodoo!', *Strange Tales* #169 (New York: Marvel, 1973).

37  The term 'voodoo' has been used to describe various interconnected belief systems and practices found in Africa and the diaspora. The Haitian incarnation combines elements of various African religious traditions with Western Catholicism. The version of voodoo that appears in American popular culture, including Brother Voodoo, is largely invented and conflates voodoo with satanism, witchcraft, and various folk traditions.

38  There is an additional sense of dislocation as after 1968 and George A. Romero's *Night of the Living Dead*, zombie films took a distinct shift away from their Haitian origins towards the flesh-eating undead most people now associate with the term.

39  See, for instance, Jean-Claude Gerlus, 'The Effects of the Cold War on US–Haiti

Relations', *Journal of Haitian Studies* 1.1 (1995), 34–56. For more on the undocumented migration of Haitians to Florida, see Christopher Mitchell, 'US Policy Toward Haitian Boat People, 1972–93', *Annals of the American Academy of Political and Social Science* 534 (1995), 69–80.

40  Len Wein (w) and Gene Colan (a), 'Baptism of Fire!', *Strange Tales* #170 (New York: Marvel, 1973). It is noteworthy that Damballah's accent is coded as Jamaican, conflating two Caribbean communities with distinct languages, histories, and practices.

41  For more on the Sino-Soviet split, see Lorenz M. Luthi, *The Sino-Soviet Split: Cold War in the Communist World* (Princeton, NJ: Princeton University Press, 2010).

42  For more on this, see Margaret Macmillan, *Nixon & Mao: The Week That Changed the World* (New York: Random House, 2007).

43  For analysis of this, see Matthew D. Johnson, 'From Peace to the Panthers: PRC Engagement with African-American Transnational Networks, 1949–1979', *Past & Present* Supplement 8 (2013), 233–257.

44  See, for instance, Luckhurst, *Zombies: A Cultural History*, and Goodrum, 'The Past That Will Not Die', in Davies and Rifkind (eds), *Documenting Trauma in Comics*.

45  For insightful analysis of this, see Fiona Venn, *The Oil Crisis* (London: Routledge, 2002).

46  Len Wein (w) and Gene Colan (a) 'March of the Dead!', *Strange Tales* #171 (New York: Marvel, 1973). For more of a discussion on zombies and postcolonialism, see Goodrum, 'The Past That Will Not Die', in Davies and Rifkind (eds), *Documenting Trauma in Comics*. The connection between Haiti and New Orleans follows the exodus of many Haitians to the US after the Haitian Revolution and the lingering fears in New Orleans about a similar slave revolt.

47  Marvel referred to them as 'zuvembies' as the term 'zombie' lacked the necessary literary prestige to pass muster with the Comics Code Authority, even after the relaxation of the Code in 1971. 'Zuvembie' drew on the work of Robert E. Howard, of Conan the Barbarian fame, whose short story 'Pigeons from Hell!', published posthumously in *Weird Tales* 31.5 in 1938, coined the term. *Tales of the Zombie*, the magazine in which Brother Voodoo was introduced, was a black and white magazine and thus outside the restrictions placed on comics. As this crossover suggests, it was very easy to circumvent the Code.

48  The difficulties in distinguishing the horror genre from the superhero are also evident in that Brother Voodoo worked with Spider-Man in *Marvel Team-Up* #24 (1974). In *Adventure into Fear* #24 (1974), Blade, similarly, fought Morbius, a Spider-Man villain and scientifically created vampire whose origin story draws on the 1958 film, *The Fly*, and its two sequels, *Return of the Fly* (1959) and *Curse of the Fly* (1965).

49  Doug Moench (w) and Tony Dezuniga (a), *Tales of the Zombie* #10 (New York: Marvel, 1975).

50  The death of a character possessed by a demon being caused by a fall also has a clear resonance with the end of *The Exorcist* (1973).

51 Quoted in David Coffey, *Encyclopedia of the Vietnam War: A Political, Social, and Military History*, ed. Spencer C. Tucker (Oxford: ABC-CLIO, 1998).
52 Lowenstein, *Shocking Representation*, 2.
53 Lowenstein, *Shocking Representation*, 2.
54 For a good overview of the whole scope of the war, see Kevin Ruane, *War and Revolution in Vietnam, 1930–1975* (London: Routledge, 1998).
55 Len Wein (w) and Jim Mooney (a), *Marvel Team-Up* #24 (New York: Marvel, 1974).
56 This might be a reference to the Tonton Macoute, the name given to Papa Doc Duvalier's secret police force. Tonton Macoute is a Haitian folkloric character who kidnaps and eats naughty children.
57 For other narrations of the violence of Haitian history that both critiques and reinstates Haiti as a dangerous place best avoided, see Henry S. Whitehead's Gerald Canevin stories in particular, most readily available in Henry S. Whitehead, *Voodoo Tales* (Ware: Wordsworth Editions, 2012).
58 Lowenstein, *Shocking Representation*, 2–3.
59 Whitehead, *Voodoo Tales*, 2–3.
60 Steve Gerber (w) and Rich Buckler (a), *Supernatural Thrillers* #5 (New York: Marvel, 1973).
61 In his preface to Christiane Desroches-Noblecourt's tremendously successful *Tutankhamen* (London: Penguin, 1965, reissued 1971, reprinted 1972), Dr Sarwat Okasha, Minister of Culture and National Guidance of the United Arab Republic (by this stage, just Egypt), stated that the book, and the discoveries it narrates: 'occupy a place of honour … amongst the revelatory moments which history vouchsafes from time to time when it lifts for a moment the mysterious curtain which has hidden from our eyes … a significant episode in man's history' (p. 9). For a discussion of the broader geopolitical ramifications of the use of artefacts as diplomatic tools, or of the lengthy imperial history that led to the fetishization, discovery, and pillaging of Egypt in the nineteenth and early twentieth century, see Roger Luckhurst's *The Mummy's Curse: The True History of a Dark Fantasy* (Oxford: Oxford University Press, 2014). The cultural memory of the American tour of Egyptian artefacts in the 1960s informs the context of what may possibly be the greatest film of all time, *Bubba Ho-Tep* (2002), dir. Don Coscarelli.
62 Brown, 'Comic Book Masculinity', 28.
63 Early twentieth-century psychic investigators found the Egyptian Rooms at the British Museum 'thoroughly haunted by malevolent spirits and elementals', and curses connected with both Ancient Egypt and the unleashing of Elementals found their way across the Atlantic as part of the Gothic element of the Egyptology craze. See Luckhurst, *The Mummy's Curse*, 143. A particularly dangerous mummy was said to have been transported on, and therefore been responsible for the sinking of, the *Titanic*. After being recovered from the wreckage, the same mummy, while again in transit, apparently sank the *Empress of Ireland* in 1914, was again recovered, and was then responsible for the sinking of the *Lusitania* in 1915. While fabrication, this story informed popular mummy

myths. See Luckhurst, *The Mummy's Curse*, 41–43, where he also discusses a contemporary rumour that was deliberately invented in order to test people's credulity of the absurd.

64 Tony Isabella (w) and Val Mayerik (a), *Supernatural Thrillers* #9 (New York: Marvel, 1973).

65 See, for instance, James Meriwether, *Proudly We Can Be African: Black Americans and Africa, 1935–1961* (Chapel Hill, NC: University of North Carolina Press, 2002).

66 Tony Isabella (w) and Val Mayerik (a), *Supernatural Thrillers* #12 (New York: Marvel, 1974).

67 John Warner (w) and Tom Sutton (a), *Supernatural Thrillers* #15 (New York: Marvel, 1974).

68 Keith P. Feldman, 'Representing Permanent War: Black Power's Palestine and the End(s) of Civil Rights', *CR: The New Centennial Review* 8.2 (2008), 193–231 (197). For a more complete discussion of the connections between Black Power and the Israel–Palestine conflict, see Michael R. Fischbach, *Black Power and Palestine: Transnational Countries of Color* (Stanford, CT: Stanford University Press, 2018).

69 Sven Beckert, 'Emancipation and Empire: Reconstructing the Worldwide Web of Cotton Production in the Age of the American Civil War', *American Historical Review* 109.5 (2004), 1405–1438 (1413–1414).

70 Beckert, 'Emancipation and Empire', 1413–1414.

71 Luckhurst, *The Mummy's Curse*, 165.

72 Mummy's curse narratives were still circulating at some scale through popular culture in the 1980s. While growing up in Norfolk, I (Mitch) used to be afraid to go to Swaffham, where the Egyptologist Howard Carter had spent much of his childhood, in case some of the 'curse' alleged to have killed Lord Carnarvon, Carter's benefactor in the Tutankhamun dig, had attached itself to the town. I had similar concerns about the mummies in the collections of the Castle Museum in Norwich. The only possible trace of curse of which I can conceive is a series of sporting failures in both locations; as anyone who has ever seen me play cricket will tell you, though, I do not need a mummy's curse to assist on that matter. I can also report that a trip to Caernarfon in the summer of 2019, while reading Stoker's *The Jewel of Seven Stars*, was only really notable for my enjoyment of the novel.

73 Nicholas Daly, 'That Obscure Object of Desire: Victorian Commodity Culture and Fictions of the Mummy', *NOVEL: A Forum on Fiction* 28.1 (1994), 24–51 (30).

74 A great deal of work has been done on Haiti but the best place to start remains the place where it all started, so to speak, back in 1938: C. L. R. James, *The Black Jacobins: Toussaint L'Ouverture and the San Domingo Revolution* (London: Penguin, 2001).

75 Groom is here referring to Stuart Clark, *Thinking with Demons: The Idea of Witchcraft in Early Modern Europe* (Oxford: Oxford University Press, 1999). Clark uses early modern supernatural belief to illuminate the intellectual and

ideological currents of contemporary debate and Groom undertakes a similar project in *The Vampire: A New History*.

76 Ronald Chetwynd-Hayes, 'The Labyrinth', in Stephen Jones (ed.), *The Mammoth Book of Vampires* (London: Avalon, 2004), 184–206 (203). Chetwynd-Hayes' story was first published in 1974.

77 Owen Davies, *America Bewitched: The Story of Witchcraft After Salem* (Oxford: Oxford University Press, 2016), 116.

78 Jason Dittmer, '"America Is Safe While its Boys and Girls Believe in its Creeds!": Captain America and American Identity Prior to World War 2', *Environment and Planning D: Society and Space* 25.3 (2007), 401–423.

# Conclusion: appropriating white male fear

In 2019, as we were writing this book, Marc Singer published his major intervention into comics scholarship, *Breaking the Frames*.[1] Comics Studies has, Singer argues, often struggled under a perceived (and, perhaps, at least partially invented) sense of marginalization within both the academic community and culture at large. This fear of not being taken seriously, Singer argues, has produced a resistance among certain comics scholars towards approaches and readings that threaten to trivialize or infantilize their subject; this has led to scholarship that seeks to understand comics in narrow terms, which ignores or consigns to history all but the most (for want of a better term) 'literary' of examples, and is thus unrepresentative of the medium as a whole. By fighting against perceived marginalization, certain Comics Studies scholars have adopted a marginalizing approach to their own subject. At the same time, Comics Studies has drawn on, and continues to enjoy a relationship with, amateur historiography and criticism through the work of the fan scholar (from which we have benefitted immensely in the construction of this volume). As a consequence, Singer argues, Comics Studies also includes works that examine more popular genres of comics uncritically, making false claims, perpetuating misconceptions, and crediting certain texts with unwarranted technical or formal innovation and/or political and social relevance and sensitivity.[2]

Horror comics have been affected by both fears of marginalisation and a tendency towards uncritical and weak scholarship. They have fallen victim to the asymmetry of critical attention – while the alternative, underground, and (more recently) superhero genres have been subject to a number of studies, horror comics have largely been either overlooked entirely or subsumed into larger histories of the medium. As a crude indicator, a search for 'horror' on the Bonner Online-Bibliographie zur Comicforschung database reveals just 53 examples of academic works that take the horror genre as their primary subject. A similar search for 'superhero' reveals 455 entries.[3]

Where studies have taken up horror, they have tacked towards the celebratory. Stephen Sennitt's history of horror comics, for example, is, in his words, 'less about such historical matters and much more an unbridled appreciation of the horror comics themselves; their gruesome stories, their lurid artwork, and their striking covers'.[4] In other studies, anti-comics crusaders, often represented by Fredric Wertham, are claimed as conservatives who broadly subscribed to the McCarthy-era distrust of art and intellectualism. If such figures opposed horror comics, such studies assume, it follows that horror comics must have been socially liberal and politically radical. Such arguments are complicated by the contents of horror comics but also by Wertham's service and activism. In addition to running a case for the NAACP that was taken up as part of *Brown v. Board of Education* in 1954, Wertham opened the Lafargue Clinic in Harlem in 1946, an institution run by multi-racial volunteers that primarily served an economically disadvantaged black community and was widely celebrated for improving race relations in New York. Wertham did far more to improve the lives of African Americans than even the most explicitly anti-racist storyline from EC – though subsequent patterns of usage of horror comics and Wertham's legacy tell a different story.[5]

The problematic alignment of horror comics with the anti-war movement, civil rights, and feminism also springs in part from the fact that underground comics creators, including those who created explicitly political and feminist comics, have often been read as the successors to horror comics in general and EC in particular. As Art Spiegelman, an underground creator and early reader of EC comics, asserts:

> After the accusations that comics were the single biggest cause of juvenile delinquency and there were comic-book burnings across America, the generation that was denied grew up to become juvenile delinquents, and then adult delinquents. And made comics and read comics.[6]

Roger Sabin, similarly, contends:

> [The CCA] stipulated 'no sex,' so the [underground] comix revelled in every kind of sex imaginable; the Code stipulated 'no violence' so the underground took bloodshed to extremes; above all the code stipulated 'no social relevance' yet here were comics that were positively revolutionary.[7]

Such assertions draw a straight line from EC's horror comics to underground titles such as *Vietnam: An Anti-War Tale* (1967) by Julian Bond and T. G Lewis and the all-female *Wimmin's Comix* anthologies, which began in 1972. Fredric Wertham and his colleagues, such arguments suggest, were right when they claimed that horror comics infected their readers with counter-cultural messages, but were wrong to condemn the comics and their effects.

Arguments around underground comics, as with horror comics, have tended to focus on a small number of texts while omitting or decentring others. Underground comics were closely aligned with the counter-culture of the 1960s and 1970s and included many examples of anti-war and feminist texts. They were a broad church, however, and contained a great deal of misogyny and racism, too.[8] By reading backwards from the examples of underground comics that most closely align with twenty-first-century socially and culturally liberal politics, we risk over-exaggerating the prevalence and impact of overtly anti-racist storylines in 1940s and 1950s horror. We risk confusing shock for politics and ignoring or eliding the genre's more problematic, and prevalent, tendencies towards misogyny and racist stereotypes.[9] As we have shown, for every horror comic that can be read as anti-racist or anti-misogynistic, there were many more that reproduced contemporary racism, sexism, and a range of other prejudices.

This work, we hope, avoids both pitfalls in the haunted house of Cold War America. We assume that horror comics of the mid-twentieth century are worthy of study, but we do not assume that the values they express align with those of a twenty-first-century intersectional liberalism, or that they espouse what is often, and problematically, referred to as 'identity politics'. We made a conscious decision early in the project to decentre the relationship between horror comics and the anti-comics crusade; Wertham and his contemporaries wrote in response to horror comics of the 1950s, but the horror comics of the 1950s were not, as a rule, written in dialogue with contemporary criticism. While some publishers took aim at Wertham and his approach, most notably EC, comics engaged with more of their climate of reception and creation than just their critics in Congress. To understand these works, therefore, we must position them in relation to the social, economic, and cultural forces in which they were enmeshed rather than channelling our discussion through the readings of a small (if influential) group of early comics scholars.

Horror comics, we believe, were counter-cultural in the sense that they opposed what their creators saw as the dominant cultural trends of their time – not necessarily in the sense that their values aligned with what came to be known as the 'counter-culture'. It is telling, for example, to contrast the content of horror comics with the work produced by The Beats, who existed simultaneously with and outlasted the boom in horror comics, were equally set on transgressing social conventions, but took a radically different approach and agenda, most notably over the question of LGBT rights. Horror comics were shockingly violent, but shock does not necessarily equate to critique. Consider, for instance, the number of conservative 'shock jocks' whose approach to controversial topics is often to hinder socially liberal policies rather than support them. As Julian Wolfreys argues, '[t]he transgressive text is not the one that shocks [...] Nothing is more banal, predictable or quotidian'.[10] The values the comics under consideration here express are rarely aligned with those of the anti-war, Civil Rights, or feminist movements. Quite the opposite: at times they articulate what appears to be an anti-racist message while simultaneously reinforcing racist assumptions. In the majority of cases, these texts are directly hostile to women, indulge in misogynistic violence, and, in Donald F. McGregor and Luis Garcia's 'Welcome to the Witches' Coven' (1972), discussed in Chapter 6, offer an explicit and direct attack on the feminist movement.[11] They attest to the ongoing impact of war but their primary concern appears to be the loss of power experienced by heterosexual white men, both individually and on a societal level, resulting from warfare, shifts in employment practice and expectation, and new concerns around sexuality emerging from the publication of the Kinsey reports in 1948 and 1953 and the sexual revolution of the 1960s and 1970s.

It is fundamental to our understanding of these concerns that we read access to fear as a form of property. The question of who experiences fear, and how seriously that fear is taken by the text, indicates how a given body of work can be read. The image of a black man experiencing fear summons a different set of associations, for example, from that of a white woman or a gay white man experiencing fear. In assessing the political dimension of fear, the positionality of both text and audience must be taken into account, opening up a range of potential readings.

In horror comics from the mid-twentieth century, images of people of colour in a role other than that of the monster are rare. Rarer still are images of people of colour experiencing fear. Indeed, as we came to write this concluding chapter, the only two examples we could think of in which a black character experiences fear (setting aside the recurrence of frightened and superstitious 'natives' in jungle settings) are Blade's mother and her friends in *Tomb of Dracula* #13 (discussed in Chapter 7) and 'The Black Witch' from *Vampirella* #7.[12]

The latter comic's protagonist, Jaol, runs in fear from a pack of rats summoned by the eponymous black witch (Figure 77). His fear lasts just two panels, however, before he reverts to the trope, described in Chapter 7, of the tough black man, and swears to destroy his tormen-tor. Subsequent supernatural scares do not faze him – he jokes that he has seen so many voodoo dolls bearing his face that he could 'open a

**77** Nick Cuti (w) and Billy Graham (a), 'The Black Witch', *Vampirella* #7

company and sell Jaol dolls'.[13] He becomes, instead, a source of fear himself – he is described in the text as 'the terror of all witches'.[14] While Jaol represents a rare instance of a black hero in a horror comic, he nonetheless falls into the same problematic tropes as Blade and N'Kantu, the living mummy (both discussed in Chapter 7); he reinforces

**78** Anon., 'The Master's Hand', *Adventures in the Unknown* #2

the stereotype, with roots in the antebellum period, of the black male as invulnerable to either physical or emotional pain. His refusal to be afraid also ultimately preserves access to fear as white property; his violence is directed, unthreateningly, towards another black character, perpetuating contemporary discussions around black on black crime and urban black spaces as places to be avoided by white people.

Women, conversely, do experience fear in horror comics; their fear, however, is complicated by invitations for complicity with their tormentors, and by the absence of convincing characterization to give their fear consequence. When, in 'The Master's Hand' in *Adventures in the Unknown* #2 (1948), Betty Saunders is pursued by monsters, for example, she clearly experiences fear (Figure 78).

Betty's body is captured with lavish detail elsewhere in the comic, with full-body shots that carefully delineate the shape of her buttocks and legs (Figure 79). Later, when she appears in bed in her nightwear, a loud noise causes a strap to slip from her shoulder (Figure 80). Given the recurring instances of the male gaze elsewhere in the comic, we might assume that readers are expected to, at least in part, side with the monsters who are pulling away her clothes; female nudity is, after all, hinted at repeatedly throughout the genre, and the female form is made to stand out visually on the page through the repeated use of block red for dresses (this was also common in the romance and crime genres). Worse, perhaps, is that through the way in which frames are constructed, the reader is positioned as a scopophilic viewer, a bystander who enjoys both the objectification of the female body and its subjection to physical and emotional threats. In this, the nature of viewing recalls the characterization of Mark Lewis, the cinematographer who

**79** Anon., 'The Master's Hand', *Adventures in the Unknown* #2

**80** Anon., 'The Master's Hand', *Adventures in the Unknown* #2

murders women while filming them in order to capture the look of fear in Michael Powell's film, *Peeping Tom* (1960).[15]

Aside from the potential erotic uses to which it is put, the stakes of Betty's fear are called into question by the fact that she is indistinguishable from almost all other female characters to appear in horror comics at the time; her sole attributes are that she is young, blonde, attractive, and subject to constant peril. Her reproducibility means that the stakes of the violence to which she is subjected are so low as to be inconsequential; regardless of what happens to her, she will return in a later issue, perhaps even a later page, equally young, equally blonde, equally attractive, and equally imperilled. In reading the misadventures of her various incarnations, one encounters the recurring suggestion that Betty somehow invites or is complicit with the violence to which she is inevitably subject. In the opening of the story, for example, a museum guards asserts, 'that Saunders girl is still upstairs **alone** ...'.[16] What should she expect, the reader is invited to speculate, if she insists, issue after issue, on entering sites of horror unchaperoned?

Such representation is consistent with horror film of the 1940s and 1950s, which formed some of the milieu feeding into these comics. Here, actors such as Evelyn Ankers appeared as a damsel in distress opposite the Wolf Man, Frankenstein, Dracula, and the Invisible Man.[17] It is telling that they, and others in similar roles, were known as 'scream queens'; the emphasis on close-ups of open-mouthed women raises further questions of erotic spectacle, suggesting, simultaneously, substitute images for sexual climax and the prospect of the male gaze fixating on, and sexualizing, the female mouth. In terms of spectacle, again, much of the appeal of *Creature from the Black Lagoon* (1954) and *Revenge of the Creature* (1955) might have revolved around the fact that Kay and then Helen, the two female leads, spend a lot of time in swimming costumes. The phenomenon of scream queens and their objectification was not missed by contemporary observers. *The Rocky Horror Picture Show* (1975) includes, at a pivotal narrative moment, the lines, 'Whatever happened to Fay Wray/That delicate satin draped frame/As it clung to her thigh', drawing attention to the sexualized representation of Wray. Another scream queen, Wray is perhaps defined by the erotically charged boat scene in *King Kong* where her director excitedly instructs her on how to scream while the rival for her affections watches in discomfort.[18]

Women's fear, then, operates as a complex nexus, entangled with sexual objectification and a number of potential subject positions, most notably that of the monster and the scopophilic viewer. Female fear operates as a climax to the narrative, but largely as sexual spectacle, not as imbued with any meaning beyond its representation. In contrast to these reader-centred readings, which are necessarily more contingent, texts frequently represented white male fear as real and of narrative consequence. When Frank Drake – a white man and property-owner with a back-story explored over multiple issues – enters Dracula's tomb in *Tomb of Dracula* #2, his experience is both shown and described by a narrative voice: 'Memories burn, stinging your eyes almost as much as the heat from your hand-held lantern ...'. The captions continue, 'by its light, you descend into the castle, deeper into the clammy darkness with each furtive step ... And there, you see what you've come so far to find ...' (Figure 81).[19] The choice of second-person pronouns and the

**81** Marv Wolfman (w), Gene Colan (a), Jack Abel (i), Denise Vladimer (l), and Roy Thomas (e), *Tomb of Dracula* #10

mounting tension over a series of panels encourages a kind of reader identification not found in either of the examples of black fear or female fear described above, but an identification that is structured very clearly around an assumed, indeed preferred, white male reader. The reader drawn into the narrative through this process wants Frank Drake to live. He wants Jaol to protect him. He wants Betty Saunders' clothes to fall off. Through such narrative tactics, readers are invited to invest in the fear of the white male protagonist.

None of the racism and misogyny we describe here, however, is inherent to the horror genre. In our introduction we balance different readings of horror, from Darryl Jones' description of the genre as a 'phobic cultural form', to George Haggerty, who reads horror as an inherently queer space that allows the exploration of transgressive identities. Rather than attempting to reconcile the two, we argue that horror does not have a single social or political function. The possibility for horror that recognizes and respects the experiences of characters other than heterosexual white men was not realized in a sustained manner in comics, however, until much later in the twentieth century.

### Horror comics after 1975

Neither horror comics nor the Cold War ended with the bounds of this study. We seek in this closing section to sketch the legacy of the comics discussed in the previous chapters, offering a brief overview of the ways in which the themes we have described above have reverberated and changed course in subsequent incarnations of the genre. One 1950s horror brand to have something of a resurgence was *Tales from the Crypt*, a television and, later, film series, which ran from 1989 to 1996. It also led to a spin-off cartoon, *Tales from the Cryptkeeper*, which ran from 1993 to 1994. The television series and cartoon both followed the style of the horror comic, with a horror host and stand-alone stories. The series was popular and garnered seven Primetime Emmy nominations, among other awards. The Warren comics brand continued until the company went bankrupt in 1983. The titles were then acquired by Harris Publishing and went on to have various afterlives; *Eerie* and *Creepy* each had a single issue under Harris but publication otherwise ceased. The properties returned to Warren in 2000 and were subsequently acquired by New Comic Company in 2007, which published a series of archival collections, and relaunched *Creepy* with new stories.

The Warren aesthetic continued as contributors migrated to other publications. One magazine of particular note is *Métal Hurlant*, launched in the US in 1977 as *Heavy Metal*. The magazine features European and American comics in the science fiction, dark fantasy, and erotica genres. Contributors include long-time Warren artists and writers such as Richard Corben and Terrance Lindall, who have created comics largely in keeping with the Warren style. Corben's dark fantasy series *Den*, in particular, is largely plotless and revolves around heterosexual male fantasies of sex and violence. Paul Gravett, charitably, describes *Den* as 'prone to charges of sexism and cliché'.[20]

Even as certain themes persisted, significant changes were afoot in the comics industry of the 1980s. While Warren went under, Marvel and DC continued to cater to the tastes of their core demographic. Increasing shifts to direct market distribution meant that comics were, in the main, consumed by a readership made up (or conceived by publishers to be made up) largely of white, middle-class, heterosexual men. Any lingering pretence that mainstream superhero comics might cater to any other audience almost completely vanished. Mike Deodato, who drew *Wonder Woman* from 1994 to 1995, once asserted that during this period, '[e]very time the bikini was smaller the sales got higher'.[21] The comics that emerged during the 1980s and 1990s ran parallel with artistic developments that positioned comics as 'adult' graphic novels worthy of serious cultural attention. In the context of the majority of genres, 'adult' meant often hugely violent, sexualized, and misogynistic content that quite often took the themes of the horror comics discussed here and dragged them into the murky shadows of the 1980s Cold War endgame. With the threat of nuclear war ever present, as in the Able Archer crisis of November 1983 when the USSR mistook a NATO training exercise for Western mobilization against them, 1980s culture was awash with imagery of nuclear destruction.[22] Even upbeat pop, such as the 1984 classic '99 Red Balloons' by Nena, showcase how small the gap was between setting the charts alight, and setting the world alight.[23]

We would not wish to suggest, of course, that the 1980s and 1990s were a period of unmitigated hawkish rhetoric and misogyny – this was, after all, the same period that gave us, among others, the comics art magazine *RAW* (1980 to 1991), Chris Ware's profoundly melancholic *Jimmy Corrigan: The Smartest Kid on Earth* (1995), and Joe Sacco's comics reportage *Palestine* (1993). Nonetheless, even as dramatic changes were taking place at what was then the fringes of the comics world, the majority of superhero comics during the 1980s and 1990s, including ground-breaking works such as Frank Miller's *The Dark Knight Returns* (1986), tended to offer various shades of violence meted out by heterosexual white men, often against those who were coded as people of colour, genderqueer, or both. This was equally true of comics that included horror elements. The *Spawn* comics from Image included a black protagonist (albeit one who is in costume so often, and whose body is so badly scarred, that his blackness is easily forgotten) much along the same lines as Blade and Jaol described above – he is an avenging figure who both reinforces the myth of the resilient black body and engages in battles against the supernatural, thus externalizing real world problems into a fantasy environment and alleviating a white audience of any sense of complicity in existent systems of oppression.

Changes were also ongoing in the wider culture and society. The Culture Wars, the AIDS crisis, and increasingly fraught domestic and international relations have been covered in detail elsewhere.[24] New technologies for home video distribution led to what was described in the UK as a 'video nasties' panic, a restaging of the crisis around horror comics of the 1950s for the new technology and distribution methods of the 1980s. Narratives and images in these films and comics of the 1980s engaged with anxieties around shifting gender roles, crises of sexuality, and continuing issues of racial inequality and police brutality. Many superheroes came to offer fantasies of an impenetrable male body, mirroring both anxieties over AIDS and an idealized form of the white, heterosexual, male body politic that, similarly, maintains a stable identity in the midst of cultural upheaval.[25] Comics, then, continued to explore many of the same themes as before, but adapted to new forms, in new places, and in dialogue with new factors, both domestic and international.

For much of the 1980s and 1990s mainstream comics, including those with horror elements, continued to be primarily concerned with white male fear. This did not remain the case forever. A notable turn in the horror genre was the 1993 introduction of DC's Vertigo line, which included titles such as *Hellblazer* (1988–2013, 2019–present), *Preacher* (1995–2000), and *The Sandman* (the series began in 1989 and is ongoing).[26] Vertigo sought to engage creative teams who, in the words of editor Karen Berger, represented the 'edgier' and 'smarter' fringes of comics publishing.[27] The Vertigo line was originally designed to offer a space for comics with content that did not align with CCA standards. Over time, however, the series became a home for prestige comics. This involved technological processes such as permanent binding, distribution through bookstores, and a higher standard of writing and art than found elsewhere in the industry at the time. A key acquisition for the Vertigo line was Neil Gaiman's *Sandman* series, which uses many of the visual trappings of horror comics; the work of artist Sam Kieth, in particular, evokes the mid-twentieth-century horror style and features horror hosts, Cain and Abel, from *House of Mystery* (1951–2011) and *House of Secrets* (1956–1976). Unlike earlier incarnations of the horror genre, however, the *Sandman* series has proven to speak for, and to, a readership other than heterosexual white men. As Rachel R. Martin states, Gaiman 'crafts tales about characters other than men, stories with fully developed female protagonists, and narratives showing those not fitting into a simplified gender binary. He depicts girls conquering worlds and saving adults […], women acting as superheroes and anti-heroes […], and beings who occupy spaces as both/neither man and/or woman'.[28] The series, in an almost unheard-of turn, engaged a sizeable female readership.[29]

Comics have undertaken further developments in the twenty-first century. Of the Warren properties, the titular protagonist of *Vampirella* proved to be more enduring than *Eerie* and *Creepy*. In part, this was because the character suited the turn, described above, which popular comics took towards increasingly concupiscent and violent art in the late 1980s and 1990s. The character reappeared in a publication by Harris, both as reprints and new stories, beginning in 1988, and in various titles over the following years. In 2010, the character was acquired by Dynamite Entertainment, which has since published several *Vampirella* series, many of which have deviated from the style of previous decades. Jeremy Whitley's version of the character from 2017 is perhaps the furthest the character has drifted from her original incarnation. Whitley, working with artist Andy Belanger, did not make use of the iconic red costume and consciously avoided the male gaze.[30] He asserts that when dealing 'with sexiness or sexuality with Vampirella, it's making it about what she's doing, not how we're framing it' – the character's sexuality emerges through her words and interaction with other characters, rather than costume and poses.[31] He also chose to place the character in a long-term monogamous relationship with recurring character Vicki Vincente so that, unlike previous incarnations, 'she won't be set up to seduce every other person that pops up on the page'.[32] As discussed previously, Vampirella has historically hinted at same-sex attraction. The introduction of a long-term and narratively significant lesbian relationship, and the move away from sexualized art, however, brought the character decidedly into what Adrienne Resha calls the 'Blue Age' of comics, where the introduction of digital sales, most notably through ComiXology, has encouraged publishers to create comics that appeal to individuals other than the traditional market of heterosexual white men.[33] This turn into the Blue Age has led to, as will be explored below, a re-examination of many of the horror properties discussed in this book.

This opening of comics beyond what has, for several decades, been their core demographic, has allowed writers and artists, like Jeremy Whitley and Andy Belanger, to restage and reinterpret the tropes of horror property. The possibility of horror comics that allow people of colour, women, and members of the LGBTQI community access to fear moves us beyond questions of an erotic gaze to an 'interpretive gaze' that still takes bodies as its object but examines them through the lens of the 'representational importance of correct demeanour and deportment', a space where social norms are defined and reinforced – and, potentially, challenged through the creation of oppositional texts or reader practices.[34]

Horror comics, as we have sought to demonstrate, invite and attempt to direct certain reactions from their readers, but invitations do not have to be accepted. To return to the earlier quotation from *The Rocky Horror Picture Show*, it continues, 'How I started to cry/Cause I wanted to be dressed just the same'. Here, the speaker acknowledges the male gaze through lingering over the sexualized representation of Fay Wray, but simultaneously queers the image by stating that he wishes to be dressed 'just the same' as the female object of his erotic gaze. This unites some of the apparently disparate approaches mentioned at the start of this chapter, showing how horror can be both conventional – reinforcing the male gaze as active and female bodies as passive erotic objects – and transgressive, a space for negotiating queer identities, depending on the use to which that eroticization is put by the bearer of the gaze. The invitation extended by the text can be accepted as it stands or transformed. The presentation of the eroticized female body for the gaze of an assumed white male reader might work towards the creation and curation of a heteronormative space that upholds patriarchy, but there is no guarantee what readers will do with that space once they are in it. As Harry M. Benshoff notes, 'horror stories and monster movies, perhaps more than any other genre, actively invoke queer readings, because of their obvious metaphorical (non-realist) forms and narrative formats which disrupt the heterosexual status quo', suggesting that the projected disciplinary functions of horror might fall down as readers look to the genre for camp excess, discovering in its frequent rending of normality the repeated creation of non-normative spaces.[35]

Horror comics of the mid-twentieth century, then, were not by conscious design a queer space. The readings of them, and the works that respond to them, however, often are. The *Sandman* series and later incarnations of *Vampirella* occupy horror properties of the mid-twentieth century and transform them into queer spaces. In his 2018 Drink 'n Draw sketchbook, artist Ken Wong includes a drawing titled 'Vampirello (John, Vampirella crossplay)' that features cosplayer TwinkyBoots as a gender-swapped Vampirella (Figure 82).[36] These queer and feminist reworkings of mid-twentieth century horror suggest that there is nothing inherent in the genre or medium that prevents the expression of fear beyond that experienced by white heterosexual men; horror, after all, has given us *Interview with the Vampire* (1994) and *Get Out* (2017), and comics have given us *Fun Home* (2006) and Kamala Khan as *Ms Marvel* (2013–present). The multiple evolutions of horror comics found

**82** Vampirello (TwinkyBoots, Vampirella crossplay) from 'Sketch Nights at Anyone Comics'

**83** Charles Burns, 'The Smell of Shallow Graves', *Raw* #2.2

in the works of creators such as Neil Gaiman and the floor of comics conventions do not exonerate their source material – a space that is liberated for some will still continue to serve a simultaneous disciplinary function for others, and horror still continues to confer deviant status on those it renders horrific, however those communities might contest and appropriate its imagery.

One artist to engage with the horror style was Charles Burns who, in 1990, published 'The Smell of Shallow Graves', a four-panel comic drawn in the style of 1950s horror. In the story, deceased and decomposing teenagers sneak into their parents' homes at night to re-create the existences they had in life (Figure 83). The teenagers' skin is pockmarked and discoloured and the parents are shown with furrowed brows worrying as they sleep. The story is open to multiple readings: it is about puberty as body horror, a theme that Burns develops in his series *Black Hole* (1995–2005); it can also be read as a commentary on a generational divide; it is an ironic account of the ways in which, during the 1950s, comics were accused of turning children into monsters, and the ways in which the decades to follow saw profound conflicts between parents and their teenage children; it is also a reworking of the familiar trope of suburbia as a site of horror.

Read as a commentary on the horror genre, in Burns' story white suburban America has birthed, and failed to destroy, monsters. In one sense, then, the comic mediates themes from the comics it parodies – the white male fears of invasion and of being replaced. The second panel shows an image of a Lichtenstein-esque sleeping woman as monstrous figures stalk behind her suggesting, in a familiar trope, white women in need of rescue. The monsters, however, are benign; they want to watch TV and make sandwiches. The white man who appears in the final panel stands with his back to us, watching as a zombie hand appears to wave at him from the ground. We experience the comic not through the eyes of a victim but, instead, through the source of his fear. The comic is not, at its heart, about horror, but alienation and the experience of monstrosity, of living on the fringe of an opulent society that would rather you did not exist. Similar 'outsider' genres directed at teenage rebellion against the suburban norms of their parents borrowed the trappings of horror and horror comics, most notably punk, with bands such as The Ramones channelling the aesthetic of 1950s horror comics in their career retrospective, *Weird Tales of the Ramones*, which included a comic as part of the package, and The Cramps, who drew on horror imagery more broadly (see, for instance, *Bad Music for Bad People*).

The theme of sympathy with the monster was not new: indeed, Cynthia Erb positions *King Kong* (1933) as a film that 'encourages identification with King Kong as a rather mysterious animal figure whose domain is violated by an arrogant white male', meaning that the film's 'call to identify with the position of tormented outsider has historically been answered by spectators outside the "mainstream", including international, gay, black, and feminist' audiences.[37] Horror of the 1970s, as we have argued, continued to expand this notion as it widened the space for white men as monsters and, consequently, is a move that elicits more empathy for the monster from the assumed white male audience. Burns' ambulatory teenage corpses, however, offer something quite different from the tortured and repentant protagonist of *Monster of Frankenstein*. They, too, want to experience suburban life in all of its safe mundanity. They occupy the shadows and fringes of suburban America because they know that its inhabitants fear them, and because they know that fear turns people into monsters.

In fighting monsters, the US took insufficient care to see that it did not itself become a monster; worse, it enshrined the monstrosity of structural racism and misogyny already present in American society as a good, not as something to be managed and ultimately reformed. If fear is only the property of white men, and fear turns people into monsters, Cold War horror comics bear a harsh lesson for the creative teams and their preferred audience of white men.

## Notes

1 Singer, *Breaking the Frames*.
2 A further gulf lies, Singer argues, in the fact that these two factions of comics scholars often ignore one another's work. In writing this book we have, we hope, avoided this phenomenon. We have sought to offer an appropriately scholarly lens (and, as such, have been judicious in the deployment of personal anecdotes and horror puns – which is to say, Mitch put them in, and Phil, the killjoy, took most of them out) and yet have benefitted tremendously from the dedication and work of people such as William Schoell (*The Horror Comics*) and Jim Trombetta (*The Horror! The Horror!*).
3 These numbers are broadly indicative of trends but do not represent a thorough study – we typed in the key term and then looked through the entries to determine how many directly concern the genre in question. We did not search for synonyms, publisher names, titles, characters, etc., nor did we eliminate texts which are outside of our area of study such as horror manga or American horror comics published after 1975. Comics, similarly, have largely been overlooked in academic studies of horror; they do not feature in the areas of interest for the journal, *Horror Studies*, for instance.
4 Sennitt, *Ghastly Terror!*, 10.
5 See Beaty, *Fredric Wertham and the Critique of Mass Culture*.
6 Joseph Witek (ed.), *Art Spiegelman Conversations* (Jackson, MS: University Press of Mississippi, 2007), 302.
7 Sabin, *Adult Comics*, 171.
8 Robert R. Crumb's satirical comics 'When the Niggers Take Over America' and 'When the Goddamn Jews Take Over America', which had originally appeared in the underground publication *Weirdo* (1981–1993) were reproduced, without irony, in the neo-Nazi magazine *Race & Reality*. Crumb's aesthetic commitment to offence has led to several texts that contain overtly racist and misogynistic imagery. While we can charitably read such imagery as satire or an exploration of taboo (as with Art Spiegelman's entries to the Iranian newspaper *Hamshahri*'s Anti-Semitic Cartoon Contest) they nonetheless contain the capacity for unironic readings. Crumb is perhaps the artist most commonly associated with the underground. One does not need to search far to find other artists whose work does not align with the feminist or Civil Rights movements. Manuel 'Spain' Rodriguez's works, for example, are unambiguously misogynistic. He presents women as sexual objects and misogynistic violence as a source of humour.
9 Terrence R. Wandtke, for example, celebrates Neil Gaiman's *Sandman* series as a horror comic that features a genderqueer character while remaining largely silent on the misogyny and anti-feminist images which were a staple of horror comics for much of the twentieth century. See Wandtke. *The Comics Scare Returns*.
10 Julian Wolfreys, *Transgression: Identity, Space, Time* (London: Palgrave Macmillan 2008), 12.

11  McGregor and Garcia, 'Welcome to the Witches' Coven', 57.
12  Cuti and Graham, 'The Black Witch', 22–28. This is not to say that there were not others: just that we did not see any that featured black characters experiencing fear. Given the number of comics we looked at, this means that images of black characters experiencing fear form a tiny minority in these texts.
13  Cuti and Graham, 'The Black Witch', 26.
14  Cuti and Graham, 'The Black Witch', 26.
15  For a detailed discussion of this, see Clover, *Men, Women, and Chain Saws*, 168–181.
16  Anon., 'The Master's Hand', *Adventures in the Unknown* #2 (New York: B&L Publishing Co, 1948). Emphasis in original.
17  Admittedly, Lon Chaney Jr appeared as all of her antagonists but while he changed, Ankers was essentially the same character in each film.
18  Richard O'Brien and Richard Hartley, 'Fanfare/Don't Dream It' from *The Rocky Horror Picture Show* (1975).
19  Marv Wolfman (w), Gene Colan (a), Jack Abel (i), Denise Vladimer (l), and Roy Thomas (e), *Tomb of Dracula* #10 (New York: Marvel, 1973).
20  Paul Gravett, 'Richard Corben: Getting Over the Underground', *Paulgravett. com* (18 February 2009), retrieved from https://web.archive.org/web/2009 0218131355/http://www.paulgravett.com/articles/013_corben/013_corben.htm (accessed 10 June 2020).
21  Mike Deodato quoted in Newsarama staff, 'Interview with Mike Deodato' (2006), archived at www.comicbloc.com/forums/archive/index.php?t-29878. html (accessed 19 May 2017); Brian Mitchell Peters maintains that William Messner-Loebs' writing during this period articulates queer identities but is belied by the art. See Brian Mitchell Peters, 'Qu(e)erying Comic Book Culture and Representations of Sexuality in Wonder Woman', *CLCWeb: Comparative Literature and Culture* 5.3 (2003), 1–9.
22  For more on Able Archer, see Larry Burriss, 'Slouching Toward Nuclear War: Coorientation and NATO Exercise Able Archer 83', *International Journal of Intelligence, Security, and Public Affairs* 21.3 (2019), 219–250.
23  For the uninitiated, Nena and her friend release 99 red balloons into the sky, triggering a fear of attack that sparks a military response. The song ends with her standing 'in this dust that was a city'. The song reached #1 in the UK and #2 in the US.
24  See, for instance, Andrew Hartmann, *A War for the Soul of America: A History of the Culture Wars* (Chicago, IL: University of Chicago Press, 2019); Randy Shilts, *And the Band Played On: Politics, People, and the AIDS Epidemic* (New York: St. Martin's Press, 1987).
25  See Philip Smith, 'Reading Aaron Diaz's Wonder Woman', *Literature Compass* 14.5 (2017) e12384.
26  For a discussion of Vertigo and its impact, see Julia Round, '"Is This a Book?" DC Vertigo and the Redefinition of Comics in the 1990s', in Paul Williams and James Lyons (eds), *The Rise of the American Comics Artist: Creators and Contexts* (Jackson, MS: University Press of Mississippi, 2010), 14–30.

27  Dana Jennings, 'MEDIA: At House of Comics, a Writer's Champion', *New York Times* (15 September 2003), 2.

28  Rachel R. Martin, 'Speaking the Cacophony of Angels: Gaiman's Women and the Fracturing of Phallocentric Discourse', in Tara Prescott and Aaron Drucker (eds), *Feminism in the Worlds of Neil Gaiman: Essays on the Comics, Poetry and Prose* (Jefferson, NC: McFarland, 2012), 11–31 (12).

29  Randy Duncan and Matthew J. Smith (eds), *Icons of the American Comic Book: From Captain America to Wonder Woman, Volume One* (Santa Barbara, CA: Greenwood, 2013), 648.

30  Jeremy Whitley (w) and Andy Belanger (i, c), *Vampirella Vol. 4* (Mount Laurel, NJ: Dynamite, 2018).

31  Jeremy Whitley, 'Interview: Jeremy Whitley Takes a Bite of VAMPIRELLA', *Comicsity* (19 October 2017), retrieved from www.comicosity.com/interview-jeremy-whitley-takes-a-bite-of-vampirella/ (accessed 13 January 2019).

32  Whitley, 'Interview'.

33  Adrienne Resha, 'The Blue Age of Comic Books' Comics Studies Society Conference, Urbana, IL, August 9 2017.

34  John Walter, 'Gesturing at Authority: Deciphering the Gestural Code of Early Modern England', *Past & Present* (2009), Supplement 4, 96–127 (123).

35  Benshoff, *Monsters in the Closet*, 6.

36  Ken Wong, 'Sketch Nights at Anyone Comics' *Origamicomics.com* (18 October 2018), retrieved from http://origamicomics.com/2018/10/sketch-nights-anyone-comics/?fbclid=IwAR1GPTMD1AOQqzA6c7SMXchkm6mae_zmhEmsF86v-LcnLBPWsc0DkirGCcsM (accessed 10 June 2020). Ani Mia has cosplayed as an Asian Vampirella and Maki Roll has cosplayed as a black Vampirella.

37  Erb, *Tracking King Kong*, 14. Similarly, *Creature from the Black Lagoon* posits the Gill-man as the victim of white male scientists who penetrate the womb-like space of the Black Lagoon, against the wishes of the local population, to inflict violence on the body of the international Other. Another film directed by Jack Arnold, *It Came from Outer Space* (1953), also positioned the horrifying bodies of the aliens as sympathetic, albeit still as the source of visual spectacle. It is the normative white bodies, and the mob McCarthyite violence in which they threaten to engage, which are the true source of horror in this film.

# Bibliography

**Primary sources**

*Books and comics*

Abrahams, Terri (w), and Ed Robbins (a), 'Eleven Footsteps to Lucy Fuhr', *Vampirella* #3 (New York: Warren Publishing, 1971).

Anon., '8.30', *Witches Tales* #25 (New York: Harvey Comics Group, 1954).

Anon., 'Cavern of Doom', *Tomb of Terror* #3 (New York: Harvey Publications, 1952).

Anon., 'Corpse of the Jury', *Voodoo* #5 (New York: Four Star Publications/Farrell Publications, 1953).

Anon., 'Death Is a Dream', *Ghost Comics* #4 (New York: Fiction House, 1952).

Anon., 'Death Pact', *Tomb of Terror* #3 (New York: Harvey Publications, 1952).

Anon., 'The Demon of Devonshire', *Ghost Comics* #7 (New York: Fiction House, 1953).

Anon., 'Dimension IV', *Witches Tales* #13 (New York: Witches Tales Inc., 1952).

Anon., 'Dirt of Death', *Ghost Comics* #4 (New York: Fiction House, 1952).

Anon., 'Dungeon of Doom', *Chamber of Chills* #6 (New York: Harvey Publications, 1952).

Anon., 'Fatal Steps', *Witches Tales* #9 (New York: Witches Tales Inc., 1952).

Anon., 'Fog Was My Shroud', *Voodoo* #16 (New York: Four Star Publications, 1954).

Anon., 'Found: The Lair of the Snow Monster', *Tomb of Terror* #6 (New York: Harvey Publications, 1952).

Anon., 'The Frenzy of Sheila Lord', *Beyond* #5 (New York: Ace Magazines Inc. 1951).

Anon., 'Gallows Curse', *Voodoo* #14 (New York: Four Star Publications, 1954).

Anon., 'Gateway to Death', *Witches Tales* #16 (New York: Harvey Comics Group, 1952).

Anon., 'Hammer of Evil', *Voodoo* #15 (New York: Farrell Publications, 1954).

Anon., 'Happy Anniversary', *Chamber of Chills* #19 (New York: Harvey Publications, 1953).

Anon., 'The Haunted One', *Voodoo* #1 (New York: Four Star Publications, 1952).

Anon., 'Hollow Horror', *Fantastic Fears* #6 (New York: Ajax-Farrell, 1954).

Anon., 'It', *Witches Tales* #10 (New York: Witches Tales Inc., 1952).

Anon., 'King of Hades', *Voodoo* #11 (New York: Four Star Publications, 1953).

Anon., 'Mannequin of Murder', *Witches Tales* #17 (New York: Harvey Comics Group, 1953).

Anon., 'Mask of the Monster', *Voodoo* #10 (New York: Four Star Publications/Farrell Publications, 1953).

Anon., 'Massacre of the Ghosts', *Witches Tales* #2 (New York: Witches Tales Inc., 1951).

Anon., 'The Master's Hand', *Adventures in the Unknown* #2 (New York: B&L Publishing Co, 1948).

Anon., 'Midnight Limited', *Witches Tales* #16 (New York: Harvey Comics Group, 1952).

Anon., 'Nightmare Merchant', *Strange Fantasy* #7 (New York: Farrell Comics, 1953).

Anon., 'Payoff Blues', *Ghost Comics* #6 (New York: Fiction House, 1953).

Anon., 'The Shelf of Skulls', *Voodoo* #1 (New York: Four Star Publications, 1952).

Anon., 'Shower of Death', *Witches Tales* #12 (New York: Harvey Comics Group, 1952).

Anon., 'The Snake Man', *Chamber of Chills* #22 (New York: Harvey Publications, 1951).

Anon., 'Snow Beasts', *Tomb of Terror* #4 (New York: Harvey Publications, 1952).

Anon., 'Star of Doom', *Witches Tales* #17 (New York: Harvey Comics Group, 1953).

Anon., 'The Survivors', *Tomb of Terror* #6 (New York: Harvey Publications, 1952).

Anon., 'The Thing that Walked at Night', *Ghost Comics* #9 (Fiction House, 1953).

Anon., 'The Torture Jar', *Witches Tales* #13 (New York: Harvey Comics Group, 1952).

Anon., 'The Valley of the Scaly Monsters', *The Beyond* #2 (New York: Ace Magazines, 1951).

Anon., 'Wax Museum', *Tomb of Terror* #3 (New York: Harvey Publications, 1952).

Anon., 'The Werewolf', *Voodoo* #1 (New York: Four Star Publications, 1952).

Anon., 'Werewolf Hunter', *Ghost Comics* #3 (New York: Fiction House, 1952).

Anon., 'The Witch Who Wore White', *Witches Tales* #8 (New York: Harvey Publications, 1952).

Anon. (w), and Harry Lazarus (a), 'Vampires? Don't Make Me Laugh', *The Clutching Hand* (New York: Best Syndicated Features Inc., 1954).

Balmer, Edwin, and Philip Wylie, *When Worlds Collide* (New York: Frederick A. Stokes, 1933).

Bellin, Edward (w), Fred Kida, George Roussos, and Joe Kubert (a), *Eerie Comics* #1 (New York: Avon, 1947).

Biafra, Jello, and East Bay Ray, 'Kill the Poor', as performed by The Dead Kennedys (1980).

Bolte, Charles G., *The New Veteran* (New York: Reynal & Hitchcock, 1946).

Burns, Charles, 'The Smell of Shallow Graves', *Raw* #2.2 (1990).

Check (i), Sid, 'Death Sentence' *Tomb of Terror* #14 (New York: Harvey Publications, 1954).

Church, Jane, 'Whatever Turns You On', *Vampirella* #4 (New York: Warren Publishing, 1970).

Cohen, Sol (w), and Everett Raymond Kinstler (a), 'The Thing in the Mirror', *Psycho* #1 (New York: Skywald Publications, 1971).

Conway, Gerry (w), Gene Colan (a, i), John Costanza (l), and Stan Lee (e), *Tomb of Dracula* #1 (New York: Marvel, 1972).

Conway, Gerry (w), and Mike Ploog (a), *Werewolf by Night* #2 (New York: Marvel, 1972).

*Creepy Archives*, vol. 9 (New York: Dark Horse, 2011).

Cuti, Nicola (w), and Billy Graham (a), 'The Black Witch', *Vampirella* #7 (New York: Warren Publishing, 1970).

Cuti, Nicola (w), and Jack Sparling (w), 'Snake Eyes' Town', *Vampirella* #8 (New York: Warren Publishing, 1970).

Elvgren, Gil, *Out on a Limb* (St Paul, MN: Louis F. Dow & Co., 1937).

Elvgren, Gil, *Tail Wind* (St Paul, MN: Louis F. Dow & Co., 1942).

Elvgren, Gil, 'Target for Tonite', *Esquire* (military edition, March 1944).

Fairclough, Peter (ed.), *Three Gothic Novels* (London: Penguin, 1986).

Feldstein, Al (w), and Joe Orlando (a), *Weird Fantasy* #18 (New York: EC Comics, 1953).

Fox, Gardner (w), Eugene Colan (a), Tom Palmer (i), Artie Simek (l), Roy Thomas (e), 'Death to a Vampire-Slayer!', *Tomb of Dracula* #5 (New York: Marvel, 1972).

Fox, Gardner (w), and Dan Dakins (a), 'New Girl in Town', *Vampirella* #5 (New York: Warren Publishing, 1970).

Friedrich, Gary (w), and Dick Ayers (a), *Sgt Fury and His Howling Commandos* #64 (New York: Marvel, 1969).

Friedrich, Gary (w), Mike Ploog (p), John Verpoorten (i), Artie Simek (l), and Glynis Wein (c), *Monster of Frankenstein* #4 (New York: Marvel, 1973).

Friedrich, Gary (w), Mike Ploog (a), John Verpoorten (i), Artie Simek (l), and Glynis Wien (c), *Monster of Frankenstein* #5 (New York: Marvel, 1973).

Gaines, Bill (w), Albert B. Feldstein (w), and Graham Ingels (a), 'Mournin' Mess', *Tales from the Crypt* #38 (New York: EC Comics, 1953).

Gaines, Bill (w), Al Feldstein (w), and Joe Orlando (a), 'Midnight Mess!', *Tales from the Crypt* #35 (New York: EC Comics, 1953).

Gaines, Bill (w), Al Feldstein (w), and George Roussos (a), 'Indian Burial Mound', *Tales from the Crypt* #26 (New York: EC Comics, 1951).

Gerber, Steve (w), and Rich Buckler (a), *Supernatural Thrillers* #5 (New York: Marvel, 1973).

Gerber, Steve (w), and P. Craig Russell (a), *Adventure into Fear* #24 (New York: Marvel, 1974).

Glut, Don (w), and Billy Graham (a), 'Rhapsody in Red', *Vampirella* #2 (New York: Warren Publishing, 1969).

Glut, Don (w), and Dick Piscopo (a), 'Queen of Horror', *Vampirella* #2 (New York: Warren Publishing, 1969).

Glut, Don (w), and Mike Royer (a) 'Last Act: October', *Vampirella* #1 (New York: Harris Publications, 1969).

Glut, Don (w), and Tony Tallarigo (a), 'Spaced-out Girls!', *Vampirella* #1 (New York: Warren Publishing, 1969).

Goodwin, Archie (w), Gene Colan (a), Tom Palmer (i), John Costanza (l), and Stan Lee (e), *Tomb of Dracula* #3 (New York: Marvel, 1972).

Goodwin, Archie (w), and Jose Gonzales (a), *Vampirella* #12 (New York: Warren Publishing, 1971).

Goodwin, Archie (w), and Don Heck (a), *The Invincible Iron Man* #27 (New York: Marvel, 1970).

Graham, Billy (w, a), 'I Wake Up Screaming!' *Vampirella* #3 (New York: Warren Publishing, 1970).

Griffin, John Howard, *Black Like Me* (New York: Houghton Mifflin Harcourt, 1961).

Gutwirth, Maurice (w), and George Appel (a), 'The Mystery of Lunablanca', *The Beyond* #2 (New York: Ace Magazines, 1951).

Herndon, Larry (w), and Tony Williamsune (a), 'One Way Trip!', *Vampirella* #6 (New York: Warren Publishing, 1970)

Hewetson, Alan, *Psycho* #13 (New York: Skywald Publications, 1973).

Hewetson, Al (w), and Francisco Javier Gonzalez (a), 'I Am Dead: I Am Buried', *Nightmare* #12 (New York: Skywald Publications, 1973).

'Hoover Calls Panthers Top Threat to Security', *The Washington Post* (WP Company LLC, 16 July 1969).

Howard, Robert E., 'Pigeons from Hell', *Weird Tales* 31.5 (May, 1938).

Iger Studio, 'Crawling Evil', *Journey into Fear* #10 (New York: Superior Publishers, 1952).

Iger Studio, 'Tusks of Terror', *Voodoo* #10 (New York: Four Star Publications, 1953).

Isabella, Tony, 'Introducing Brother Voodoo: The Creation of Marvel's Most Mysterious Superhero', *Tales of the Zombie* #2 (New York: Marvel, 1973).

Isabella, Tony (w), and Val Mayerik (a), *Supernatural Thrillers* #9 (New York: Marvel, 1973).

Isabella, Tony (w), and Val Mayerik (a), *Supernatural Thrillers* #12 (New York: Marvel, 1974).

Jones, Stephen (ed.), *The Mammoth Book of Vampires* (London: Avalon, 2004).

Kanigher, Robert (w), and Ross Andru (a), *Superman* #216 (New York: DC Comics, 1969).

Kanigher, Robert (w), and Werner Roth (a), *Superman's Girl Friend, Lois Lane* #106 (New York: DC Comics, 1970).

Kennedy, Stetson, *I Rode with the Ku Klux Klan* (London: Arco, 1954).

Khoury, George, 'The Thing About Man-Thing', *Alter-Ego* #81 (Raleigh, NC: TwoMorrows Publishing, 2008), 26–28.

Kida, Fred, 'The Strange Case of Hen-Pecked Harry', *Eerie Comics* #1 (New York: Avon, 1947).

King, Stephen, *Carrie* (New York: Doubleday, 1974).

King, Stephen, *Pet Sematary* (New York: Doubleday, 1983).

Krigstein, Bernard, 'Master Race', *Impact* #1 (New York: EC Comics, 1955).

Lee, Stan, 'The Spider's Web', *The Amazing Spider-Man* #76 (New York: Marvel, 1963).

Lee, Stan (w), Jack Kirby (a), 'Grottu, King of the Insects!', *Strange Tales* #73 (New York: Marvel, 1960).

Lee, Stan (w), Larry Lieber (w), Jack Kirby (a), 'Fin Fang Foom!', *Strange Tales* #89 (New York: Marvel, 1961).

Lee, Stan (w), Larry Lieber (w), Jack Kirby (a), 'Gorgolla! The Living Gargoyle!!', *Strange Tales* #74 (New York: Marvel, 1960).

Lee, Stan (w), Larry Lieber (w), and Jack Kirby (a), 'I Fought the Colossus', *Strange Tales* #72 (New York: Marvel, 1959).

Lee, Stan (w), Larry Lieber (w), Jack Kirby (a), 'Taboo! The Thing from the Murky Swamp!', *Strange Tales* #75 (New York: Marvel, 1960).

Le Fanu, Joseph Sheridan, *Carmilla* (London: Richard Bentley and Son, 1872).

Levi, Primo, *If This Is A Man and The Truce*, trans. Stuart Woolf (London: Abacus, 1979).

*LIFE Magazine*, 22 May 1944.

Lovecraft, H. P., 'He', *Weird Tales* (September, 1926).

'The Madhouse Murder Mystery', *Amazing Mystery Funnies*, volume 2, number 3 (New York: Centaur Publications, 1939).

McGregor, Don (w), and Luis Garcia (a), 'Welcome to the Witches' Coven', *Vampirella* #15 (New York: Warren Publishing, 1972).

McLaughlin, Jim, 'Cult of the Undead', *The Beyond* #4 (New York: Ace Magazines, 1951).

Moench, Doug (w), and Tony Dezuniga (a), *Tales of the Zombie* #10 (New York: Marvel, 1975).

Morrell, David, *First Blood* (Lanham, MD: M. Evans, 1972).

Murdoch, Drew (w), 'The Ghost Gallery', *Ghost Comics* #2 (New York: Fiction House, 1952).

Nakazawa, Keiji, *Barefoot Gen*, trans. Project Gen (San Francisco, CA: Last Gasp, 2004).

O'Brien, Richard, and Richard Hartley, 'Fanfare/Don't Dream It', as performed by Tim Curry in *The Rocky Horror Picture Show* (1975).

O'Brien, Tim, *The Things They Carried* (Boston, MA: Houghton Mifflin, 1990).

O'Neil, Dennis (w), and Neal Adams (a), *Green Lantern co-starring Green Arrow* #76 (New York: DC Comics, 1970).

Parente, Bill (w), and David Sinclair (a), 'Forgotten Kingdom', *Vampirella* #2 (New York: Warren Publishing, 1970).

Rice, Anne, *Interview with the Vampire* (New York: Knopf, 1976).

Rice, Ken, 'The Ghost Who Stole a Body', *The Beyond* #2 (New York: Ace Magazines, 1951).

Riesman, David, Nathan Glazer, and Reuel Denney, *The Lonely Crowd* (New Haven, CT: Yale University Press, 1950)

Roche, Ruth (w), Robert Webb, and David Heames (i), 'Corpses ... Coast to Coast!', *Voodoo* #14 (New York: Four Star Publications/Farrell Publications, 1954).

Rosen, R. Michael (w), and Jack Sparling (a), 'A Slimy Situation', *Vampirella* #3 (New York: Warren Publishing, 1970).

Roth, Philip, *American Pastoral* (Boston, MA and New York: Houghton Mifflin Company).

Seabrook, William B., *The Magic Island* (New York: Dover Publications, 2016).

Skeates, Steve (w), and Ken Barr (a), 'Out of the Fog ... Into the Mist', *Vampirella* #8 (New York: Warren Publishing, 1970).

Sparling, Jack (a), '4... 3... 2... 1... Blast Off! To a Nightmare!', *Vampirella* #3 (New York: Warren Publishing, 1970).

Spiegelman, Art, *Comix, Essays, Graphics, and Scraps* (Selerrio: Editore-La Centrale dell'Arte, 1999).

Spiegelman, Art, and Hillary Chute, *Metamaus* (New York: Pantheon, 2011).

Sprigle, Ray, *In the Land of Jim Crow* (New York: Simon & Schuster, 1949).

Stoker, Bram, *Dracula*, ed. Roger Luckhurst (Oxford: Oxford University Press, 2011).

Stoker, Bram, *The Jewel of Seven Stars* (London: Heinemann, 1903).

Thompson, Hunter S., *Fear and Loathing in Las Vegas* (London: HarperCollins, 2005).

Thompson, Hunter S., *Hell's Angels: The Strange and Terrible Saga of the Outlaw Motorcycle Gangs* (New York: Random House, 1967).

Vampirello (TwinkyBoots, Vampirella crossplay) from 'Sketch Nights at Anyone Comics', 18 October 2018.

Voltaire, Frank (w), Jack Katz (a), and Frank Giacoia (i), 'Beware Small Evils', *Nightmare* #3 (New York: Skywald Magazines, 1971).

Walpole, Horace, *The Castle of Otranto* (Oxford: Oxford University Press, 2014).

Warner, John (w), and Tom Sutton (a), *Supernatural Thrillers* #15 (New York: Marvel, 1974).

Warren, James, 'An Editorial to the President of the United States and all the Members of Congress – on behalf of our readers, most of whom are from 10 to 18 years old', *Vampirella* #7 (New York: Warren Publishing, 1970).

Wein, Len (w), and Gene Colan (a), 'Baptism of Fire!', *Strange Tales* #170 (New York: Marvel, 1973).
Wein, Len (w), and Gene Colan (a), 'Brother Voodoo!', *Strange Tales* #169 (New York: Marvel, 1973).
Wein, Len (w), and Gene Colan (a), 'March of the Dead!', *Strange Tales* #171 (New York: Marvel, 1973).
Wein, Len (w), Tony Isabella (w), and Val Mayerick (w/a), *Supernatural Thrillers* #10 (New York: Marvel, 1974).
Wein, Len (w), and Jim Mooney (a), *Marvel Team-Up* #24 (New York: Marvel, 1974).
Wein, Len (w), and Berni Wrightson (a), 'Swamp Thing', *The House of Secrets* #92 (New York: DC Comics, 1971).
Wells, H. G., *The Shape of Things to Come* (London: Gollancz, 2017).
Whitehead, Henry S., *Voodoo Tales* (Ware: Wordsworth Editions, 2012).
Whitley, Jeremy (w), and Andy Belanger (i, c), *Vampirella Vol. 4* (Mount Laurel, NJ: Dynamite, 2018).
Williamson, Al, Larry Woromay, and King Ward (i), 'The Flapping Head', *Forbidden Worlds* #6 (New York: American Comics Group, 1952).
Wolfman, Marv (w), Gene Colan (a), Jack Abel (i), Denise Vladimer (l), and Roy Thomas (e), *Tomb of Dracula* #10 (New York: Marvel, 1973).
Wolfman, Marv (w), Gene Colan (a), Tom Palmer (i, c), and John Costanza (l), *Tomb of Dracula* #12 (New York: Marvel, 1973).
Wolfman, Marv (w), Gene Colan (a), Tom Palmer (i, c), John Costanza (l), and Roy Thomas (e), *Tomb of Dracula* #13 (New York: Marvel, 1973).

### Films
*Abbott & Costello Meet Frankenstein* (1948), dir. Charles Barton.
*A Clockwork Orange* (1971), dir. Stanley Kubrick.
*Alien* (1979), dir. Ridley Scott.
*Blood Fest* (1963), dir. Herschell Gordon Lewis.
*Bonnie and Clyde* (1967), dir. Arthur Penn.
*Brides of Dracula* (1960), dir. Terence Fisher.
*Bubba Ho-Tep* (2002), dir. Don Coscarelli.
*Carrie* (1976), dir. Brian De Palma.
*Cat People* (1942), dir. Jacques Tourneur.
*Circus* (1936), dir. Grigori Aleksandrov and Isidor Simkov.
*Creature from the Black Lagoon* (1954), dir. Jack Arnold.
*Curse of the Fly* (1965), dir. Don Sharp.
*Deathdream* (1974), dir. Bob Clark.
*Deliverance* (1972), dir. John Boorman.
*Demon Seed* (1977), dir. Donald Cammell.
*Dracula* (1931), dir. Tod Browning.
*Dracula* (1958), dir. Terence Fisher.
*Dracula's Daughter* (1936), dir. Lambert Hillyer.
*Dracula vs. Frankenstein* (1971), dir. Al Adamson.

*Dr. Jekyll and Mr. Hyde* (1931), dir. Rouben Mamoulian.
*Dr. Jekyll and Mr. Hyde* (1941), dir. Victor Fleming.
*Face at the Window* (1939), dir George King.
*Footlight Parade* (1933), dir. Lloyd Bacon and Busby Berkeley.
*Frankenstein* (1931), dir. James Whale.
*Frankenstein Meets the Wolf Man* (1942), dir. Roy William Neill.
*Freaks* (1932), dir. Tod Browning.
*Get Out* (2017), dir Jordan Peele.
*Godzilla* (1954), dir. Ishiro Honda.
*Guess Who's Coming to Dinner* (1967), dir. Stanley Kramer.
*Halloween* (1978), dir. John Carpenter.
*House of Dracula* (1945), dir. Erle C. Kenton.
*House of Frankenstein* (1944), dir. Erle C. Kenton.
*Interview with the Vampire* (1994), dir. Neil Jordan.
*I Spit on Your Grave* (1978), dir. Meir Zarchi.
*It Came from Outer Space* (1953), dir. Jack Arnold.
*It's Alive* (1974), dir. Larry Cohen.
*I Walked With a Zombie* (1943), dir. Jacques Tourneur.
*King Kong* (1933), dir. Merian C. Cooper and Ernest B. Schoedsack.
*Kong: Skull Island* (2017), dir. Jordan Vogt-Roberts.
*Live and Let Die* (1973), dir. Guy Hamilton.
*London After Midnight* (1927), dir. Tod Browning.
*Mystery of the Wax Museum* (1933), dir. Michael Curtiz.
*Night of the Living Dead* (1968), dir. George A. Romero.
*Nosferatu* (1929) dir. F. W. Murnau.
*Peeping Tom* (1960), dir. Michael Powell.
*Pet Sematary* (1989), dir. Mary Lambert.
*Plan 9 From Outer Space* (1959), dir. Ed Wood.
*Psycho* (1960), dir. Alfred Hitchcock.
*Rambo* (1982) dir. Ted Kotcheff.
*Revenge of the Creature* (1955), dir. Jack Arnold.
*Return of the Fly* (1959), dir. Edward Bernds.
*Robot Monster* (1953), dir. Phil Tucker.
*Rosemary's Baby* (1968), dir. Roman Polanski.
*Son of Dracula* (1943), dir. Robert Siodmak.
*Son of Frankenstein* (1939), dir. Rowland V. Lee.
*Straight Jacket* (1963), dir. William Castle.
*Straw Dogs* (1971), dir. Sam Peckinpah.
*Taxi Driver* (1976), dir. Martin Scorsese.
*The Amityville Horror* (1979), dir. Stuart Rosenberg.
*The Best Years of Our Lives* (1946), dir. William Wyler.
*The Black Cat* (1934), dir. Edgar G. Ulmer.
*The Blob* (1958), dir. Ivan Yeaworth and Russell Doughton.
*The Bride of Frankenstein* (1935), dir. James Whale.
*The Brood* (1979), dir. David Cronenberg.

*The Cabinet of Dr. Caligari* (1920), dir. Robert Wiene.
*The Crazies* (1973), dir. George A. Romero.
*The Curse of Frankenstein* (1957), dir. Terence Fisher.
*The Devil Doll* (1936), dir. Tod Browning.
*The Exorcist* (1973), dir. William Friedkin.
*The Fly* (1958), dir. Kurt Neumann.
*The Fury* (1978), dir. Brian De Palma.
*The Hills Have Eyes* (1977), dir. Wes Craven.
*The Invasion of the Body Snatchers* (1956), dir. Don Siegel.
*The Last House on the Left* (1972), dir. Wes Craven.
*The Leopard Man* (1943), dir. Jacques Tourneur.
*Them!* (1954), dir. Gordon Douglas.
*The Mad Doctor* (1933), dir. David Hand.
*The Man Who Laughs* (1928), dir. Paul Leni.
*The Mummy* (1932), dir. Karl Freund.
*The Mummy* (1959), dir. Terence Fisher.
*The Omen* (1976), dir. Richard Donner.
*The Plague of the Zombies* (1966), dir. John Gilling.
*The Rocky Horror Picture Show* (1975), dir. Jim Sharman.
*The Texas Chainsaw Massacre* (1974), dir. Tobe Hooper.
*The Thing From Another World* (1951), dir. Christian Nyby.
*The Unknown* (1927), dir. Tod Browning.
*The Vietnam War* (2017), dir. Ken Burns and Lynn Novick.
*The Village of the Damned* (1960), dir. Wolf Rilla.
*The Wolf Man* (1941), dir. George Waggner.
*Universal Horror* (1998), dir. Kevin Brownlow.
*Way of the Dragon* (1972), dir. Bruce Lee.
*White Zombie* (1932), dir. Victor Halperin.

### Secondary sources

Adams, Rachel, *Sideshow USA: Freaks and the American Cultural Imagination* (Chicago, IL: University of Chicago Press, 2001).
Adorno, Theodor, and Max Horkheimer, *Dialectic of Enlightenment*, trans. Edmund Jephcott (Stanford, CT: Stanford University Press, 2002).
Aldeman, Bob (ed.), *The Tijuana Bibles* (New York: Simon & Schuster, 2006).
Althusser, Louis, *Lenin and Philosophy and Other Essays* (New York: Monthly Review Press, 2001).
Arata, Stephen D., ' "The Occidental Tourist": *Dracula* and the Anxiety of Reverse Colonization', *Victorian Studies* 33.4 (1990), 621–645.
Arendt, Hannah, *Eichmann in Jerusalem* (New York: Viking Press, 1963).
Armstrong, Louis, Dave Brubeck, and Iola Brubeck, *The Real Ambassadors* (Monterey Jazz Festival, 1962).
Arndt, Richard J., *Horror Comics in Black and White: A History and Catalogue, 1964–2004* (Jefferson, NC: McFarland, 2013)

Bakwin, Ruth Morris, 'Psychological Journal of Pediatrics: The Comics', *Journal of Pediatrics* 42.5 (1953), 633–635.

Baldick, Chris (ed.), *Gothic Tales* (Oxford: Oxford University Press, 1992).

Barker, Martin, *Haunt of Fears: The Strange History of the British Horror Comics Campaign* (London: Pluto Press, 1984).

Barnett, Vincent L., 'Hammering Out a Deal: The Contractual and Commercial Contexts of *The Curse of Frankenstein* (1957) and *Dracula* (1958)', *Historical Journal of Film, Radio and Television*, 34.2 (2014), 231–252.

Barron, Neil (ed.), *Fantasy and Horror* (Lanham, MD: Scarecrow Press, 1999).

Bassett, Mary T., 'Beyond Berets: The Black Panthers as Health Activists', *American Journal of Public Health* 106.10 (2006), 1741–1743.

Bastién, Angelica Jade, 'Vulnerability and the Strong Black Female Archetype', in Kelly Sue Deconnick (w), Valentine De Landro (a), and Kelly Fitzpatrick (i), *Bitch Planet* #7 (Berkeley, CA: Image Comics, 2016), n.p.

Bazin, Andre, 'Metamorphosis of the Pin-Up Girl', *What Is Cinema? Vol. 2* (Berkley, CA: University of California Press, 2005), 159–162.

Beaty, Bart, *Fredric Wertham and the Critique of Mass Culture: A Re-examination of the Critic Whose Congressional Testimony Sparked the Comics Code* (Jackson, MS: University Press of Mississippi, 2005).

Beckert, Sven, 'Emancipation and Empire: Reconstructing the Worldwide Web of Cotton Production in the Age of the American Civil War', *American Historical Review* 109.5 (2004), 1405–1438.

Beckman, Karen (ed.), *Animating Film Theory* (Durham, NC: Duke University Press, 2014).

Benshoff, Harry M., *Dark Shadows* (Detroit, MI: Wayne State University Press, 2011).

Benshoff, Harry M., *Monsters in the Closet: Homosexuality and the Horror Film* (Manchester: Manchester University Press, 1997).

Benton, Mike, *The Comic Book in America: An Illustrated History* (Dallas, TX: Taylor Publishing, 1989).

Benton, Mike, *Horror Comics: The Illustrated History* (Dallas, TX: Taylor Publishing, 1991).

Berebitsky, Julie, 'The Joy of Work: Helen Gurley Brown, Gender, and Sexuality in the White-Collar Office', *Journal of the History of Sexuality* 15.1 (2006), 89–127.

Berlatsky, Noah, *Wonder Woman: Bondage and Feminism in the Marston/Peter Comics* (New Brunswick, NJ: Rutgers University Press, 2015).

Berman, Marshall, *All That Is Solid Melts Into Air: The Experience of Modernity* (London: Penguin Books, 1988).

Bernard, Richard M., and Bradley R. Rice (eds), *Sunbelt Cities: Politics and Growth Since World War II* (Austin, TX: University of Texas Press, 1983).

Bhabha, Homi K., 'Of Mimicry and Man: The Ambivalence of Colonial Discourse', *October* 28 (Spring 1984), 125–133.

Biagi, Shirley, and Marilyn Kern-Foxworth, *Facing Difference: Race, Gender, and Mass Media* (Thousand Oaks, CA: Pine Forge Press, 1997).

Blake, Linnie, *The Wounds of Nations: Horror Cinema, Historical Trauma, and National Identity* (Manchester: Manchester University Press, 2008).

Blumberg, Arnold T., ' "The Night Gwen Stacy Died": The End of Innocence and the "Last Gasp of the Silver Age"', *International Journal of Comic Art* 8.1 (2006), 197–211.

Booker, Keith M. (ed.), *Comics Through Time* (Santa Barbara, CA: Greenwood, 2014).

Boyd, Jerry, 'Taste the Blood of Vampirella: A 40th Anniversary Tribute', *Back Issue* 36 (2009), 20–27.

Brown, Gurley, *Sex and the Single Girl* (New York: Bernard Geis Associates, 1962).

Brown, Jeffrey A., *Black Superheroes, Milestone Comics, and Their Fans* (Jackson, MS: University Press of Mississippi, 2001).

Brown, Jeffrey A., 'Comic Book Masculinity and the New Black Superhero', *African American Review* 33.1 (1999), 25–42.

Burk, Robert Fredrick, *The Eisenhower Administration and Black Civil Rights* (Knoxville, TN: University of Tennessee Press, 1984).

Burriss, Larry, 'Slouching Toward Nuclear War: Coorientation and NATO Exercise Able Archer 83', *International Journal of Intelligence, Security, and Public Affairs* 21.3 (2019), 219–250.

Butler, Eric, *Metamorphoses of the Vampire in Literature and Film: Cultural Transformations in Europe, 1732–1933* (Rochester, NY: Random House, 2010).

Cannadine, David, *Ornamentalism: How the British Saw Their Empire* (London: Penguin, 2002).

Carnevale, Nancy C., ' "No Italian Spoken for the Duration of the War": Language, Italian American Identity, and Cultural Pluralism in the World War II Years', *Journal of American Ethnic History* 22.3 (2003), 3–33.

Carroll, Noël, *The Philosophy of Horror: Or, Paradoxes of the Heart* (London and New York: Routledge, 1990).

Carter, Dan, *Scottsboro: A Tragedy of the American South* (Baton Rouge, LA: Louisiana State University Press, 2007).

Cavarero, Adriana, *Horrorism: Naming Contemporary Violence* (New York: Columbia University Press, 2009).

Cavell, Stanley, *The Claim of Reason* (New York: Oxford University Press, 1979).

Césaire, Aimé, *Discours sur le colonialisme* (Paris: Éditions Réclame, 1950).

Chafe, William, *The Paradox of Change: American Women in the 20ᵗʰ Century* (Oxford: Oxford University Press, 1991).

Chang, Iris, *The Rape of Nanking: The Forgotten Holocaust of World War II* (New York: Basic Books, 2012).

Chauncey, George, *Gay New York: Gender, Urban Culture, and the Making of the Gay World, 1890–1940* (New York: Basic Books, 1994).

Chute, Hillary, *Disaster Drawn* (Cambridge, MA and London: Harvard University Press, 2016).

Clark, Leisa A., Amanda Firestone, and Mary F. Pharr (eds), *The Last Midnight: Essays on Apocalyptic Narratives in Millennial Media* (Jefferson, NC: McFarland, 2016).

Clark, Stuart, 'Inversion, Misrule and the Meaning of Witchcraft', *Past & Present* 87.1 (1980), 98–127.

Clark, Stuart, *Thinking with Demons: The Idea of Witchcraft in Early Modern Europe* (Oxford: Oxford University Press, 1999).

Clover, Carol J., *Men, Women, and Chain Saws: Gender in the Modern Horror Film* (Princeton, NJ: Princeton University Press, 2015).

Cocca, Carolyn, *Superwomen: Gender, Power, and Representation* (New York: Bloomsbury Academic 2016).

Coffey, David, *Encyclopedia of the Vietnam War: A Political, Social, and Military History*, ed. Spencer C. Tucker (Oxford: ABC-CLIO, 1998)

Connolly, Paula T., *Slavery in American Children's Literature 1790–2010* (Iowa City, IA: University of Iowa Press, 2013).

Coste, Françoise, 'Conservative Women and Feminism in the United States: Between Hatred and Appropriation', *Caliban: French Journal of English Studies* 27 (2017), 167–176.

Costello, Brannon (ed.), *Howard Chaykin: Conversations* (Jackson, MS: University Press of Mississippi, 2011)

Costello, Matthew J., *Secret Identity Crisis: Comic Books & the Unmasking of Cold War America* (London and New York: Continuum, 2009).

Cotter, Robert Michael 'Bobb', *The Great Monster Magazines: A Critical Study of the Black and White Publications of the 1950s, 1960s, and 1970s* (Jefferson, NC: McFarland, 2008).

Creed, Barbara, 'Horror and the Monstrous-Feminine: An Imaginary Abjection', *Screen* 27.1 (1986), 44–71.

Cuordileone, K. A., ' "Politics in an Age of Anxiety": Cold War Political Culture and the Crisis in American Masculinity, 1949–1960', *Journal of American History* 87.2 (2000), 515–545.

Daly, Nicholas, 'That Obscure Object of Desire: Victorian Commodity Culture and Fictions of the Mummy', *NOVEL: A Forum on Fiction* 28.1 (1994), 24–51.

Davidson, Olga M., and Ferdowsi, 'The Text of Ferdowsi's Shahnama and the Burden of the Past', *Journal of the American Oriental Society* 118.1 (1998), 63–68.

Davies, Dominic, and Candida Rifkind (eds), *Documenting Trauma in Comics: Traumatic Pasts, Embodied Histories, and Graphic Reportage* (London: Palgrave Macmillan, 2020).

Davies, Owen, *America Bewitched: The Story of Witchcraft After Salem* (Oxford: Oxford University Press, 2016).

Davies, Owen, *The Haunted: A Social History of Ghosts* (Basingstoke: Palgrave Macmillan, 2009).

Davis, Blair, *Movie Comics* (New Brunswick, NJ: Rutgers University Press, 2017).

Desroches-Noblecourt, Christiane, *Tutankhamen* (London: Penguin, 1972).

Dickey, Colin, *Ghostland: An American History in Haunted Places* (London: Penguin, 2016).

Dittmer, Jason, ' "America is Safe While its Boys and Girls Believe in its Creeds!": Captain America and American Identity Prior to World War 2', *Environment and Planning D: Society and Space* 25.3 (2007), 401–423.

Du Bois, William Edward Burghardt, *Color and Democracy* (San Diego, CA: Harcourt, Brace and Co., 1945).

Dudziak, Mary L., '*Brown* as a Cold War Case', *Journal of American History* 91.1 (2004), 32–42.

Duncan, Randy, and Matthew J. Smith (eds), *Icons of the American Comic Book: From Captain America to Wonder Woman, Volume One* (Santa Barbara, CA: Greenwood, 2013).

Dworkin, Andrea, *Pornography: Men Possessing Women* (New York: Penguin, 1989).

Ehrlich, Paul, *The Population Bomb* (New York: Sierra Club/Ballantine Books, 1968).

Epstein, Helen, *Children of the Holocaust: Conversations with Sons and Daughters of Survivors* (New York: Bantam Books, 1980).

Erb, Cynthia, *Tracking King Kong: A Hollywood Icon in World Culture*, 2nd edn (Detroit, MI: Wayne State University Press, 2009).

Eyerman, Ron, *Cultural Trauma: Slavery and the Formation of African American Identity* (Cambridge: Cambridge University Press, 2001).

Feldman, Keith P., 'Representing Permanent War: Black Power's Palestine and the End(s) of Civil Rights', *CR: The New Centennial Review* 8.2 (2008), 193–231.

Fiedler, Leslie A., *Love and Death in the American Novel* (New York: Stein and Day, 1966).

Firestone, Shulamith, *The Dialectic of Sex: The Case for Feminist Revolution* (New York: William Morrow and Company, 1970).

Fischbach, Michael R., *Black Power and Palestine: Transnational Countries of Color* (Stanford, CT: Stanford University Press, 2018).

Fisher, Eugene, and Leon Klenicki (eds), *Spiritual Pilgrimage: Texts on Jews and Judaism* 1979–1995 (New York: The Crossroads Publishing Company, 1995).

Foner, Philip S., 'Why the United States Went to War with Spain in 1898', *Science and Society* 32.1 (1968), 39–65.

Friedan, Betty, *The Feminine Mystique* (New York: W. W. Norton & Company, 1963).

Gabor, Mark (ed.), *The Pinup: A Modest History* (New York: Evergreen, 1972).

Gage, S. J. L., 'The Amerasian Problem: Blood, Duty, and Race', *International Relations* 21.1 (2007), 86–102.

Galbraith, John Kenneth, *The Affluent Society* (Boston, MA: Houghton Mifflin, 1958).

Gateward, Frances, and John Jennings (eds), *The Blacker the Ink: Constructions of Black Identity in Comics and Sequential Art* (New Brunswick, NJ: Rutgers University Press 2015).

Gerlus, Jean-Claude, 'The Effects of the Cold War on US–Haiti Relations', *Journal of Haitian Studies* 1.1 (1995), 34–56.

Glenn, D. Micheal, Jean C. Beckham, Michelle E. Feldman, Angela C. Kirby, Michael A. Hertzberg, Scott D. Moore, 'Violence and Hostility Among Families of Vietnam Veterans with Combat-Related Posttraumatic Stress Disorder', *Violence and Victims* 17.4 (2002), 473–489.

Glover, David, and Scott McCracken (eds), *The Cambridge Companion to Popular Fiction* (Cambridge: Cambridge University Press, 2012).

Goleman, Daniel, *Emotional Intelligence, Why It Can Matter More Than IQ* (New York: Bloomsbury, 1995).

Gomez, Betsy (ed.), *She Changed Comics: The Untold Story of the Women Who Changed Free Expression in Comics* (Berkley, CA: Image Comics, 2001).

Goodrum, Michael, ' "Friend of the People of Many Lands": Johnny Everyman, "critical internationalism", and liberal postwar US heroism', *Social History* 38.2 (2013), 203–219.

Goodrum, Michael, ' "His Greatest Enemy – Intolerance!": The Superman Radio Show in 1946', *Scan: Journal of Media, Arts, & Culture* 5.2 (2008), retrieved from http://scan.net.au/scan/journal/display.php?journal_id=118 (accessed 16 June 2020).

Goodrum, Michael, *Superheroes and American Self Image: From War to Watergate* (Farnham: Ashgate, 2016).

Goodrum, Michael, ' "Superman Believes that a Wife's Place Is in the Home": *Superman's Girl Friend, Lois Lane* and the Representation of Women', *Gender & History* 30.2 (2018), 442–464.

Goodrum, Michael, Tara Prescott, and Philip Smith (eds), *Gender and the Superhero Narrative* (Jackson, MS: University Press of Mississippi, 2018).

Gotham, Kevin Fox, 'Urban Space, Restrictive Covenants, and the Origins of Racial Residential Segregation in a US City, 1900–1950', *International Journal of Urban and Regional Research* 24.3 (2000), 616–633.

Grant, Barry (ed.), *The Film Reader* (Austin, TX: University of Texas Press, 1986).

Gravett, Paul, 'Richard Corben: Getting Over the Underground', *Paulgravett. com* (18 February 2009), retrieved from https://web.archive.org/web/2009 0218131355/http://www.paulgravett.com/articles/013_corben/013_corben. htm (accessed 10 June 2020).

Greer, Germaine, *The Female Eunuch* (London: Paladin, 1971).

Groensteen, Thierry, *The System of Comics*, trans. Bart Beaty and Nick Nguyen (Jackson, MS: University Press of Mississippi, 2007).

Groom, Nick, *The Vampire: A New History* (New Haven, CT: Yale University Press, 2018).

Haggerty, George E., 'Literature and Homosexuality in the Late Eighteenth Century: Walpole, Beckford and Lewis', *Studies in the Novel* 18 (1986), 341–352.

Hajdu, David, *The Ten Cent Plague: The Great Comic Book Scare and How It Changed America* (New York: Farrar, Straus, and Giroux, 2008).

Halberstam, Judith, *Skin Shows: Gothic Horror and the Technology of Monsters* (Durham, NC and London: Duke University Press, 1995).

Hall, Jacquelyn Dowd, 'The Long Civil Rights Movement and the Political Uses of the Past', *Journal of American History* (2005), 1233–1263.

Handlin, Oscar, 'The Modern City as a Field of Historical Study', in Alexander B. Callow Jr (ed.), *American Urban History: An Interpretive Reader with Commentaries* (Oxford: Oxford University Press, 1973), 17–36.

Hanley, Tim, *Investigating Lois Lane: The Turbulent History of the Daily Planet's Ace Reporter* (Chicago, IL: Chicago Review Press, 2016).

Hanley, Tim, *Wonder Woman Unbound* (Chicago, IL: Chicago Review Press, 2014).

Hartmann, Andrew, *A War for the Soul of America: A History of the Culture Wars* (Chicago, IL: University of Chicago Press, 2019).

Heffernan, Kevin, *Ghouls, Gimmicks, and Gold: Horror Films and the American Movie Business, 1953–1968* (Durham, NC and London: Duke University Press, 2004).

Hierholzer, Robert, Jan Munson, Carol Peabody, and John Rosenberg, 'Clinical Presentation of PTSD in World War II Combat Veterans', *Hospital & Community Psychiatry* 43.8 (1992), 816–820.

Hofstadter, Richard, *The Paranoid Style of American Politics* (New York: Alfred A. Knopf, 1968).

Hoganson, Kristin, *Fighting for American Manhood: How Gender Politics Provoked the Spanish-American and Philippine-American Wars* (New Haven, CT: Yale University Press, 2000).

Hoppenstand, Gary, 'Editorial: Today's Televised Circus', *Journal of Popular Culture* 40.3 (2007), 407–408.

Howe, Sean, *Marvel Comics: The Untold Story* (New York: Harper Collins, 2012).

Hughes, Julie, and Nathan Abrams (eds), *Containing America: Cultural Consumption and Production in 50s America* (London: Bloomsbury, 2000).

Hughes, Robert, *The Shock of the New: Art and the Century of Change* (London: Thames & Hudson, 1991).

Humphreys, Reynolds, *The American Horror Film: An Introduction* (Edinburgh: Edinburgh University Press, 2002).

Hutcheon, Linda, with Siobhan O'Flynn, *A Theory of Adaptation*, 2nd edn (New York: Routledge, 2013).

Jacobs, Jane, *The Death and Life of Great American Cities* (New York: Vintage, 1961).

James, C. L. R., *The Black Jacobins: Toussaint L'Ouverture and the San Domingo Revolution* (London: Penguin, 2001).

James, M. R., *Collected Ghost Stories*, ed. Darryl Jones (Oxford: Oxford University Press, 2017).

Jancovich, Mark, *Rational Fears: American Horror in the 1950s* (Manchester: Manchester University Press, 1996).

Jeffries, Dru, *Comic Book Film Style* (Austin, TX: University of Texas Press, 2017).

Jennings, Dana, 'MEDIA: At House of Comics, a Writer's Champion', *New York Times* (15 September 2003).

Johnson, David K., *The Lavender Scare: The Cold War Persecution of Gays and Lesbians in the Federal Government* (Chicago, IL: University of Chicago Press, 2004).

Johnson, Matthew D., 'From Peace to the Panthers: PRC Engagement with African-American Transnational Networks, 1949–1979', *Past & Present* Supplement 8 (2013), 233–257.

Jones, Darryl, *Horror: A Thematic History in Fiction and Film* (London: Arnold Publishers, 2002).

Jones, Darryl, *Horror Stories: Classic Tales from Hoffman to Hodgson* (Oxford: Oxford University Press, 2014).

Jones, Darryl, *Sleeping With the Lights On: The Unsettling Story of Horror* (Oxford: Oxford University Press, 2018).

Joseph, Paul (ed.), *The SAGE Encyclopedia of War: Social Science Perspectives* (Thousand Oaks, CA: Sage Publications: 2014).

Joshi, S. T., *Unutterable Horror: A History of Supernatural Fiction*, 2 vols (New York: Hippocampus Press, 2012).

Karasik, Paul, and Mark Newgarden, *How to Read Nancy* (Seattle, WA: Fantagraphic Books, 2017).

Kennan, George, *Democracy and the Student Left* (London: Hutchinson & Co., 1968).

Klaniczay, Gábor, *The Uses of Supernatural Power: The Transformation of Popular Religion in Medieval and Early Modern Europe* (Cambridge and Oxford: Polity Press, 1990).

Koppes, Clayton R., and Gregory D. Black, *Hollywood Goes to War: Patriotism, Movies and the Second World War, from 'Ninotchka' to 'Mrs. Miniver'* (London and New York: Tauris Parke, 2000).

Kraft, Robert, 'Archival Memory: Representations of the Holocaust in Oral Testimony', Holocaust Representations Since 1975, conference held at Chester University, 18 September 2009.

Kramer, Paul A., *The Blood of Government: Race, Empire, the United States, and the Philippines* (Chapel Hill, NC: University of North Carolina Press, 2006).

Kunzle, David, *The Early Comic Strip: Narrative Strips and Picture Stories in the European Broadsheet from c.1450 to 1825 (History of the Comic Strip, Volume 1)* (Berkley, CA: University of California Press, 1973).

Kurlansky, Mark, *1968: The Year That Rocked the World* (London: Vintage, 2005).

Lendrum, Rob, 'The Super Black Macho, One Baaad Mutha: Black Superhero Masculinity in 1970s Mainstream Comic Books', *Extrapolation* 46.3 (2005), 360–372.

Levitt, Steven D., and Stephen J. Dubner, *Freakonomics: A Rogue Economist Explores the Hidden Side of Everything* (London: Penguin, 2007).

Lipsitz, George, 'The Possessive Investment in Whiteness: Racialized Social Democracy and the "White" Problem in American Studies', *American Quarterly* 47.3 (1995), 369–387.

Loewen, James W., *Sundown Towns: A Hidden Dimension of American Racism* (New York: New Press, 2005).

Lowenstein, Adam, *Shocking Representation: Historical Trauma, National Cinema, and the Modern Horror Film* (New York: Columbia University Press, 2005).

Lowenthal, David, 'Earth Day', *Area: Institute of British Geographers* 4 (1970), 1–10.

Luckhurst, Roger, *The Mummy's Curse: The True History of a Dark Fantasy* (Oxford: Oxford University Press, 2014).

Luckhurst, Roger, *Zombies: A Cultural History* (London: Reaktion Books, 2015).

Luckhurst, Roger (ed.), *Science Fiction: A Literary History* (London: British Library, 2017).

Lundberg, Ferdinand, and Marynia F. Farnham, *Modern Woman: The Lost Sex* (New York: Harper & Brothers, 1947).

Luthi, Lorenz M., *The Sino-Soviet Split: Cold War in the Communist World* (Princeton, NJ: Princeton University Press, 2010).

Macmillan, Margaret, *Nixon & Mao: The Week That Changed the World* (New York: Random House, 2007).

Madrid, Mike, *The Supergirls: Fashion, Feminism, Fantasy, and the History of Comic Book Heroines* (Minneapolis, MN: Exterminating Angel Press, 2009).

Mailer, Norman, *Prisoner of Sex* (New York: Little Brown, 1971).

Maraniss, David, *They Marched into Sunlight: War and Peace, Vietnam and America, October 1967* (New York: Simon & Schuster, 2004).

May, Elaine Tyler, *Homeward Bound: American Families in the Cold War Era* (New York: Basic Books, 2008).

May, Lori (ed.), *Recasting America: Culture and Politics in the Age of Cold War* (Chicago, IL and London: University of Chicago Press, 1989).

McCloud, Scott, *Understanding Comics* (Northampton, MA: Tundra Publishing, 1993).

Melley, Timothy. *Empire of Conspiracy: The Culture of Paranoia in Postwar America* (Ithaca, NY: Cornell University Press, 2000).

Menu, Jean-Christophe, *Krollebitches, de Franquin à Gébé Broché* (Brussels: Les Impressions Nouvelles, 2016).

Meriwether, James, *Proudly We Can Be African: Black Americans and Africa, 1935–1961* (Chapel Hill, NC: University of North Carolina Press, 2002).

Messerschmidt, James W., 'The Forgotten Victims of World War II', *Violence Against Women* 12.7 (2006), 706–712.

Mitchell, Christopher, 'US Policy Toward Haitian Boat People, 1972–93', *Annals of the American Academy of Political and Social Science* 534 (1995), 69–80.

Morgan, Marabel, *The Total Woman* (Old Tappan, NJ: Spire Books, 1973).

Nama, Adilifu, *Super Black: American Pop Culture and Black Superheroes* (Austin, TX: University of Texas Press, 2011).

Napier, Susan J., 'Panic Sites: The Japanese Imagination of Disaster from Godzilla to Akira' *Journal of Japanese Studies* 19.2 (Summer, 1993), 327–351.

Naremore, James, 'American Film Noir: The History of an Idea' *Film Quarterly* 49 (1995–1996), 12–28.

Nesfield, Victoria, and Philip Smith (eds), *The Struggle for Understanding: The Novels of Elie Wiesel* (New York: SUNY Press, 2019)

Ngai, Mae M., 'The Architecture of Race in American Immigration Law: A Reexamination of the Immigration Act of 1924', *The Journal of American History* 86.1 (1999), 67–92.

Nyberg, Amy Kiste, *Seal of Approval: The History of the Comics Code* (Jackson, MS: University Press of Mississippi, 1998).

Orwell, George, 'Boy's Weeklies', in *George Orwell Essays* (London: Penguin Classics, 2000), 78–100.

Oshinsky, David M., *A Conspiracy So Immense: The World of Joe McCarthy* (Oxford: Oxford University Press, 2005).

Padmore, George, *Pan-Africanism or Communism? The Coming Struggle for Africa* (London: D. Dobson, 1956).

Paul, William, *Laughing Screaming: Modern Hollywood Horror and Comedy* (New York: Columbia University Press, 1994).

Peirse, Alison, *After Dracula: The 1930s Horror Film* (London: I. B. Tauris, 2013).

Peters, Brian Mitchell, 'Qu(e)erying Comic Book Culture and Representations of Sexuality in Wonder Woman', *CLCWeb: Comparative Literature and Culture* 5.3 (2003), 1–9.

Phillips, Kendall R., *Projected Fears* (Westport, CN: Praeger, 2008).

Phoenix, Mike, *Comics' Second City: The Gateway History of the American Comic Book* (self-published, 2012).

Poole, W. Scott, *Monsters in America: Our Historical Obsession with the Hideous and the Haunting* (Waco, TX: Baylor University Press, 2011).

Prescott, Tara, and Aaron Drucker (eds), *Feminism in the Worlds of Neil Gaiman: Essays on the Comics, Poetry and Prose* (Jefferson, NC: McFarland, 2012).

Prince, Dennis L., and Andrew P. Yanchus, *Aurora Monster Scenes: The Most Controversial Toys of a Generation* (Drexel Hill, PA: StarComm, 2014).

Radcliffe, Ann, 'On the Supernatural in Poetry', *New Monthly Magazine* 16.1 (1826).

Radcliffe, Ann, *The Romance of the Forest* (Oxford: Oxford University Press, 1999).

Rainwater, Lee, *Behind Ghetto Walls: Black Families in a Federal Slum* (Abingdon: Routledge, 2017).

Reumann, Miriam G., *American Sexual Character: Sex, Gender, and National Identity in the Kinsey Reports* (Berkeley, CA: University of California Press, 2005).

Reyes, Xavier Aldana (ed.), *Horror: A Literary History* (London: British Library, 2016).

Reynolds, Simon, *Rip It Up and Start Again: Postpunk 1978–1984*. (London: Faber and Faber, 2005).

Rhodes, Gary D., *White Zombie: Anatomy of a Horror Film* (Jefferson, NC: McFarland, 2001).

Rigby, Jonathan, *American Gothic: Sixty Years of Horror Cinema* (London: Reynolds and Hearn, 2007).

Roach, David, and Jon B. Cooke, *The Warren Companion: The Definitive Compendium to the Great Comics of Warren Publishing* (Raleigh, NC: TwoMorrows Publishing, 2001).

Roberge, Erika M., Nathaniel J. Allen, Judith W. Taylor, and Craig J. Bryan, 'Relationship Functioning in Vietnam Veteran Couples: The Roles of PTSD and Anger', *Journal of Clinical Psychology* 72.9 (2016), 966–974.

Rogin, Michael, 'Liberal Society and the Indian Question', *Politics and Society* 1.3 (1971), 269–312.

Rones, Philip L., 'Moving to the Sun: Job Growth in the Sunbelt (1968–1978)', *Monthly Labor Review* 103.3 (1980), 12–19.

Rosen, Ruth, *The World Split Open: How the Modern Women's Movement Changed America* (Old Saybrook, CT: Tantor Ebooks, 2012).

Rowlands, Alison, 'Witchcraft and Old Women in Early Modern Germany', *Past & Present* 173.1 (2001), 50–89.

Ruane, Kevin, *War and Revolution in Vietnam, 1930–1975* (London: Routledge, 1998).

Ruth, David E., *Inventing the Public Enemy: The Gangster in American Society, 1918–1934* (Chicago, IL: University of Chicago Press, 1996).

Sabin, Roger, *Adult Comics: An Introduction* (London: Routledge, 1993).

Sadowski, Greg (ed.), *Four Color Fear: Forgotten Horror Comics of the 1950s* (Seattle, WA: Fantagraphics Books, 2017).

Saunders, Frances Stonor, *Who Paid the Piper? The CIA and the Cultural Cold War* (New York: Granta, 2000).

Savage, Jr, William W., *Commies, Cowboys, and Jungle Queens: Comic Books and America, 1945–1954* (Middletown, CT: Wesleyan University Press, 1990).

Scanlon, Jennifer, 'Sexy from the Start: Anticipatory Elements of Second Wave Feminism', *Women's Studies* 38.2 (2009), 127–150.

Schiff, Stacy, *The Witches: Salem, 1692* (New York: Little, Brown and Co., 2015).

Schlesinger, Stephen, and Stephen Kinzer, *Bitter Fruit: The Story of the American Coup in Guatemala, Revised and Expanded* (Cambridge, MA: Harvard University Press, 2005).

Schoell, William, *The Horror Comics: Fiends, Freaks, and Fantastic Creatures, 1940s-1980s* (Jefferson, NC: McFarland, 2014).

Sennitt, Stephen, *Ghastly Terror! The Horrible Story of Horror Comics* (Manchester: Critical Vision, 1999).

Shilts, Randy, *And the Band Played On: Politics, People, and the AIDS Epidemic* (New York: St. Martin's Press, 1987).

Silver, Alain, and James Ursini (eds), *Horror Film Reader* (New York: Limelight Editions, 2000).

Silverman, Kaja, *Male Subjectivity at the Margins* (London: Routledge, 1992).

Singer, Marc, *Breaking the Frames* (Austin, TX: University of Texas Press, 2019).

Skal, David J., *The Monster Show: A Cultural History of Horror* (New York: Faber and Faber, 2001).

Sklaroff, Lauren Rebecca, 'Constructing GI Joe Louis: Cultural Solutions to the 'Negro Problem' During World War II', *Journal of American History* 89.3 (2002), 958–983.

Slotkin, Richard, *Regeneration Through Violence: The Mythology of the American Frontier, 1600–1860* (Middletown, CT: Wesleyan University Press, 1973).

Smith, Philip, 'Reading Aaron Diaz's Wonder Woman', *Literature Compass* 14.5 (2017) e12384.

Sommer, Richard M., and Glenn Forley, 'Dyn-o-Mite Fiends: The Weather Underground at Chicago's Haymarket', *Journal of Architectural Education* 61.3 (2008), 13–24.

Spector, Rachel. E., *Cultural Diversity in Heath and Illness*, 6th edn (Upper Saddle River, NJ: Pearson Prentice Hall, 2004.)

Stevenson, John Allen, 'A Vampire in the Mirror: The Sexuality of Dracula', *Publications of the Modern Language Association of America* (1988), 139–149.

Stickney, John, 'Four Doors to the Future: Gothic Rock Is Their Thing', *The Williams Record* (24 October 1967).

Stitch, Sidra, *Anxious Visions: Surrealist Art.* (New York: Abbeville Press, 1990).

Strömberg, Fredrik, *Black Images in the Comics: A Visual History* (Seattle, WA: Fantagraphics, 2003).

Takaki, Ronald, *Double Victory: A Multicultural History of American in World War II* (New York: Back Bay Books, 2001).

Tilley, Carol L., 'Seducing the Innocent: Fredric Wertham and the Falsifications That Helped Condemn Comics', *Information and Culture: A Journal of History* 47 (2012), 383–413.

Topliss, Iain, *The Comic Worlds of Peter Arno, William Steig, Charles Addams, and Saun Steinberg* (Baltimore, MD: Johns Hopkins University Press, 2005).

Trombetta, Jim, *The Horror! The Horror!* (New York: Abrams ComicArt, 2010).

Tudor, Andrew, 'Why Horror? The Peculiar Pleasures of a Popular Genre', *Cultural Studies* 11.3 (1997), 443–463.

Turk, Katherine, 'Out of the Revolution, into the Mainstream: Employment Activism in the NOW Sears Campaign and the Growing Pains of Liberal Feminism', *Journal of American History* 97.2 (2010), 399–423.

Tyrrell, Ian, *Transnational Nation: United States History in Global Perspective Since 1789* (London: Palgrave Macmillan, 2015).

Van Ells, Mark David, *To Hear Only Thunder Again: America's World War II Veterans Come Home* (Lanham, MD: Lexington Books, 2001).

Venn, Fiona, *The Oil Crisis* (London: Routledge, 2002).

von Eschen, Penny M., *Satchmo Blows Up the World: Jazz Ambassadors Play the Cold War* (Cambridge, MA: Harvard University Press, 2006).

Wainstock, Dennis, *The Decision to Drop the Atomic Bomb* (Westport, CT: Praeger Publishers, 1996).

Wall, L. L., 'The Medical Ethics of Dr J Marion Sims: A Fresh Look at the Historical Record', *Journal of Medical Ethics* 32.6 (2006), 346–350.

Waller, Willard, *The Veteran Comes Back* (New York: Dryden Press, 1944).

Walter, John, 'Gesturing at Authority: Deciphering the Gestural Code of Early Modern England', *Past & Present* (2009), Supplement 4, 96–127.

Walton, Michael, *The Horror Comic Never Dies* (Jefferson, NC: McFarland, 2019).

Wandtke, Terrence R., *The Comics Scare Returns: The Contemporary Resurgence of Horror Comics* (New York: RIT Press, 2018).

Weatherford, Doris, *American Women and World War II* (New York: Facts on File, 1990).

Weber, Cynthia, *Faking It: U.S. Hegemony in a 'Post-Phallic' Era* (Minneapolis, MI: University of Minnesota Press: 1999).

Weiss, Daniel S., Charles R. Marmar, William E. Schlenger, John A. Fairbank, B. Kathleen Jordan, Richard L. Hough, and Richard A. Kulka, 'The Prevalence of Lifetime and Partial Posttraumatic Stress Disorder in Vietnam Theater Veterans', *Journal of Traumatic Stress* 5 (1992), 365–376.

Weldon, Glen, *The Caped Crusade: Batman and the Rise of Nerd Culture* (New York: Simon & Schuster, 2016).

Wertham, Fredric, *Seduction of the Innocent* (London: Museum Press, 1955).

West, Mark I., *The Japanification of Children's Popular Culture: From Godzilla to Miyazaki* (Lanham, MD: Scarecrow Press, 2009).

Westbrook, Robert B., *Why We Fought* (Washington, DC: Smithsonian Book, 2010).

White, Walter, *A Man Called White* (New York: Viking Press, 1948).

Whitted, Qiana, *EC Comics: Race, Shock, & Social Protest* (New Brunswick, NJ: Rutgers University Press, 2019).

Williams, Linda (ed.), *Porn Studies* (Durham, NC and London: Duke University Press, 2004).

Williams, Paul, and James Lyons (eds), *The Rise of the American Comics Artist: Creators and Contexts* (Jackson, MS: University Press of Mississippi, 2010)

Winkler, Allan M., *The Politics of Propaganda: The Office of War Information 1942–1945* (New Haven, CT: Yale University Press, 1978).

Witek, Joseph (ed.), *Art Spiegelman Conversations* (Jackson, MS: University Press of Mississippi, 2007).

Wolfreys, Julian, *Transgression: Identity, Space, Time* (London: Palgrave Macmillan, 2008).

Wolk, Douglas, *Reading Comics: How Graphic Novels Work and What They Mean* (Cambridge, MA: Da Capo Press, 2008).

Wood, Robin, 'Return of the Repressed', *Film Comment* (July–August 1978), 25–32.

Wood, Robin, *Hollywood from Vietnam to Reagan* (New York: Columbia University Press, 1986).

Wood, Angela K., 'African Americans and Their Distrust of the Health Care System: Health Care for Diverse Populations', *Journal of Cultural Diversity* 14.2 (2007) 56–60.

Worland, Rick, 'Dark Shadows 1970: Industry, Anxiety, and Adaptation', *Journal of Popular Film and Television* 40.4 (2012), 169–180.

Wriggins, Jennifer, 'Rape, Racism, and the Law', *Harvard Women's Law Journal* 6 (1983), 103–141.

Wright, Angela, *Britain, France, and the Gothic, 1764–1820: The Import of Terror* (Cambridge: Cambridge University Press, 2013).

Wright, Bradford W., *Comic Book Nation: The Transformation of Youth Culture in America* (Baltimore, MA: Johns Hopkins University Press, 2001).

Wright, Richard, *White Man Listen!* (Garden City, NY: Doubleday, 1957).

Wylie, Philip, *Generation of Vipers* (New York and Toronto: Muller, 1942).

Wynn, Neil A., *The African American Experience During World War II* (New York: Rowman & Littlefield 2010).

Yu, Eric Kwan-Wai, 'Productive Fear: Labour, Sexuality and, Mimicry in Bram Stoker's *Dracula*', *Texas Studies in Literature and Language* 48.2 (2006), 145–170.

**Internet Sources**

Asbley, Bill Ayers, Bernadine Dohrn, John Jacobs, Jeff Jones, Gerry Long, Home Machtinger, Jim Mellen, Terry Robbins, Mark Rudd, and Steve Tappis, 'You Don't Need a Weatherman to Know Which Way the Wind Blows', *New Left Notes* (18 June 1969), retrieved from https://archive.org/details/YouDont NeedAWeathermanToKnowWhichWayTheWindBlows_925 (accessed 13 August 2019).

British Library, 'Gothic novel *The Castle of Otranto*, by Horace Walpole', retrieved from www.bl.uk/collection-items/gothic-novel-the-castle-of-otranto-by-horace-walpole#sthash.83xwktBX.dpuf (accessed 23 May 2017).

Burke, Edmund, *On the Sublime and Beautiful* (New York: Bartleby.com, 2001), retrieved from www.bartleby.com/24/2/202.html (accessed 26 February 2018).

Carroll, Rory, 'Woman at Centre of Emmett Till Case Tells Author She Fabricated Testimony', *The Guardian* (27 January 2017), retrieved from www.theguardian.com/us-news/2017/jan/27/emmett-till-book-carolyn-bryant-confession (accessed 29 July 2019).

Embury-Dennis, Tom, 'Trump Tells Fake Story About US General Slaughtering 49 Muslims Using Bullets Dipped in Pig's Blood, in Resurfaced Video', *The Independent* (19 March 2019), retrieved from www.independent.co.uk/news/world/americas/us-politics/trump-muslims-general-pershing-pigs-blood-video-a8829676.html (accessed 28 January 2020).

Federal Writers' Project, retrieved from www.loc.gov/collections/slave-narratives-from-the-federal-writers-project-1936-to-1938/about-this-collection/ (accessed 26 May 2020).

Huie, William Bradford, 'The Shocking Story of Approved Killing in Mississippi', *Look* (24 January 1956), 46–50, available at 'Killers' Confession', *American Experience: The Murder of Emmett Till*, retrieved from www.pbs.org/wgbh/americanexperience/features/till-killers-confession/ (accessed 29 July 2019).

McClancy, Kathleen, *Back in the World: Vietnam Veterans through Popular Culture* (unpublished dissertation, 2009), retrieved from https://dukespace.lib.duke.edu/dspace/handle/10161/1658 (accessed 26 May 2020).

Miller, John Jackson, '*Amazing Spider-Man* Sales Figures', *Comichron* (n.d.), retrieved from www.comichron.com/titlespotlights/amazingspiderman.html (accessed 26 May 2020).

Miller, John Jackson, '*Vampirella* Sales Figures', *Comichron* (n.d.), retrieved from www.comichron.com/titlespotlights/vampirella.html (accessed 26 May 2020).

Motley, Jr, Hubert, 'Black History in Comics: EC Comics "Judgment Day" the Anvil that Needed to be Dropped', *Groonk[dot]Net* ಠ_ಠ (n.d.), retrieved from www.groonk.net/blog/2010/02/black-history-in-comics-ec-comics-judgment-day-the-anvil-that-needed-to-be-dropped/ (accessed 30 July 2019).

Reid, Robin T., 'The History of the Drive-In Movie Theater', *Smithsonian Magazine* (27 May 2008), retrieved from www.smithsonianmag.com/arts-culture/the-history-of-the-drive-in-movie-theater-51331221/ (accessed 4 December 2018).

Towlson, Jon 'Why *Night of the Living Dead* Was a Big-Band Moment for Horror Movies' (29 October 2018), retrieved from www.bfi.org.uk/news-opinion/news-bfi/features/night-living-dead-george-romero (accessed 8 March 2019).

Whitley, Jeremy, 'Interview: Jeremy Whitley Takes a Bite of VAMPIRELLA', *Comicsity* (19 October 2017), retrieved from www.comicosity.com/interview-jeremy-whitley-takes-a-bite-of-vampirella/ (accessed 13 January 2019).

Wong, Ken, 'Sketch Nights at Anyone Comics', *Origamicomics.com* (18 October 2018), retrieved from http://origamicomics.com/2018/10/sketch-nights-anyone-comics/?fbclid=IwAR1GPTMD1AOQqzA6c7SMXchkm6mae_zmhEmsF86vLcnLBPWsc0DkirGCcsM (accessed 10 June 2020).

# Index

9 781526 179005